Jalebi Management

Jalebi Management

All stakeholders can enjoy a bite

SHOMBIT SENGUPTA

r Response
Business books from SAGE
Los Angeles ▪ London ▪ New Delhi ▪ Singapore
www.sagepublications.com

First published in 2007 by

Response Books
Business books from SAGE
B1/I1, Mohan Cooperative Industrial Area
Mathura Road, New Delhi 110044

Sage Publications Inc
2455 Teller Road
Thousand Oaks, California 91320

Sage Publications Ltd
1 Oliver's Yard, 55 City Road
London EC1Y 1SP

Sage Publications Asia-Pacific Pte Ltd
33 Pekin Street
#02-01 Far East Square
Singapore 048763

Published by Vivek Mehra for Response Books, typeset in 12/15 pt Agaramond by Star Compugraphics Private Limited, Delhi and printed at Chaman Enterprises, New Delhi

ISBN: 978-81-7829-745-3 (PB)

The Sage Team: Sugata Ghosh, Gayatri E. Koshy, Rajib Chatterjee, and Sanjeev Kumar Sharma

For
Renee Jhala

contents

acknowledgments

I would like to thank my friends from different parts of the world who have supported me, during the past two years, in this venture: in France, Bernard Gaud, Julia Cherol, Dorothee Massolier and Bernard Binette; in USA, Dr Romy Borooah; from India, Avik Dutta, S. Raghavendra Prakash, Prahalada Rao, D.S. Anil, Iqbal Ahamad Usmani, Gajendra Singh, R. Prakash, Dr Aradhana Kotoky, Chandra Gopalan, Hemant Sikka, Ravindra A. Manerkar and Dr Satchidananda Ray; in Germany, Debjit Chaudhuri; and in Spain, Jose Morera.

introduction

Living, bathing, breathing and scribbling consumer and customer sensitivity for the organization, I asked myself, will I be true to my subjects if I neglect them in my *jalebi* journey?

Human society is the pivot of business. Notwithstanding the size, stature, geographical location or innovating capacity of your organization, you cannot grow your business in isolation from people and social ramifications.

Consumers across the world say they don't understand business jargon. My mission is for everyone to read and understand the expressions of *Jalebi Management*.

So allow me, dear management practitioner, to describe from time-to-time different concepts practised in corporate management in language that your mother, children or friends outside the world of business would understand. Reading about business in consumer words may help you connect better with your consumer and customer.

My adventurous journey to Paris and the world of business started from a refugee colony named Sahidnagar in West Bengal, 33 years ago. As part of my work, I have empathized emotionally with the joys and pitfalls of different societies across the world. This has propelled me to enjoy psychological nuances in varied social settings, while being grounded in economic rationality.

This book is for those who, like me, believe in the keystone of passion, and relish optimism in life.

take off on jalebi!

*Make your organization into a unique palatable sweet that
everyone wants to bite into*

Forever positive is sweetness in any format: sweetheart, sweet
dessert, sweet nothings, sweet tooth and sweet-meats like the
jalebi. The fascinating character of the *jalebi* lends credence to
my *Jalebi Management* concept of upbeat values. Let me invite you, the Chief Executive Officer (CEO), and all your
employees, consumers and shareholders to enjoy a bite of my
Jalebi Management.

Not familiar with a *jalebi*? Soaked in sugary syrup, it looks
like the American snack called pretzel, but it's asymmetrical.
The *jalebi* represents the sweet desire of a billion plus people
of India, about 60 percent of whom are below 20 years of age.
Representing this melting pot of multiple cultures, multiple
languages, multiple religions, multiple kinds of food, India is
a future global power that will majorly impact global business.
Associating the *jalebi* with business may give you a divergent
perspective to understand your universe in a different way.
The core of this *Jalebi Management* recipe is the blend of the
ocean of humanity with industry.

How can the *jalebi*, so common in India and a few oriental
countries, weave global business? The sophisticated developed
countries are zeroing in on India and China for markets, manufacturing and development. *Jalebi Management* is a way of
handling tomorrow's overly competitive business world. It will
help you win markets in both economically emerging and
developed countries with a creative business strategy.

If you are reading this *Jalebi Management* saga sitting in the different cultural backgrounds of Melbourne, Osaka, Paris, or San Francisco, you may never have heard of a *jalebi*. India has been reflected to you with spiritual gurus, snake charmers, or Maharajas eating monkey brains as Spielberg's mega success *Indiana Jones* shows. The world where these images were created has since changed.

The sophisticated developed countries now need the consuming habits of the billions living in emerging economy countries. They need to sell them what's in the stockyards of their manufacturing houses. They also need to outsource the work of managing the back-end of their businesses to low-cost intellectual slaves in emerging economy countries.

Historically, Western management knowhow evolving from Caucasian innovative capacity, marketing attitude and social norms have influenced the business practices of emerging economy countries. This knowhow does not take into account, conform to, or seamlessly mesh with, the societal aspects of the billions in developing economies.

million vs. billion paradox

The scale of a million people and their way of functioning is very different from the billion population scale. An airport or railway station of a sophisticated developed country which is populated by millions not billions is large, almost like a nearly vacant exhibition gallery. In contrast, in such functional zones in billion-peopled India or China, the crowds will not allow you to see any free space. A million people country has sharp focus and discipline akin to the military. Their 'million-mindset' is unidirectional in approach. A billion people country has the 'billion-mindset' that takes care of many small aspects, and so becomes multidirectional.

Living and working in both million and billion people countries I have realized that a million-mindset person looks at those in a billion people country through his own million-mindset perspective. When the billion realization hits him, its nuances go beyond his capability to comprehend. Not having understood the logic makes him feel inadequate at not being in total control of the situation. Generally, he would find it difficult to integrate with the billion people culture.

In contrast, being able to adjust is a major characteristic of billion-mindset people, like the Chinese and Indians who live in USA. Just imagine, if the same number of Americans were to stay in China or India, would they be able to flow with the social and business norms there? In a reverse BPO (business process outsourcing) location, would Americans have the capacity to learn to communicate in perfect Indian or Chinese languages without an American accent?

If you are the manufacturer of the world's fastest train, the TGV in France, or the rapid German ICE train, your commercial coup can come from commuters in a billion people's country. But you need to customize the million-mindset innovation for usage in a billion people country. This means incorporating the billion-mindset numerical as well as their psychological, sociological, geographical and economic requirements. Have you designed for overload? Is the seating flexible to accommodate more? Can the entry point count people? Does a red light come on when the passenger limit has been crossed, as in an elevator? If your sophisticated technology has these parameters it can be applied for the billions.

The billions in India and China have different cultures, but both carry thoughts and actions relevant to the billion-mindset. They are very tolerant of the varied others around them. They think in terms of adjustment and family, instead of taking independent actions as people in the West are prone to do. In both India and China demands for new management techniques are now getting created, either for their masses or to provide support services for the sophisticated world. Budding new techniques of addressing the business culture of the billions will give a new direction to handling business in emerging markets.

The emerging new management knowhow for the billion-mindset will indicate the changes in work culture that the West has to adapt to. The Eastern mindframe of wholesale imitation of all Western management practices must also change. My *Jalebi Management* is meant to indicate this new organization culture. It distinguishes the million and billion-mindset platforms in tomorrow's global business.

On a chilly November day in 1973, three days after I had landed in Paris with just $8 in my pocket, I was walking down the street, hungrily savoring my new surroundings, when suddenly, what did I see? Lo and behold, a pyramidical building block of *jalebis*! It was in a North African sweet shop in the 14th district. I was thrilled!

In that entirely new Parisian culture I had jumped into, with new food habits, no language to express myself, where no crowds jostled inside a bus, there were no squatters, everybody was huddled in black or grey overcoats, no *lungis (sarongs)*, pyjamas, skimpy *dhotis* (loin cloth), colorful *sarees* or *dupattas* (scarves). Not even a soul relieving himself on the roadside, no cows or abandoned dogs, no rickshaws or hawkers with *bhelpuri* and *pani puris*, the street snacks of my native country. Here a man and woman publicly kissing and hugging drew nobody's attention except mine. I understood these hot gestures to be a cold country's remedy to heat up the street. Its obvious I had become quite clinical within three days. But suddenly discovering *jalebis* in this never-before-seen environment was like a dream.

I impulsively strode in to ask the price. Could it be 15 French Francs (Rs 30 in rupee value then) per *jalebi*? Or did I mistakenly read 1.5 Francs I wondered, reminiscing my art school life in Kolkata when *samosas* and *jalebis* were standard affordable fare wherever we went for sketching. The shopkeeper indicated in no uncertain terms: ten open fingers with both hands and again five open fingers. I lost my prestige on the spot as I couldn't afford a 15-Franc *jalebi*.

A big French bread, enough for lunch, costs just 1 franc, table wine is only 4 francs. It was shocking that a *jalebi* could be so luxurious as to be 15 francs. This had to be different, I consoled myself, it was a Parisian *jalebi*. As my desire level did not match my means, I took advantage of not knowing French, pretended non-comprehension and left. But I noted the shop's location for a hopeful future visit to fulfill my *jalebi* eating dream.

After two months, I got a sweeper's job in Mr Francois Martineau's lithographic print shop in Cachan, about 10 kilometers from Paris. My salary was 500 francs a month in place of the minimum salary of 3,500 francs because I had no formal work papers yet. It was a very kind gesture on Mr Martineau's part to pay me 500 francs salary from his personal account. Among other French employees, the print machine conductor here was an Algerian called Djamal. Djamal became my first friend at work because he helped me get over my helpless intimidation that arose from not yet understanding French language and culture. We communicated through gestures and hand drawings. It was my big pleasure to take Djamal to buy a 15-franc *jalebi* with my first month's salary.

Anticipating delicious taste, I bit into the *jalebi*. Sweet honey syrup trickled into my mouth. It was indeed a very strange flavor, far too sugary for my enjoyment. That's when I understood that a *jalebi* is so unique that not only are two *jalebi*s different in shape, but the *jalebi* changes its taste and appeal from culture to culture.

My first Parisian *jalebi* experience was an eye-opener. In subsequent years in Paris, through several jobs and my own consulting enterprise in management strategy for corporate houses across the world, I realized the importance of being as unique as a *jalebi* while operating in the established environment of global business norms. Somehow I've always attributed *jalebi* traits to the organizations that are my clients.

In over three decades of management experience in developed countries, I have observed that every different layer in an organization understands the practical aspects of business. However, in most economically emerging countries, there exists a hierarchy of business castes. There is top management and several layers of workers who function in silos as though firewalls of status exist. India's heritage of English *babu*dom, which encouraged clerks (*babus*) to become kowtowing sycophants to the rulers, still holds sway. For personal growth, an employee tries to satisfy different management layers. This becomes his most important job, with thoughts on consumer sensitivity and market competition sliding far away from him.

Post Indian Independence, a licence had to be obtained from the Government to do business. This 'Licence *Raj*' continued the *babu*dom legacy of the British *Raj* (monarchy). The Indian economy before 1991 was 'protected' as foreign companies were barred from operating in the country. Sheltered from global markets, Indian companies did not realize how an open market economy operates. They theorized from Western management books, listened to erudite Western professionals to get ready-made solutions, but deeper understanding of the breadth of the billions escaped them. That's why their theories did not percolate down to the performing bottom layers and solutions remained unimplemented.

Every organization's individual character is distinct. No organization, like no individual, or no *jalebi* is like another. Nor are organizational layers temperamentally alike. An organizational culture must be interconnected, built with experience, be flexible and open to tread new avenues. Trying to carbon copy the culture and processes followed by developed countries will never work in India because Indians have not been exposed to every step of the West's industrial revolution and evolution.

To become globally competitive, India can use extreme discipline and customize the world's best management practices for its multi-diverse people. But the discipline and work culture must be uniquely billion-mindset driven. Collectively Indian business houses need to undergo wholesome struggle to displace non-productive old values and achieve the ambition of becoming world famous, aspirational, innovative and growing powerhouses.

big bang displacement

Century after century, different European theoreticians have come up with theory after theory. A few were appreciated and practically applied. Mediocre conservatives who didn't understand out-of-the-box theories tried to destroy them. It was largely in the 20th century that most of these past theories on different aspects of civilization were validated and applied. The unparalleled struggle experienced through the two World Wars, disgraceful Nazi SS (*Schutzstaffel* meaning protected squad) torture of Jews, the Pearl Harbour attack and bombing of Hiroshima forced a new era of counter survival tactics. This struggle culminated in a melting pot of innovation that used many old theories to build new avenues like Big Bang that led to the Milky Way emerging from cosmic collisions.

The Wars ignited incredible innovation that has led to differing thought processes to facilitate better living comfort. By 1945, Western Europe, USA, Japan, and China found their socio-cultural and economic life being totally displaced from their past ways of living. The technology highway aided and speeded up new global business relationships. Such mental and physical displacements gave rise to Big Bang like innovations. My view is that both natural and man made displacements have positive or negative impact.

what is displacement?

People get displaced for reasons like political disturbance or economic reform and recession. Innovation can displace people's needs and desires. Here, people don't want to go back to the old system. For example, when we can make photocopies, we'd rather not have a carbon copy; when the CD is here, why return to the vinyl musical disks? The exception, of course, is music collectors or professional disk jockeys.

successful displacement

Check the team composition of the creators of the atom bomb and hydrogen bomb. Their common factor? Most of them were Jewish. From Albert Einstein onwards, they immigrated from Germany, Hungary and Austria; except Oppenheimer who was an American-born Jew. The pain flowing in the spirit of these scientists was Nazi torture and bloodshed of 6 million Jews, 4 million gypsies, homosexuals and the disabled. Through their work they revenged this ravage of an entire race.

My belief is that the struggles of the 20th century compelled scientists to combat fear and persecution with invention. They innovated as never before, dipping into knowledge that had existed in earlier centuries.

From 1920 to 1945, a huge sociocultural and economic displacement followed the economic recession. As a people, Americans cultivate a sense of belongingness for their country. Immigrants from across the world feel a welcome that is not experienced by immigrants in any other country. They maintain the individuality of their origin yet identify themselves with the American populace. These positive displacements happen in spite of the fact that Caucasian Americans had dislodged the native Indian Americans, and have been extremely racist with people of African origin. Their unstinting confidence of being able to blend in an intellectual melting pot has made Americans the strongest nation on earth.

non-integrated displacement

France has a diametrically opposite example. Six million North Africans form 10 percent of France's population. When the French colony of Algeria attained independence in 1960, France enticed Algerians to come for manual work. French infrastructure had to be rebuilt after World War II and the depleted French population was not ready for manual labor. Considering this an opportunity to enjoy glamorous European living and comfort, Algerians, Moroccans and Tunisians flooded into France. Initially they considered this move to be of economic advantage, not as mental displacement to become a French citizen.

The French Government had demarcated areas where they gave the North African community the opportunity to be together in France. This created a kind of isolation from mainstream French society.

The immigrants live here by their own rules. My Algerian friend explained that a typical father-to-daughter command used to be: 'Consider this home to be in Algiers. Outside our four walls is the foreign country, France where women are easy going. When you go out for an errand, return straight home. Don't look to the left or right. If I see you anywhere else, I will stab you to death.'

Being part of the worker class in my first few years in Paris, I befriended many North Africans. They enjoy seeing the romantic Indian silver screen pair of Nargis and Raj Kapoor in 1950s and 1960s Hindi films. They find Indian civilization to be closer to theirs than European culture. They treated me like their folkloric brother.

This fraternal relationship got me invited one day to a family occasion in an Algerian friend's home in north Paris. I arrived at 4 P.M. at Cour Neuve to a very small home shared by 10 family members. Festivities started by first slaughtering a sheep inside the house. Then they cleaned and prepared the animal for roasting whole in front of the guests. More friends joined us, and we were about 40 people squeezed into the tiny room. The lamb was cooking in the center, surrounded by a musical soiree with darbuka, bendir and Rai songs.

It was a fantastic evening. I felt I was dreaming or playing a part in the Arabian Nights. The revelry went on till the wee hours of 4 am; the neighbors were unperturbed by the party. In the French neighborhood I lived in, 65 rue Didot in Paris 14th district, such an ambience and event would have been impossible. My Algerian friends say they follow all the customs and rituals of their home villages here, without a worry about conforming to foreign living norms. The French who migrated from Europe and the original French people do not understand this and fear to enter such a North African complex. In today's generation there will be many people of North African descent who are French nationals, but they are North African in discipline.

Even after three generations, Algerians haven't made a mental shift to embrace France as their own. Moroccan and Tunisian labor have similar feelings. About 1,000 North African families occupy each large multi-storied building. Attractive in 1960, these habitations are insecure hubs now. Aggressive, jobless third-generation immigrants commit violence, rape, burglary and hooliganism. The French establishment finds it difficult to understand the depth of their culture. Occidental France has deep-rooted Catholic culture that is very different from Islam. This cultural chasm belies any displacement.

Zinedine Zidane was not given much attention prior to his propelling France into victory in the World Football Cup in 1998. He may be an example of how many barriers North Africans may have to cross in France. Arabs were not visible in French electronic media 10 years ago. Zidane and singer Khaled changed the rules with their extraordinary talent.

Zidane's fabulous 1998 World Cup performance shot him into overnight fame, and incredibly transformed the product marketing climate in France. People experienced a culture shock that even Christian Dior signed up Zidane for his advertisements, exclaiming: 'An Arab promoting the most aspirational, international, French fashion brand!' His talent made this North African a media hugging celebrity, and the French accepted this per force. Does Zidane feel himself a displaced Algerian or a Frenchman?

I remember, the Socialist Government in the 1980s tried to integrate North African immigrants by using the exceptional talent of singer Khaled. To get the French to accept him, his first album was released with his photo in the middle and an advertising slogan that said, 'These are not Arab songs.' But actually they were all Arab songs.

The Socialist Government tried very hard to displace the attitude and behavior of both the French and immigrants to mutually understand and recognize each other. Unfortunately French Caucasians psychologically harbor racist tendencies against North Africans. The extreme right converted this bias into a political opportunity saying, '*Les francais d'abord, les immigrants dehors,*' meaning 'French first, immigrants outside.' So the social fracture continues.

Undercurrents of French parochial vocabulary such as '*J'aime pas les Arabes* (I don't like Arabs)' further alienate the immigrants. Democratic France with the human right dictum of 'Liberty, equality, fraternity' still has no elected immigrant Member of Parliament (as of March 2007). The social distance has become so grave that 2005 saw the start of immigrant riots breaking out across the country. The French are very scared of the North African population and don't know how to handle them. This example shows displacement gone awry.

In contrast, my personal integration in France is devoid of racism. Through my professional graduation from worker to high corporate executive to businessman today, I have enjoyed relationships with people across the board without ever feeling segregated. French high society in both business and in cultural interactions has given me unstinted support and respect for my work and thought process. Unlike a Christian or Muslim whose inability to deviate from a religious root can result in a head-on clash, a Hindu has no religious box he cannot escape from. On a wider perspective, I would say the dogma-less, open Hindu culture enabled me to adjust.

The US encourages different quarters for Koreans, Chinese, Puerto Ricans and other immigrants, and yet they are not entirely free of racism. Unlike a proud American immigrant, immigrants to France have two constraints:

(*i*)   Being American is very important in America's recent cultural collage. People work hard and achieve economic success without facing racial barriers. In contrast, the culture of hard work is not obvious in France. Social compensation for being jobless is more than adequate. This diminishes the passion for work. Immigrants can take advantage, feed on the dole and not work.

(*ii*) Immigrants rarely feel they belong as French Catholic heritage is not very inclusive. France may need to rethink its parochial culture, be open to blending to make immigrants spontaneously say, 'I am French, so I am above religion.' French culture and thought have always gone beyond any barrier, from Pascal's theory to Gustave's Eiffel Tower to the TGV design.

Another displacement without integration: Political displacement creates refugees. A refugee with a horrific previous situation will choose to start a new life. Nobody wants to return to the unpleasant old; but sentiments of their country of origin stay imprinted in their minds. My Vietnamese colleagues in Paris spoke about their terrible experiences as boat people. Whole families fled afloat boats with unknown destinations. The vessels sailed for days; food became scarce. Weak passengers were allegedly killed so the others could eat them and survive. Survival under such sickening situations after escape from political torture made the boat people take asylum in France.

The Vietnamese and Chinese have their own localities in France. They are not aggressive, nor do they disturb anyone, but they still do not think they are integrated into French culture in spite of having gained French nationality. Population growth since 1950 may have largely come from immigrants, not the original Caucasian people of France.

Both North African and Vietnamese communities feel geographically displaced by force, so they emotionally return to their roots. People's attitude and behavior cannot be displaced into the migrant country if the mind continues to look back at the displaced root. Such unsatisfactory displacement creates disintegration. It is indeed dangerous for socio-economic stability and work culture. It's preventing the French from taking forward the *avant-garde* movement they are historically famous for.

chaos of political displacement

My father and millions of Bengali Hindus had to suddenly leave East Bengal as refugees during Independence from the British in 1947. They considered religious partition as artificial and shameful, motivated by politicians who brought Hindu and Muslim fundamentalists from other Indian states to infiltrate and ignite Bengal. They cite how the people rebelled against the controversial previous attempt at partition by Lord Curzon in 1905, and how in 1971 Muslim and Hindu Bengalis combined to fight Pakistan to liberate Bangladesh. East Bengal became East Pakistan in 1947, and after 1971, became an independent nation called Bangladesh.

Was Bengal always too difficult to control? Chronic upheavals here perhaps prompted the British to shift their capital from

Calcutta to Delhi in 1912. Of course Delhi was also topographically more suitable for better administrative control of greater India as proved by the Mughals who preceded the British. In my view, the Indian *Raj* that followed the British anticipated that Bengalis would numerically exceed the number of elected Parliamentarians from the Hindi-speaking belt. This fear prompted the break up of East and West Bengal, a tactical solution to India's partition favoring a section of leaders.

Our refugee colony in West Bengal was on squatted, abandoned land with no amenities like water, sanitation or electricity. A disturbing childhood memory I have is of a man from the municipality who would come around every year tom-tomming a drum slung around his neck. In a loud, dramatic voice he would threaten forfeiture of the land we had squatted upon if we failed to inscribe our presence in India by marking attendance in the municipality office on a regular basis. I used to rush to ask my grandmother why we were going to be thrown out of our home. She would fabricate many tales to make me feel secure and forget the dramatic message of the percussionist.

Such force-fit displacement alienates immigrants from integration. Landless and houseless immigrants have increased since 1947; most do not accept the state of West Bengal as their home, nor India as their country. This is another displacement characteristic where people just cannot mentally adjust, thinking they have somehow been deceived.

Sociocultural non-integration has made India's West Bengal totally unbalanced and economically underdeveloped. After 1947 the Left party consoled immigrants with socio-psycho comfort of bringing them under their shelter.

A third generation Bengali migrant is still likely to name a village or district in East Bengal as his origin. With economic reforms and a technology revolution sweeping across India, perhaps the fourth generation Bengali immigrants will feel India to be their country. That's when real displacement will take place.

· The three scenarios in three continents prove that displacement will remain incomplete until immigrants and people in their host country are mentally and socially integrated:

(*i*) Positive: Jewish immigrants to North America,

(*ii*) Negative: North African and Vietnamese immigrants in France, and

(*iii*) Chaos: East Bengal immigrants into West Bengal.

Receiving honor and acceptance as did the immigrant Jewish scientists in the US, helped them displace mentally and socially. They gave their very best to innovate and grow in their adopted country. With no opportunity to participate in French social culture, North Africans have created a social fracture. Migrant East Bengalis feel duped, so they do not care to use their intellectual acumen to make West Bengal flourish like they should have.

Let's compare how the maverick *jalebi* with its obviously spiraling character comprises an integrated holistic system. Displaced persons may enter a country or new recruits from other organizational cultures can enter your company, but do you round off all uneven edges like a *jalebi* does? A *jalebi* connects at different fragile points to get bigger and bigger. The moral fiber in any country or corporate culture can also grow when thought is not confined within the box.

Your process may have a regular temperament, but it has to be activated by different individuals, all of whom have their own behavior. The *jalebi* provides the perfect balance. From its central form to its irregular extremities, the taste of the *jalebi* is uniform. Imitate it.

wholesome struggle to build new avenues

Some people make themselves victims of struggle, others use struggle as a challenge to totally change their lives, as 20th century

Europeans have done. World War I witnessed human loss of 9 million, over 51 million died in World War II including killings from Nazi atrocities. My childhood struggle in abject poverty pales in the face of this enormous life struggle. I became conscious of this after visiting Auschwitz concentration camps in Poland that first time in 1990.

Films of Nazi torment of Jews were more Hollywoodian cinematic expression for me than reality, until Auschwitz opened my eyes to the horrors humans can resort to. The Nazis tortured and sucked innocent Jewish people into becoming dry dead shells, drained of emotions, relationships and family bonding. The recollection of Szpilman, the pianist who survived the Nazi camp was starkly narrated on film by director Roman Polanski, himself a victim in a Nazi concentration camp. From the passion and genius of the director and protagonist, their struggle to survive those beleaguered times is obvious in the film 'The Pianist'.

India faced no death squad struggle

India has not faced any real life threatening mass struggle especially in the last two centuries. The British *Raj* divided India to rule it. They encouraged scraps among local ruling princes to come to blows, and magnified the existing class and caste systems so they could sit on judgment. As a country India never did fight a real opponent; this increased the tolerance level of its people. Inefficient political leaders have converted tolerance into a religious showcase. If you put frogs in hot water they will not die, they will jump to survive. Did Indians ever have to jump to escape a tormenting situation?

Actually India's independence in 1947 was probably a fallout from the turbulence the British experienced in their home country. World War II and Nazi dictatorship frightened the world into uniting towards a civilized society. Britain's people and Army seemed unwilling to continue with repression in the Empire, so freedom for India was inevitable. Even Sir Winston Churchill who led the Allies into victory was not chosen to steer Britain as Prime Minister in peace time. He won the election, but his party lost the power to rule. England understood that colonialism and dictatorship are not too different from one another.

I see distinct similarity between British imperialism and Nazi dictatorship:

(*i*) The British injected English culture into their colonies across the world. Like slow poison they used more than two centuries to convert people into thinking like them, changing their original values and thought processes.

(*ii*) The Nazi regime wanted first and foremost to have dominating power over the white races of the world. Their method of perfecting the ruling Aryan class was to eradicate those they believed to be too inferior to have a right to live on earth. This led to their fifteen-year spree of mass torture and killing in Europe.

If you objectively read German or British history, their ruling instincts were more or less the same. The Germans employed the hard dose of extermination while the British used the soft dose of cultural transformation.

The hard dose of destruction tactics boomerangs on the perpetuators, as recorded in Germany's historical archives. In mid-2006, over 60 years after the Nazis ruled Germany, when Pope Benedict went from the Vatican to Auswichtz, he apologized for Nazi human crimes. Being a son of Germany he felt the need to do so before he could talk of world peace.

In World War II Churchill led the Allied Army against Hitler, yet in speeches he'd utter, 'The British Empire will not tolerate that.' For him this was a fight of the Empire versus a dictator. In such a statement, where is the difference between colonial mentality and fighting to protect humanity and democracy?

History has proved that a soft dose has lasting impact. Britain's obsession with imperial pelf gets no less attention even from their Left wing governments. Britain and erstwhile colonies in the Commonwealth of Nations, still kowtow to Buckingham Palace, Lady Di and Camilla, giving them superior majestic stature. Why did independent India invite Lord Mountbatten, the last British Governor-General to remain as her ceremonial head for a year? The strong influence of the soft dose is obviously at play.

India eulogizes tolerance as a religion. But has tolerance helped displace the country's subjugated outlook? Have Indians aggressively moved to create unique differentiation globally, either through a commercial or innovative act? Without having undergone wholesome struggle, the monotony of life stills ebbs and flows in India. The British instigated independent monarchies to quarrel, and created the supreme ruling nation state of India. I've never understood why our first democratic general election took place in 1952 even though we achieved freedom in 1947.

The economic reforms of 1991, revised since Rajiv Gandhi had introduced them in the mid-1980s, came as suddenly as Independence did in 1947. The liberalized economy changed the country's perspective. Indian industrial tycoons did not initially recognize this change and the opportunities it threw open until WTO knocked on the door. Their lack of competitive killer instinct in business has a reason. From India's independence movement came the hand *charka* (loom spindle) as a symbol of protest. This was more a philosophical concept against being colonized than a business or the country's growth vision. But in the fervor of seeking freedom, the *charka* ended up giving active direction to people in general and to the business community in particular.

Business succeeds with competition, speed, creating differentiation and with organizational discipline. It has evolved through handmade products to mechanical, industrial and technology applications. The *charka* symbol does not reflect this path of business development and is a dissonance in the world of technology today. If you cage a tiger he loses aggressiveness, as did Indian business in the Licence *Raj* post Independence.

The vision of a genius is lateral, a big thought that sustains for the long term. Six hundred years ago Leonardo da Vinci outlined a vision of how people could be flying. Through the six centuries that this thought has existed, it has now metamorphosed into today's airplane. This vision has combined human curiosity to knowledge, leading to improvement in living conditions and creation of economic wealth. In our contemporary economy where IT is booming, the political act of the *charka* is not relevant.

The need of the hour for Indian companies is displacement with wholesome struggle in organizational culture. Pre-1991 was a business culture sans competition, so no real struggle. Indian business leaders should take global competition as the real struggle. By creating pressure through 'self struggle' they can conquer business over globally reputed companies across the world.

My *jalebi* journey from my art college life in the streets of Kolkata upto the Parisian *jalebi* in a North African sweet shop impelled me to discover the world of business with the ever-growing rings that form the *jalebi* culture. A *jalebi* is so simple and tasty. This simplicity is its biggest goodwill. It makes people understand easily, straining less effort. In this *jalebi* story unfolding for you here, you may find essential factors that relate to whichever vertical your business is in.

Those of you not in business could surely be *jalebi*s lovers too. Have you experienced a *jalebi* making process? I am translating my global experience in corporate value creation and in strategizing within management complexity into this *Jalebi Management* book for you to bite into. Discover and enjoy multiple forms of *jalebi* making with your very own sensorial familiarity, either with your million-mindset or your billion-mindset.

create discomfort

Is *jalebi* street food? Ask for it in a sophisticated Indian 5 star hotel and you'll throw the restaurant manager into total discomfort. An intelligent, courteous chef will request you to return on an appointed day, saying he'll make *jalebi* especially for you. Yes, I've experienced many such promises! That's because *jalebi* needs preparation time for good fermentation to make it crunchy and tasty.

Similarly, no organization or vendor can find instant solutions, not even one producing instantly consuming products. Every individual being different, an organization needs to proactively use multiple dimensions of consumer sensitivity. A given preparation time to season internal operations is required, just like the *jalebi* does, to make a palatable consumer-sensitive delivery.

Delicious *jalebi* is versatile, enjoyed by the roadside, in upper class homes, in high-end hotels, for breakfast, lunch, tea, snacks and dinner. An unsuspecting chef is discomfited by your sudden request for a *jalebi*; likewise, as the CEO you should generate discomfort in every functional area. Sensitize employees about the consumers' versatile requirements. When you surpass a consumer's expectations to reach her desire level, you will touch latent social trends.

Social mores dictate consumerism. An organization not relating to social trends becomes laid back; consequently, business can shrink. Employees need to undergo a certain amount of discomfort in trying to connect to the latent perspective so as to create business differentiation in the market.

Organizational discomfort means pushing the whole organization towards change that leads to strategic innovation which differentiates, sells better and raises profit. Western societies have implicitly mastered discomfort in their hunger to discover the new and for better living. Stretching thought into lateral areas, they have gone beyond the obvious. Before I select six telling areas later in this chapter to illustrate how they made a difference in changing the world, let's look at the way we individually shock-absorb discomfort.

Of the innumerable activities outside your workplace, with family, friends or in social gatherings, something suddenly can disturb you. Your personal life has many surprises you absorb as part of the trend. You may not even notice it, as it becomes implicit; you expect it. In time, such social discomfort, so different from India's non-liberalized days, can even convince you that you enjoy it.

Look at your 18-year-old daughter's low-cut trousers. They're precariously hugging her hips, the T-shirt is barely covering her belly. To establish a trend, she's creating discomfort in the parent in you, and in the social environment. Fifteen years ago, a middle class Indian girl would think it immodest dressing. Will you admonish your child's new dressing style? Wouldn't you rather understand her new ways and become a liberal parent?

If you're over 40, you'll remember your young life in India with stringent home return timings, no grace period for girls. It was an adventure escaping parents and neighborhood spies for that secret love affair, or even to converse with the opposite sex! A 25-year-old today easily introduces romantic relationships to parents who may feel discomfited at the variance from their childhood, but accept the change as the contemporary way to be.

In contrast, when it comes to the workplace, predictable routine reigns supreme, keeping the employee in total comfort zone. The conventional workplace has imposing dogma employees easily distance themselves from. They don't expect or want flexibility from 'The Company.' They resist change, become risk averse, and refuse to go along with any discomfort in the working system.

Your consumers may be similar to your belly-baring daughter. Why then must you oppose discomfort at work? Only if an organization, whether it's small, medium or big, continuously perpetuates discomfort within the workplace, can it meet success.

discomfort brings innovation

The whole organization needs to feel a certain discomfort to set innovation in motion. Keeping the antenna up for the not-so-obvious is the only way to win the business game. Discomfort propels you to know that your achievement to date is not a throne to sit pretty upon, or to command the market from. Being self-righteous in business can jeopardize your long-term business existence. When knowhow is easily accessible in every domain nowadays, an unexpected challenger can shake up the traditional market at any time. Apple's iPod did just this, disrupting Sony's undisputed leadership in the audio-video player market.

Sony may never have imagined that Apple could cross its threshold to get into the music territory. Having vibrated the mass consumption electronic market with trendy musical products these last 50 years, Sony may have overlooked creating discomfort for itself. iPod is no rocket science, just extreme consumer sensitivity in managing music. iPod's outstanding concept of being a trendy pocket music dictionary has made it an addiction.

Following World War II, Japan's strategic business step was very clear: The war has broken us, let's not waste initial reconstruction time with fundamental innovation the West has already done.

Japanese products in the 1960s were perceived to be of very low quality. When they improved in the 1970s, Europeans would caricature them as 'copy masters.' The West failed to beware of the fact that the Japanese imitated to better the original as renovation. The Japanese innovated by establishing a marketing approach to product design. They minutely studied Western innovation, sociology and psychology, concentrating on how consumers approached and used products. Then zeroed in on the concept of miniaturization as the consumer-friendly solution of gaining consumer proximity.

Europeans paid no heed to this 'marketing of design,' but consumers were clearly endeared to innovative smallness in product design. French automobile companies did attempt marketing a small car to change the American culture of bigness, but it was the Japanese who succeeded in indulging Americans with small cars, compact motorbikes and electronic gadgets. Miniaturization has tremendous universal appeal anywhere in the world. The Japanese own the concept and enjoy its proximity with the masses.

Miniaturization evolved from the Japanese tradition of minimalism, the religious Buddhist way of life, the symbolic form of bonsai art. A bonsai plant is genetically pure; in miniature format, its authenticity remains intact.

If I were to mime Japanese miniaturization this is how it would be (see Figure 2.1): The European symbol for perfection is akin to the palms of both hands joining, finger on outstretched finger. This symbol of a perfect unbreakable joint is applicable for any sophisticated manufacturing process. What the Japanese have done is slightly twisted the two joined palms so that the outstretched fingers from one hand touch the edges of the other. This now enables the fingers to fold on the back of the palm, allowing a snug hug of the two hands. This coziness is miniaturization. This principle applies in every product of Western origin that the Japanese have miniaturized.

Figure 2.1 European perfection in innovation and Japanese renovation is miniaturization

European Perfection in Innovation	Japanese Renovation is Miniaturization
Both palms joining, finger on outstretched finger 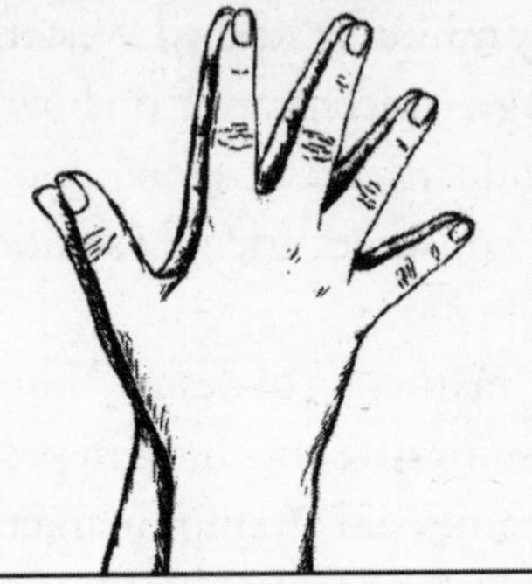	Snug hug of two palms, fingers behind palms 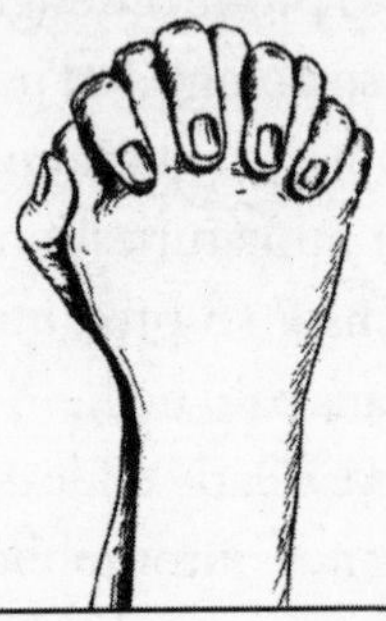

With spectacular renovation of Western innovation, the Japanese have now achieved global leadership in many connoisseur European businesses such as cameras, motorbikes, automobiles, electronic entertainment systems among others. As Europeans busied themselves conducting analysis after laboratory analysis, the Japanese concentrated on surprising the global consumer by breaking local tradition. It was as though Philips invented, and Sony marketed. Caught unawares by the iPod in this century, Sony may surely be working in intense discomfort now for another breakthrough marketing innovation to regain their market.

Through Europe's 2000 years of Judeo-Christian history, Western society has developed through the discomfort route. Hygienic living comfort was at the root of this culture. When a Roman king would conquer any country, the first infrastructure constructed in the new place would be the water supply system. This bygone water circulation system, still visible today, displays their finicky compulsion for civilized living practices. The rulers used to stretch the social system with total discomfort to achieve the art of good living through innovation.

discomfort led to many innovations

Before the advent of science and scientific instruments, Galileo sat under a tree, figured out the concept of heavenly bodies structured into planets and tried to prove it to a disbelieving public. His anti-establishment thoughts were much ahead of his time. Similarly Newton too had sat under an apple tree and proved the theory of gravitation.

Six hundred years ago Leonardo da Vinci's anti-establishment temperament was directed towards the service of humankind. The ability to think laterally, and the desire to live comfortably and hygienically are not God given traits, but manmade practices of Western civilization. People created discomfort by demanding comfort and thus created the ethos of forward-looking vision.

Osmosis of thought among painters, writers, filmmakers and inventors from the 19th century created significant discomfort. Paintings and lithography were used to record historical events. Suddenly in 1826 French inventor Joseph Nicephore Niepce clicked photography in and opened up a new chapter in the thinking process of the West.

Photography dislodged painters from their prime status, rendering them disposable. This discomfort gave birth to newer styles of art beyond the realism of portraits, still life, landscapes, and religious interpretations in canvas or frescos. Vincent van Gogh in 1888 created the Expressionist style of art. Monet introduced Impressionism in 1897, while Picasso and Braques brought Cubism.

In 1929 Salvadore Dali and Max Ernst made Surrealism a recognized style, while Mondrian in 1940 made abstract paintings popular. The American artist Andy Warhol launched Pop art in 1960, and by 1965 Vasarely established the Graphic form as art. This evolution of art will be further elaborated in the first of my selected six controversial areas that have since made great business and economic sense.

Painters, writers, film directors and inventors were very vision-ary and really astonished the world. *Elephant Celebes*, a 1921 oil painting by Max Ernst shows a robotic man walking. Such robots didn't exist then. Writer H.G. Wells predicted tanks, warfare and the atom bomb in 1913 in his book, *The World Set Free*. Inspired by these futuristic forms, film director William Cameron Menzies made *The Shape of Things to Come* in 1936. The movie showed air warfare and the atom bomb for the first time. And in 1945 Leo Szilard actually invented the atom bomb that looked incred-ibly similar to Max Ernst's robot painting of 1921.

The invention of laser lights again demonstrates osmosis of thought. Painter, philosopher and writer Man Ray created, in 1931, a current-like illumination over a semi-nude woman's body to express her character. In 1937, scientist Albert Einstein theorized the process of 'stimulated emission' which makes laser possible. Film director Fred M. Wilcox made *Forbidden Planet* in 1956 showing human evolution with electric beam effects. Gordon Gould subsequently invented the optical light laser in 1958.

The discomfort that photography and cinema created was very visible. Prominent FBI agent J. Edgar Hoover was totally against realistic documentary films. His concern that television and cinema had political influence over Americans led him to encour-age the House of Un-American Activities Committee (HUAC) to investigate into the entertainment industry. In 1950, a list of 151 writers, directors and performers was culled from FBI files and American Communist Party publications, and these people blacklisted for supposedly being members of subversive organ-izations. He alerted the American people that such films were propaganda that encouraged antisocial elements in the country.

Hoover was totally unhappy when Charlie Chaplain made *The Great Dictator* on Adolf Hitler and other films on American society. In 1952, when Charlie Chaplain had gone to London with his fourth wife Oona, American authorities informed him that he would not be allowed to return to USA.

Hoover's disquiet came from Nazi use of cinematography to inspire people to annihilate Jews and other 'undesirables.' In 1943 Hitler, who considered Jews of less human substance as they were not Aryans, said to his aide, Joseph Goebbels, 'In nature life always works immediately against parasites; in the existence of peoples that is not exclusively the case. From that results the Jewish danger. So there is nothing else open to modern peoples than to exterminate the Jews.' For propaganda purposes, SS filmmakers used films to keep such evidence that they did not consider as crime, but a necessity. This made Hoover suspicious of people who used the film medium.

I feel it is important for large emerging countries like India to understand that European culture developed through an excellent fusion of discomfort thoughts shared among writers, philosophers, painters, inventors and musicians in every era. Invention or innovation is rarely the upshot of concentration on a single subject. A painter's palette is not just a carrier of colors, it powerfully blends and transfers inspiration to grow different intellects. This blend of intellect morphs into tremendous inventive and innovative power.

People in the West have the capability to create self-struggle that generates thought, which leads to a vision and materializes in human development. This passion to take on discomfort by the horns, disintegrate it, and move forward, was prevalent in all domains. In some ways this was the maturing of the West.

If we were to go back to Harappa and Mohenjodaro, the East was far ahead. Perhaps discomfort is the sign of extremely affluent societies, or is it a sign of all societies? We develop, we destroy, and develop again. Perhaps that is how nations, societies and even organizations grow.

In the case of organizations, the destroyed item could be replaced by renovation. Develop, renovate to change myself, and innovate to change the world.

Why do billion-mindset countries need to imbibe discomfort? From consulting with emerging country companies, I find they pay scant heed to Japanese and Western companies, approaching them very casually as peripheral competition. When a globally reputed company (GRC) unveils a competing product, the Indian company complacently questions, 'Will it succeed?' instead of finding a better alternative to the GRC's offering. They fail to check out the root cause of GRC's success, and perhaps just quick-fix their deliverables for short-term gains. Their further questioning of whether Indian consumers are ready to buy into sophisticated innovation is quite baseless and judgmental. Consumers with money are always open to alternative choice and better options.

The Japanese, since the 1950s, have been exceptional in seeing things differently. They link microscopic observation to quality in product development.

I remember seeing Japanese groups traveling around Europe in the early 1970s, always with cameras. Their collective discipline makes them process the microtones of their observation into high quality deliverables. Microtone is a Western musical term where multiple instruments play different chords with different tones to arrive at a harmonious melody. Should there be a mistake in these different chords or tones, the melody output will be corrupted.

That is why during the period a subject is being observed, the Japanese don't allow any criticism. The subject must be kept intact and understood in a holistic way, without distorting its image or substance with preconceived thought baggage.

When something already exists it would have gone through different processes, struggles and exhaustion. If you observe with curiosity, you fulfill the objective of going in-depth into the subject. Only questioning without understanding every step will make you a good school teacher who does not innovate.

The Japanese delve into the total package, not its surface. Having thoroughly understood its complexity, they top-up with added value. The object's first and fundamental innovative system is kept intact. The Japanese reinvented the European motorbike in a Japanese style and conquered the world with it.

The piano is a good example of Japanese renovation. This sophisticated European acoustic musical instrument needs perfection at every stage. Although the German piano is acclaimed the best in the world, look at which piano is the most popular with rock, pop, classical singers or musicians on stage anywhere in the world today. It's the Japanese Yamaha, its brand blinking on the piano's side, showing itself off in any music program. Is India capable of producing a world-class product one day that will replace the best that is available?

We are proud to be an intellectual society in India. But can our collective intellectual power, not individual intelligence, help us attain world-class business processes and products? The billion-mindset economies need to grow a disciplined business mentality that can dissect success. To challenge the market, our professionals must collectively understand how and why innovation happened in developed countries. This will orient them towards the very foundation of the innovation mechanism.

South Koreans are following the route the Japanese took, with fantastic visible results. They are already competing globally and taking leadership in areas like hybrid steel, consumer dur-ables, electronics and the automobile business.

In my experience in China, I find Chairman Mao Zedong has sharpened focus on their national character of discipline even outside politics. Discipline was taken to torturous heights even in the prestigious Peking Opera in earlier days. Unwanted orphans were brought here at a very tender age, physically tormented with disciplined training and transformed into famous stage musicians and singers. Adolescent students who manage to escape, invariably return to their focused training. That's because they crave the spontaneous adulation they see Peking Opera stage performers evoke in the public.

Chinese product quality may still be embryonic. With stringent discipline, positive mindset and following in Japanese footsteps they will overcome their current deficiency and stigma with radically improved inherent quality within 5 to 10 years.

In 2002 Jean Michel Jarre, the laser and electronic entertainment master musician, made a spectacular concert called *Forbidden City* at the Red Square. Jean Michel is the son of the celebrated music director, Maurice Jarre, whose *Dr Zhivago* and *Love Story* have become the world's standard in easy listening. Jean Michel Jarre's concert was unique because he wove together the Beijing Symphony Orchestra, Chinese National Orchestra, Beijing Opera chorus and notable Chinese rock musicians in a two-hour open air Western music concert.

In normal course Western performers bring their own musicians. This successful direction of Western music with Chinese musicians amazed everyone as even traditional Chinese instruments were played in Western style. A billion Chinese viewers saw the show live on stage and TV. Enjoying the musical program on DVD, I watched with interest the capability of the Chinese to enter a new realm with calculated ease. Their command over discipline and curiosity proved to me that China will be the future business driver of the world.

To my dismay I have discovered a school of thought in India that needs to only understand failures, not to learn from them but as standalone case study subjects. They don't enquire about how successful companies have achieved their triumph.

Failure in a company could have several reasons ranging from misjudging market potential, strategy that does not match the organization's culture or marketing, vendor management, production, procurement and sales activation, to just plain wrong communication. There is no reason to suggest that applying a similar strategy in another company under different conditions will result in failure. You'll never know the root cause of any failure in detail as nobody will reveal it. But success can be emulated because everyone proudly shares winning case studies. Examining the wins is more useful for directing business wins.

Business is not a sportsman's life that's effective for a maximum of 10 to 15 years. The failure of a high quality product needs to be studied with curiosity, and from all angles. If you bring positive energy into a failed subject you may refuel its success. Was the French Concorde a failure? Was it not extreme innovation that could fly over Mach 3, close the distance from one country to another in half the time of normal aircrafts? In business, the word failure does not work.

The Japanese are now working on a supersonic aircraft to be launched in about 15 years. Their attempt is to reduce sound and increase seats. They have failed twice, but have recently made a successful trial.

Business is not akin to questions and answers (Q&A) in a school or workshop. A hangover from our theoretical and pedagogic education, the Q&A mentality does not allow the subject to move forward. The mind of a consumer or customer is not predictable, nor is the innovative world or the competitive environment written in a book. Business grows encircling these phenomena, not with questions.

The Q&A culture has seeped into India's Hindi films as well. Most movie dialogs give advice rather than create new paradigms of knowledge, intellectual advancement or art form. The masses get no food for thought watching the films. Innovation in business has to be a passion of curiosity to change the world with, not to question it.

In the open markets of the world's emerging economy countries, end consumers are enjoying a heightened lifestyle with GRC product offers. As an industrial house here, you may modernize your business to compete, but unless you inquire into your global competitor's origin of success, your market growth will merely touch the surface, and not sustain.

six domains that changed the world through discomfort and grew the economy

Out of countless activities that have caused discomfort in the world, I have identified six dominant fields that I believe have dramatically changed human perception. These six selected inflections have made deep inroads into psychological and sociological spheres, which then have culminated in business aggrandizement. People initially resisted these specific fields, making them controversial. Yet they have become memorable for their tremendous commercial success. My six chosen subjects are:

1. Painters have magnified the field of imagination. Before the advent of photography when paintings had represented reality, if an exceptional painter deviated from reproducing realistic form, he was considered anti-society or just plain crazy. Post the monotony of realism in the 19th century, paintings spawned from the discomfort that seeped into the community of Western artists. The first form in the evolution of art was Expressionism followed by Impressionism.

Expressionism is the artist's interpreted form of a realistic subject. It creates a pictorial form in spite of being twisted as per the artist's imagination. Vincent van Gogh's paintings were quite realistic when he was in his motherland, Holland. Look at his *Potato Eaters* in 1885. The atmosphere of the painting was very dark and gloomy, reflecting his background amongst the working class miners in the Netherlands. He came to France in 1886, and a radical change was seen in his palette. His *Sunflowers* painted in 1888 is bright and cheerful, interpreted quite unlike any other artist's expression. It does not look like a photograph.

His failure was van Gogh's discomfort, which fueled the paintings he did in France to become hallucinating in expression. Discomfited with his interpretations, society failed to recognize his genius, so his talent did not figure in any radar. During his lifetime van Gogh sold only a single painting. Eccentricity and madness made him commit suicide in 1890 at the age of 37.

After his death, van Gogh's work was somehow discovered. Europe's openness towards artistic talent is interesting. The extremely high value of his paintings today has created wealth for van Gogh's collectors and museums in different parts of the world. This creator of discomfort left behind an *avant-garde* vision of color with brushstrokes on canvas.

Van Gogh's discomfort was transformed to ideology in a new era of art philosophy. His art is kept alive and magnified for the world to appreciate even after a hundred years of his death. Can business be compared to van Gogh? Are we capable of reviving a neglected dead shell of a brand or company after its tangible presence is gone?

An Impressionist painter executes reality in semi abstract form. Unlike Michelangelo who was a realistic artist, Claude Monet painted his thoughts. Monet painted *WaterLilies* in 1897 from his French style county house at Giverny, 74 kilometers from Paris. His lily pond had an imaginative character, a new light much above its basic reality. People visit Monet's house amidst wild vegetation which itself is like a canvas that is said to be the genesis of Impressionism in 1870s.

As the Expressionist and Impressionist art epochs were building up, Pablo Picasso and Georges Braque introduced discomfort at the turn of the 20th century by starting the Cubist movement. A totally new style influenced by tribal art, Cubism simultaneously interpreted the essence of an object, human being or nature from multiple viewpoints. Picasso worked with the human character whereas Georges Braque's Cubism was more with objects and nature.

Braque and Picasso shared a close partnership in the same studio for a few years in 1908–12. They were 'roped together like mountaineers,' said Braque. Picasso was very impetuous and Braque had a sense of order. Their joint ideas unearthed and contributed an immense cultural treasure. Their vision of Cubism created discomfort in the art world at that time.

Surrealism and the Dada movement were discomfiting jerks of the 1930s. Surrealism is realism in an imaginative world. This style had its roots in the Dada movement, an artistic and literary movement in Western Europe in 1916–23. Dadaists wanted to discover authentic reality by abolishing traditional culture and aesthetic forms. Their disgust for bourgeois values and despair over World War I made them anti-establishment.

Evolving through the phases of Cubism, futurism and metaphysical painting, Salvador Dali joined the Surrealists in Paris in 1929. The group comprised of painters Max Ernst, Yves Tanguy and Andre Breton, and filmmaker Luis Bunuel, a classmate of Dali's who has since come to be known as the most *avant-garde* filmmaker of the last century.

With artistic form that draws upon psychology and weaves into society's drama, Luis Bunuel chose France to locate his masterpieces in. He uncovered French society in surreal dimension. He was a Spaniard, but his reading of French bourgeoisie was more minute than French filmmakers. In his film *That Obscure Object of Desire* he wanted to simultaneously reveal the 'untrue' character of a successful businessman, and check how far the audience sees his *machismo* storyline.

The businessman narrates how his love for his *au pair* (live-in maid) was unrequited, that she cruelly taunts him. Actually, two actresses play the single role of the maid in the film, but the businessman could not differentiate between them, and most often, nor does the audience. The girls provoke him with desirable acts to prove his professed love was untrue, that his only desire was sexual enjoyment. The film's message is when money and sex reign supreme, love and refinement are waylaid.

Using a platonic platform, Surrealism displayed strong artistic craft and skill to become a controversial movement. Surrealist paintings have a nostalgic character that evokes layers and layers of imagination residing in the human subconscious mind. Although Surrealism did not acquire mass appeal at that time, it established itself as the subliminal foundation of the conservative society.

Surrealism carried over to modern times characterizes Georges Lucas' 1977 film, *Star Wars*. The sets and the facial character of the protagonist were influenced by the 1930s surreal sculptures and paintings of Max Ernst. Stephen Spielberg's *ET*, a mega success among the masses, also interpreted the surrealist vision of Max Ernst and Salvador Dali. The big thought of Surrealism ignited the subconscious layer of human beings. People across cultures in the world, from children to adults, enjoyed and could connect with *ET*.

Surreal influences instigated business too. When Hollywood was turning dull and dreary, Surrealist fiction films changed both the platform and fortunes of the cinema industry worldwide.

The art form can juice up a company's vision into thinking very differently. Even as artists influenced thought processes, manufacturers made surrealist dreams into reality. Surrealism is evident in dream products like Mercedes' bionic car or a mobile telephone-cum-camera-cum-computer-cum-music bank in your hand.

The Western world is intensely involved with the lateral thinking of their artists. These influences reveal continuity and consistency across art, music, film, fiction, industry and business. The imagination of painters created discomfort, leading to significant human development to enhance the art of living.

2. Musical devices have generated a new style of business as personal and collective hedonism through discomfort. Artists alone did not create discomfort, inventors of music playing devices also contributed to shaking up society to take a leap. History traces the personal music device to Thomas Edison's innovation of the speaking phonograph in the 19th century. This inspired

Emile Berliner, a German in USA, to invent a music-playing gadget for consumers in 1877. The gramophone was born, additionally representing lifestyle and home decor till 1939. Columbia Music Company introduced Europeans to double sided 78-rpm records in 1923.

In 1948 Columbia came up with the 12 inch, 33-rpm vinyl record that could play several songs for 25 minutes. Competitor RCA Victor came up with the single, the fast-selling 45-rpm, 7-inch record that started music charts. The single that consumers most bought became a chart buster. The economic success of musicians is totally dependent on these chart busters.

In 1930, Bell Telephone Laboratories invented magnetic tape recording. Using Armour Research Foundation, German design and expertise, Ampex Corporation produced the first professional tape recorder in 1948. Philips introduced the compact cassette and portable tape recorder using a small cartridge in 1962; and took the compact disk to the mass market in 1982.

Before 1877, entertainment was not a lucrative industry like it is today. For over a hundred years western inventors have created continuous discomfort with musical devices that helped bring new art forms from one corner of the world to another. The restlessness of artists since Impressionism and Expressionism influenced inventors like Thomas Edison to give birth to a new value in civilization that touched every individual. Consumers were titivated with the phonograph to gramophone, record player to tape recorders, Walkman to MP3 to iPod. New entertainment innovations like the Bose and Dolby systems came up too.

The musical world transformed invention into a money-spinning industry generating immense wealth for manufacturers, performers, producers and promoters worldwide. A variety of singers, musicians, entertainers and stars destroyed life's monotony and increased people's desire level. This established a new source of economic power that has been phenomenal.

3. Singers and musicians have, through discomfort, made a break-through in the entertainment business. They have infused new thoughts that have heightened collective and personal human emotion. Western music's evolution from medieval, renaissance, baroque to the classical opera, operetta and philharmonic symphony to today's rock, rap and jazz happened amidst immense discomfort in the Western musical world. Most Western classical masterpieces emerged from Eastern and Western Europe since 1740. Georges Handel was among the precursors who set the foundation of Western classical music.

Simultaneously from the 1600s, African music from the enslaved African community in USA opened another musical chapter with rhythm as the base. Black music started as spiritual, and evolved incorporating worksongs, ragtime and minstrel shows during the American Civil War from 1861 to 1865. Blues and Dixieland were born in the late 1800s, while jazz and gospel began in early 1900s. After World War II the black influence invented rock and rap music.

African American gospel music, the collective humming voice of the black community in church was not considered aristocratic by Caucasians. Over centuries they were used to hearing songs sung in characteristic monotone as in country music. In the 1950s Elvis Presley created a new musical era of discomfort when he brought black gospel music and rhythm into mainstream society as rock 'n' roll. He also broke the rules of musical performance and disapprovingly got dubbed 'Elvis the Pelvis' for gyrating suggestively, moving his hands and legs while on stage.

Elvis followed his father's profession of being a truck driver; he worked for Crown Electric Company. One day he stopped his truck at Memphis Recording Studios where he had heard that anyone could record a 10-inch acetate for $4. He was 19 years old, totally smitten by music, and enthusiastically recorded his own composition 'My Happiness.' That was the beginning of an extraordinary journey to be crowned the King of Rock 'n' Roll.

When television shows censored his rhythmic leg movements as too sexy, Elvis concentrated on rhythmically moving the upper part of his body. He wanted his music to stir up everybody's dancing shoes because the atmosphere after World War II was very morose. His sensational singing style became extremely controversial, with American puritans taking a jab at Christianity and calling it the devil's music. Elvis was unique in that nobody was ever neutral about him. The shock of this negative–positive current made him the rock 'n' roll phenomenon of all time.

Another discomfort in music came from the Beatles in 1962. John Lennon, James Paul McCartney, George Harrison and Richard Starkey (who took the name of Ringo Starr later) were born into working class obscurity in post war Liverpool, a dingy depressed town where money was scarce. They took the world by storm, and Beatlemania became a worldwide cult. Even the Queen of England honored them with the MBE in Buckingham Palace in 1965.

An *Evening Standard* interviewer queried John Lennon about religion, and his apolitical reply was: 'Christianity will go. It will vanish and shrink. I needn't argue with that. I'm right and I will be proved right. We're more popular than Jesus now; I don't know which will go first, rock 'n' roll or Christianity.'

Pandemonium broke loose. Disk jockeys in the southern American states encouraged a God-fearing youth to destroy Beatles records and memorabilia at bonfire rallies. Within a week, 30 US Bible Belt radio stations banned the Beatles from airplay. Lennon created discomfort at the risk of breaking his own group's career at the height of their success.

The shock was momentary though. Lennon inspired a whole generation to think fearlessly, openly and clearly. He also touched a raw, discomfiting nerve in a social atmosphere stifled with a telling generation gap. In a world tired of domination, discipline, prudishness and morality, the genuineness of the Beatles was powerfully refreshing. Millions of young and old fans world-wide still uphold the Beatles as the perpetuators of 'All you need is love.'

Musicians and singers comprised a new kind of creature who emerged to kill gloominess and depression in Europe and America in the second half of the 20th century. They deliberately brought discomfort with a message. Singer Mick Jagger, at over 60, is still creating discomfort with 'I can't get no satisfaction.' He's taken a *40 Licks World Tour* to wake up newer generations across the globe.

There was a cliché that the Punks were less a musical genre than a state of mind. In their discomfort creating heydays from early 1970, being a Punk fashion victim became fashionable. The Punks remained an underground music sect upto 1976. They demonstrated individualism and even revolted against older sub-cultures like hard-rockers and hippies. Being an anarchistic, anti-power movement, the Punks were amazingly successful in establishing a trend that influenced industry and lasted beyond their generation.

The Punk culture was different from the introverted hippies who distanced themselves from society's woes to find hallucin-ating relief in drugs. The hippies fell out of society's tolerance level when it was discovered that drugs caused incurable diseases such as AIDS. The Punks, in contrast, were individually aggressive, but for 30 years they have been considered the trend that brought color into European fashion and music.

Singer Nina Hagen personifies their daring, rebellious char-acter as the Mother of Punks. To magnify Punk philosophy, she unashamedly masturbated in a TV talk show, proving that rebels always emerge to create discomfort and kill society's monotony.

The Punks influenced both music and fashion with breakaway characteristics and tremendous business gain. The distinctive peculiarity of Punk hair styling killed hair lacquer which came to represent old people. They introduced the young generation to hair gel, and manufacturers responded with innovation to meet new demands.

Let me digress a bit from music to share my personal Punk experience. One day at the end of the 1980s a person by the name Pierre called me in my Paris office to say, 'I want to meet you personally. I have tried contacting your HR head, but he asked me to send my CV. Unfortunately I don't have a CV that will satisfy the establishment. But I am creative, and I am sure you will like me.' Such provoking words obviously touched me as well as Caroline, my incredibly efficient and warmhearted personal assistant. She set up my meeting with Pierre.

Pierre walked in with a safety pin pierced on his cheek. In the 1980s, body piercing was practically unknown. Pierre tried to chameleonize himself to conform to establishment ways. He was a Punk of few words, and I found his creative power to be out-of-the-box. His was a perfect fit in my creative department where his fascinating thought process and execution capability contributed to strategizing for our international clients. His superior intellect and vast knowledge came from copious reading of any and every book.

Pierre had extreme likes and dislikes. He could make lightning changes in his affections if he felt discomfited. I gave him total liberty to express his eccentric self, but also challenged him to abandon his community. I grew very fond of Pierre the person, except for his sinister streak of aggression, which was too much to stomach.

Trying to maneuver into my reserved office parking space one winter morning, I faced the incessant problem of double-parking by visitors. Pierre happened to enter just then and saw my unhappy plight. You can't imagine what he did. He swished open a pocketknife, and even before I could react, with practiced precision he slashed the tyres of four cars blocking my path.

My exasperation over parking immediately turned to fury at Pierre's action. His intention to help me was somehow noble, but aggression is all he knew. 'These are the real hypocrites!' he shouted. 'Why don't they respect the outsize parking signs the establishment has put up? They surely read, so they are devoid of honesty and integrity. Only anti-establishment anarchists like me can punish such deceit!' I was dumbfounded.

Like a nomad, Pierre used to stay in different places. He listened very carefully to my suggestion of renting an apartment, and did so in his own rebellious way. He preferred using candlelight, but not for economic reasons as French nuclear energy generated power is possibly the cheapest in the world.

I found mysticism in Pierre. He was truthful to the point of sadism. As he gesticulated at an internal meeting, I noticed a serious burn injury had made a hollow behind his palm. He explained it away nonchalantly as his girlfriend's passion mark. She had angrily jabbed her cigarette butt there because she didn't want to live his fantasy of making love atop a public dustbin on a cold night. He accepted her passion, convinced that this pain was just another way of making love.

Pierre worked at our Paris office for almost six years. His appearance gradually changed, he became a gentleman dressed in white. His parents once called me; I told them Pierre's ingenious talent will never change. When he left, it was to discover new pastures in South East Asia as France, he said, was becoming too boring for him. I will never forget the discomfort that oozed out of Pierre. His very rebellious being explained to me how to see things differently in a certain area.

Music purchase was not such a thrill in small neighborhood record stores with limited collections, where the owner would prescript music. Richard Branson changed that. He magnified the music buying experience by introducing choice and the self service concept. A gigantic music indulging Virgin Megastore gave consumers an unthinkable opportunity to enjoy multicultural, multilingual, multi sound and multi-voice music, and be in tune with the trend. Born in 1950, Branson founded Virgin as a mail order record retailer in 1970, opened a record shop in London's Oxford Street and a recording studio in Oxfordshire. The first Virgin artist he promoted, Mike Oldfield, sold over 5 million copies of the recording 'Tubular Bells' in 1973. The Virgin Group hasn't looked back since, expanding beyond international music Megastores to other businesses. Their individual involvement on several mega floors also opened up their purse strings, making Virgin a mega success.

The flourishing entertainment business worldwide is a perpetual discomfort-creating machine. Being a perfect performer is never enough; the masses will endow you with commercial success only if they can remember the discomfort you created in reaching out to them.

4. Sex has the power to disturb upfront, but is enjoyed secretively. It embellishes living style and grows businesses through discomfort.
The American recession from 1930 saw the rapid growth of the mafia movement. Sex and bootlegging flourished to become prime businesses like never before.

The Catholics managed to keep sex under wraps upto the 1960s. As per their dogma, sex outside marriage is taboo, and marriage is merely a matter of procreation. Over the centuries this prohibition has inspired writers, philosophers and painters to create discomfort at high ground level.

Austrian painter Gustaf Klimt (1862–1918) found no favor with establishment art critics. They said his paintings were too sensual and erotic, his symbolism very deviant and pornographic. Feeling his integrity as an artist undermined and under threat, Klimt formed The Secession Movement in 1897 to expose talented but unconventional young artists to society. He published a magazine that brought foreign art into Vienna. Controversial in his time, he posthumously shot into fame in 1920s. Today his paintings are recognized as masterpieces.

Western intellectuals played with sex, transforming basic pornography to high-class eroticism through philosophic adventures. Post 1970s erotica influenced Western society through music, cinema and literature. By creating great societal discomfort, John Lennon established his love and peace theme with his second wife, Yoko Ono, by publicly portraying their lovemaking and birth of their baby Sean.

Let's go from real life to reel life in *Emmanuel*. Emmanuel was a desirable woman flying to Thailand to meet her husband, when suddenly on the aircraft a stranger makes love to her. Details of their intrepid sexual act performed surreptitiously even as other passengers sat unawares behind them were shown as sophisticated eroticism, not pornography. This film ran for decades and made a great deal of money.

In 2003, Italian film director Bertolucci made *The Dreamer* which combined cinema, sex and politics. A portrait of a brother and sister who are film buffs at the time of the French student revolution in 1968, the story daringly depicts lovemaking as creative art in the incestuous French bourgeoisie.

The siblings play a game of enacting scenes from classic films, daring each other to recognize the film. Whoever's answer is wrong has to give a forfeit. One day when the brother lost the game, his forfeit was to masturbate in front of a film actress's picture he kept inside his cupboard. An American friend they had invited to be their houseguest was entirely shocked to see this scene, especially the sister examining the sperm on the picture with her fingertips.

The day the American lost a game, his forfeit was to make love with his friend's sister. The film had earlier established the siblings sleep together in the nude at night, but this sexual act with the American deflowered the girl. In extreme emotion the lovers discover the blood, and devour each other in the passion of first love. In total curiosity, the brother raptly watches the love scene.

In another scene, recreating childhood under a tent, the naked three happily party and fall asleep. Suddenly the parents arrive, having interrupted their vacation in response to the children's SOS messages for money. The audience empathy focuses on the parents who return to witness a home in total disarray, the children and friend drunk, naked and passed out. Distraught, confused and with no courage to disturb the scene, they just write a check and leave.

Through the three friends Bertolucci exposed French upper class hypocrisy, and how an American puritan can never really understand the undercurrents and complexity of relationships in European society. But the film's true revelation is the sincere intellectual involvement of young people with the ideologies of Mao Zedong and Che Guevara in the 1968 student revolution.

The cabaret has become a part of the sex business today. This French innovation started as a singing club peppered with colloquial speech and jokes. The 19th and 20th centuries saw writers, painters and musicians living in Montmarte, atop a hill with a panoramic view of Paris, lead several cultural and intellectual movements. Montmarte remains the most vibrant open-air artistic place in Paris, and the hallmark of the world's art.

Singer Aristid Bruant (1851–1925) personified the Montmarte café concert scene north of Paris. His cabaret was a small space that entertained people with slang, gossip and songs that celebrated the prostitute and those wanted by the law. When the bourgeoisie came, he'd address them as 'pigs,' 'scoundrels' and worse. Bruant would himself lead an audience chorus escorting every woman who entered his club Le Mirliton, called Lapain Agile today, by singing 'Oh how pale she is.' Other musicians here would spontaneously compose lyrics and music. Artist Toulouse Lautrec was his regular consumer. His famous poster of a girl with the red scarf was designed for this cabaret.

Bruant was a bourgeois by birth but his father's death forced him to enter the working class. Having discovered the cafés, he was initially shocked by the coarseness of popular conversation. But he soon embraced street language to make scathing satire of the comfortable classes and sad laments on the struggling poor.

The cabaret acquired its sexual hue after the World War II. With nude stage dancers, music and song it graduated from being soldier entertainment to dramatic commercialized stage performances for attracting tourists.

Latin Europeans used to mock American films of 30 years ago as being prudish about sex, claiming that even the screen kiss on European films had more inner depth. According to them, Hollywood has realized the box office does not jingle with dry historical films, so they remake European films, exaggeratedly introduce love and violence and join two sentences with 'f..k.' The story of adultery in Claude Chabrol's French film *Infidel* ends with the husband murdering his wife's lover under intriguing circumstances. The American version changed the film's focus to the sexual relationship between the wife and her lover with near-pornographic portrayal such as sodomy under a public staircase.

All businesses that can be connected with sex, such as lingerie products, have also experienced a boom. Since Roman times when nylon stockings did not exist, the garter had faithfully served western women as inner wear in their complicated, puritanical dressing mode. Used to clip on thigh length stockings, the garter was swept up by prostitutes as an erotica-evoking element in the 20th century when prostitution became legal. With sexy postures they openly bared their very flimsy garters in front of brothels, converting the garter into a symbol for prostitution. Moulin Rouge in Paris was among the prominent music halls and brothels for the affluent where women wore garters to entertain men. Subsequently, the garter fell from grace and became unsophisticated.

In 1980 it bounced back into fashion for weddings or as party dress or street wear for the young.

Similarly the brassiere, an inner garment, came into center stage in 1968 with public bra-burning sessions in different parts of the world in support of the feminist cause. Women avowed they will no longer be caged or girdled, but fashion picked up the gauntlet and made the bra an external garment. This societal disturbance proved a money-spinner. The business of skimpy women's wear continues to boom.

Sex has tremendous power to achieve; people enjoy sex even if it is virtual. Beauty pageants, whether international, national or local, are outsized events that generate big bucks. They propel the sexuality of beautiful girls, making one of them a star and opinion leader on whose words business grows. The fashion business has the power to demonstrate suggestive sexuality on stage and bestows the license to wear minimalist garments as fashion. In short, sex, in spite of the imminent danger of sexual disease, melts business to create money.

5. Through discomfort, automobiles are driving industrial evolution towards lust. In the 14th century the Italian painter Martini designed a man-propelled carriage on a piece of paper. He called it 'automobile.' Auto means self in Greek, and mobile means moving in Latin. Martini's innovative name 'automobile' has inspired people in subsequent centuries to innovate on this self-propelled machine. Even Henry Ford, at the end of the 19th century could not find a better name than the powerful one that Martini coined. Here again was a painter's vision ahead of his time. He may have had to hide his thought during his lifetime to avoid discomfort.

In the 15th century Leonardo da Vinci created designs and models for transport vehicles. The automobile he attempted to power with modified clockwork mechanism is remarkable, intensely researched and one of his best-known inventions. Leonardo's thought evoked total discomfort in his time. Nobody could think it possible. But psychologically people always wanted to move faster than walking. Leonardo's mechanism lay buried upto 1771 when Nicolas Joseph Cugnot built the Fardier, a three-wheeled, steam-powered, 2.3-mph vehicle for the French minister of war. This earliest ancestor of the modern automobile was a cumbersome machine with a top speed of 2mph. It caused the world's first automobile accident when it went off control and demolished a garden wall. Louis XV pensioned Cugnot with 600 Francs annually upto the 1789 French Revolution. Cugnot died a poor, exiled man in 1804. His drawing can still be seen in a French museum.

The automobile thought slept again until the 4-wheel physical ignition carrier came out. Karl Benz from Germany created the first true automobile in 1885–86.

Running on steam, electricity and gasoline, different people invented different styles of automobiles. In the 19th century they started as objects of art with rare, limited editions. As more people gained access to it, the automobile became the most physically exciting sport, just like human or animal fights in the Coliseum in Roman times, or Formula 1 today. Since the 1960s, the automobile has become mass consumption.

As per post World War II treaties, the Japanese were forbidden to manufacture weapons. So they chose to develop gadgets for human need and created discomfort by challenging the Western world. In the 1970s most European automobile manufacturers sold a bare shell of a car; customers had to spend about 30 percent more to make the car road-ready. The Japanese observed that customers disliked this system. So they stormed Western markets by offering the novelty of cars already equipped with air conditioning, auto radio and other features. The customer's pleasure at being handed the key and driving away his new car from the showroom was immense. The Japanese brought joy to customers, but created total discomfort in the automobile industry. European protectionism raised a protesting head, but to no avail.

For the Western world, the automobile evokes passion. People fantasize nomadic sexual adventures in the automobile. A quantitative research with 10,000 British women in the 1960s revealed that making love in the car is their most secret desire and exciting fantasy. This inspired manufacturers to customize for extreme pleasure, both for driving and making love. Designers collaborated with comfortable interiors. The popular open-air drive-in theaters in USA have become a euphemism for making love in the car. Harold Robbins depicted this in *The Betsy*. The pleasure of driving has been stretched to a very personal passport to freedom. In a disciplined social system that conditions people not to display emotion, your subconscious mind may not be so averse to making love inside the car.

Automobile evolution was a total discomfort in different decades and centuries. The discomfort Western manufacturers experienced with Japanese customer sensitivity changed the rules in the automobile sales game. The Koreans are again creating manufacturer discomfort with extreme customization. Skoda, the Czech brand considered very low class yesterday, has created enormous discomfort for other manufacturers by establishing premium value today. Automobile manufacturers continually create discomfort; and consumers enjoy the ensuing benefit features as their new passion toy.

6. *Technology has helped to realize human fantasy through discomfort.* The first freely programmable computer was born in 1936. IBM, the mainframe manufacturer who deployed computers for high tech industries, globally led the computer business as Big Blue.

Then along came the colorful, mysterious Apple. Inviting consumers to bite into individual small computers, Apple subliminally conjured up Adam and Eve's pleasure of the forbidden fruit in the prohibited Garden of Eden. IBM was socially branded as Big Blue because of its color, size of equipment and the entirety of business processes it controlled in an organization. It was unimaginable that IBM's large business could be challenged by a tiny new company, offering reduced business machines for an even smaller purpose, that of a personal computer. Steve Wozniak and Steve Jobs released the first personal computer, the single circuit board Apple I, on April Fool's Day, 1976. That unleashed total discomfort in the industry.

IBM followed Apple into personal computing in 1981, but it was IBM that coined and popularized the term PC for personal computer. Within four months of the IBM PC launch, *Time* magazine named the computer as 'Man of the Year'.

Technology has given the world a new religious order, that of the code. In most activity domains, efficiency and perfection go through the filter of a technology chip. The innovation of electricity changed people's lives; technology made the world upside down. When automation was introduced in the workplace, technology became the enemy of people, throwing large numbers into discomfort with the fear of losing their jobs. In time the induction of technology increased, as did its discomfiting pressure on the human mind. Who would have thought of technology in traditional areas like marriages? You can now conduct weddings in cyberspace through the Internet rather than by calling on the neighborhood priest. Inspite of human beings trying to protect their habits, technology is creating its own avenues, very much like nature's storms and waves, and changing our lives significantly.

My six examples of innovation prove that discomfort happened century after century, but in the final analysis, discomfort served the need of human development.

Indian consumers are exposed to discomfort from many quarters. Two years ago when I saw a newspaper displaying Madonna and Britney Spears kissing in a public concert I wondered how Indian women would perceive such a picture. Men get quite disturbed seeing a physical homosexual act, but women in the West have generally accepted lesbianism. They feel no discomfort watching two women make love.

Surprisingly, from my different consumer interactions we undertake as part of our working process, I got the answer that Indian women would enjoy such a fantasy. In Indian culture, women are taught never to be honest about their desires, but to suppress them. With international exposure, will Indians indulge in such adventure? Does taboo apply today? Although socio-economic depression may suppress carnal instincts, human beings across the world enjoy fantasizing.

If Indian consumers are accepting the discomfort of sexual expose, are Indian manufacturers keeping pace by addressing them with new understanding? Indian organizations need to desperately enter this discomfort zone of analyzing the deeper impact of human psychological and sociological aspects and bring it into business. This will enable them to act on the liberalization of human desire as per today's market.

Indian organizations fail to create internal discomfort. Their self-questioning includes: Will it work? Is our Indian consumer advanced to this level? Do we have the capability to do that? Will everyone in the organization support this discomfort? Will the trade accept this discomfort? By sadistically defending their inaction, Indian organizations avoid discomfort.

GRCs are proactively playing with discomfort. Having experienced discomfort and its positive results, they will continue to intensify it. When organizations attempt changing their culture to better serve consumers, they go through dramatic discomfort. But consumers are oblivious of the discomfort your organization experiences. They just expect and demand quality products and services. Think of your wife/husband, mother, sister, brother, son as consumers, and whether the result of your organizational transformation meets with their desire. Sometimes what for you is discomfort may be of little consequence for them.

The protected economy has paralyzed the competitive killer instinct of Indian industry. In today's competitive global scenario, making a normal shift may not be adequate. A radical transformation is required to upgrade intellectual human capital along with a working process that co-opts and drives the consumers' latent trend.

The basis of human evolution has always come from discomfort. Whatever position you may have in the organization, push your management, both subordinates and superiors, to express their composed thoughts on discomfort, exactly like you had asked a sophisticated five star hotel to serve you a *jalebi*. By unearthing discomfort in social or market experiences, you can help your organization worship discomfort, and change its protected economy working style.

Unfortunately, extreme economic pressure has made love and affection very artificial in today's Western society. Additionally, the fear of AIDS makes them feel vulnerable and insecure. In countries like India where earning a livelihood is the priority, a conjugal relationship may become mechanical after some time. To prevent that, it's necessary to always create discomfort to re-vibrate a couple's world of fantasy and love. Such discomfort will create curiosity and break any monotony of married life. In the rush to meet economic growth, India's heritage of a certain mental peace should not be allowed to crumble away. It is the social responsibility of Indians to integrate the rich philosophical insights of the country in the future development of business.

Food, sex and spirituality are vital human acts that will always need discomfort to re-ignite passion and make life vibrant. How can a *jalebi* help you here? Try introducing it unexpectedly at a moment not related to enjoying food, such as at a heated debate at office, or while cheering your favorite football team at the stadium. Because the moment is unrelated and there is discomfort on how to eat a sticky spiral when you are totally preoccupied with something else, you will enjoy the *jalebi* better.

exercising with discomfort

There is no single way of driving discomfort into an organization's culture. Discomfort lies in the hands of society and the masses. Compared to the past, the West today is saturated of discomfort, and somehow snoozing in material comfort. People are preoccupied with sex-related disease, terrorism, social fracture; the *avant-garde* character is missing. Europe is passing through a dull phase now, with desire plummeting to the level of need. They fear the future economic power India and China can amass with the onset of development; they worry about how that will harm their economy. Even when no physical danger exists, Europeans somehow create discomfort in society as though it's a need.

To combat the billion-mindset power, Western society will need to ignite another profound wave of discomfort. As their discomfort-creating root exists, growing the branch and fruit will not take time. Just look at how fast the European Union is enlarging in spite of every independent country not thinking alike.

Discomfort in the 19th and 20th centuries was limited to the Caucasians. A new type of discomfort will now emerge to understand and cope with emerging new non-European power states. The Europeans are yet to understand the mixture of races that make up North American culture. Likewise, Americans need to put in effort to understand Eastern cultures.

I visualize tremendous pressure from the extreme right wing of Western society in the near future. Unemployment is growing, but poor productivity is making European countries hire immigrants to support labor-intensive work. That raises political issues, so the new method is to outsource to India and China. Simultaneously, the initiative of people to work is deteriorating in the West.

If you look back at history, Nazism was born in the lap of German recession. The extreme right has always taken advantage of economic reasons like unemployment and recession, to hook people through psychological rationale. Socialism will try to fight racism in future, but the biggest weapon to overcome chaos would be to go in for immense innovation or invention.

Let's come back to your business. For exceptional organizational growth you need to revive your strategic planning session to deal with discomfort as a project (see Table 2.1). Discomfort is pinpricks in your backside—you just cannot ignore it, you have to deal with it in a hurry.

Table 2.1 discomfort framework

DISCOMFORT FRAMEWORK	©
Discomfort Zone	
WHAT	**HOW**
Deliberately curious	Create the obligation to dramatize things to see them differently
Value lateral thinking	Apple vs. gravitation
Make the unstated obvious	Fungus = Penicillin
Belief in commercial value	Timeless diagonal reading of usage benefit
Change work culture	Prioritize discipline to structure creativity to result in a process that facilitates mass scale change
Sense of urgency	Continuous reduction of cycle time
Time bound	Days driven
What is Comfort zone?	
Continuous incremental improvement	

Unless people in management are deliberately pushed to dive into discomfort zone, discomfort will remain a gossip metaphor rather than serious action. Initially, it would be an immensely esoteric thing to do. But you'll soon realize that by penetrating into discomfort you become the actor rather than the audience. After a certain effort discomfort becomes your chronic link that delivers exceptional growth.

Outside of routine, that maintenance part of business, create a task force with a clear objective to provoke in a given timeframe. Surprise the market with a deliverable that disturbs. To avoid possible dissonance within the organization, everyone need not be told of the discomfort project. This discomfort creating team must be totally aligned with the end consumers' latent trend, having understood their lifecycle, lifestyle and trend. This will comprise their route to market success.

Discomfort is a man-made approach, but sometimes Nature thrusts it upon us. Involving the psychological aspect of people, their lifestyle and the trends they absorb, discomfort constantly evolves. In any selling approach, whether it is through discomfort or in normal circumstances, three factors impact the subconscious of consumers anywhere in the world. There is a mechanism to understand this impact which is through Consumer Lifecycle, Consumer Lifestyle and Trends.

lifecycle

The psychological deliberations and obsession of human beings comprise their link to their individual lifecycle. All over the world people are more and more nurturing self-centeredness, searching for individual meaning and for independence. That's why factoring in the psychological attitude of consumers and their behavior is an infinite direction to building an organization's culture (see Figure 2.2). A person's lifecycle is self-centric. It covers his fundamental ego and everyday personal routine, how he eats, sleeps, makes love, works, entertains or gets entertained, takes responsibility, distributes affection. He owns this biosystem, which is perpetual in his life, making it a cycle. Some things may change in the course of his lifespan like food habits, working style or entertainment. But always trying to get back to somehow reconstructing his cycle is his lifecycle.

The psychological aspect of every individual is like a fingerprint, each is very different from any other. The psychological

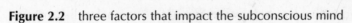

Figure 2.2   three factors that impact the subconscious mind

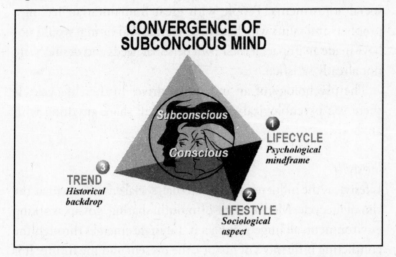

parameters are so profound that if, as an organization, you don't find the mechanism to understand it, you will always remain distanced from the sensitivity of consumers and customers.

In reality the psychological aspect of consumers and customers is stretchable like a chewing gum. It is not enough for an organization to buy a process or materials, build the infrastructure, or take high caliber people. The thrust has to be on entering the psychological nodal points of the consumer and customer's thought and action.

Not everyone in an organization cares to consider the psychological attitude and behavior of consumers and customers. But it's worth remembering that quantitative research data alone is of little worth in an innovative paradigm. Collecting quantitative social data is like the proverbial counting of sheep where the sensitivity of human psychology is not recorded. Such research merely serves as the barometer of where you are and where the business potential lies. It does not tell you whether to go and how to go, for both of which you need the psychological paradigm to proceed.

Individual psychology is essential for personal well-being and social adjustments. People with great humanitarian feelings, prophets and saints who believe in sharing and caring, would not have made an impact if their own personal needs and desires were not already satisfied.

The psychology of an individual drives his/her lifecycle. If there is a psychological gap, nobody will share anything with anybody.

lifestyle

Lifestyle is the influence of the external, social environment at the rim of lifecycle. Media, word-of-mouth, sharing, gossip, working environment, all hugely impact it. Lifestyle emerges through the conflicting influences of history, the present and the future. It is transmitted through society, different classes of people, from one place to another.

In every country, lifestyle grows at all society levels alongside economic affluence, be it for the striving, the aspiring or the affluent class. This sociological parameter is manifested by living style, showing off, greediness, jealousy, envy, and influences from different angles.

An organization cannot run business today without being at the heart of this societal phenomenon. If isolated from lifestyle, the organization becomes introverted, backward looking, and associated only with the past. To become a top-of-mind topic in lifestyle, a brand has to increase its awareness.

The social context is always visible. It is easier to get in here compared to penetrating the psychological mindframe. But you need extreme curiosity to get on board. An organization trying to watch society needs to dive in with snorkeling equipment and watch the habits and behavior of different social fishes. To really understand the sociological paradigm, be careful not to be presumptuous about your own knowledge while watching.

In the snorkeling analogy, you wear widescreen glass goggles that protect your eyes from water and give you clean visibility. The mouth-breathing equipment can keep you underwater without choking you, for any length of time. In this comfort you can see the activities of several shoals of sea fish without disturbing them. You don't have to be a swimmer or expert diver to watch this underwater panorama, you just need curiosity to see what's below the surface. In the same way, you can snorkel society to see and absorb social ways more closely and clearly.

trend

What is the trend? A trend has a distinct character and forms in the backdrop of history. It is related to economic power, is a multidirectional catalyst that takes life forward or back. A trend emerges mainly from the human manifestations of being anti-establishment. Social rebels want to be so different that people stop in their tracks and contemplate on their activity. Being a reverse wave, it stuns people creating discomfort in society. An individual can be impacted by the trend soberly, subtly or exuberantly. It depends on the individual.

Different types of trends emerge at different times. A trend can sometimes overpower society where a large number of people fall in its current. The advent of denim jeans was such a trend where the poor, rich, middle class, executives, farm hands, almost everybody went through the trend.

In business, it is important to understand the trend as consumers and customers will draw for you the path of the latent trend. Having an inkling of the future allows you to direct your business in the right growth path. The trend has a tremendous cyclic effect from history. Although technology is creating a futuristic trend which people have not been associated with before, a trend takes the future as a hook to climb from, even as it is anchored in the past.

A brand needs to be at the core of the trend to absorb and anticipate the future, and to drive the latent trend.

A trend is a non-stop wave that has an undercurrent. It is extremely difficult to swim against the undercurrent. Trying to do so can be very laborious, and it can drown you. Similarly if your business is not riding the trend it may fall into the undercurrent.

Even if watching and absorbing global trends does not connect to you as a businessman, you need to voluntarily enter this sphere. In whatever business you may be, whether Business-to-Business (B2B) or Business-to-Consumer (B2C), you need to take the initiative to see and deploy the world's trends in your business.

Business-to-business means two business houses simultaneously buying and selling between each other, or only buying or selling. In abbreviated business language this is B2B which deals with customers. Who is the customer? The customer is a buyer you know in a limited circle, whom you may address individually. Customer relationship is more business-to-business in a limited circle, which is easier to capture than the consumer circle.

Who then is the consumer? The ocean of human beings, the individuals over whom you will not have physical control are consumers. Your organization has to create a wave to connect to consumers. Business-to-consumer or B2C is the traditional approach, such as industry to human beings.

Are you, for example, isolated from today's trends such as hip hop, iPod, Rbk, Niketown, Fcuk, Smart car, Swatch, homosexual marriage, Bose sound, Starbucks, health and fitness, all of which are linking cords to any business? Connecting well to trends like these will help you generate the latent trend. You may even establish a new world trend where people will follow you.

A latent trend can never be generated from a vacuum. It's the better cook of current and past trends that becomes the latent. Managements that intellectually understand the world of business and can translate it to a philosophical mode can create the latent trend in business. This is an absolutely different creature.

When you relish a *jalebi* in a sophisticated banquet, discomfort oozes out from two simultaneous angles, nostalgia and snobbery. Nostalgia brings back the forgotten, inviting aroma and taste of a *jalebi* you may have savored on the street a long time ago. Snobbery comes into play if you are consciously cultivating yourself to mingle in that society where caviar and smoked salmon are common fare. Their influence would grow your curiosity about a *jalebi*.

Societal discomfort can be compared to the swirling effect of a *jalebi*. If you can interlink the discomfort in society's lifecycle, lifestyle or trend, and weave its balance into the organization in a circular whirling motion, all *jalebi* bites become delicious. When an organization's intangible energy is free flowing yet balanced with its surroundings, whatever step that organization takes, it will be commercially viable.

After an initial success, the discomfort project you have initiated should be projected to the whole organization as their own case study. It will show how everybody in the organization can be in the discomfort zone to kill complacency. This will help your organization to continuously renovate, which means, 'I change myself.' Out-of-the-box innovation means, 'I change the world.'

beauty of the curse

Organizations may need to pay attention to the flashpoints in a society. Areas where emotions are high consequently become entry points or business opportunities. Uttering curse words is a metaphor of discomfort. But such profanities should not end up as mere provocation, they should be exploited for business gain.

There has to be some substance behind swears that tickle. In business parlance, provocation should make people understand an insight, and that should lead to the consumer or customer's buying act. That's my concept of the PUB Reflex: to Provoke, to Understand, to Buy. When a marketer can grab the consumer's attention in a cluttered market, and the consumer understands the benefit of the offer, only then will she buy into the product or service.

Look around the world's street language, and you will see how different business cultures have been emerging amidst curses aplenty. *Jalebi Management's* advantage is that everyone can understand its concept. You can easily get a *jalebi* in every Indian town; every socio-economic class hungers for it, and savors its bite. When visiting the market for the company, do you ferret out such *jalebi*-enjoying destinations and study their colloquial language?

Benetton case study

Luciano Benetton transformed his company when he changed his brand from Benetton to United Colors of Benetton. The brand that's thrived on expletives stands for anti-racism. The shock value of his provocations is so extreme that it shakes up the shackles that bind civilized society. But the point he raises is a serious social cause. Being a Caucasian, he alerts his fellow men to the racism ingrained in their minds. He proved that curses and abuses could be stretched to a very distant point to defend a social cause.

Till the 1970s, racism went unbridled. Even poverty-stricken Caucasian countries like Italy, Spain and Portugal were considered inferior; the French would arrogantly dub Portuguese to be good only as concierge of condominiums. African or Arab communities hated the 'high and mighty white attitude' which oftentimes led to violence.

In such an atmosphere, fashion designer Benetton had the caliber, vision and the guts to use abusive visual communication with anti-racism as his platform. Fashion traces its origins to royalty that distinguished itself from the proletariat; it has no obvious connect to racism. By whipping up collages of different cultures to create a difference and distinction, Benetton created total discomfort. He turned the sophisticated world of fashion upside down.

Not only did his anti-racism pitch disturb the Establishment, Benetton fought for social justice, humanitarian rights and political causes, winning appreciation from liberals, intellectuals and the young. He plastered Western cities with daring, controversial visuals and attracted people of all societies to become his buyers. The platform he ultimately created is so large and intense that nobody can imitate him.

United Colors of Benetton established a brand that is always linked to colors, whether in clothing or in uniting the human race comprising different skin colors. His messages never abused anyone, but his images always exposed the totally taboo. Just imagine an outsize billboard in a prime metro's prime area exhibiting innumerable male and female sex organs of multiple colors and races, with nothing else but a sign-off at the corner saying United Colors of Benetton. You may publicly denounce such a picture, but wouldn't you be curious to openly see the United Colors of sex for your personal hedonism? Would anyone even think about such an outrageous picture, never mind seeing it?

Whenever evolution reaches a peak, an eruption takes place and we tend to look back at what we left behind. In pre-civilization times people roamed naked and looked at any number of sex organs the way we look at faces today. Civilization covered that up. Dressing the body up has since evolved so much that your personality is now created by what you wear.

Benetton billboards communicate people's subliminal desire to see the unmentionable such as a symbolic white and dark horse making love. This sexual fantasy with the opposite color is hidden, especially the colored person's revenge through sex over white supremacy. Benetton proves that a desirable object can break racism. He also spoke out against the high incidence of incest in societies.

You may not apply such confrontational tactics in your own business, but it's interesting to look at the trend. For the different purposes they pursue in life, your consumers are surely enjoying products that have extremely thought-provoking messages. You could say companies like Benetton are not relevant for your business, and completely ignore them. By doing that, you are totally missing out on the consumer's deeper insight, which is a part of society, not subjective or individualistic. You will consequently fail to analyse and understand the fantasies of your end consumers that are being addressed by several different domains of industry. Perhaps you should consider studying such companies in a workshop. Or do a case study on how they manage to mesmerize the public.

Fashion codes change every year, but the professional success of United Colors of Benetton is its single message magnified to overwhelming proportions. For over a quarter century, it has not bored people. The media mileage his communication gets is incredible. Just a few confrontational billboards in a country, and the media automatically start different kinds of debate. Millions of people, shocked, disturbed or supportive of the pictures, watch these TV debates at prime time.

No company can hope for such mileage even if they invest huge sums of money. Protests and turbulence have frequently knocked his door. But the cacophonous attentions his unrelenting salvos receive establish that people love to be provoked. People enjoy public exhibition of their unstated desires, and are keen to openly indulge in controversy to keep life dynamic.

When so many humanitarian causes have received the Nobel Prize, I'll not be surprised if Benetton is nominated for the Nobel for his philosophic message of United Colors of Benetton, an established icon of anti-racism today.

cursing moments

Abusive communication is the psychological, sociological and anthropological essence of human emotion. People curse in excitement or in stress; such emotions loosen their purse strings to spend money as well. A product or service offer would do well to be associated here. It is very rare for people to curse in bereavement.

Extending their personal life practice of playing the woman's role, many homosexuals have given heightened meaning to fashion culture. In mentally making a gender shift, they have carefully condensed the aura around womanhood, and acquired a keen and subtle understanding of the female sex. This cerebral segregation allows homosexuals to portray fashion for women in very provocative, naïve and distinctive ways. The immense intangible content they create entice women with: 'Change your habit, create a different look.'

Let me elaborate different moments when people love to curse. What is the deeper insight of the curse? A part of human hedonism, the curse is an orgasmic act. Anger at somebody inspires a curse, an extremely welcoming action comes through a curse, self depression intrigues a curse, sociocultural colloquialism invites a curse, intense sexual intercourse ejaculates through a curse, and over intoxication can lead to a curse.

A curse is a *sutra*, a process like the Kamasutra is for sexual positions. Abuse can be considered to have six internationally recognizable *sutra*s. Civilized society may want to hide it, but a curse is the most enjoyed, used and abused expression in every social level in every country. Let's analyse below the six Curse *Sutra*s I have identified as a given habit of human life.

1. anger curse

Violence drives people to become like uncontrollable wild animals. People react to anger through physical aggression or use the weapon of the curse. Some people's belligerence can become so intense that physical torture needs the accompaniment of a weapon. If he doesn't find any tool, a curse replaces that need. The anger curse umbrella has five patterns:

the exotic anger curse
When society shows disapproval, you curse in chosen circumstances only. A curse erupts spontaneously when holding the car steering wheel in a traffic jam, or as you drive past any neighborhood disturbance. This curse discharges pleasure and achievement. It feels exotic.

curse to discharge anger

When you absolutely need to communicate that expletive, your expressively peppered message gives that feeling of accomplishment. You cannot physically harm people but you can meaningfully curse them.

A curse can convey very deep and heart rendering meanings in different countries. When a very important thought needs to be put into words, but articulation is poor, how do you bridge the gap? In France I experienced that the inner meaning of a curse can be so powerful that even Shakespearean language cannot replace it. For example when a corporate meeting lengthens to become a marathon session, the topic is not just exhibited and discussed threadbare, but people unnecessarily masturbate around it. At the end there's no solution for specific implementation. The next day people describe such a meeting as *'enculer les mouches,'* meaning 'We have tortured ourselves enough to f..k a mosquito.'

curse for extracting pleasure when angry

Nothing can stop you from cursing; it's the only pleasure in life that doesn't cost money. Any defeated situation in your life extracts a curse from you for the person who has done you in or the person who has achieved over you.

anger curse of achievement

When revenge cannot be taken by any other means, you curse and automatically experience a temporary achievement.

the curse of aggression

Those who physically torture others find their expression of aggression incomplete without a curse. At the aggressive moment, they curse to multiply the pleasure they derive from aggression.

Listening to curses from different cultures is quite astounding. A rap-singing group became controversial for their French slang band name *'Nique Ta Mere'* which means 'f..k your mother.'

Following an outraged legal attack, they changed their name to use its acronym NTM. Their popularity continued to soar. NTM is known for hostility towards the police, violent lyrics, and legal battles with French authorities. The group is outspokenly critical of racism and class inequality in French society. Their musical style is hardcore rap with hip-hop influence and later funk, soul and reggae. The song '*1993...J'appuye sur la gachette*' (I've got my finger on the trigger) featured violent criticism of the police. The French police took them to court, but NTM won. A second police encounter happened in 1995 when the group made further derogatory comments in a live concert, and advocated violence against the police. This time the court sentenced them with imprisonment for 6 months.

NTM gambled with the judicial system only because a considerable section of the public was in their favor. This proves that the public enjoys vulgar language.

2. the extreme welcome curse

I have a fascination for the Punjabi society in India. They are frank, joyful, open. At a very serious corporate meeting one day, a senior executive stepped out of the conference room perhaps for a bio-break. Suddenly we could hear some scuffle-like loud thumping noise outside, and choice uncivil words: '*Saale paape! Kya haal chaal hai, behenchod! Tu kaha mar gaya tha?*' ('You so-and-so! How have you been, you sister f..ker! Where were you dead for so long?' Totally shocked I rushed out in concern. The scene that greeted me is indelible in my mind. Two well-built handsome men of the Punjab in '*pucca* suited-booted' gear, back thumping, beaming, hugging each other tight, exchanging a string of diatribes in total congenial surrender.

I discovered in them the extreme welcome curse. That bosom friend you are so fond of, when he shows up after a long duration, or makes a fraternal move that brings you extreme pleasure or benefit, you will respond with an emotional curse. This is a token of love and intimacy between two long lost buddies.

curse of hypocrisy in a welcome

Cultural ambivalence can lead to insecure business transactions. After heavy negotiations, a French client of mine got his way in a surprise 3-hour business lunch to welcome his newfound partner. Without realizing the possible consequence of business loss, his executives impolitely celebrated among themselves in jocular French: '*Je L'ai bien baise celui la*' meaning 'I f..ked him and got exactly what I wanted.'

Unfortunately, businessmen from every country can sense sincerity; the clinched deal ran into bad weather. Being able to say '*Je L'ai bien baise celui la*' behind an opponent's back comprises true enjoyment, but in business it can cost you dearly.

3. depression curse

It's natural to be depressed sometimes. A curse-filled monologue is an effective antibiotic solution for despondency because any opportunity to curse gets rid of the undesired down-in-the-dumps feeling. Solid cursing refreshes you out of your misery making you really feel good once again.

No management theory to date has recognized that consumers love the language of the curse. Does an IT networking solutions provider setting up a luxury hotel's sophisticated software program ever worry about the consumer's curses when he cannot access services through the network? Here's a hypothetical scene: 'Welcome back sir!' the hotel doorman says, and the guest is happy. In the lobby a queue has formed as the new receptionist doesn't know how to quickly register guests. The front desk manager comes to help but fails to find the guest's name in reservations.

He asks for the guest's business card, and sure enough a four-letter expletive is ejected. It's his 69th visit to the same hotel and he's not even recognized! He may not articulate them, but the sound of four-letter words play in the guest's mind.

Having collected his room swipe key card, he finds it's not working. His boiling nerves curse, 'What a f..king door.' Once finally inside, the air conditioner could not be adjusted. He was taken back to the −25 degree temperature of Moscow from which he had just escaped. In this cold New York hotel he tries calling maintenance, but nobody replies. Did the IT design architect ever imagine a guest unnerved when his software fails? His design may have cleared quantitative research on customer tolerance, but microscopic customer diagnosis under diverse situations was ignored. Product development engineers need to factor in customer anger moments to dramatically increase their passion in designing. Proactively magnifying and synchronizing design will bring them in line with customer need and desire parameters.

Thousands of customer research systems exist in the world. But drilling into the customer's subconscious mind from where curses emerge can provide a different platform as food for thought.

4. sociocultural colloquialism curse

The Yankee American culture of peppering speech with curses dates back 300 years. It is considered cowboy heritage. Curse words used in normal dialog brightens up a conversation making it punchier. Indian languages also have this curse sutra.

When curse expressions from different countries is translated, they may have lateral not literal meaning. Americans spontaneously say, 'Oh f..k!' or 'shit' while French would say '*Merde!*' meaning shit. Colloquial curse words reflect a country's inner socio-historical latitude and attitude.

France, considered among the most cultured of societies, has a proverb: '*pensee et application*' meaning 'thought and application.' Living in France I learnt and absorbed the unbeatable mechanism of the French thinking process. It uniquely incorporates innovation and philosophy.

Fundamental thinkers like Pascal, Pierre and Marie Curie and Pasteur have emerged from France. French innovations such as Concorde and TGV have vastly contributed to the world's progress. The French know they are in the 'think big' mode, and equally acknowledge that they don't devote themselves in application. Over the centuries, of the many innovations emanating from France, very little was converted to business that powers world markets. Closeted parochially in their geographical hexagon, France does not engage in global public relations to publicize the country's innovative power. Other countries have converted their innovative recipes into application and business.

Here's an example: French inventors Joseph Nicephore Niepce and Louis Jacques Mande Adgurre ushered in modern photography in the 1820s. It was American John Wesley Hyatt who commercially used celluloid photography in 1868, and George Eastman invented dry photographic film for commercial use in the Kodak camera in 1888. In contrast, American inventor Thomas Alva Edison commercialized most of his innovations like the motion picture camera and the light bulb, and created one of the most successful corporations, General Electric.

Rich philosophical discourse has been endemic in France, led by thinkers like Voltaire (Francois-Marie Arouet), Charles Baudelaire, Rabelais, Victor Hugo, Emile Zola and Marcel Proust upto Albert Camus and Jean Paul Sartre among others. Implicit in French culture are questioning, mocking and lampooning of everything to provoke thought, including abuse in refined language. French style comprises the bi-polarity of the aristocratic chic, and 'Rabelaisian' meaning the good life, good food and good down-to-earth abuse.

The much-imitated, 16th century satiric masterpiece, *Gargantua* and *Pantagruel* by French monk, physician, humanist scholar and writer, Francois Rabelais was in the mock-quest tradition. The author would parody religious orders, lawyers, Sorbonne pedants and almost every power-group. He was censored and condemned, but his abusive language climbed aboard culture as 'Rabelaisiean.' His exuberant writing style combining humor, sex and scatology can be illustrated in his search of the ideal toilet paper. The answer? The neck of a goose, well downed!

Among my favorite intellectual diversions was comic actor Colouche on TV, radio or the theater. His outrageous views, tongue-in-cheek acidic reactions to current anti-people issues made people understand a subject from different angles, allowing them to laugh at themselves at even the most serious of times. He brightened up history, philosophy and politics with humor and anecdotes, linking them to daily life.

'I am the pivot for the poor. I always raise their morale,' he said, churning up French society with scathing abuse yet hilarious banter. He once mocked the Government by becoming a candidate for the French Presidency.

Mixing sarcasm, contradiction, wit and abuse, his act ripped up the absurd: 'The art of saying the real without uttering a lie is to shut your mouth.' He actually uprooted many hidden subjects that cause discomfort and go unsaid in society. The grass roots connected to his caricatures spiced with swear words and naughty jokes that uprooted societal paradoxes: 'What goes inside dry and hard, and comes out soft and wet? The answer? Chewing gum.'

He'd pick typical French idiosyncrasies, simple happenings in unemployment, sports, entertainment, health, and twist them: 'I enjoy watching others work; where the gynecologist works, others enjoy.' In over 25 years of poking cynical fun at the establishment, immigrants, different professions, this middle class man endeared himself to an entire nation and became a legend. His fatal motorcycle accident at the age of 45 left France bereft of a witty supporter of the common man.

Malaca: I entered the cheery world of Greek curses through one of my clients in Athens, a leader of the Greek food business now. While researching consumers throughout Greece to understand the deeper intonations of their lifecycle, lifestyle and the trend, I often heard the word *malaca* accompanied with great laughter and bonhomie. I don't speak Greek, but I knew this was an important thread in their cultural fabric. Participating with my team and interpreter in consumer interactions, business and retail audits, I was curious to find that certain people further elaborated *malaca* as *haga misu malaca.*

I was thrilled to discover that *malaca* means asshole, and *haga misu malaca* is 'go f..k yourself, asshole!'

Following the research, we started different interactions in the client's organization. We would start in English and after sometime they would chatter away in Greek. I got fed up and shouted, *Malaca!* You can't believe the appreciation I got! Coming as I did from France, they had considered me a Frenchman, somehow different from them. *Malaca!* immediately put me on even keel, making me an insider in their midst. When they veered off into Greek again, the salvo I directed their way was, *Haga misu malaca!* Tumultuous delight erupted. Now my inclusion was com-plete and forever.

Through my ongoing consultancy with this company from 1985 to 1995, I intermittently used their foul language to break the ice or make a point. In tough meetings with the Managing Director when certain hard-hitting decisions had to be taken, or when difficulties persisted in implementation I would throw in Greek abuse for good measure. The team was particularly thrilled as I was the only person they saw address such words to their promoter Managing Director. The MD, who has since become a very good friend of mine, enjoyed together with his team, listening to their curse words in my French accent. I have understood that this is not quite a curse for the Greeks, but punctuation in a sentence.

5. intense sexual act curse

Let me illustrate this Curse *sutra* by narrating an unbelievably intimate experience I perchance saw in Paris. Internationally reputed painters frequented the lithography studio I worked in. A famous French painter used to bring his model, a beautiful, slim African woman. When everybody was out at lunch, they would go to the print shop's first floor room adjacent to my workplace. Intrigued at hearing loud shouts interspersed with whispering sounds, I peeped through the keyhole and saw them make love.

I was a greenhorn, fresh out of India, with no French vocabulary. I quickly wrote down the phonetics of their passionate utterances to find out the meaning of those fascinating words. The artist was fervently poetic; his partner would say, *'o oui! o oui!'* meaning Oh yes! Oh yes! My French friends helped me unscramble his groaning, rasping doggerel awash with the choicest sexual expletives: 'I want to p..s on the cutting edge of your asshole! I want to deflower you! Whenever I f..k you, I want to rape you! I want to block all your holes!' The climax was a guttural yell resounding through the studio keyhole: 'My big p...s will kill you!'

During normal social interaction with us, this artist is never intense, never uses vulgar language. The worst swear word we've heard from him was *'merde.'* But the sex moment inspires him to reach the heights of coarse speech. Here the curse becomes intimate articulation at a very personal level.

trapping fashion victims
French Connection United Kingdom (FCUK) is an apparel brand created to trap victims of fashion. The United Kingdom has not had a link to the French since Waterloo, but FCUK branding

has created this association internationally. How would you react to a beautiful girl wearing a 'FCUK me' T shirt? With fun, sensuality, social perversion, rupture or discomfort? Shy and rebellious people express themselves buying FCUK garments, so both exhibitionist label and wearer communicate.

Such uncivilized language connects instinctively to the masses. FCUK mingles the FCUK expression in all communication including human resource recruitment and company financials, linking abuse to desire and sexuality. How does FCUK percolate its message in Arab countries that prohibit explicit statements? Their shop name is the expanded version 'French Connection.' The mannequin's unzipped jacket has FC on the left side and UK on the right. Their target consumers, who are exposed to the brand from electronic media, immediately recognize it. Surrogate advertising increases appetite for purchase.

People crave the unconventional, and secretly enjoy being rebellious. So when a large establishment high street store in London's glorious Regent Street loudly displays the words FCUK, aficionados are there to pay for and enjoy their branded products year after year. Everything depends on your brand's presentation, how you package it for consumption.

6. over-intoxicated curse

When people drink more that they can stomach, intoxication makes them spiritual, aggressive or romantic. Strangely enough, these states also bolster their courage to curse unabashedly.

Gainsbourg forever
For 50 years, the French art and culture scene was over-intoxicated with Serge Gainsbourg, renowned and revered singer, artist, poet and writer who incited social drama. Unfortunately, being only French-speaking, he couldn't muster up fame in the English-speaking world stage.

Meshing abuse with philosophy and intellectual refinement, this incredible eccentric has become a cult figure inspiring and connecting to every generation. His provocative song '*1969, year of erotic*' ignited graphic sexual imagination and gained popularity at the height of the non-compliant hippie movement. To provoke erotica he directed a scantily dressed Brigitte Bardot to move suggestively on a brute Harley Davidson bike and sensually sing, 'I don't know anybody, I only know my Harley Davidson. I turn on the ignition, it revs up, so I don't need anybody, I only need my Harley Davidson.'

Gainsbourg revolted against French tax laws when he appeared on TV, displayed a 500 Franc note, took out his cigarette lighter and burnt up 75 percent of it. Burning currency is illegal. He kept the 25 percent stub, and said, 'The government takes 75 percent of income as tax. Is it used for any humanitarian or social purpose?'

At a concert, Gainsbourg got tall and lean Bamboo, his Philippino second wife, to wear tight jeans and dance half nude, showing her beautiful upper portion to the public. He introduced her saying, 'A man is privileged. At 55 years I can marry a 24-year-old girl, and nobody feels insulted. But if our ages were reversed, people will call me a gigolo.' His socially offensive abuse established Gainsbourg as an *avant-garde* philosophic entertainer. He made a film lying side by side in bed with his daughter as they both sang. The public was confused. Was the bed relationship incest or art? Called *Charlotte Forever*, the film was immensely controversial. It also established a bright career for his daughter who has since become a great actress.

In a prime-time variety program on French television, Gainsbourg came on stage to greet special guest Whitney Houston. Taking her hand, in a heavy French accent, he very softly said, 'I wanth thu fock yu.' The audience gasped because he spoke English on French TV, something he's never done. With a 'What? What? What?' Whitney pretended she didn't understand him, although she seemed to enjoy the compliment. TV presenter

Michele Drukker tried to deviate the subject but Gainsbourg, who's written most of his songs and poems on sex, repeated himself.

Gainsbourg is considered the most creative and unique poet of 20th century France. His artistic expressions went through sex, love, curses and his erotic husky voice. He's even made an album with the sound of his own farts. In spite of a public image of being overtly intoxicated with cigarettes and alcohol, he imposed a philosophical abusive character to French culture, which is still minting money for the French entertainment business.

Most men heartily participate in my six Curse *Sutra*s. Women don't use swear words, but do enjoy listening to curses not directed at them.

Masculinity expresses itself in physical, pragmatic terms with a possessive tendency. Its image in a man's subliminal mind would possibly be represented by speed in action and making winning moves. Romance would be translated as very physical love. But a women's subconscious mind is subtle, surrounded with restraint and natural beauty. Love would be reflected by a caress. Except for 'page-3' showoffs or feminists, women are not on-the-face like men, and so are rarely 'curse driven.'

one world curse book

You may not swear, but everyone tends to love the universal language of curses. Unfortunately no university in the world has taken care to make a 'one world curse book.' Such a book could put together curse words from every country, with explanations about the moment and circumstances under which different kinds of curses manifest. Such cross-country, cross-cultural insight is rich material for organizations to understand consumer sensitivity.

Making the effort to understand people in their lifecycle, lifestyle, and as they imbibe trends, can make organizations grow.

This psycho-socio-historical background will indicate a new route of emotion, which is the Curse *Sutra*. Understanding the depth from where curses emanate could become a totally different angle to making the consumer offer appropriate.

What can the culture of curses bring you in business? A curse is the trigger of a civilization's multidimensional perspective. You can acquire tremendous knowledge by investing time on this subject. The Curse *Sutra* will help in selling durable products, automobiles, FMCG, cosmetics, fashion, or IT hardware.

A curse in hand is a fatal weapon that's subconscious. It does not physically kill your business opponents. If you are curious to understand human lifecycle, lifestyle or trend as inputs for your business, you will find their association with the curse to be very high. This is true in every country.

In silent private lifecycle moments people love to sink into the six curse *sutra*s. In social lifestyle it becomes a mark of distinction. Trends that emerge from the lap of history are peppered with message-rich curses that communicate powerfully. A futuristic curse does not exist because who would want to waste a curse that nobody understands?

Whether covering a frustrating moment or a thrilling one, the curse works just so. To understand an individual in society who happens to be your consumer, your organization cannot neglect research on the human recipe that thrives on the delicious, upfront language of the curse.

We all know that without consumers business cannot exist. The homily to understand is that cursing is inherent in consumer language, lifecycle and lifestyle. For example, a male gynecologist's concentration on female sex organs is for a diagnosis that's driven by a process. A husband will never consider this as violation of social norms. The analogy I draw is that the curse and sexuality can play a diagnostic role in different cultures. Diagnosing the curse will help in understanding consumer sensitivity at large.

Don't shy away from cursing. Just think of it as a ring of the *jalebi*. It touches the lives of people of different socio-cultural and economic strata. It has the strength and power to keep its taste for all of them. The curse also occupies a prime place in the thinking process of *Jalebi Management*.

The *jalebi*'s swirly movement has reveled in society's discomfort and observed the beauty of the curse. Let's see how the *jalebi*'s bite can become a jagged byte as it goes into the next chapter.

the jagged edges I see in business

People associate with discomfort or a palatable curse at an individual level. An organization associates with people by looking at them as consumers or employees. Do you see an insensitive jagged edge there? Let's see if the *jalebi* can come to the rescue.

The *jalebi*'s peculiarity is its idiosyncratic gaps that can have jagged edges, yet it is decidedly an irregular roundel. *Jalebi Management* encourages every organization to have its unique smell, with an inherent design that makes them all very different. Giving the masses a mysterious sweet bite, and motivating employees to bite once, and one more time again, could be a unique way to overcome jagged edges and manage the organization.

The three inter-linked prerequisites to run a business are:

(*i*)   The masses
(*ii*) The employees (who are from the masses and become people inside an organization)
(*iii*) The organization.

The masses need organizations to help them live better through products or services, and to find jobs that make them employees at these organizations. Therefore, the organization is the powerhouse in business.

An organization's vital need is to anchor people: the masses will buy the products and services the company creates, and employees will help create and sell those products. Unfortunately, organizations carry many jagged, insensitive edges that are not healthy for future business or for the community. Let me sensitize you to these jagged edges that concern people in organizations.

1. the masses

the masses can love or hate

As an organization that wants to grow and profit, do you take the initiative to enter the unarticulated, frustrated paradigm of consumer and customer sensitivity?

People enjoy the rapid change that improved technology brings, and benefit from it. But quick, unexpected changes also create hidden, psychological disappointment. Sophisticated developed countries are yet to understand that there is a drawback in using technology advancement as an excuse for frequent product upgrades. Consumers love the new versions technology throws up, but not if they feel victimized. Intermittent upgrades are increasingly being seen as what I call 'technology pollution.'

Product lifespan in a consumer's hand has drastically reduced. An automobile's span of life has come down from 15 to 3–5 years; a refrigerator's from 40 to 5 years. Technology driven hardware or software barely lasts 6 to 8 months. The masses accept such quick obsolescence because they just cannot control their temptation to acquire high-tech alternatives. In the technology market, there appears to be concerted propaganda about the desirability of technological advancement. Consequently it becomes necessary to change whatever you bought a year earlier as that has become antiquated.

Manufacturers pretend they have no control over the technology blitz. Hype for the new initially excites consumers; they don't see any gap. Instead they often empathize with technology's creative dimension, and its need to continuously move up. When consumers can no longer afford to keep up with the technology-marketing tide, will they feel the jagged edge of becoming a victim? This is an underwater, unstated feeling today.

Digital quality normally has no variance. The low cost, pirated product is technically not inferior to the original expensive DVD. Is the consumer happy to spend money on form, not content, especially as it's not a personal or intimate product? Organizations that unnecessarily release high-priced products instead of giving consumers value for money actually encourage piracy. Instead, a marketing judgment could have been made. Volume sales, when planned at inception, can actually compensate a reduced market price.

A consumer bonds better with an inexpensive pirated DVD that gives the same result as the original. She feels righteous about having beaten the system that was trying to somehow cheat her. On a rational level, consumers don't care about the legal issues of piracy. They just appreciate a logical price. So when authentic DVD and CD labels cry themselves hoarse about being hoodwinked by piracy and appeal for justice, consumers may pay lip service to fair dealing, but it cuts no ice with them.

How long will new technology tempt consumers? You buy a mobile phone for $1,000. After 8 months the price reduces to half. A new model with a new gadget emerges. The consumer's subconscious resentment is, 'Why didn't I wait for 8 months?' Did she feel cheated? Advanced technology is good, but what about the economic jerk you feel in keeping up with it? The shock of sudden price reduction will erase a customer's emotional bond with the product and brand, and forever lose its pride of ownership. Over-consumption of technology products can make people disloyal to a brand, or to a product segment.

As advanced technology is rapidly reducing product cost, a corporate buy-back/exchange policy for technology products will encourage higher per capita consumption. It will also make a brand credible. A used technology product can be taken back at a value that depends on its age and condition; simultaneously a new product is offered at a lower-than-market price.

Durables such as a telephone, computer, palm top, TV, CD player, mobile music device and hi-fi set should be very careful about abusing people's confidence. If they do, a parallel repair or refurbish market can emerge in future to attract price conscious people. Those driven by status will always go for new things, but a manufacturer can lose major value and volume market share from almost-new repaired or refurbished products. Corporations that engage in drastic price cuts at short intervals will never be seen as good corporate citizens.

version culture

Hollywood started the version culture. Once a mega film is successful with the masses, it is used as a formula to reproduce sequels. This generates box office demand. Versions drag entertainment into manifesting itself as mass industrial production. People perceive this as reducing cinematography from being an art form to becoming soap opera driven by newer versions. Unlike art that's unique and cannot be reproduced as mass consumption, people get conditioned to the characters and genre of the versions, and can guess what's coming in the next film. Subconsciously, people feel distanced from the version culture as it does not have the stamp of originality.

Hollywood's version culture has stormed different businesses today. It is very visible in the IT domain.

The moment any computer software is upgraded, the set of engineers and scientists working in your organization will hear of it in their profession, and request for the new version. The current output may be satisfactory, but speed and added features is what the software user is after. His mental makeup is that he will fall short of fashion in the eyes of his peers unless he keeps up with technology advancement. Also of course, his professional curriculum vitae may get contaminated without working knowledge on the latest version.

New versions may be materializing every year or two now. You will feel the financial burden of succumbing to technology improvements when these changes become quarterly or monthly in future. Advancement is indispensable, but when you blindly chase versions you lose the emotional link to technology innovation.

Today's techno-savvy generation is losing the value of emotional attachment influenced by frequent technology upgrades. They do not value what they buy because it will soon be discarded. Cohabiting with the value of impermanence, they have become vulnerable to being attached to almost nothing in life.

Such swift technology changes can at best bring incremental improvement. The French would call this as another form of *encule les mouch*. Real renovation needs requisite time for an existing model to stabilize before it is re-launched in the market. Titillating consumers with incremental changes is like hypnotizing them with a few bells and whistles. Industry should stop taking percentage-increase-in-technology into the market. Product performance should become stable before unsettling consumers with numerous new versions.

As a manufacturer or product designer, you need to remove professional bias before diving into multiversion remakes, and put yourself in the customer's shoes. You need to experience and understand her woes. If you can find, feel and measure the jagged discrepancy in her mind, you will obviously step into the platform of real innovation. You can certainly make the difference by stopping incremental refurbishment that perpetuates the version culture.

marketing as manipulation

The million-mindset people in Europe generally believe marketing to be pure manipulation that sells a product by fooling people. Marketing is sometimes even considered a vulgar weapon to overdose and bulldoze the masses with. It is not seen as an economic strength that serves organizations and the society.

The private labels of hyper or supermarkets in the West started by exploiting the consumer's mistrust for marketing. Organized retail brands are called private labels. In Europe they are sold only inside their own outlets without any license to advertise in public media. Private labels duplicate most fast moving consumer goods and sell the products at least 25 percent lower in price than the big brands. A new range of shops like Leader Price in Europe and Dollar Store in USA emerged to espouse high discount prices. This anti-marketing force against over-priced branded products is a growing business sect in all sophisticated developed countries.

Americans in general are business driven and attuned to marketing. In its 300-year-old Caucasian civilization, marketing occupies an embellished social stature, and has become almost a religion. When heritage is at a discount, people use scale and wealth to establish their history. Americans assign power and recognition when money is quoted. The success of Donald Trump, Bill Gates, George Lucas, Hugh Hefner, Stephan King or Bob Dylan is glorified in terms of wealth.

In every aspect of life, be it business, films, writing, music and even literature, success is measured in scale and money. 'Best seller' was coined to market literature through quantitative measurement of a specific number of books sold. Should a book be equated to a consuming product's multi-mega sale, like beefsteaks sold in kilos in a hypermarket? Shouldn't 'highly read' replace 'best seller' to define this category that grows intellect or creates fantasy? Being in the Top 5, Top 10 or Top 50 of the musical hit parade originated here to measure a singer's commercial success. Entrenched as positive endorsement in American culture is money, size and scale for all subjects.

My observation is that the US context of marketing means being clever and intelligent enough to make money. The more marketing oriented you are in any domain, the more respect you gain from society. Making money is crucial and not negotiable, and having money translates to being on top of everything. Commerce drives marketing making it a revered subject at both the workplace and in business schools.

American big city lifestyle is dazzling, its cost of living is getting out of reach, but the American farmer is strapped, he cannot make ends meet. Across the country, farmers are unable to make a living in their own farms. As per a research finding, they consider theirs to be the country's most neglected profession, with agricultural imports destroying their earnings. They corporatize their farms, stay in joint families to save on earnings and taxes that do not match the high American living standard. American corporate farming outsources farm produce from small farmers who make around $1.4 million on 3,000 acres land. The actual earning from that farm can amount to a meager $70,000 per year for the joint family inclusive of taxes to be paid.

American farmers say that large American corporations have no qualms about importing cheap foreign produce to gain higher profits at their expense. The farmer resents getting short-changed by the consumer who rejects his high priced American produce for imports. This undercurrent of hard times in American farms is likely to reverse their livelihood dependence on agriculture.

When manufacturing of Western branded products is outsourced to an emerging economy country, a few American and European consumers doubt the product's quality. But anti-marketing consumers for whom brands mean some marketing brush up with no real substance, are quite happy to get such cheaper products.

To win consumer confidence it may so happen that globally reputed companies (GRC) will showcase and justify their outsourced infrastructure to increase their reliability factor. Somewhat in the same lines, manufacturers had made long TV commercials in the 1960s to prove the value of their post-War industrial products.

Also post the War, large Western manufacturers took up mass production of consuming products, but failed to take environment protection initiatives until public pressure fell on them. The growing consuming society is becoming very aware of civic responsibilities. The ecology has become a jagged edge for GRCs now. Using environment friendliness as a marketing tactic to prevail over the consumer's sensitive emotion must have concrete substance.

The world is waiting for highly innovative environment friendly products with outstanding sensorialism. The company that makes the first move to fulfill this future need of society will have a bright future. Already, caring for the environment is being integrated as business strategy. In million-mindset countries where basic civic and hygienic sense is high, it is easier to take ecology measures.

Entering billion-mindset societies where civic sense and hygiene are far away, how should GRCs deploy eco-friendly action? Definitely not by considering billion-mindset countries as mere consumption baskets. Care needs to be taken to ensure that recycle-able product materials are used. Otherwise consumers living in billion-mindset countries will find their homes and dustbins cohabiting 20 years down the line.

Today GRCs who are good corporate citizens in their own countries have entered India and are housed in large buildings. But have they checked to see whether the overflowing, foul smelling dustbins in front of their offices and outlets have been cleaned? Or are they waiting for consumer revolt to start becoming environment friendly? The garbage that comprised of plastic sachets of Indian consuming products has now become international, with GRC sachets and other packaging brands vying for space.

Different industries have to develop their own sensitivities towards its public. As a business leader you must strive for business growth; at the same time you can help bring social harmony by the way you conduct business. With refined sensitive discipline your organization can avoid creating more jagged undercurrents in society.

2. employees: the people inside different styles of organizations

leadership streak of the corporate pilot

From my experience of how the capital market views listed companies, five types of promoters can be identified:

- Promoter as a god
- Conservative promoter
- Democratic promoters
- Institutional non-visible promoters
- Individual inventive promoter

Let's look at promoter employers and what they offer to the quality of human capital, products and services and organizational values and promise.

quality of human capital

Whether an organization is small, mid-size, big or gigantic, the quality of its human capital is a decisive factor for its sustainable growth and profit. A company attracts and bears responsibility towards its talent, vendors, partners, shareholders and the financial community.

Recruiting talent is complex in a country like India where market opportunity is ample. Tables have turned from the days when jobs were scarce. Today talent looks at an organization's people management quality, checks to see if he or she will have enough space to breathe and grow his personal career, or will be given the right accountability for growing the company. In turn, the mindset of global employers has changed too. When business survival makes them go global, they are open to getting the best brains from anywhere in the world.

Let's find out how the five types of promoters approach the talent pool.

promoter as a god

When a promoter becomes paternalistic, interferes in the organization's every action, expects to resolve every issue and so acquires a make-believe halo to hover over the human race, he wills himself to be a god. If senior or top management become his bag carrier, he bothers not to dissuade them. On the contrary, he feels such a gesture clinches his position of being a god.

An organization of this kind can attract top talent only with a big remuneration package. Those who want a comfortable life without being responsible for major decisions get convinced to join here. The lower management finds great security here as loyalty is the only major expectation from them. Instead of working to deliver high quality to consumers or customers, they spend time satisfying the super god and other junior gods. Unfortunately, with such a modus operandi, it becomes difficult to develop talent.

conservative promoter

He is open-minded and tries to portray himself as very liberal. But in his mind he carries a fishing rod with a casting wheel. He releases more fishing line to show his liberal stance, and allows employees to perform using their best judgment. With the mental fishing rod tightly in his grip, he reels in any employee-fish the moment he becomes too powerful. The rolling sound of the wheel in the fishing rod allows him to verify where all his other employee-fishes are moving. At the time he considers appropriate, he takes deliberate action to pull in his employees.

Should an employee-fish be going off-line, a big jerk on the fishing rod will get him off the hook. In management parlance, this is called the promoter's push. But if the employee-fish decides to unhook himself, the jerk he will get in the struggle would certainly wound him. He may carry that scar for some time in his career.

A conservative promoter undoubtedly produces very good talent. Employees of such organizations feel good up to a certain level as they can avail the best facilities and training, and are encouraged to grow and perform. Such employees become very valuable in the job market. In fact on reaching a senior level, these employees start fishing around themselves, as they are aware of better prospects for higher level jobs elsewhere, the equivalent of which they may not be allowed to handle in their present company.

If a high quality professional at the higher echelons starts asking unsolicited questions after experiencing certain precedents, the conservative promoter may not entertain him. A separation may ensue. Every so often the conservative promoter needs to establish his control over his company. He psychologically needs to feel he is the real boss, and often seeks such market recognition.

democratic promoters

When two or more promoters create a company, they start by amalgamating the best practices of all the different organizations they had previously worked in. The sharing value is incubated within the company from inception. The market and talent pool see such an organization as democratic and very professional based on the track record of the individual promoters. Employees find this to be an agreeable place to work and grow, and very easily get attracted here. The condition of course is that they will gain in market value.

In general democratic promoters are collectively very shrewd. One promoter normally becomes powerful as the public face of the organization. In spite of its democratic ways, this organization secretly creates clones to cultivate people with similar thinking who will not usurp power.

institutional non-visible promoters

This comprises the most enthusiastic workplace in employee perspective, if work principles and organizational credo are clearly defined. A professional with ambition and aptitude to fit into organizational credo, knows he can join here as a trainee to become its CEO or managing director someday. So climbing to the top by commandeering promotions takes precedence over everything else. Clones exist here too, but they are self-created. They follow a role model to move up the value chain for a life-size career.

Such an organization breeds battalions of high quality talent so competition becomes rife and intense here. Vendors, partners and future talent get easily magnetized to this company because the market sees it to be very professionally managed.

individual inventive promoter

When a promoter ingrains innovation into his organization's heart, and different layers of employees share this inventiveness, it draws talent like bees to honey. Creative and inventive talents ferret out such a place to work in. It stretches their innovative potential. They don't bother about whether the company is listed in the stock exchange. Even if the promoter has an overriding influence in the organization, people are drawn to his innovative genius, not his personal attitude. Here employees are very committed to the discipline of innovation. In fact innovative power has the capacity to rule the market under any circumstance, and this fascinates vendors, future talent and partners.

Promoters can definitely be sub-classified into categories beyond these most common five I have identified. But for the long term, it's the quality of human capital that counts for delivering sustainable, profitable business.

An individual coming for his/her first job is entrenched in family, societal and college culture. He/she has to change to absorb long, addictive work hours in an organizational culture that influences and seasons both his/her professional and personal life.

As a promoter, you carry a huge responsibility for the kind of organizational culture you build as that shapes your human capital. Today managers spend at least 10 hours a day at the workplace; his work starts to mirror his work environment. It's important to inject human sensitivity in this culture as it drives employee enthusiasm for work and their hawk eye on quality.

quality of products and services

Taking these same promoters, let's see how they customize their deliverables for customers and consumers.

promoter as a god

Organizations run by a god-like promoter is often seen as monopolistic, industrial business. Power, lobbying and political influence can overshadow quality here. They maintain a standard quality system in products and services, and a high standard in the quality of infrastructure and production capability. Normally their size of business can grow to be very big.

conservative promoter and democratic promoter

As these companies are proactive and aggressive, they put in the necessary quality processes for their products or services to score high on customer or consumer satisfaction. These promoters normally do not get into monopolistic business. They are business-to-business or business-to-consumer.

institutional non-visible promoters

Product and service quality has to be outstanding as they face shareholder pressure. These promoters seek differentiation as a primary criterion for business to bring in heavy returns.

individual inventive promoter

Such a company will always score higher among the 5 types of promoter companies in terms of product quality and service. The sound business of Bose, smaller than any world electronic giant, is an example. Bose has proved that without being in the capital market, a fundamentally innovative company can conquer consumer mindshare across the world.

Bill Gates is another cult-like individual inventive promoter. The public sees him as an extraordinary human being who maintains down-to-earth relationships in spite of running a monopoly business like no other has ever done before. He ensures outstanding product quality and continuously innovates to create cannot-do-without experiences for his consumers. He is aware of public distaste for monopoly business, so he has made it his mandate to deliver world class, undoubtedly out-of-the-box, and extremely consumer friendly products.

A thin line of danger is inherent in such an organization. The innovative gene of the promoter becomes very difficult to replicate in perpetuity. For the business to sustain, you need to institutionalize a creative process for innovation. The web pattern of the innovative promoter's mind has to be extracted and a design process created for future use. Inheriting generations must be careful that their reference of his mind-web captures his innovative perspective, and does not result in their taking a retrograde step.

In his lifetime, the innovative promoter's parallel agenda should be to design the systems and functioning of his mind-web. The next generation needs to connect to his thinking process, not grasp his output. Institutionalizing his mind-web functioning will ensure that the inventive promoter's visioning capability remains with the organization when it changes its character after two or more generations. Companies like Kodak or HP would certainly have benefited if they had their inventive promoters' direction translated for today's output.

organizational values and promise

How do these five types of promoters approach their work framework that comprises of employees' attitude, behavior, action and delivery? This organizational value program filters to arrive at an organizational promise to the customer and consumer.

promoter as a god
Such a company would normally adopt a generic, readymade mission, vision, quality program adapted from a management book. So gauging the effectiveness of organizational values and promise is difficult.

conservative promoter
Being aware of being professional, the conservative promoter will try to project integrity, stringent discipline, quality, excellence, and consumer and customer satisfaction.

democratic promoter
A democratic promoter will try to project lifestyle at the workplace. He will instill a certain discipline and care for employees' careers, share values, and give freedom to ensure consumer satisfaction.

institutional non-visible promoters
Here operational efficiency with rigorous processes is as important as employee development and a stringent delivery promise.

individual inventive promoter
They try to make things better than what people actually need.

If you want to transform your organization, you will need to ladder and balance the quality of the rational, functional and emotional attributes of your human capital, products, services, and organizational value and promise to evaluate your core essence for its market potential. This quality varies among the five different types of organizations. Check out the ReFinE process (see Figure 10.10) to verify where your organization fits.

3. the organization

western imperialistic social and business attitude

Population is decreasing in the West, as also passion for hard work. But their imperialistic living style and cost of living are on the rise. Within Europe there are differences in business orientation: the North has a formal business attitude, mid-Western Europeans have rigor and precision, Eastern Europe has a folkloric pattern while Latin Europeans are casual, parochial and fight among themselves in their countries. Their common factor is active trade unions that have created rules and regulations to scale up leisure and social protection.

Take the working class in France: paid holidays were first granted in 1936 when work time was 58 hours per week. Today organizations are bound by law to give 6 weeks of paid holiday, and working time has reduced to 35 hours a week. Survival without a job, on social security dole, is not tough either. The working class is not particularly motivated as social security is sufficient. So immigrants readily step into their shoes.

Such paralytic conditions have compelled the Western business community to engage in global outsourcing. Started as an alternative when backward integration was becoming very expensive, outsourcing has now come to stay as the cost efficient solution.

United Kingdom is a small country that markets imperialism in an organized manner. This business has since become global. Their cultural infusion into their colonies was akin to slow poison that finally consumed their subjects. It was just a handful of British traders who spread the English culture into India. Nobody faults an Indian who does not speak his own mother language correctly, but if he should use improper English, he will lose his social status. Implementing the British way of life in a colony was the finest marketing action of the British race. Whichever country they went to, they drove the indigenous people to adopt and swear by English culture.

The UK has played a critical role in bringing Northern Europe and USA close to each other. The English language undoubtedly helped. Soldiers from the countries of the Allied army lived and fought together from the base camp of World War II. This alliance seems strong even with the two governments having different ideologies today, America is conservative, the British leftist. What's prompting this proximity is unclear. Were Karl Marx to rise from his grave today, he may be prompted to add a new chapter in his book, *Das Kapital*, for such an alliance. For now, American economic imperialism, with UK in its pocket, has a base platform for both right and left wings in Europe.

Both displaying an imperial business attitude corroborates my view of negligible difference between dictatorial and colonial power. Imperialism very diplomatically pushes emerging economy countries to follow their model by default. This becomes another form of colonial slavery. Of course physical slavery is abolished, but slavery has migrated to the intellectual level today.

In global fora, European leaders invariably raise immigrant issues in their countries. In the next breath they appreciate the advantage of outsourcing from emerging economy countries, but not very openly for fear of trade union pressure at home. In sum, Europeans feel totally sandwiched between cheap labor in India and China, and the American pressure of gigantic global business vision. Conversely, Americans are frightened in exactly the same way with the power of United Europe and the low cost labor and economic growth potential of the billion-mindset countries.

European political leaders wanted to re-establish Caucasian Europe after the War. So many European countries invited immigrants mainly from their colonies, like France had asked North Africans, to build infrastructure. Indians and Pakistanis responded to England. Upto 1970 people from Italy, Portugal and Spain were considered low cost workers in masonry and construction in North Western Europe. The French would boorishly retort to bad workmanship, saying: 'Why are you working like the Portuguese?' They are still derogatively using the slang word 'butter' when talking about North African Arabs.

In the 21st century, Causacian integration is experiencing a new jagged edge from Eastern Europe. But this is likely to get sorted out in a shorter timeframe, like Italy, Portugal and Spain being at par now, as their common factor is being Caucasian. But the jagged edge between oriental Arabic and occidental Caucasian may still take some time to smoothen.

The war victims in Europe reckoned that a united Europe would have the strength to take on business opportunities, expand geographically and challenge the American dollar power. After World War II, Europeans, mainly the intellectuals, feared the jagged edge of American economic colonialism. This led to the creation of the EU and Euro currency. Unfortunately, the Euro is based more or less on Germany's high cost of living, so it has in turn become a jagged edge for other European countries. In challenging the dollar, the Europeans are still neglecting to strategize how they will integrate with non-Caucasian immigrants.

The billion-mindset countries are now downloading jagged new complexities in the front yard of Americans and Europeans. India and China are overpowering them with issues relating to unemployment, outsourcing and organized immigration.

octopus opportunity for slavery

Technology has dramatically facilitated the democratic power of people. The Western imperialistic classes and sophisticated developed countries still maintain a sophisticated living style, employing lower cost labor and infrastructure as support. What exactly are they getting? On a platter emerging economy countries are serving them an octopus business opportunity which comprises of:

(*i*)   Workers in large numbers
(*ii*)   Low cost knowledge workers
(*iii*) Motivated workers
(*iv*)   A smiling society
(*v*)   Huge base of consumers
(*vi*)   Low cost infrastructure
(*vii*) Avoiding industrial pollution in their own countries
(*viii*) Low cost of production

The discrepancy is that low cost labor is also the mass consumer. Their huge potential for mass consumption or being shareholders needs to be recognised. The billion-mindset mentality is rapidly changing. Not much longer will they remain subservient; tomorrow they will command the world markets.

Indian labor classes from metros to rural areas are just boarding the economic jetliner. Where no telephone figured in their waking hours, rural people are today experiencing the advanced mobile phone in their hands. That big, solid black instrument that sometimes rang in the rich farmer or trader's place suddenly has no status or relevance. Technology has inducted democracy by showering a large population with aesthetic mobile telephony handsets. It has made living easier. It is educating children at a faster pace. Clearly, this is an indicator of how people's aspirations will move up. The combination of education and technology is poised to bring in economic wealth for the billions.

Will this next generation accept a work culture associated only with low cost? Matching up to the living style of sophisticated countries may take a decade, but before people get demotivated, India should stop representing itself to the world as low cost in every domain, whether in labor, intellect or infrastructure. Low standard of living and low labor cost may give high profitability percentage to Indian or Chinese companies, but the concept of low cost is not sustainable as operational efficiency for the future.

Mao Zedong's Cultural Revolution equalized all social layers, made the Chinese disciplined and hardworking; but it simultaneously suppressed their intellectual advancement. In my view this situation will change after two decades. The Indian subcontinent in contrast, without such life-changing socio-political upheaval, and with exposure to Anglophone education and culture, has given Indians a strong inclination towards high-rise lifestyles. For the next two decades India will lead over the Chinese in knowledge work for the Western imperialists.

Intellectuals in sophisticated countries have started becoming aware that the jagged edge they have to be wary of is the powerful global influence emerging from billion-mindset people.

GRC pressure on companies in emerging economy countries like India

Consumerism is growing faster in India than the capability of industrial houses to cope with it. GRCs (globally reputed companies) have entered offering consumers perceptible quality and choice. Their pressure is obliging Indian companies to enter into the vast ocean of consumer and customer sensitivity.

A *jalebi* has a sensitive character too. From preparation to cooking, to reaching it to the consumer's hand, before it enters the mouth, the *jalebi* is very delicate indeed. It can break easily. The deliverables from Indian organizations need to be just as sensitive to satisfy the subtle needs of consumers and customers.

Unfortunately Indian manufacturers hadn't quite factored in consumer desire until GRCs opened the floodgates of consumption. There are a few business houses that are currently not facing GRC pressure either because GRCs did not get FDI (foreign direct investment) or are still not paying attention to India.

Among these are the newspaper publication business, airlines in the domestic sector, bicycles, 1, 2 and 3 star hotels, mass scale hypermarkets and supermarkets and the jewelry business. If these industries become lax and take it easy for another 5 to 10 years, they'll have the carpet pulled from under their feet.

The mental make-up of consumers is changing because of exposure to variety and high value GRC items. So even if your business category is not in the GRC radar yet, you cannot afford to leave the quality of your product or service below GRC standards. GRCs benefit consumers with extreme customization. Their quality is reliable, and products consumer friendly. They visibly display global success to provide confidence. This influence has totally changed Indian consumers who now expect such benefits even in the areas where GRCs are not present.

When expectation levels rise, consumers get conditioned to a certain quality that translates to aspiration. So consumers find the products and services not yet upgraded to GRC standards to be devoid of value. When only the price point matters, the products are considered to be of basic need. They will not pay extra for quality for what is less aspirational.

As Indian companies, you should take this drastic GRC pressure as your real struggle today. Your challenge in this global competition should be to proactively innovate, and become sensitive to the consumer. Making your product or service of global standard even without GRC pressure on you can make you ready for the sophisticated western or developed country market. This will help you make your company a GRC.

mushrooming of retail

An example would be the mushrooming of organized retail and mall development in India. Retail business actually needs to increase just three major factors

(*i*)   traffic
(*ii*) conversion

(*iii*) shopper wallet share increase

(*iv*) repeat purchase (retention)

Unfortunately in India, organized retail strategy appears to be driven by the real estate business model. Mall builders are quick to occupy prime real estate in the country, perhaps to barricade the GRC retail business that is yet to come. The retails give shoppers an enjoyable pastime. They are yet to focus on consumers leaving the outlet with loaded shopping bags.

It is obvious that when GRCs enter, they may not get today's prime places. With shopper sensitivity, efficient management of logistics and brand value, they are capable of attracting people even to abandoned areas. They will transform these into new prime places. What is missing in today's sophisticated, air conditioned malls in India?

Product selection and versatile presentation must connect to the psycho-socio parameters of Indian shoppers of diverse cultures. If you talk to 20 shoppers at any time in any organized retail, you will find many different cultures, languages and geographical differences. The organized retail business is not addressing this multiplicity. So conversions are not happening easily even though shoppers in the retail have disposable income.

Imperial GRC power can overwhelm. Their global repute connects to shoppers. Price sensitive Indian brands get neglected as they do not enter the shopper's desire level.

Understanding and deploying socio-behavioral factors need not await the GRC's arrival. Organized retail needs to cater to this aspect accurately, as the shopper can easily pick up similar products in the unorganized market at every street corner. How long will Indian malls remain a tourist place that's fantastic for a weekend outing?

competing with remuneration

GRCs are breaking the rules of the job market in India. Employee remuneration is seen to have seriously gone up without commensurate justification of deliverable quality. Its comparable to how Western tourists pay exorbitantly to hawkers and transporters, disturbing the ability of local people to pay those rates. The fallout is unmet high expectations, and people trying to unnecessarily cheat foreigners.

You cannot prevent pay packet democracy, but you can find a route to protect its consequences. The only remedy I can see is for Indian companies to become GRCs. They must expect and extract the best from their employees' and accordingly improve the status of employees.

Indian companies that directly compete with GRCs should not benchmark their remuneration with other Indian companies. In the unprotected economy, why will competent people stay with companies that do not value them as much as others would? Having experienced it, developed countries know by default that low labor cost is a short-lived situation. Saturation will soon seep in. GRCs are already setting a trend of changing their outsourcing partners very often and flitting from one country to another.

By continuously squeezing costs, making large profits and temporarily satisfying shareholders, Indian companies may miss out on their vision. They should invest for innovation to brighten up the future. The West can rightly claim superiority because they have strong innovative power. India and China need to work at creating incredible innovation within a short time. Otherwise their countries will only be consuming societies, viewed as cheap labor.

The real threat lies in your corporate vision not being accurate. Your organization may get tempted to take the opportunities cheap labor brings in, but are you walking down tomorrow lane? GRCs are setting up their India offices to market their products locally and globally. Work content being executed here ranges from innovation to fabrication. Most of their hires are local. Why are Indian companies not waking up to the power of their own captive, innovative human capital? They do not recognize that their manpower base has vast opportunities now.

Developed countries are also shifting manufacturing bases and other labor related work to countries with manpower that's competent and cheap. These economically emerging countries are acquiring global skills that can bring them at par with developed countries. In the global perspective, low cost labor comprises just a timeline in the economic progression of a nation.

hygiene and civic sense

Is the consumer's hygienic living comfort a part of corporate initiative? Developing hygienic sense is a sensitive criterion that needs addressing. In most Indian companies, there is a big difference in the upkeep of the toilets, the general workplace conditions and canteens for senior and junior management and workers. The lower you go, the more pathetic it becomes.

An organization's responsibility is to significantly improve these areas and maintain the same hygienic cleanliness everywhere. This will change the mentality of workers, making them understand that consumers and customers must be served in a hygienic, civic platform. Your employee himself could be your consumer or shareholder. The whole organization must have an outstanding, hygienic environment to inspire people to work. Addressing these issues entails no heavy investment or recurring cost. It's a matter of discipline and sensitivity to cleanliness.

Most eating places for the general public in an emerging economy country, save a few sophisticated restaurants, have unhygienic conditions. Check out a sophisticated retail store. Imagine the feeling a worker would have who sees the product he helped make in his disheveled factory selling in this dreamy context. He perhaps can't even imagine it could come from his shopfloor. Exporters of different goods go through a radical change of attitude and tough, mandatory compliance rules as required by their foreign oursourcing partners. Can businesses in India take the initiative to make theirs a beautiful workplace?

I don't understand why Indians who bathe and pray everyday, dress so well, are reputed to be hospitable, lack in hygienic civic sense. In the staircase landing of a large apartment complex in Mumbai, I saw ceramic statues of gods and goddesses on every floor. Observing the general decline of Indian culture nowadays, I commented to my colleague, 'What a good decoration idea!' He laughed, 'There was no choice but to place such statues here. People were spitting on the walls!' Each extremely clean, exclusive apartment had fabulous décor. Why do such people neglect their civic sense?

Perhaps industrial bodies similar to Confederation of Indian Industry can finance an independent body with stringent discipline to sensitize and monitor organizations to implement hygiene in offices and their surroundings, from the shopfloor to the middle management floor. The top management floor is always clean. Unhygienic working environment, irrespective of organization size, is totally antisocial behavior. I can assure you that by visibly improving hygiene, your quality and productivity will be higher than normal. Your entire organization will incline towards deeper customer and consumer sensitivity.

One hears of many new initiatives regarding airports and metros, but nobody is enquiring about the improvement of sewage and disposal systems in the cities and towns.

The way consumption is growing in India, care should be taken about dustbin clearance. Industry can take the initiative to sensitize the government and municipality to avoid dustbin heaps in front of every locality. The entry of GRCs post economic liberalization saw all salary levels rise, but I am not sure the hygienic sensitivity across the different layers has gone up. There should be stringent discipline and measurable initiatives to help employees improve their hygienic sense in their personal living style.

Hygiene is the biggest evolution in human development as it addresses consumer sensitivity. You may be afraid to eat a *jalebi* cooked in unhygienic conditions if you are sensitive to hygiene. You may get tempted but you will not dare to try it for fear of de-stabilizing your digestive system. When conditions are hygienic, you'll want to try it.

Just think about an unhygienic *jalebi*, a broken *jalebi*, an unsticky *jalebi* of imperfect taste or a dried up *jalebi*. Then try to smoothen the jagged edges of the organization with that just-what-the-doctor-ordered *jalebi* that reaches out to all. The masses plus employees will enjoy a crunchy, yummy bite.

renovation and innovation

To bring significant differentiation, you need to effectively renovate your existing product or service. For quantum growth, you need to establish valuable innovation that can change human life.

Renovation makes the old come alive just as *Jalebi Management* has resurrected a syrupy fried pastry that's shaped like a tubular swirl. Historical reference to *jalebis* being served in a feast is found in Jinasura, a Jain work dated AD 1450. Two early and well-known 17th century manuscripts, a science of cooking and a work on dietetics by Bhojana-Kuntala of Raghunatha, describe the *jalebi*'s preparation in exactly the same way as it is made today. The Soundarya Vilasa of Annaji, a Kannada poem dated 1600, mentions the 'jil-abi' as an item of food served at Ishwara *puja* (prayer).

According to Hobson-Jobson, *jalebi* is 'apparently a corruption of the Arabic zalabia or Persian zalabia.' If this is correct, it entered India quite early. Notwithstanding its origin, *jalebi* has been around for centuries, renovating itself with every epoch and culture; encouraging innovations in taste and looks with different ingredients and shapes like *jangiri* and *imurti*.

In a similar analogy, an organizational culture of continuous renovation and innovation will sustain growth that ripples like a *jalebi*.

Penetrating into French culture that's deep-rooted, I found their renovation/innovation thought process, and fundamental invention over centuries to be quite unbeatable. Fascinated at how they renovate history, art and living style, and change human life with path-breaking innovation, my curiosity was further aroused to observe and inculcate European culture in every aspect of my personal and professional life. To professionally succeed, I honed my creative thought process to mingle with their masses. In doing so my personal learning curve has climbed like greased lightning.

Immigrants in the West generally have two ways of living:

(*i*)   Get a good job, improve lifestyle and living comfort, surround yourself with people of your country of origin, try to exactly live the culture you are used to, and continuously criticize the country you have migrated to.

(*ii*)   Immigrants like me have followed a second route. Integrate, understand and act according to Europe's longstanding tradition and history, but philosophize as per our own origins. The objective is to discover Western history and society from a new angle in daily life. Being in this culture-absorbing category, I am enjoying a fascinating value of life.

Renovation, France has taught me, is 'I change myself' and innovation means, 'I change the world.' Living in Europe, the process and philosophy of renovation and innovation are now entrenched inside me.

The French believe renovation and innovation blossom into action only when social life improves. They attribute a philosophical character to renovation and innovation, which pervades the art form inherent in French culture. *Pensée unique* which means 'think in a unique way' is an unshakable French trademark that has helped them to be extremely creative and out-of-the-box.

Averse to vulgarizing art, they somehow believe mixing it with business is not tenable. The French scoff at the typecast American tourist who, instead of marveling at an era's architecture, wonders about how much it would cost to reconstruct the Eiffel Tower or Versailles Palace today. They think Americans have a money-centric culture.

Conversely, the French are deficient in promoting their high thoughts into commercial success. They have yet to lucratively spread their renovation/innovation knowledge as processes the world can use. Being a lover of French sensitivity and intellectual sparkle, I believe that renovation and innovation can be efficacious when applied as a process for business coherency. It can bring sustainability and growth.

renovation

The French renovate scientific inventions, historical architecture in buildings, artistic works, and refurbish legends through unbelievable theatrical enactments and story telling. The approach has passion, and is fundamental with four key facets:

- Refreshing history
- Transcending history to the next era
- Solidifying the base
- Self change

The 21st century is already inscribed with the blend of cultures. In earlier centuries, artistic expression was prioritized; detailing was minute. In today's fast moving social climate the micro details of any subject get waylaid. Renovation can determine a new dimension of life by intermingling what's valuable in history with what's prized in contemporary life.

The billion-mindset countries have traditional legacy and several kinds of valuable possessions. Co-opting the renovation process they can achieve a significant commercial or sociological leap. Renovation requires them to have a powerful thought process, philosophical vision and a sensitive potent message.

the Louvre, a philosophical touch to renovation

Will a transparent pyramid shaped structure anywhere in the world be recognized as a new interpretation of the history of Egypt? The fantastic fiber-glass pyramid in Paris' Louvre Museum is renovation par excellence. It is not easy to superimpose two cultures, the French and Egyptian, and to ultimately create a new cult with the blend. The Louvre's grandeur as the carrier of art and culture of all time gives it superior advantage to absorb foreign symbols to create a new dimension for the world to enjoy art. We are in a century where technology can completely kill the anthropological perspective. But here both are given paramount consideration. We view what had existed and what's here today before we start something totally new.

The Louvre, the world's most renowned museum housing the best collection of art, with masterpieces dating back at least 200 years, was losing its dynamism. French President Francois Mitterrand's idea of renovating Louvre museum shocked the traditionalists. His opponents ignited the masses saying the huge government investment was public money being thrown away. People were disturbed that a foreign architect was inflicting an Egyptian pyramid on a historical French monument. I actively shared this controversial renovation experience with the French populace between 1985 and 1989.

Chinese born American Ieoh Ming Pei, the architect famed for the Kennedy Library in Boston, USA, was chosen to renovate the Louvre. Pei's proposition was to make a 71 feet high glass pyramid in the Louvre's courtyard.

The French establishment was aghast. They found it totally absurd that the Egyptian pyramid culture was being imported into an art treasure trove of the world's best Renaissance masterpieces. When Mitterrand accepted Pei's structural design of unusual arrangements in geometric shapes, it conjured up both provocation and displeasure.

This renovation totally changed the Louvre's face value. The underlying thought was to blend modern architecture and materials with the old civilization that the Louvre represented. Global visitors now have superb functional accessibility. They now have flexibility in being able to freely circulate inside to enjoy the philosophy of art at their own pace. A basement was created in the courtyard, and daylight flooded in through the transparent pyramid over it.

During the renovation period, the Louvre was assigned a special status with focused temporary branding: '*Grand travaux du Louvre*' meaning 'Grand work at the Louvre.' In spite of the storm surrounding it, such communication aroused great curiosity, making people think. Slowly but surely, everybody got aligned to considering the renovation as a masterwork of great and grand dimensions. Today the Museum together with its environment has become a precious, contemporary harbor of the blend of art and commerce. Revenue increasing activities here include fashion shows by *haute couture* designers, and addition of several entry points to ease tourist traffic. Its changed name of Pyramide du Louvre has proved that timely renovation with a contemporary code can reactivate a played out attraction, rendering it more vibrant and open to commerce.

'The modernization of art is the goodwill of society, as art and culture will always be alive,' said President Mitterrand when commissioning Pyramide du Louvre in 1985. It was completed not in his first Presidential term but when he was re-elected and remained President for 14 years.

I've observed that Europe never abandons its history; its heritage spots are just contemporarized to connect to contemporary generations. By commercializing the surroundings of historical monuments, life is injected into them. Entertainment concepts and shopping can draw traffic to historical places that are otherwise very expensive to maintain. Once their vicinity becomes vibrant they pull in traffic, acquire commercial value, and automatically attract funds from business houses and tourists for continuous maintenance.

the Indian scenario

It is very disappointing that India's historical features languish in obscurity. The Government's Archeological Department is yet to display vision in contemporizing heritage monuments in a trendy form. India Gate in New Delhi looks desert-like all day. With a more or less similar arch of triumph, look at the Avenue Champs des Elysees in Paris. France has turned it into the world's very precious avenue where both history and commerce combine to bubble.

Contemporary India proudly talks of centuries old cultural history; but not much attention has been given on how to revitalize this heritage. Ancient architectural monuments are being demolished or defaced by hooligans for lack of protection. Poor upkeep is collapsing them into abandoned havens for snakes where a few tourists visit from time to time. Little wonder then that despite our rich heritage, India attracted a miniscule 3.92 million, just 0.5 percent of the world's 808 million tourists arrivals per year, whereas France has 76.92 million arrivals, which means 9.5 percent of global share in 2005.

Billion-mindset India and China with thousands of years of history hanging here and there need to take up scientific renovation of historical architecture. These assets will then transform to goodwill. Their rapid growth into modernity can become vulnerable without people's pride in their traditional roots. Renovating and making visible their past will sensitize people to distinguish themselves with their origin in modern times. Heritage can be transformed into a qualitative advantage in their social and business approach.

Renovation is not about demolishing the past in favor of the new, like Dubai's Palm City on the sea. When the classic dimension is revitalized in contemporary taste, the polish glamorizes ancient treasures. Emerging economy countries can tap Europe for detailed learning. The Government could appoint a Minister of Renovation to autonomously run the show without bureaucracy. Architects and restorers alone may not be enough; engineers, anthropologists, philosophers, historians, and business professionals must get involved in such renovation.

With today's modern technology and new materials, the country's legacy could be renovated in classic contemporary style, making historical sites into functional and happening everyday places. The intermingling of varied cultures from Harappa, Mahenjodaro, Buddha, Emperor Ashoka, Hindu Maharajas, Jains, Sikhs, Parsis, Mughals, the British, Portuguese and French have combined to create the kaleidoscope that is India. These cultures were not just transplanted here. They entered, intermingled and immersed into the country's unique blend of people and customs co-existing with nature.

The Muslims, British, Portuguese or French in India retained their original cultures, yet they acquired a certain Indian flavor quite unique from their origin. As in Hindu custom, Muslim marriages in Gujarat use turmeric to decorate and smoothen the bride's face and body. Islamic India alone practices this social custom. The British *babu*dom culture exists in India only. The Goan culture of songs has a distinctive Portuguese legacy. In erstwhile French principality Chandan Nagar outside Kolkata, there still exists Dosco Bakery that makes French handmade bread. It's available from 4 to 6 P.M. because in the days of yore, that's when the French were ready for dinner. Even now St. Joseph's

Convent gets a regular supply of this French bread called *Nouko Roti* meaning 'bread like a boat.' Over centuries of intermingling with conquerors and visitors, India has acquired many dimensions of the blending of cultures. This is steadily getting wiped out for lack of archiving and renovation.

Take the example of the Portuguese explorer Vasco da Gama (1469–1524), the first person to sail directly from Europe to India. He was buried for some time at St. Francis Church in Kochi, Kerela. In 1539 his remains were returned to Portugal and re-interred in Vidigueira. St Francis Church has an exotic character totally unlike any church in Portugal. The sea, fishermen in their oriental boats, the wonderful picture of an occasional Indian Christian marriage, together they give an out-of-this-world feel in a Catholic house of prayer, which I have never experienced in Europe. As modern India has no significant innovation, its historical places, from architecture to social culture, can be renovated and showcased as a dynamic selling point. This will prevent the next generation from becoming cultural orphans.

the US approach

Renovation is a European culture, not American. Crossing Beverly Hills, I went looking for the heritage homes of Hollywood stalwarts. What I found instead were old homes bulldozed by new actor-occupants to construct their own new landmarks for society to recognize. American culture is recent, molded by money, power, speed and living comfort. Europe's 2000-year-old Judea-Christian culture continuously shakes up history to modernize it. Doing so they somehow maintain the authenticity of Caucasian culture through its past ingenuity and glory of discovery.

American history is short; its mixed communities have not anthropologically absorbed the culture for renovation. But for more than a hundred years American corporations have displayed strong renovation in business. There are different examples of brands translating their century-old experience into history to give birth to trends that form the link of generations. Old brands like GE, Coca-Cola, Tropicana, Bell, Kellogg's, Citibank, Pepsi, Harley Davidson, Proctor & Gamble have continuously renovated themselves, from the back-end of their organizations upto all consumer touch points, to match with the trend of different epochs. These giant American brands have acquired world fame and social acceptance because of being around for a wide span of time. But more importantly, they have always engaged in renovation to be close to their consumers and be in tune with the times.

business renovation in Europe

Following its destruction in the World War II, Germany was rebuilt from scratch. That is why its architecture is new. Side by side Germany undertook phenomenal renovation in its manufacturing systems, so 'Made in Germany' continues to be equated to supreme quality recognized by global communities.

Many European luxury brands like Channel, Cartier, Louis Vuitton, Mont Blanc, Burberry's are hallucinating the world. Continuous renovation of their product portfolio, while preserving tradition, has enabled them to dominate with phenomenal brand value. Technology can create the new, but technology cannot create heritage brands. Renovation is used to scale up a unique heritage virtue and connect it to contemporary trends. So the luxury business has a timeless base which is above the product's physical features.

Having renovated several international brands that date back to more than a century, I've found different challenges in different countries. When I modernized a 250-year-old French brand, the owner of the company had to take permission for its change from the French Cultural Minister. That's because the age of the brand made it a part of French heritage.

The origin of the *jalebi* goes back hundreds of years too. It blends with the trend through minor renovations but has never lost its heritage. Its age-old attraction is to invite a bite whether it is big or small, hot or cold, crisp or juicy, yellow or multi-hued. You may not be able to find the individual creator of the *jalebi* as it's become a cultural part of Indian society. Over the decades and centuries the *jalebi* has been continuously kindled in the stoves of different people. It's possible the *jalebi* had different tastes through the ages, but the shape has kept its link. This social transmission has kept the *jalebi* as a dynamic indulging dessert.

innovation

Let's return to Paris for the counterpart to renovation, which is innovation. At another Parisian right bank corner, an area replete with ancient architecture on the east side, they created the Cultural Center of Georges Pompidou. When Georges Pompidou became the President in 1969, it was his desire that the visual arts coexist with music, cinema, books, and audio-visual as a research library. He took Italian architect Renzo Piano and British architect Richard Rodgers to innovate another controversial, fully steel structure that would stand out in sharp contrast to its 300-year-old neighboring buildings.

Centre Pompidou is a million sq ft in area with four main branches and its construction began in 1972. The distinctly industrial structure has a glass façade covered with steel pipes, frames and walls, encircled by transparent tubes. To this day people feel for it in extremes, either love or hate.

The unique design has modern utility products contrasting with Expressionist-style evergreen old paintings done in early 20th century. The beautiful terrace of restaurants is half glass and half open so you enjoy your dinner with a 360-degree view of illuminated old and new Paris. There was innovation in moving up from the ground to the sixth floor too. The external circling elevator, the like of which you may not see anywhere in the world, gives you a wide view of Paris.

The innovative character is outstanding; Pompidou Center is situated in the heart of an old locality, alongside stores and facades hundreds of years old, that have been renovated to keep alive the allure of their period. This extremely modern building would be all the rage even in the most sophisticated areas of the New World like Manhattan, New York. But will it have the same charisma? Absolutely not! The charm of innovation gets a distinct power when it is surrounded with heritage that has been renovated.

Sudden innovation without any reference to the past does not create a breakaway, lasting impact. Consumers appreciate the value of an industrial, scientific, entertainment, artistic or every day consuming product only when it has a thread that connects it to its legacy. To become credible, new things need social acceptance. For example, when international brands carrying their worldwide reputation entered India, they immediately got recognition and gobbled up market share. Even newly developed Korea could bring in sophistication with LG and Samsung.

Indian manufacturers did not quite realize any emergency when economic reforms were announced in 1991. They felt no urgency to renovate their product quality in the competitive platform of GRCs. So in people's mind, the essence of their old brands did not change. They continued to carry the weight of pre-liberalized days, and were perceived as non-competitive and backward. Without initial renovation, if innovation is placed atop the old, it does not carry the consumer's trust. The brand subsequently becomes local and price sensitive, and GRCs ride over it from every angle. What gets trampled is brand image along with growth, profitability, the consumer's attachment and high aspiration for the brand.

Where then are the lacunae? India does not figure in the chapter on innovation in any consuming area. If you are an Indian staying in India, look at your environment, your socio-economic life. You will find India has not contributed in the paradigm of innovation in modern living, at the workplace or in any social aspect. Indian manufacturing companies need to care about what the consumer perceives.

In the last 16 years since economic liberalization, Indian manufacturing companies have been reluctant to make a radical change in their product offering. They look for growth always in incremental steps. In the competitive scenario with GRCs, can consumers confidently accept a premium value Indian proposition when they find no historical base and social endorsement of quality excellence? Indian manufacturers had presumed that Indian shoppers are not ready to pay a high price for high quality. This theoretical undervaluation of the Indian consumer's desire for newness deflected them from introducing breakaway offerings. Consequently they have been unable to get consumer mindshare and have not established a radical difference from what they had on offer before the economic reforms.

What can be done when a country's origin does not reflect innovative power? Master the platform of displacement, and change the literal and lateral substance of the product. That's what Japan did following their crushing defeat after World War II. Now LG and Samsung from Korea are becoming displacement masters. Just think about how ingeniously they have integrated their name in the sophisticated developed western society. Could Europe even imagine, 15 years ago, companies like these being in their midst?

When economically emerging countries do not have the legacy of industrial excellence, they can anchor their product and brand to consumer mindspace only by building a breakaway strategy. The strategy could be radical organizational transformation on a highly sensitive product development platform in conjunction with the consumer's latent trend. Only with change in people's working culture can a breakaway strategy be driven.

The Europeans and Americans established their industrial superiority in the 19th and 20th centuries. The Japanese started after World War II. The Koreans followed them into the superior level in the last 10 years. These were steps in achieving manufacturing excellence. To get global acceptance, the approach of economically emerging countries has to be that much more superior than companies in countries considered to be superior.

The real challenge for BRIC (Brazil, Russia, India, China) countries is to take the pressure of being able to succeed in sophisticated developed countries. If a product and brand can achieve at least 30 percent of its business from the extremely demanding Western market, it will prove that the organization has uplifted the quality of its manpower and product development. That logical backpressure within the company will rapidly improve its value chain. Industrial evolution is no longer a factor today. It is possible for a marketing innovation to change your business profile within a short span of time.

Innovation in marketing is an intelligent tactic to increase business. Marketing innovation means increasing the comfort level of the masses by showing a radical new avenue of living or working style through products or services that are extremely consumer friendly. Japanese or Korean companies grabbed this vast opportunity of mastering innovative marketing and became GRCs.

What is the recipe for innovative marketing? Think of a painter's big canvas as global social culture. Create a collage on this canvas by superimposing different sociocultural grains. While doing so, you will suddenly find a certain form of innovation has gotten created. This is marketing innovation. Marketing your products through innovations in marketing can make your bottomline very healthy. In parallel, you can start fundamental R&D innovation for the future.

Whatever your business may be, if you follow the discipline, creativity and process route, you can definitely enter the GRC arena. How to successfully innovate in marketing and connect to consumers is the total science of Branding.

Because of the supremacy of GRCs in India, Indian manufacturers are hurtling towards link-less innovation. They are getting vehicles designed from Italy, hiring famous foreign actors for motorbike advertising campaigns or making TV designs so different that consumers don't connect with that trend. This is a big mistake.

New product innovations from a brand is very important, but not before steps are taken to clean up the old stable. What the consumer is familiar with must be brushed up so she is convinced to come with you when you come up with an innovation. It is like the old traditional *jalebi* sweet. Does it not give you a juicy palatable taste with a link to tradition even as you freshly make it in any modern context?

renovation and innovation can be deployed in three platforms

- **Displacement platform:** Displacement is a total change in course, with no desire to go back to the old.
- **Rupture piatform:** Rupture is a desire to break away from market monotony. In doing so, can return to co-opt and comtemporarize history.
- **Maintaining aspiration platform:** Maintaining aspiration is continuous improvement, a desire to preserve a value that is recognized as effective and premium.

displacement

In economically emerging countries, economic reforms push manufacturing companies to displace their offerings so as to take on emerging opportunities and competitive challenges. The displacement mode gets a company to pursue a new line of business, and not return to the old business.

Japan's Toyota encountered a very successful displacement after 79 years of existence. From being a company that made looms with the family name of Toyoda, the company name was changed to Toyota as the corporate name, and the market opportunity of manufacturing trucks was taken up. In 1927 Toyota audaciously copied the European car.

A strong innovative power can create displacement in both sophisticated markets as well as in economically emerging countries. In the 1950s and 1960s the Japanese showed the world that miniaturization with aesthetic sophistication and extreme consumer friendliness can displace any fundamental European or American innovation.

Europeans were very negative about everything Japanese, but the US recognized their prowess in deploying technology with a consumer sensitive approach. Keen to win over Europe, the Japanese through an act of displacement, delivered to customers, accessorized, road-ready cars of quality with consumer friendly features and services. European car dealers said Japanese spare parts are more expensive, will take three months to arrive, and their car insurance is costlier. But consumer sensitivity won the day.

Economically emerging BRIC countries need to learn about displacement in the manufacturing business. Incremental improvement will not bring success to companies that have survived, totally isolated from competition, in protected economies. The challenge is to create displacement that's significant and perceptible in any country, and so surpass Japanese, Korean, European and American products. Unless they pursue the displacement route, BRIC countries and Africa will become mere suppliers to sophisticated markets, and not be able to hold their own in manufacturing excellence.

The iPod is a recent example of displacement that came through very basic software logic. It drastically changed personal entertainment and has since acquired cult status among youngsters across the world. Challengers to the iPod have been many, like Sony's Network Walkman and Microsoft's Zune, perhaps with more advanced features. But Apple's iPod got first mover advantage and an enigmatic following. This is an excellent example of innovation in the displacement platform in sophisticated markets where entertainment instruments are saturated.

When innovation has mass and global appeal it becomes revolutionary. The iPod follows this school. Unlike the East, the West has produced performing artists who follow their own cultures but have been sought after in most countries across the world.

Displacement in music has been happening since different centuries in Western Europe. In the last 60 years entertainment artists such as Bob Dylan, the Rolling Stones, Beatles, John Lennon, Maria Callas, Pavarotti, Elvis Presley, Jean Michel Jarre or Zubin Mehta have displaced traditional music. They can go anywhere in the world to perform to people of different cultures. People hunger for their musical shows.

This kind of revolutionary displacement in music that attracts varied world people has always come from the West. That's because they follow stringent discipline, creativity and process even while being in the platform of displacement. You can visibly see a link between Thomas Alva Edison and Steve Jobs. Edison brought in displacement by innovating the gramophone to record the human voice, while Jobs did so by creating an independent on-the-move library of music and film through the iPod.

Society's habits and inclinations can inspire innovators to come up with inventions to entice people. Why the iPod? Nobody told Steve Jobs to create an iPod. But he realized that music fans who listen to many different musical styles could discover a value here. Having understood European society where no individual listens to only one or two kinds of music, I can very easily connect to iPod's success. It created a personal mobile pocket library of thousands of different styles of musical pieces to listen to at my leisure. Today the marketing innovation that is the iPod attracts and appeals to people from all cultures.

One of the displacement examples I have experienced is BSN Corporation transforming to Danone. In 1970s and 1980s, BSN of France grew through acquisitions. Operating in 14 different product categories, BSN could not garner global focus and remained a narrow French multi-domain conglomerate. Profitability was very low. So a strategic decision was taken to focus on only three product categories connecting to health. These were dairy, beverage and biscuits.

Displacement happened in terms of strategy: reducing from 14 to 3 category verticals, and change in name. Danone achieved the global business that had escaped BSN for 30 years. Within 15 years of passing through the displacement route, Danone is today an admired global food brand with the value of health, a turnover of 13 billion Euros and outstanding profitability.

The masses in BRIC countries obviously have several cultural habits that manufacturing companies could exploit in business. Have they considered translating some cultural habit into a business perspective so that a new product or service can attain world success? Companies in economically emerging countries must metamorphosize to prioritize displacement. Being able to renovate an old product in the displacement platform proves they have authenticity. It creates the link for future innovation to happen.

Work cultures can also do with total displacement, especially in manufacturing companies of protected economies like India. Employees must radically change their thinking, attitude to teamwork and external partner association so they do not regress to earlier times. Are they abreast of evolving trends their consumers are immersed in? In tune with consumer needs and desires? Do they understand youth flair?

An organization that's insensitive to local and global consumers must turn itself upside down through perceptible work culture displacement. The displacement platform starts from an organization's human capital. When internal displacement takes place, employees get in sync with their consumers.

Professionals of over 45 years, say in India, will obviously have tremendous domain knowledge, experience and expertise, but may not match the trend of the market. The 18 to 25-year-olds who represent the young that's driving the market should be allowed to question them. The experienced elders will automatically get the opportunity to displace their thinking, functioning and deployment of different transaction processes.

Protected Indian companies forced to jump directly into the competitive WTO find themselves at the crossroads. Take the Chetak scooter brand that enjoyed exceptional consumer bonding. Its low cost mode of travel was valuable for individual and families alike when the country's transportation system and road conditions were very poor. Chetak was aspirational for all Indians then. Its renovation through the displacement platform could have been a great opportunity to encash its historical aspiration value. Instead, this scooter was pulled off the market, and its manufacturer started manufacturing non-heritage products from scratch.

The fallout of Chetak's manufacturer not displacing itself to milk the scooter opportunity saw the entry of Activa from Honda. With new technology, Activa stole Chetak's thunder. It proved the scooter still had a market.

In comparison, look at Japan's Corolla car. Renovating itself several times, the brand has existed for more than three decades and become the highest selling car in world automobile history.

how an organization can deploy the displacement platform for products and services

Displacement is extremely tough work; it cannot be done through an incremental process. It impacts the organization's working culture, product development, upto its delivery. Its positive thrust proves that the previous processes, transactions and culture were ineffective and futile, necessitating a move away from them to achieve growth and business success.

What is the kind of manpower involvement necessary for effecting displacement? First, a strong **core team** who has deep intellectual knowledge, persuasive character, capability to deliver with great teamwork. The CEO's job is to build a core team from internal talent. If a dearth of expertise exists, new people must be inducted to form the team before the project starts. Members from different functional areas must comprise the core team. Their mandate would be to facilitate change for effective consumer delivery within a given timeframe.

The character of a product or service can reflect displacement in the market. That's why its more realistic to simultaneously develop two or three displacement projects the impact of which can be quickly seen by the market.

Managing time is a crucial factor to develop displacement platform products. From the initial stage, every aspect of product development needs to be plotted on graph paper like a blue print. Once all activities upto delivery time are allotted, this becomes the master plan. This blue print masterminds investment, vendor management, tooling, manpower, business case manifestation and quality. Even if such detailed preparation takes one or two months, don't hesitate to do it as recording every activity is essential for proper management and on-time delivery.

Second, **cross functional teams** must be created by the core team. The competencies of different team members must converge to deliver as per the displacement platform.

Third, **dedicated teams** must be formed to work under the cross functional teams. These dedicated teams will work on specific components within a function to take forward the displacement initiatives.

The work of the taskforce comprising the core team, cross functional teams and dedicated teams should not get disturbed by the organization's existing ongoing business.

When organizational displacement is geared towards consumer sensitivity, it will naturally impact growth and profitability. So it needs to be ignited as an intense, time bound project. It definitely cannot happen within a 2–4 week timeframe. The task force needs a big thrust and must have persuasive power to continuously connect to the top management and get their support.

At the time of launching and immediately after the launch, products or services cannot afford to have any fault or discrepancy. Their quality, consumer sensorialism, sophistication, aesthetics and price must be super blended. Coordination and planning must anticipate and address every minuscule issue.

The displacement taskforce can be the champions of organizational culture change. The CEO's challenge would be to orchestrate continuity of ongoing systems, and simultaneously give extreme priority and encouragement to the displacement taskforce.

The moment displacement delivery is launched, another job begins for the CEO and the taskforce. The whole organization becomes its first consumer. Employees need exposure to the new displacement development which has now become the company's future. This way, organizational culture will follow displacement characteristics in future deliverables.

The momentum generated when launching displacement should be used to change the culture of the organization. Don't wait for the annual financial results to check the effect of displacement and innovation. Continue to sensitize people to change their work culture in the new direction. The displacement process is not immediate; it has a lead time for performance to show.

Innovation driven by displacement should incorporate tremendous research and consumer sensitivity so it has 90 percent assurance of absolute success. Financial projections may not materialize immediately, but will do so subsequently. The discipline, creativity and process you establish during this displacement project is your real and long-term goodwill.

Sooner than later the displacement temperament will upgrade the organization culture, and it can become a global player. The timeframe for effecting displacement should not go beyond 9 months for fast moving products and upto 24 months for complex engineering products.

rupture

When all players are fighting in the same platform and competition is rife, people's usage and habits become the same, making things boring for the consumer. There is not much choice or scope to create a difference in the intrinsic quality of the product or service. To overcome this situation, create a rupture through renovation. A successful example of rupture is the new Volkswagen Beetle.

Frequent fundamental innovation may not be possible in durable products, automobiles, home appliances, entertainment and hardware products that use digital technology. That's why a rupture in styling is very essential to create differentiation in the product's appearance. Such a rupture can be cyclic. The design difference can be brought back to make the product or service acquire a contemporary feel. The rupture could be futuristic, or it could be retro. The new Volkswagon Beetle is rupture using a retro style.

LG's refrigerator door with it's leaf-designed handle is a futuristic, well-thought-of rupture. The handle is more frequently touched than any other part of the refrigerator. Creating a rupture on the handle creates an obvious consumer touch.

Incremental innovation takes place continuously in IT hardware and telephone accessories. This is cyclic rupture. The mobile phone is a recent phenomenon so there is no attempt at being retro here. Most hand phones look quite futuristic. After 20 years people will revert to the past with a contemporary twist.

There is severe competition in branded food and grooming, beauty and cosmetic products, including from private labels of large retailers in developed countries. The consumer's mind can very easily change in this very vulnerable market. If a brand appears generic, a strong visible rupture can make it so disturbing that nobody can copy it easily. Should an imitation appear, the market would clearly perceive the imitator as a copy. Most importantly, a rupture will succeed if it has a hidden benefit for the consumer.

Apparel and fashion accessories come in and out of fashion. This periodic back and forth movement is continuous rupture.

Consumer related service industries like banking, insurance and telecom have very similar offers. Continuous rupture in communication is necessary here, as also different manifestations of the services on offer. It is important to retain a fine balance between the danger of communication overdose which can pollute society with monotonous repetition, and getting a single, powerful focused message across through a rupture.

To break a life of routine and daily habits, people tend to seek excitement. Communication media and entertainment come into play here, stimulating society with ruptures.

how an organization can deploy the rupture platform for products and services to keep a strong bottomline

Only a few with foresight would be sensitive towards rupture in an organization. That's because rupture disturbs; the zone of comfort gets misbalanced. Should you have the passion for rupture that builds, ignite the subject, but keep your morale and stamina tight. You'll be attacked from different angles, even unexpected quarters.

Rupture is difficult for an organization to absorb as it can disrupt at the initial stage. Deliberately accepting rupture before it showers its obvious benefits requires an innovative mental spirit.

In normal course, continuous incremental improvement is the standard for development of a product or productized service. Make a stark break and introduce the rupture platform.

Rupture platform as strategy is required for four types of companies. (*i*) It's easy for an organization that's continuously delivered premium value to introduce rupture. Somewhere through its decades of existence, rupture would have been there for the organization to have acquired its global premium value and stature. Such an experienced company is likely to have a readymade process and experience of rupture. (*ii*) But if organizational complacence makes it lose its rupture metaphor, it could lose its premium stature. (*iii*) Another type of company could be without any culture of rupture. (*iv*) A new generation company needs rupture to excite the market.

Getting senior management acquiesce to enter the rupture platform will not be easy and simple. As a leader you need to develop 5 to 10 case studies of how creating a rupture made a difference to positive topline and bottomline growth in different companies. Simultaneously you have to keep a track of society to find out the different areas where rupture is emerging and evident.

You may soon be disappointed as people in your organization may not be able to align with rupture. When rupture cannot be translated through the binary process, discomfort can become totally esoteric. A strong persuasive communication skill will now become necessary to convince your colleague.

Rupture is very visible and has physical substance. It has to be measurable, so be careful not to make it conceptual. Show your team how rupture proliferates in society to excite people. They will then understand how your company's product or service is getting monotonous in this changing scenario.

Rupture is very visible, physical and practical. Being perceptible at a social level, rupture is the most important factor to take into account in economically emerging countries.

Check out how rupture has dynamized business verticals unrelated to your business. Your senior management may let you down citing such examples to be a waste of time. You can educate your colleagues by pointing out that your own consumers are using these rupture products. These products unrelated to your business are changing the way consumers live and approach everything. So your business should use any such rupture product as a reference of the consumer's habit and usage.

Sometimes it may be difficult to find a rupture example in business related to yours. Like you, your competitors may be dull and static, giving you no reference of change. If your business is becoming flat, try going back down history lane, you may find rupture there.

Make it clear that your delivery needs the rupture platform for better growth and profitability. Then it is not the continuous incremental improvement. It's imperative to appreciate that there is a difference between rupture and continuous incremental improvement.

When your products become very generic in the market, consumers become bored of them. Co-opt your colleagues to see the need for rupture, and make a pictorial presentation to others in the organization on how you will deliver on this platform. You may even need to use an illustrator who can simultaneously draw rupture features on your product so everyone understands the proposition at a very physical level. Anticipate questions and don't leave any scope for non-believers to make holes in the rupture process. Then take everybody's sign-off on implementing the rupture.

After your team has agreed to utilize the rupture platform, make them understand there is no going back, and that this decision is not negotiable.

The next step is cost involvement, product costing, market viability and the marketing aspect of the product of rupture. While initiating the rupture project, introduce the concept in a ceremonial way. Avoid likely negatives, give no opportunity to break the rupture. Create emotion for it, ensure no delay in the final rupture delivery. Buy-in from your internal consumer is half the battle won in the marketplace. So make sure all employees admire the rupture and compliment you on incorporating it.

maintaining aspiration platform

Luxury goods and alcohol brands need to establish their authenticity and so become credible in the market. The premium value of alcohol comes from the seasoning time it spends in the barrel. The brand's seasoning knowhow has to reflect in the look. The cost of luxury products far exceed its real cost. The premium cost gets justified as added value because of the legacy that adds source credibility to the brand.

Even if you have outstanding new products in the luxury line, you cannot overnight create a luxury product brand. Having ultra modern technology Mercedes could have created a totally new brand for a new product. But it's no mystery that they went back a hundred years to reopen the chapter of the Maybach brand. Named after one of its founders, Maybach from Mercedes is now the most luxurious passenger automobile of the 21st century. A reputed manufacturer like Toyota can easily create a car similar to Maybach, but Toyota can never recreate Maybach's legacy of authenticity without acquiring a similar brand.

Authenticity is the crucial factor that comes into play. Maybach magnifies its connection to the history of the company, and presents itself in a contemporary platform.

For premium products and world famous brands, continuously maintaining aspiration of their products and brands is the key to retaining their quality and super premium image. Creating a rupture or displacement in such an area may generate a very negative result.

In India, China, Korea, Russia, Brazil, African countries and even Japan, brands do not have the requisite legacy that will put them in the platform of maintaining aspiration. Developed countries like Korea and Japan have realized that they can win the market through rupture, or by taking the route of displacement. But they are yet to arrive in upscale global reckoning to be in the maintaining aspiration platform.

To be in the platform of maintaining aspiration, a brand needs to have been established with (*a*) outstanding quality that's perceptible to the consumer, (*b*) for a long period of time, (*c*) with a certain culture attached to it, before consumers really accept it, and (*d*) its unconditional superior premiumness as a luxury position.

Organizations can own the maintaining aspiration platform only after they receive consumer approval on their ability to deliver premium value and aspiration beyond the consumer's expectation.

To illustrate, let's take two comparable models: both Toyota's Lexus and Mercedes have more or less similar features and consumers in the same income group. Lexus continually brings in consumer benefit advantages with best value for money. However, when it comes to pricing, the consumer is still willing to pay more for a Mercedes.

Living through a century, Mercedes built up product quality and aspiration at an incredible level of desire. Not only was their quality orientation a cut above, they have always anticipated to continuously surprise the consumer. In the rational engineering areas that are hidden from the consumer's direct gaze or knowledge, they have severely upgraded performance and machine quality. This commendable strategy keeps them unquestionably on top.

To their detriment, most organizations across the world avoid the initiative to improve such hidden areas. They concentrate instead on increasing value in consumer visible points only. Intrinsic product or service contamination starts this way, leading to slow erosion in market value.

Being visionary, companies like Mercedes better their deliverables from the market benchmark without consumers ever asking for it. The brand thus creates the legacy of high consumer confidence. Subsequently, if a brand lke Mercedes should ever develop a defect, consumers will consider it as a one-time shortcoming. They will never register it as a chronic flaw.

Mercedes is in the maintaining aspiration platform. It cannot suddenly make a rupture or displacement the way Lexus can do. If Mercedes tries a rupture or displaces itself, its heritage will be obliterated in the consumer's mind. In such an event, competitors will try to commoditize the new Mercedes offer to demolish the superior segment Mercedes sits on today.

Were I to make Mercedes a suggestion, what would I say? Never discount your legacy while planning your strategy; and never complacently allow your superiority to affect your product development. Technology drives engineering superiority today. When technology is available to all, it is a vulnerable strength that protects no one. The way its supremacy was used in the last century may not be applicable in the same way in the 21st century.

A Mercedes consumer would have been located in a very sophisticated, rich country in the last century. More and more citizens of what was considered the third world have the capacity to buy luxury goods today. If Mercedes maintains its product development value like the German football team comprising only Caucasian Germans, they will lose out on the feel, breath and sensitivity of other races capable of buying a Mercedes.

While keeping its legacy, Mercedes should welcome society's blend in the 21st century. Even as it remains in the maintaining aspiration platform, Mercedes' product development can adopt the value of globally blending the human race as their differentiated approach.

Western Europe has a legacy of innovative power in every domain like music, literature, art, science and consuming products. That is why a brand's association with the centuries-old culture of the West gives it credibility that the world takes for granted. Economically emerging countries need to understand every microtone of Europe's inherent innovative power derived from their distinctive culture. When Americans want to showcase authentic value, they return to their sophisticated European roots. The historical authenticity of the US mass market falls somewhere between cowboy culture and Native Indian culture.

India, China, Russia, Brazil and African countries are yet to establish their legacy of innovation. To get noticed by consumers, there has to be displacement first. The rupture platform can follow to surprise consumers decade after decade. It may take up to 50 years to reach the maintaining aspiration platform.

An apt example is Lenovo, the Chinese company that acquired the hardware business of American IT giant IBM. Lenovo continued to sell the laptop computer as IBM Think Pad for a considerable time. Taking consumer mindshare away from IBM's computing value and technology legacy with Lenovo brand may not be very easy. Lenovo has to create a strong displacement in product quality, look, touch, feel and image to become credible and get recognition in world markets.

A superior perception brand like IBM has gone into Lenovo's unrecognized value. In the current situation Lenovo does not have the credibility that IBM had to take the maintaining aspiration platform. So Lenovo's real challenge can be to take the displacement platform and introduce a terrific consumer benefit that IBM could not bring, particularly today when computer hardware is becoming very basic. With out-of-the-box displacement in their domain they can create brand credibility in superior value only.

how an organization can deploy the maintaining aspiration platform for products and services

The maintaining aspiration platform is very relevant to most European product and service brands and a few American ones. In their sophisticated home markets where growth levels are getting saturated, these brands have to think out-of-the-box, fundamental innovation. They need to bring a new way of consumption in consumer lifestyle. People in these sophisticated markets can appreciate a totally new rupture or displacement product from a brand with a link to the past. But for the global market, these brands cannot play with rupture or displacement in their core products.

Let's say a radical rupture or displacement from Louis Vuitton gives a fancy exotic look to a core product in its home market. Consumers from a BRIC (Brazil, Russia, India, China) country may find this fancy look to resemble low price ethnic products in their own country. Will this consumer pay such large sums of money just for the brand name when the product resembles a low price product he is familiar with? Consumer appreciation of sophisticated luxury brands can be different in out-of-home markets. The core product must maintain premium value, which is its real credential.

Brands from BRIC countries have no choice but to take the displacement route to succeed in world markets. By providing superior quality, miniaturization, sophistication and highly competitive pricing, Japanese and Korean brands have displaced their image in the world. These brands are just a notch behind sophisticated Western brands in consuming products. BRIC countries wrongly believe they cannot bring premium quality in low price products. This surely is a cultural deficiency in marketing. Low price does not mean a product has to be low profile with lower aspiration. Let me give a few examples of how low price products can be highly aspirational.

There is a huge difference in the pricing of watches Tag Heuer, Omega, Cartier or Rolex with Swatch. But in the consumer's mind Swatch is not considered of lower aspiration in spite of its price being lower that the others. But I am not sure you can do the same to measure the global aspiration level of Kelton or Timex brands, which were launched as low cost watches much before Swatch.

Swatch swung ahead creating a cult and trend, leaving many older and expensive brands far behind. Swatch's high aspiration was not deterred by its low price. BRIC countries should not think that pricing is the decisive factor. You have to create a difference between product pricing and consumer aspirational value.

The Japanese and Koreans have understood this aspect very minutely and unfailingly deliver outstanding quality, miniaturization and sophistication in aesthetics. They have created a global reputation for assiduous mass customization by being easy to use. Western countries can pick up positive cues from the Japanese and Koreans to effectively function in their maintaining aspiration platform. While keeping their authenticity, Western brands can customize their products to become more user-friendly.

Renovation and innovation are two sides of a coin. No company engaged in business can go with one without the other. If a philosophical transmission of renovation and innovation has not taken place at a strategic level, you will find your product or service will become more and more generic and low profile. You may have spent large sums of money for new technology or new manpower, but if you have not addressed proper renovation or innovation at the core on time, your bottomline may reflect very poorly. The tragedy would be your amassing revenue growth, but without growing profit.

Achieving high profitability depends on your qualitative action, from strategy planning to delivery. The culture of renovation and innovation will lead to qualitative improvement of your value chain. Don't always concentrate on the quantitative perspective. Numbers can be effective when used to quantify highly qualitative, consumer sensitive, measurable value.

Renovation and innovation of an organization's deliverables and human capital, which propels all deliverables, are linked. Renovation in human capital means you change the culture of your existing people towards the latent trend. Innovation means you have attracted high caliber people who will help the organization as change agents.

The specific purpose of a knowledge bank is to maintain a permanent encyclopedia on how to implement organizational renovation and innovation through discipline, creativity and process. In your organizational displacement journey, keep a record of all displacement steps, perhaps on film so it will be useful in future. When you buy a DVD, oftentimes there is a bonus film where the filmmakers talk about the making of the movie. In that spirit, you can make a film on how displacement happened in your organization.

If you are contemplating initiation of renovation and innovation in business, don't forget the deeper meaning of the *jalebi*. The *jalebi* can ride any wave to make your business premium and you a GRC. A freshly made *jalebi* is irresistible and inviting. Cooked on the roadside a *jalebi* gets renovated because it has no industrial process; it is handmade. In an elegant place, a chef who has worked in India can make an innovative *jalebi* on the spot.

I had mentioned that renovation is 'I change myself,' and innovation stands for 'I change the world.' A futuristic innovation is possible sitting anywhere in the world. But innovation with an umbilical cord to the past cannot happen everywhere. When such innovation sits on the authenticity of renovation, it absorbs the total power of both. In business, renovation cleans the vital space and makes the space sturdy. Vital space is the bread-and-butter earning of an organization. The vital space then becomes the uncontaminated foundation pillar that can take the load of future innovation.

vital space in business

The renovation process can help an organization make its vital space powerful. A company sustains on the strength of its existing people, culture and product, and their relation to the market, from retail animation upto the time the product reaches the consumer's home. Employees have a certain skill and experience that can be harnessed, just like the *jalebi* dough is best when it is appropriately aged and fermented. Fermentation ensures the *jalebi* fluffs a bit so the sweet syrup flows in it with ease. The syrup supply line of the *jalebi* maintains its authenticity. Your organizational delivery can flow similarly to maintain what's vital in your business.

In the human progression pyramid (see Figure 6.1), the base comprises the instinct for survival which ladders from food to the need for sex. These two vital layers indicate strength, violence, peaceful co-existence and physical energy. They are essential for living creatures, whether human or animal.

The third layer is atomic discharge related only to human beings. It is pleasure and ingenuity divided into two: violence leveraging our animal character; or harmony of life which is fundamentally non-violent and could be active or inactive. Its energy is spirituality, the higher equilibrium of human order in body, mind and spirit.

The fourth layer is that of luxury with affluence to enjoy life either lavishly, or in a low profile or economic way. At this layer you have choice.

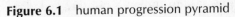

Figure 6.1   human progression pyramid

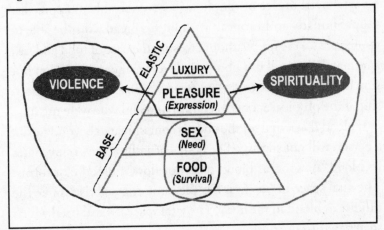

Intellectual violence grows from different sources: economic poverty, a political cause, hankering for quick achievement, being anti-establishment, or just people indulging their hidden crass characteristics. People capable of intellectual violence are not inferior. They mastermind, sometimes surreptitiously, with superior intellectual acumen; others may have no choice but to suffer the power they amass. Mafia gangsters in the 1930s were such people. They considered their principle to be right for society, although they individually sinned by taking human lives. They even declared that whatever right they may subsequently do, none of them would ever go to Heaven; Hell will always be reserved for them.

Your economic affluence may qualify you to be in the luxury layer, but you may choose to live frugally, just fulfilling your survival (food) and need (sex) layers. Alternatively, you could be economically less endowed but a climber that fulfills the dream of affluence with a strong commitment to education. Unlike traditionally wealthy families, the climber has a powerful new economic path in today's world of technology. In fact everyone can aim to riches now, unless political storms destabilize a country's economy.

The vital space is basic need. If an Indian is not satisfied with his vital need of rice or *roti*, he will never be able to appreciate soup. Similarly an European without his bread won't be able to appreciate ice cream. Without crossing the base of food and sex, a human being will not be able to leverage mental love. I'm not sure how effective platonic love would be in a conjugal relationship if the physical act between husband and wife were missing.

If blood that's vital for the body is contaminated beyond repair, a person will not survive. The body naturally always rejuvenates its blood. As soon as blood does not flow, a blood clot forms. The vital space in business has the same characteristics like the fluidity of blood in the body. The vital space is a real need which society has to nurture.

Human activity being central to business, the human progression layers are applicable in business too. Without fulfilling hunger, man does not think about sex. Similarly, your business cannot graduate to the next pleasurable layer unless your current cash cow, the survival layer of your business, is renovated. I have equated 'vital space' to mean the base of your business, a combination of the survival and need layers.

Very often business houses are impatient. They want to enter the pleasurable or luxury layer of business without solidifying their survival factor, the 'vital space' of their business.

Here's a typical scenario: Your base business is growing year after year, but low profit demoralizes you. Next door, an emerging business is witnessing high profit. That's the temptation. In a quick, opportunity-grabbing temperament you may enter that business to earn high profit in a shorter span of time than your current business.

But wait! Before putting your current business in the back burner, did you check whether it could deliver better if an alternative best practice is applied? Or if the delivery time and method were altered? Perhaps your delivery offer has to renovate radically because some unrelated business is eating into your market, and you haven't noticed. In fact, you may be totally insensitive to such a happening.

If your consumers or customers have shifted, it means you lack microtone proactiveness. Is your business of obsolete technology, or have the habits of people changed? You have to understand your business and its interplay in the competitive environment of business that's both related to, or unrelated to yours. To revive an unprofitable business, you certainly need mental strength and a 'creative business strategy.'

Strategy is a war term borrowed by business. But it is not fully compatible. Wars are fought over a limited time, not indefinitely. But at any given time, sustaining business is the most important factor.

There is a difference between traditional business strategy and 'creative business strategy.' In traditional business strategy you are being generic; not practising anything better than your competitor in related or unrelated businesses. But a creative business strategy, also useful at wartime, is a stratagem known only to the top brass. It's a macro gambit to win the war in the critical moment.

Creative business strategy differentiates you from run-of-the-mill strategy planning. Bringing creativity into business supersedes benchmarking with the best, where quantitative data specifies how a similar company became successful under similar market conditions. It's dangerous to follow such an analogous path because your data may not be as complete or comprehensive, so the desired result may escape you.

When you analyze your company's strengths in the competitive scenario to see what is feasible, build your own ingredients and create your own weapons, you can assess your individual internal and external environment. You can consolidate your business by refining your 'vital space.'

An organization is known by its vital space, which is its existing market offer. In general, a company's vital space accounts for a minimum 40 percent to 60 percent of its annual revenue. Sometimes it can go up to 70 percent. This valuable business source is the company's foundation. It is connected to the market, trade and partners, consumers and customers. The vital space can become so mechanical that organizations often remember just to milk it, not to nurture it.

Instead, hunger for topline growth makes organizations indulge in superficial repositioning, diversifications that are either flavor-of-the-season or unrelated to its vital space. Such topline growth is not real; it just cannibalizes the vital space and totally compresses it. A shrinking vital space increases the cost of complexity and creates roadblocks to profit and growth. Investor confidence subsequently reduces, and a crisis erupts to acquire high quality professional talent to manage the show. New people often get into new ventures that eat into the vital space, and contaminate it. And this hampers real growth. Why is that so?

A shrinking vital space weakens an organization's core competence, the captured essence of which is its intellectual goodwill to expand. If a company considers it so easy to transpose core competence into a diversified business, it shows that the company has blindly worked only on the physical aspect of its deliverable.

The primary objective of a creative business strategy concentrates on how to continuously address and grow the vital space. In your business, establish the vital space visibly. It can hypnotize your employees towards growing it, making it vibrant and dynamic to gain quantum business that sustains.

An organization's vital space is often its comfort zone. Vital space activities invariably become everyday routine habits in the organization's lifecycle. You may not want to disturb the vital space for fear of upsetting the applecart on its way to market. But by not touching it, you really can't gauge how far back you are stepping. Your offer will soon be attacked or devoured by low price products or services, aggressive competitors, or unpredictable competition driven by modern technology.

In business, vital space is considered the existing consumers' foothold. It connects to the organization's intellectual capital. Without continuous microtone observation and nurturing of your vital space, you will never really know when and why your consumers change their mind and shift to other offers.

I have developed the vital space concept to sensitize organizations to their regular cash cow business. Like a conjugal relationship, vital space needs constant care and attention to remain exciting and fulfilling. The organization's flirtations with unrelated diversification, superficial repositioning and flavor-of-the-season diversifications provide, like extra marital sex, only fleeting enjoyment, and trouble thereafter.

Indian companies appear very reluctant to create self struggle for reviving their existing business. Have they really comprehended the vast difference in being an assembler or trader, versus being an aspirational, core competence-driven, consumer or customer sensitive manufacturing company? For example, a courier service can simply have messengers, or it can self-struggle to establish a cocooning and elegant courier service culture that talks about hard work to make the customer extremely happy.

A business can face any of these four vital space contamination cases:

Case 1: The category is widening in perspective, but you are not
Case 2: The category is stagnant, you are also stagnant
Case 3: The category is de-growing, you are also de-growing
Case 4: The category is de-growing, but you are growing

case 1: the category is widening in perspective, but you are not

In the market's undercurrents a totally new product category that's beyond your imagination and estimate may have emerged, and you may be unaware of it. Ignorance of the market's real picture can stop your growth. The fire under your vital space starts now. This is when you need to shake up your organization by introducing the creative business strategy. If at this stage complacency surrounds you, don't wait to cut off such hidden cancer. Renovate the organization immediately using the displacement, rupture or maintaining aspiration platform as per the specific requirement of your brand reputation.

case 2: the category is stagnant, you are also stagnant

If you are the market leader, you have the humongous task of reviving the stagnation that's setting in for the entire category. Should you be a challenger in the market, take the opportunity to ride on the revival.

Whether a leader or challenger, divide the market by focusing sharply on your consumer segment. Redefine your proposition with the punch of renovation and adequate innovation. Be more target specific by layering price as per product wedges. Dynamic visible versions can be created by segmenting and micro-segmenting for the market. In revitalizing your vital space, take care to avoid innovation that's delinked from your vital space. Segmentation has to be latent consumer or customer trend driven, not introverted and industrial.

case 3: the category is de-growing, you are also de-growing

It's a dangerous sign when both the category as well as your business are de-growing. Obsolescence can be a cause. Without hesitation, you absolutely need the displacement platform to revive your vital space. Innovate your backend, but ensure your external face shows that fundamental renovation has taken place. This way, the link with your vital space is maintained.

case 4: the category is de-growing, but you are growing

You face the biggest peril when only your business is growing in a deflated market. People in your company tend to wallow in this seemingly spectacular growth. And complacency grows from here. Be sensitive, take quick action to identify any deficiency in your offer. You may have some time to react, but your backend will need innovation even as the public sees a link to your vital space as in case 3.

Sometimes, of course, vital space can totally diminish or become obsolete, the way carbon paper lost its prime position when photocopying machines were invented. When obsolescence sets in, the intellectual capital of that business can be transformed to a new area. From Toyoda loom to Toyota automobile was a successful shift. In such a situation there is no choice but to change your skin while keeping your intellectual property intact. In most cases, when vital space is nurtured at the appropriate time with strong renovating commitment, the old company transforms to become always contemporary.

Over the decades, on-the-move music with CDs, cassettes or other audio devices has been synonymous with Sony Walkman brand. But an avoidable contamination entered Sony Corporation's vital space in the form of Apple's iPod. Riding the leadership wave, Sony had perhaps become complacent and neglected microscopic market watch, how people's desire in entertainment is changing, how continuous technology upliftment can impact efforts to satisfy this desire. The real dilemma was in the symbiosis between technology and entertainment.

In the 30 years since their Walkman innovation, the designer in me was eager to see some breakaway thinking at Sony.

Perhaps they transformed mechanical systems with hydraulic ease, made sound improvements, or even modified the look, but Sony totally disappointed my expectations. Shouldn't it have been Sony, the global leader in audio music, who should have come up with a consumer sensitive iPod-like solution required to keep their vital space robust? Could Sony have foreseen such a serious underwater torpedo attack from an unrelated competitor, a computer manufacturer, disturbing their domain?

The iPod is a serious attack on the vital space of the global giant, Sony. I believe Sony wasted too much time in the art, entertainment and telephone hardware businesses instead of keeping a proper eye on their core business of the Walkman. Their dream strategy was upturned into hard-hitting market reality. It is quite amazing that having been the best marketing innovator to date, Sony neglected their field and lost out to a marketing innovation that is the iPod. Was this complacency or just bad luck?

Sony's misfortune shows an encouraging direction to organizations in economically emerging countries: never be scared to establish the new. You may be a small local company in a BRIC country, but you may perhaps have the ability to read a hidden aspect of the consumer's desire. The discovery and effort to bridge this hidden aspect could bring you global success. Should you attempt to do that, make sure it is relevant to your vital space, not de-linked from it.

Toyota's Corolla vividly displays how to care for and continually revitalize vital space. By fostering its vital space, never sacrificing on deficiency, Toyota made Corolla the world's largest selling car since the last 30 years. The Dolby system is another instance of preserving and growing vital space to win people's perception and comfort. There are many panoramic sound systems such as DTS and THX. But with continuous modernization such as Dolby Digital, Dolby has assured the public that Dolby sound will remain the benchmark for sound quality for all time.

Why is vital space an issue to reckon with? Because its stake is so colossal in the organization that if it gets a hammering, which it easily can, management must be alerted. It should not disregard the mishap and allow it to morph into a Titanic syndrome.

What is the Titanic syndrome? Luxury liner Titanic was considered impregnable. It continued to smoothly sail the Atlantic waters for a considerable time even as it suffered a damaging puncture from an iceberg. Nobody on board could even fathom that danger was around the bend, they wanted to ignore such a passé idea. Passengers continued to be misled by music even as they were being evacuated, but the Titanic did sink, as was inevitable.

Contamination in the vital space is normally, and very mistakenly, considered a minor affair, just like the Titanic's fatal fissure from hitting an iceberg. People at the Titanic failed to react immediately, they took action only when the unbelievable danger loomed large and unavoidable in front of their very eyes. Before such a catastrophe strikes an organization, or slow poison engulfs the vital space, surgery in the form of corporate transformation should be undertaken without wasting time. This is when an organization needs three simultaneous actions: (*a*) a microscope to see its defects as large as possible without arrogance; (*b*) a culture change to absorb the defect; and (*c*) a telescope to bring its vision nearer.

The vital space must always watch the radar for decreased consumption. When a flicker of fluctuation is detected, go in for immediate renovation using every available or new technology, and the creative marketing strategy. Look at multiple opportunities at a time like this. You may discover an opportunity area totally unrelated with your business, which can use your existing technology or core expertise. This captive knowhow will regain the value it lost in its existing business domain, and involve no cost. Yes, grab the opportunity of such low hanging fruit.

By seizing this prospect you may be renovating your product in such a vigorous way that it changes the whole market perception. Even as this moves the business forward, it will re-establish the pillar of your vital space while using your core competence. A strengthened vital space will satisfy the basic requirement of organizational growth. After fundamental renovation, continue to check your vital space on the radar so it can never shrink or die.

Real corporate transformation happens when you anticipate your vision. If renovation of vital space is factored in and internalized, the organization's sustainability will be very powerful and valuable.

Your hunger to go in for the next layer of growth is immensely possible after the vital space has been totally renovated. During renovation you will definitely encounter a hurdle race of difficulties, both internally and in the market. This can only strengthen your commitment and knowledge base, and help find the diversification route to build your new business strategy.

Having conditioned the organization to renovation, the next step is introspection for deep innovation. What is innovation for tomorrow's world? It may not be rocket science; just innovation that can satisfy human life with extreme benefit. Growth that's driven by vision and an empowered vital space will bring the following positives with it:

- Mindset change of existing employees
- Easier to attract talent
- Increase in investor confidence
- The advantage of synergy
- Resulting in quantum profit and growth

The audacious innovation of Lexus was possible only because Toyota always had Corolla as a cash cow in its vital space. People in industry often remark that diversifications need not link the corporation's existing value to the new world. They give the example of Toyota having created Lexus as a totally different company to manifest luxury value. This is a totally wrong understanding. Toyota's first attention has always been Corolla. The earnings from Corolla supported Lexus for competing in the luxury D category. Toyota's continuous renovation value is so high in consumer mind that it can never pull down the value of Lexus. Rather, Toyota will increase the value of Lexus.

Being a challenger, Toyota segmented the market. On the one hand Toyota created a segment just below Mercedes with the Toyota line, and on the other, challenged Mercedes with premium aspirational value through the Lexus. Toyota means reliable, so the new brand Lexus enjoyed the privilege of being associated with this positive undercurrent.

Innovation, as I had mentioned earlier, is 'I change the world.' When Lexus entered the market 30 years ago, Europeans thought the Japanese were too impudent to compete with a German car. Toyota could take up this challenge only because their vital space with Corolla was extremely robust. They had both the conviction and the investment for making the luxury line Lexus.

Real business growth vision comes from renovation that is robust, vital space that incorporates the trend, with innovation as the topping. If visioning is attempted through quantitative generic data and economic analysis, tomorrow's business will be more smoky than achievable.

For me business vision must have scalable factors that improve profit and growth. These factors reside in two outstretched hands.

One hand comprises the promise and resources that drive:

- high consumer sensitivity in all operations
- high quality and knowledgeable human capital
- continuous renovation of the existing product
- a highly processed cost design that manages vendors through a single all-purpose window

- consumer perceptive and reliable quality in all deliverables
- high aspiration delivered at any cost in any product or service segment

This leads to a differentiated corporate and brand promise that co-opts channel mindshare and powerfully communicates to the consumer. Through these resources you will, under any situation, be able to make better profit than the industry and keep your promise to the consumer. Good profit at the initial stage will give you robust muscle to grow. Just remember to maintain the scale of consistency and high profitability.

The other outstretched hand is the knowledge and initiative to convert the fast changing environment into an input. This input would have:

- the impact of technological advancement
- influence of changing trends
- global influence
- media influence
- change in job content
- international competition
- government policy change

Expect the result to be behavioral change in the channel, end consumers and the society. Be alert to bring in external qualitative influence for potential business. Innovate by incorporating the consumers' latent perspective. These are elements that will magnify your growth.

Growth is the future, growth will get you bigness, bigness will take you global, being global you become a true GRC leader. When your resources and the promise are driven by fast changing environmental trends, you will achieve the vision to empower profit and growth.

the latent perspective of business

When an organization talks about its vision, it is always an assumption. If we can fit the latent perspective of society with the organization's vision, then the vision can take a direction towards tangible results. When vision finds direction in the latent aspect of consumers in society, organic growth will fall in place. Trying to achieve the vision through inorganic growth and haphazard acquisition will always be a little dicey. In case any one of the acquired organizations is not stable, the company can suffer in the long run. There are enough and more examples of difficult integration post acquisition.

Let me have you witness a few successful companies that have very carefully nurtured their vital space decade after decade. They persist with intensive research and development work in their initial core category of products or brand expression, and have also diversified their businesses.

L'Oréal

Eugene Shueller was a young French chemist who innovated a hair color formula in 1907. He called the hair dye 'Aureole' which means 'halo' in French. His company was registered as 'Safe Hair Dye Company of France' in 1909. This was the beginning of the glory that is L'Oréal today.

From inception, L'Oréal's operating principle was research and innovation in the interest of human beauty. Today L'Oréal practically owns the global hair market in multiple ways. The vital space of hair beauty has become synonymous with L'Oréal's fundamental value, even as they have successfully developed other areas of beauty and cosmetic care worldwide. Just imagine, from hair dye which was a very negative-positive transformation, you can see the sheen of multiple colors in your hair. Even a taxi driver I met in a small South Indian town used hair color for beauty, and knew L'Oréal.

Nestlé

Born in Frankfurt in 1814, Henri Nestlé moved to Vevey, Switzerland, when in his twenties. He was a merchant and a small-scale inventor. His discovery of baby food helped mothers who were unable to breast feed. Through his experiments he created 'wholesome Swiss milk and cereal component baked by a special process of my invention.' In 1867 he fed this to a premature baby boy whose mother was dangerously ill herself. The boy survived and Henri Nestlé's reputation went sky high. This is how the company Nestlé started.

When Henri Nestlé sold his company, he transferred his personality to Nestlé's association with nurturing. The masses of the world may not know Henri Nestlé, but they recognize Nestlé through its pictorial depiction of a nest with a mother bird feeding her baby birds, and correlate the company with mother care.

From the beginning the vital space of Nestlé has been the value of milk in a caring and nurturing component for consumer benefit, whether it was condensed milk, milk powder or milk chocolate. Over time Nestlé has grown manifold with a large number of acquisitions across several countries. Nestlé has diversified business to beverage and food, but has always protected its milk value. Even an indulgence product like chocolate from an acquired company will carry Nestlé's milk value to distinguish its origin in wholesome Swiss milk.

For example, Nestlé's 1991 acquisition of British confectionary Rowntree brought the famous brand called Kit Kat into its stable, and helped its growth. Within a very short time Nestlé's solid reputation made consumers connect Kit Kit with Nestlé. Their policy to nurture milk value has protected Nestlé's vital space and infused this vital space into its acquisitions.

In actuality, Nestlé brand is the undisputed ambassador of Switzerland's valleys-and-mountains value. The image Nestlé carries to the rest of the world is blissful Swiss countryside basking in Nature, health and traditional country ideals.

Shiseido

From 1972 Japanese beauty and cosmetic company, Shiseido, has nurtured its vital space to be an art form of human physical beauty. Its philosophy is to combine eastern aesthetics with western science and business technology for the beauty and cosmetics business. Shiseido reflects the excellence of its beauty products in a pictorial art form, which has been cultivated as the company's vital space. Although their products have tremendous consumer benefit, their representation has always been as pieces of art.

In 1980 Shiseido hired Serge Lutens, a French hair and make-up artist of *Vogue* magazine, to find a form for its recognition by sophisticated European markets and internationally. Serge reinforced the beauty of art in pictorial language with Western beauty and glamor in Eastern form. This was understood internationally as an expression of premiumness. It represented Shiseido's fundamental renovation with continuity in its vital space.

Shiseido's founder had always been very particular about inculcating the purity and excellence of Western European cosmetic beauty culture in his complex Japanese traditional beauty products business. Shiseido's 1920 and 1930s products had Eastern charm and acceptance. But for consumers sitting in New York, Paris, Rome, London, Stockholm, Moscow, Dubai, Buenos Aires, Sydney, Mumbai, these cosmetics were unfamiliar and oriental. Being sensitive about catering to worldwide consumers, look at how Shiseido redesigned its Zen brand. The visual approach in 1964 was a traditional lacquer packaging design from a 16th century motif of Kyoto temple. In 2000 it was redesigned to become more contemporary. It captured the pure new quintessence of the Japanese spirit. But it continued to be based on the traditional eastern sense of beauty.

The distinctive, clutter breaking 'Shiseido style' is focused on art nouveau design with touches of art deco and arabesque.

Shiseido's refined European design gradually grew into a unique style that can be seen at any international beauty showcase, whether in an airport terminal or departmental store.

Shiseido's art form advertising poster from 1916 upto today carries the same essence of a company in continuous renewal activity linked to its vital space. Shiseido's traditional excellence in communication and image creation has evolved to reflect the company's culture and philosophy. These are among its most important intangible aspects. Shiseido's platform of beauty in art form is its vital space for its brand mission, core property and focus.

As these examples show, there are many ways to feed vital space. L'Oréal is continuity of its business origin in today's trend, even after 97 years of existence. Nestlé is continuity of the core, which is the value of milk. This is interpreted in today's business in every country they are present in as the legacy of its source credibility in health. Shiseido is continuity of the art form that is the brand's holistic approach and personality.

Since its inception, *Jalebi* has also been a pictorial art form. This art form is its vital space. Any sweet-maker who crafts the *jalebi* in any contemporary situation, has to be indoctrinated to the *jalebi's* art form. If you don't maintain this art form, the *jalebi* loses its identity. Whatever different or sophisticated ingredients you may experiment with in a *jalebi*, you cannot destroy its form. You may change its color, you may alter its flavor so it tastes somewhat different from the traditional *jalebi*, but its shape will show that you are in the *jalebi* category.

The meaning of *Jalebi Management* starts from the competence of your resources and your promise. These are the ingredients to make a juicy *jalebi*. When the basis of the *jalebi* is good, no matter how trends can alter your working environment, the *jalebi* remains a delicious bite for everybody.

The *jalebi's* timely renovation through the ages has endeared it to everyone. It is somehow always part of the trend and does not look backdated even in a sophisticated futuristic atmosphere. It is the perfect imagination of vital space that you go looking out for, whether you have too little money, or more than enough money.

In business, make your vital space like a *jalebi* that never gets old and is always sumptuous.

seven

generic market battlefield

Shriveling the bottomline by neglecting their vital space is a malaise many companies across the world suffer from. Volume sales may give revenue, but not with commensurate profit at the end. Business size and scale contribute towards getting recognition, but net profitability is the only earning that makes real business sense.

Low price competitors are quick to attack products or services from an established brand, turning the brand into a generic one. This happens when buyers, perceiving no difference between an established brand and low priced competitors, refuse to pay a premium for the brand's reputation. This tragedy of not being associated with superior quality makes yesterday's good brand into a mediocre one. The brand retrogrades to a non-specific standard, loses its premiumness in consumer or customer mindspace. This commoditizes a brand, making it generic in the market. It's a global syndrome that makes business vulnerable.

In sophisticated countries, the private labels of organized retail, low priced brands created by regional manufacturers, and cut-rate Chinese products assail reputed FMCG and other brands. Big brands resort to advertising to curtail their plunge towards a generic character. Advertising creates awareness, but unless done sensitively, it may not highlight the brand's intrinsic quality differentiation.

Low priced IT software is mushrooming. For companies providing outsourced IT services, the power of size has become the name of the game to beat cost arbitrage.

Low aspiration, poor quality products are associated with the generic condition. Price is the only sensitive factor here. If the generic condition stabilizes, business in that category becomes vulnerable and without unique value.

Everywhere in the world, the tendency is to look at market opportunity from a standpoint of quick earnings. Traders in general don't care about sustaining quality. They seek out ways to make money with huge volumes on goods that have a demand, irrespective of quality. Sensitive to both price and quality, consumers check for market options. After the first trial and upon benchmarking, if a product is detected to be of deficient quality, the consumer will never sacrifice quality to return to the low price product.

You can even brand *jalebi*, a generic product, by giving it a specific benefit. This could hypothetically be health. Such a quality assurance will radically change the *jalebi*'s perception while keeping its taste intact.

Creating a specific brand for homemade Indian traditional bread, called *roti,* is not easy. People are loath to change their age-old habits. Attempts to brand the *roti* have not met with much success upto now. Why? Because the mystique of branding has not been addressed. To destroy its price sensitive generic character, manufacturers need to come up with an alchemy that consumers instantly connect to, and accept.

With good R&D, it is possible to industrially produce *roti* on a large scale; you may very easily find trade distribution facilities too; but changing consumer usage habit from handmade to readymade bread is the challenge. Only a very 'creative business strategy' will allow a generic product to become a brand. A creative business strategy obliges you to verify every business angle, from the points of the consumer's touch, feel, edible enjoyment and health benefit, to your back-end processes. This is an exercise in microtone creativity, and its exposure cannot be superficial.

A simple marketing proposition will not shift the consumer's mind to becoming comfortable with an industrial *roti*. You need to measure every aspect of the rational, functional and emotional attributes of an industrial *roti* over the traditional handmade *roti*, and get your cues on how to score higher. The chart below is an indicator:

An industrial *roti* (see Table 7.1) can reach a commanding market height when it addresses the consumer's perspective. If consumers overlook the brand in their regular purchase habit, it will not pick up momentum.

Table 7.1 branding a generic product

	HOMEMADE ROTI	BASIC INDUSTRIAL MADE ROTI	INNOVATIVE INDUSTRIAL MADE ROTI
RATIONAL PARAMETER	Confidence in the raw material	Lack of confidence in the raw material	Need enormous focus on the added value of raw materials so that it is perceptible to consumers
FUNCTIONAL PARAMETER	Highground biased psychological comfort of traditional bite	Consumers feel they are sacrificing on the product's sensorial aspect	Need consistent dramatization of the product's edible enjoyment in the health parameter upto its better digestion
EMOTIONAL PARAMETER	Visible manifestation of freshness	A total psychological barrier. Consumers consider packaged food a grand deception of freshness	1. Exceptional format of the product 2. Breakaway packaging with a material that communicates freshness 3. An intriguing name which creates mystique that's measurable in the product 4. An exceptional retail presence and activities which instantly magnify the brand, creating a hallucination 5. Breakaway advertising which focuses on the balance of rational, functional and emotional attributes

Any traditional product that serves a basic function has tremendous business potential. Because it's required on a regular basis, if you can turn a traditional generic product into a brand, it can assure continuous business growth and profitability. But you need to crack the challenge of changing the consumer's traditional habit. Will she reach for a brand for her convenience or any other benefit? You need to penetrate and understand her psychological framework before dreaming of business success with an industrialized generic product.

Taking a basic product to the market in beautiful packaging and sexy advertising cannot create the consumer's deeper need for branded products. The product's attributes need dramatic changing so the consumer connects to the offered value and stretches out to take this value.

Camembert is a basic round-shaped French cheese that's traditionally been a small sized home industry. After World War II, in an enigmatic departure, a Camembert was industrially made in an oval shape, and marketed as 'Caprice des Dieux' (Tantrum of the Gods) with the communication 'For the Lover of Cheese.' Unlike its organic home preparation, industrial Camembert carries a consistent taste all year round. 'Caprice des Dieux' brand captured the French people's imagination; it now represents France across the world as the reference of French Camembert.

Homemade Camembert's commercial success through an industrial and marketing process is an example that homemade products like the roti can emulate. There are plenty of Indian traditional products that can be revolutionized through 'creative business strategy' and backed by excellent implementation. Shake up such sleeping opportunities to create that big potential market.

Necessity had made Europeans and Americans develop the industrial process to get into business after the war. The mental spirit of entrepreneurs such as the one who made 'Caprice des Dieux' is remarkable. Choosing to take up the challenge of transforming a traditional product into a value added brand was an incredible thinking process.

By transforming basic need to convenience, innovating new needs that reach out beyond desire to the hedonistic level, Europeans and Americans have changed the world. The Japanese and Koreans have joined the same club and in this way become globally reputed companies (GRC).

By introducing the self-service concept, super and hyper-markets in the West have introduced freedom to shoppers. Earlier shopkeepers behind small shop counters would help shoppers buy. Generic products at that time were edible or household products made by regional companies constrained by scale. They may not have had specific consumer benefit. Most generic products that consumers are traditionally habituated to have since been transformed to branded products in the West. Their next logical step has been radical, such as low fat in food products. The growth of generic to specific domestic products has led to mass customization.

There are numerous and outstanding American examples of traditional products having changed to acquire branded dimensions. Simple sandwich biscuits when filled with chocolate or cream have become Oreo, cornflakes became Kellogg's, orange juice is referred to as Tropicana. Coca-Cola, a 110-year product was concocted in a backyard kettle by mixing lime, cinnamon, coca leaves, and the seeds of a Brazilian shrub. It was originally used as a nerve and brain tonic and a medical elixir. Today Coca-Cola is one of the world's recalled brands. Anybody can easily make a Coca-Cola type of drink, but he cannot make the Coca-Cola brand. It may not be seen as a health facilitator today, but for 110 years, Coca-Cola has been synonymous with Yankee culture and has shifted out from a generic category.

Andy Warhol emerged as an outstanding eccentric artist in the 1960s. Of Slovakian origin, he was born in the US. He introduced a new advertising art form, which snowballed into the American pop art movement. He amassed great fortune during his lifetime and achieved fame like no painter before him had done.

Andy Warhol magnified Marilyn Monroe's beauty and exuberance into an all-time global icon of Pop art. He made Campbell's mass consumption soup can into a piece of art which today has tremendous economic value as part of the Pop art painting collection. It has in fact become synonymous with American culture. It may attract the same price as the brand value of Campbell, or be even higher.

This painting of an industrial soup can hanging in the famous New York museum out-and-out augments the value of the Campbell brand on a daily basis. When a museum is magnifying an industrial product, its exposure definitely has far superior value, both allegorically and commercially, than any advertisement or supermarket display. The whole world can now access the same soup brand in a historical and cultural context. This is another example of transferring a generic product to a high recall brand.

Other examples of traditional food being branded are homemade chicken fry, pizzas or burgers. The world enjoys them at a very reasonable price and with easy availability.

At the beginning of the 20th century small local French and English companies converted homemade products like jams into branded categories. French brand 'Bonne Maman' meaning sweet mother is a unique recipe. It represents French gastronomy in a mass market product. The transformation of these traditional products into global brands involved breakaway thought processes that made generic products synonymous with some unique property of people's everyday need and desire.

The socio-economic crises following the war made both men and women go to work and struggle to upgrade their economic status. The post-war trend of hard work for a better lifestyle led Western society to go in for mass industrialization. Manufacturers produced mass scale domestic products without disturbing their authenticity. This was the time when the unique selling proposition (USP) concept was established. Entrepreneurs put in tremendous effort to bring some real difference in a market that needed it. Through the decades these big brand corporations have grown to become the powerhouses that now command the market.

India, China or other emerging countries need to understand the mechanism of how Western companies took the deeper challenge of branding generic products. Such a shift needs strong discipline to think very differently. They must have unconditional creativity to change the generic character of the product and rigorous process to make it commercial.

After 1980, the technology revolution started to change the market rules. Local players in different countries challenged the big brands and their recipes became vulnerable. In a blind test, consumers often could not feel any difference between international and local brands. Apart from historic legacy, the big brands have nothing to differentiate them today. Those were the days when consumers thought manufacturers had unique recipes as they commanded the market. But now consumers have multiple choices and instead, they have started commanding the market.

Manufacturers have now very considerably increased their advertising expenses to seduce consumers from the moment they open their eyes. Brands that occupy higher media space become more powerful. A media dependent brand becomes vulnerable as it takes no risk apart from advertising. It may believe everything will be achieved through media expense, but in reality it contributes more to communication pollution than consumer benefit. Exceptional media expense may bring awareness, but it may not increase consumer desire if the product alchemy has no unique and distinct consumer benefit.

India plays a significant role in promoting film and sports stars as brand ambassadors to boost up brands at a terrific expense. The predicament has become so acute now that marketing and advertising managers of brands many a time compete among themselves to use different stars. They also relish the opportunity of hobnobbing with the stars, and the power of directing them in short advertisements. Such media expense attempts to hallucinate the consumer who may enjoy the star performance, but oftentimes does not recall the name of the brand advertised.

When a brand continuously spends huge sums of advertising money, it obviously loses its substance. Money meant for upgrading product quality goes to drive media instead. The regular investment of deeper product innovation is ignored to showcase big stars. The biggest tragedy Indian brands face is that a large number of companies are compensating the deficiency of their products' rational benefit through brand ambassadors.

A rational attribute is the non-visible factor which, in general, consumers cannot see upfront at the moment of purchase. The engine or chassis is not visible when you are buying the car. You cannot appreciate its longevity, but have to trust the authenticity of the manufacturer. Using it day after day you will discover its quality. This rational authenticity of trust exists in every domain of business.

Take a food product example. If a brand's promise is to provide health, the consumer cannot upfront see or appreciate the quality of ingredients used. The taste may be good, packaging may be attractive, its advertisements may be very emotional but if the unseen rational factor of good quality ingredients is not provided, the brand becomes vulnerable. To compensate the deficiency of negligible differentiating consumer value, a celebrity is pulled in as brand ambassador. Brands that go in for such advertising make themselves very fragile. Consumers see the same actor selling a car, chocolates, wall paint, pens and soft drink. Is he building long lasting value for these brands? I am not sure.

After the economic reforms when carbonated soft drinks re-entered India, they threw in large sums of money to occupy every advertising space, from the television screen to even the public toilet. This influenced other manufacturers to put in big money in the media for all varieties of businesses. Have other manufacturers understood that the big carbonated drinks brands have no other choice because they are all 'advertising products.' They do not have any substance as benefit other than excitement. Carbonated drinks can create proximity by seducing people at their moment of stress, depression, or in hot weather. Their ambition is to part-ner people by being within hand's reach. My prediction is that carbonated drink is not a product of the 21st century. In 30 to 40 years it will diminish in the world, except in USA.

North America, by heritage has been a country with a high level of excitement and stress in all aspects. Everybody can freely carry around firearms. Coca-Cola matches very well in this stress-ful society where everybody is always looking for an antibiotic solution in every domain. Coke spontaneously resurrects this soci-ety of stress, depression and excitement. This same kind of stress, social fracture, depression, and quest only for money that exists in the US may not be very prominent in other nations.

Towards the end of the last century, a new chapter opened, that of technology explosion. Technology brought in total democracy in the world of business where products and services are of generic character in most domains.

Branding means mystifying a generic product with a value that's superior so that it can generate sufficient net profit. Asso-ciating with the consumers' lifecycle, lifestyle and trend, a brand can grow by increasing per capita consumption and arresting new consumers without being attacked by generic categories.

Americans have successfully shifted many a generic product or service to the brand culture. They have mastered the brand-ing platform by dramatically making a micro-angle added benefit perceptible to consumers. A branding exercise always needs to portray a certain elevated aspiration to any socio-economic layer.

As seen in Figure 7.1, tradition is the horizontal axis while the trend dominates as the vertical axis. Unlimited technological advancement is taking the trend on such rapid rise every year or two that it's becoming difficult to scale up or keep pace with it.

Figure 7.1 a platform that's optimal can sustain leadership

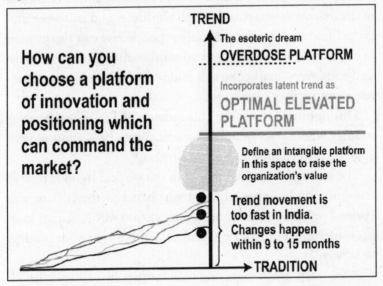

If you move along with the current trend, you can become obsolete tomorrow. If you cannot keep pace with today, your business will diminish. Even being just atop the current trend will make you obsolete in the near future, as there's no telling where the competitor ambush will be in. If your organization works on the current timeframe to get better bottomline result, you would not be building that intangible aspect in your earning that has premium value. So the consumer or customer may not find a differentiating value in your brand. What, then, should you do? Create an empowered team who can foresee your business from an elevated situation, and take an option on the extended vertical line, beyond today's trendlines.

Trying to reach the highest point of the trendline can be an overdose and an uncalculated gamble. The aspirational gene in your brand can become totally esoteric there. Yet staying on the trend is not a strategy for sustainable success. You need a trade-off.

Between the current and overdosed parameter of the trend there is an optimal level, which also has the latent perspective.

This optimal layer is the filter of your microtone understanding of the market as you pass through consumer and customer life-cycle, lifestyle and trend. This latent perspective can also be used to calculate how you will carry your innovative products, mobilized employees, marketing and trade customization into tomorrow's competitive playing field.

This optimal level is the culmination of Emotional Surplus strategy where your brand value will always be surplus to generate surplus volume and profit surplus.

The strategy in the battlefield of the vertical trend is how to continuously maintain equidistance between the current and optimal trend layers in future. Doing so, you will anticipate market leadership and avoid any generic condition on your product or service.

A few years ago, interacting with farmers in a research in different North American states, a west coast farmer explained to me how, in just an acre of land, he cultivates profit surplus. He grooms the simple tomato in a different way that produces heirloom tomatoes and gives him a selling price that is over four times higher than the basic tomato. This demonstrates how targeting the optimal layer can bring Emotional Surplus value to both you and your consumers. With miniscule land holding, the farmer anticipated consumer desire for a specialized produce. In an extremely competitive market comprising big farmers and exotic imports, he differentiated by creating higher product quality and made his profit surplus.

Americans have, interestingly, mastered the art of generating intangible value from this optimal layer. In Europe, apart from Germany, organizations in various industries have failed to draw upon this optimal layer for their business strategy. The Japanese and Koreans are riding very high on this optimal layer, while India and China have not yet understood it.

In spite of being associated with so many fundamental innovations in the world, Europeans have failed in commercial success from two angles: either overdosing the proposition which global masses cannot easily connect to; or being in the same beat of the trend which becomes generic after a certain time.

The last 60 years have seen several European brands, from diapers to fast food chains, being buried because of pressure from American branding power in the optimal layer, followed now by Japan and Korea. European luxury goods undoubtedly have an edge over the world in the optimal layer of aspiration, but they couldn't manage mass production like the Americans, Japanese and Koreans. India and China should absorb how the globally reputed companies have addressed the optimal layer as strategic option; they should not erroneously think that magic and money power built those brands.

India's IT software development industry has become well known worldwide for delivering diligent service at a low price. Most of the quarter results of IT companies talk about volume increase that's reflected in their financial result. But are these IT companies creating a difference apart from their size, flexibility and low cost?

Let's return to the *jalebi*, what is its intrinsic character? It's differentiation; no two *jalebi*s will ever look alike. Likewise, your IT organization should not look like just another generic brand sunk into cost arbitrage. Aside from being sensitive to consumers and employees alike, it should realize its own potential and chase its fulfillment.

When will an Indian company proudly state that it has made a difference by creating high intellectual property (IP)? An IP so outstanding that nobody else in the world can match it? An IP that brings in a new platform, either a new style of business or increasing people's living comfort? Most importantly, when will an Indian company create an IP that allows its parent company to command an exceptionally premium price across the world?

It's time for Indian companies to change, to pick up the gauntlet of globalization. Must finding an optimal layer to occupy, becoming a unique pathfinder, competing at par with GRCs remain distant dreams? There's certainly no need to reinvent the wheel, but when Indians imitate, they copy on the surface; unlike the Japanese who copy to make the original better. They need to struggle to enter the subject's core, or to discover how developed countries mastered this optimal layer. Understanding the mechanism of how to create the optimal layer is more important than reading a readily available case study.

Your manufacturing or service program that has unique intellectual property can lag behind with a generic business profile unless you capture the optimal layer. If a country's growth can associate with optimal layer business practices of different business houses, tremendous premium value can be created in the economy.

On the other hand, attack from local companies offering low price products and services, can affect growth for GRCs. A company that strengthens the optimal layer value proposition can become highly competitive, and generate better profit. There is more opportunity in the optimal layer scale today than 10 to 20 years ago.

You can stop your market offer from deviating towards the generic by understanding people's different purchase acts. Whether your market status is generic or premium can be fleshed out by the way customers and consumers buy.

I have classified purchase act and behavior to be of three kinds. Let's take a look at these buying ways to overcome the generic nature of the market battlefield:

(a) A brand's regular and planned repurchase has a psychological link that makes it a conditioned act.

(b) Impulse purchase is an unplanned act with an unstructured psychological anchor.

(c) Psychological involvement in periodic purchase has a momentum. This is a planned purchase act.

regular repurchase act

It's like a husband-wife relationship. Catering a brand for regular repurchase means understanding that consumers and customers consider the brand to be an extension of their family. So the brand goes through the same acts the family does, from a monotonous routine life to periodic effervescence. When on a declining slope, it can taper off from routine to boredom to divorce. The consumer and customer's psychological involvement with this category is delicate and intricate to maintain. To sustain a successful husband-wife relationship, both partners must consciously keep evolving. If their wavelengths don't connect, a psychological cut off happens. Similarly, mismatch in brand and consumer evolution results in divorce.

impulse purchase act

This girlfriend-boyfriend freelance relationship will not lead up to marriage. Impulse purchase could be a one-time act or a repeat, but it's not regular habit. The psychological dimension of consumers and customers has vibrancy very different from regular purchase. A girlfriend-boyfriend relationship always strives to maintain a certain elegance that makes things glamorous whenever they meet. It's never a boring relationship, making impulse purchase brands always sparkle in their appearance and action.

periodic purchase

Like the mistress or 'other man' relationship, this is a certain purchase, but it's not entangled with the everyday buy. The periodic purchase cycle can be mid- to long-term. An electric bulb could be a mid-term purchase, a refrigerator could be a long-term purchase. The psychological relationship with such purchase is very mature and based on being refreshed. Just like a mistress or the other man relationship has grace, this purchase is resourceful and elegant, with no boredom attached to it. To get the same consumer or customer to buy the same product after a period has elapsed, the brand has to maintain a mistress-like characteristic.

The generic market battlefield makes vulnerable the consumer and customer purchase behavior. If in your delivery you can surpass their desire with specific action that's relevant to them, these three different purchase acts can anticipate their psychological gesture. This will protect your delivery, and ensure it gets thrown in to fight the generic market battlefield.

converting the generic

When everyday consuming FMCG products are tangibly the same, creating intangibles becomes the only route to enhance profitability. Blind tests prove this similarity. Companies worldwide face the dilemma of creating differentiation and infusing intangibles into products tomorrow (see Chapter 8 on what an intangible is).

A parallel consumer rebellion is becoming obvious. With choice being aplenty, marketers promoting brands and encouraging conspicuous consumption, consumers feel like shopping victims. Radicals question big brands: why should I pay 20 to 30 percent higher price? What will the brand give to me?

Consumers today are aware that even emerging country retailers will not put a sub-standard product on the shelf; a certain base quality is expected. Neither will retailers risk diluting the retail image to sell off-quality products.

If yours is a big mass market brand, your product must have discerning superior benefit. The consumer's everyday, every moment experience with your brand and product is extremely important. You cannot explain away your high price as being on account of higher advertising or sponsoring spends. You need to create an aura of high sensitivity around your brand so that the consumer experiences the product's quality as superior, and becomes sensitive to this intangible in her usage habit.

The moment of purchase and different moments of usage are like affairs of extreme intimacy and bonding between a brand and its consumer. These moments establish whether you have merely fulfilled your consumer's need, or created an intimate link with your consumer in her sense of desire.

Take shampoo as an example. A big brand may charge the consumer a 20 to 30 percent higher price than a private label of a retailer offer, local or small player. With no rocket science inside shampoos, perhaps the rational or functional parts of your tangible quality are no superior than the smaller competitors. But you may have addressed your superiority through a well-designed container that may have some better functional system. But in absolute terms, are you giving any difference? Aren't you just improving the container against the others to create a superficial difference?

In such a predicament, if you use the ReFinE Value Ladder process (see Chapter 10), you may find different paradigms with which you can actually create differentiation to reach a quantum leap.

Should the perceptible quality of your rational, non-visible factors be high, you need to first put the rational area through the ReFinE Value Ladder. If a lab test confirms you are really unbeatable, then check your functional part. Is this reality or just a perception? You may be scoring high on a character that's become perceptible because of heavy advertising. The reality may be different; you are not at this level.

Once you know this situation, you can innovate to actually uplift your product's rational and functional benefits. If you find no competitor has rational and functional attributes higher than yours, perhaps this product has become generic; all major players are at par.

This is the stage to work at refining your product's attributes so you can command a higher price in the generic market. But how can you do this without a big advertising budget?

Put a microscope and a camera on your consumer's daily life. This will steer you away from watching shampoo usage only. Through the microscope and camera you will discover the consumers' relationship with many other activities and products that are totally unrelated to your business. Consumers may be more sensitive to emerging new products, services and solutions that have entered their lives. Against such savvy offerings, your product category may have become mundane for them.

If at this stage you release a beautiful advertisement or place a large, brilliant billboard instead of watching the consumer, at best you can just create street pollution. How will consumers get convinced that your product has a distinctive benefit?

While microscoping the consumer's life, you will get insights you may not have seen or considered as important. Possibly the system of using shampoo may not be the same in today's generation, a fact not exposed yet. Perhaps on different days, the quantity of shampoo used might differ depending on the requirement for cleaning. Is the shampoo used for taking off dust, for giving the hair a bounce, to take off hair greasiness or to prepare the foundation for hair gel?

The way a consumer pours the shampoo on her hand may have an aspiration that's not the same every day. Opening the cap may get associated with the habit of opening and closing the voguish system of the mobile phone in her hand. If sophisticated facial creams or cleansing grains are seriously gaining consumer mindshare, the shampoo could sport a hidden factor that imbibes some association of a cream. Perhaps a specialized shampoo in a small, facial cream-like container instead of a jarring vertical bottle in the toilet may make all the difference to sales.

These are elements of microtone consumer sensitivity. Think about how to generate high profitable growth in this saturated market of shampoos. Will it be by bringing new ways to beautify her hair or changing her habit?

ReFinE Value Ladder will demonstrate how you can totally change consumer perception of your product, from product inception to its container, usage pattern and daily habit. When consumer craving has reached heights that surpass necessity, you as the manufacturer will certainly miss out on her sense of desire if you continue to merely tom-tom industrial capability.

ReFinE Value Ladder helps ladder quality to become innovative in any competitive scenario. ReFinE approaches everything from the perspective of the consumers' psychological, sociological, physical usage and habit pattern. The result can be a breakaway strategy and execution. This can truly justify your brand premium and 30 percent higher price, make you aspirational and generate a better bottomline. Once your product has taken a quantum leap in ReFinE Value Ladder, it needs continuous laddering and refinement for sustaining its high score.

The luxury category price point is an intangible area, it goes beyond any justification. You will never buy a Mont Blanc pen or a Louis Vitton bag because you need it. You pay an exorbitant price, beyond its fabrication, quality standard and marketing cost. In this paradigm, a brand's intangibles associate with a human being's exhibitionist character, hedonism or sense of belongingness.

To see how genuinely higher are the rational, functional and emotional factors of the luxury category, you can do a blind ReFinE test without showing the brand. If you subsequently superimpose the brand, you will see the scale going up very significantly. It's very difficult to get consumers to recognize a brand to be in a luxury category and pay a higher price for it unless the brand has been well seasoned by time. Luxury goods are like old wine or whiskey that increases in value with age. The nuances of consumer sensitivity layers are very subtle and sensitive here, together with a high order intangible value association.

Generic service providers can always charm away a customer. They offer a very low price, thinking it's an easy, individual service industry. They approach a customer and superficially convince him of their same-service-at-lower-price syndrome. If you are a premium service provider, you can easily lose the business. That's why quality has to be visibly manifested in the service business area. Impact that's tangible can be upgraded through the ReFinE Value Ladder. Attitude and behavior are intangibles in the service business, and create the differentiation. The cost of service can be very high in sophisticated markets unlike in nascent economically emerging markets. That's because a lot of intangibles have been created around them to portray service in a superior plateau.

Highly fashionable Parisian restaurants require reservation at least a month in advance. It's a restaurant's intangible art of the table and service quality that makes its price excessive. Different wines in appropriate wine glasses will accompany the various courses of food. The wine taster's intangible approach with accompanying gestures and conversation justifies the exclusivity of the wines from different seasons and regions.

Service is impeccable on the table as every gesture carries the image value of the restaurant. If a person in your group of four is not eating, a plate will still be ceremonially put in front of him to include him. Waiters are trained to proactively keep an eye on each table to anticipate every small requirement. Along with service, the quality and taste of the food has an immaculate alchemy. So service and food quality combine to surprise the guests with thoughtful care.

This type of attention to service can only come from a structured and defined attitude and behavior that employees are trained to follow. It is possible to take this reference and use it in a processed manner in any service industry.

To appreciate the value of such intangibles, sensitivity to this kind of treatment has to be cultivated. But only the well heeled can go in for it. Those anesthetized to this service sensitivity would rather eat food outside at a substantially lower cost. Such intangible sophistication may not be available in economically emerging countries even if people have the money to spend. Collective social sophistication is an output of affluence in any society.

I am giving this example to portray a certain service quality, not the affectations of affluent society. This type of attitude and behavior in service can be scaled down for use in any type of service business to make service non generic.

Offerings from globally reputed brands did not acquire instant premium association like magic from Alladin's lamp. Their precise effort to upgrade the rational and functional attributes of their delivery helped them attain premium perception in consumer mind. An emerging country's brand must go through the pain of upgrading rational and functional quality. The brand can then achieve intangible association of premium value in the mind of the masses.

My big pain is that my favorite *jalebi* is still generic in the marketplace. So many generic products have been transformed into large global brands in the West, but nobody has taken care to give the *jalebi* a noble branding character so it will not be generic. I am eagerly awaiting the day when *jalebi* will say goodbye to the generic market battlefield.

emotional surplus strategy

My *Jalebi Management* structure brings a practical simplicity into an organization so its end consumers, employees, shareholders and all partners can sink their teeth into the delectable sweet. This delicious bite is Emotional Surplus.

In today's competitive consumer market where nothing is rocket science, the concept of unique selling proposition (USP) has negligible meaning. What's more important is how the intrinsic character of a brand can link with consumer lifecycle, lifestyle and trend. As a manufacturer, you may endow your product with some USP, but have you checked to see if consumers think of that value as unique? The market is flooded with a variety of similar products, or products unrelated to yours which can serve the consumer's same purpose in a different way.

The real, unarticulated judgment of consumers and customers resides in their subconscious. Industry with its rational way of working may find it esoteric to even think of understanding the subconscious mind of human beings. But subliminal connect is what a brand's core substance needs to seek. This substance needs to upgrade and balance its rational, functional and emotional attributes and connect to the consumer's lifecycle, lifestyle and trend. This connect is the foundation of the Emotional Surplus strategy.

from USP to ESV

The Emotional Surplus Value (ESV) is different from USP as it can sustain with a long-term perspective in any competitive scenario. I developed this business strategy from practical experience, after having worked, year after year, with people of different races and cultures, in B2B (business-to-business) and B2C (business-to-consumer) businesses, both big and small.

Most of today's businesses are facing pressure from diverse related or non-related competition, and low price categories in the market. The consequence is generic degradation of brands. A unique selling proposition has today become a 'vulnerable selling obsession' because technology has democratized the marketplace. If your organization has created Emotional Surplus value in people, products and the brand, it can overcome any vulnerable market storm to sustain your high profitable business. The natural corollary for companies is to shift from the USP concept to ESV.

After working for several companies in France from 1973 to 1983, I started my own consulting firm integrated with high caliber professionals in 1984 in Paris. Our first priority was to ensure sustainability in any thought that we bring to a client's table. The 'creative business strategy' that we instituted incorporates this element of sustainability. A creative business strategy establishes discomfort in the organization. It makes people question and debate their journey towards, and action points for, quantum growth. When everyone from the company's top to bottom layers buys into the strategy, it strengthens the strategy, making it efficacious. Never having participated in competing for any kind of professional award, my real winning spirit is to ensure that my clients always win in the marketplace. A win that is not just a short-term spark, but which can sustain their business growth decade after decade.

A product or a service needs clever investment to grow and generate money. Whatever is spent on it at any time should be considered as investment to reap long-term benefits. A shareholder's frustration, unstated though it may be, comes from a business proposition that does not sustain. In a company with a short-term goal, and strategy, with activities that change every so often to match market speed, employees fail to understand its strategic long-term focus. Vendors tend to become totally vulnerable as the client's unfocused strategy erodes their investments. Frequent change confuses consumers or customers, resulting in shareholders also losing confidence.

Operating only with tactics of short-term wins, a company's vision get truncated. Trends may change, the way we work, or the processes we work with may change, but the intangible business value you create today should multiply steadily after 3, 10, 20 years. I believe in this business vision that spells Emotional Surplus strategy.

intangibles

What are intangibles in business? At any given time there are sociocultural, economic and trend ingredients getting cooked in a cauldron in the market. Intangible flair grows from this cauldron. To create intangible content, organizational culture cannot be isolated from this social cauldron. When intangible culture is missing in business practice, you cannot enjoy high profitability.

What's intangible in a *jalebi*? For both Indians and Arabs, a *jalebi* takes you back in time, subliminally sinking you into that comfort of indulging in your very own culture. The social cauldron where *jalebi* resides distinguishes it as 'a speciality food only for those who know.' This makes the lover of *jalebi*s feel included in his ethnicity even as he rushes around in a global atmosphere at work.

How much can tinkering with operational efficiency grow an organization? Operational efficiency has a spring. The more you stretch it, the less sensitive it becomes. The spring can end up as a straight wire. Businesses need to appreciate intangibles because that's what bestows them with the differentiation to conquer the market.

A creative business strategy can very powerfully demonstrate the intangible. Intangible value is very fragile. It cannot sustain based on intuition or mandatory routine productivity. Organizations must understand how to consciously create and carefully nurture and protect their intangibles. This will break conventional working culture and pave the way for dynamic growth.

There's nothing intangible about approaching a bunch of bananas, yanking out one and munching on it. But when a sophisticated French restaurant takes the same banana to make dessert, you get into intangible zone. Check out this dish: on an ivory white plate, a wee bit of hot chocolate is placed in the shape of an elongated upside down heart. A fine green piping surrounds the heart as though encasing it with freshness. Two peeled bananas subtly meet at the top thinning part of the heart with fine sprinklings of nuts and butterscotch over them alone, not on the perfect chocolate heart they are delicately parked on. Neatly next to them is a twirl of whipped cream topped with a thin chocolate ribbon forming four petals of a flower. The entire dish is served with a sprig of fine fresh leaves aside a bunch of golden ripe bananas on the table.

The ingredients for this dessert may cost about $4–5, but nobody will question why the dessert is priced at $25 in this Parisian restaurant. That's because the restaurant has already established its food character to be intangible, much beyond any basic ingredient.

In business, intangibles comprise the most important and valuable factors. The goodwill of an organization is always appreciated on the basis of its intangibles. Only when a consumer or customer first appreciates this intangible, will he be ready to pay a premium for it. Better profitability, better share price, better market capitalization are all related to intangibles.

But the paradox is that, worldwide, business houses very often fall short of realizing this. They fail to consciously create, nurture and worship the intangible in every function in their work culture.

People generally better appreciate the tangible. It's physical and easier to understand than the intangible aspect. Often the intangible can appear to be scary to deal with, as it demands lateral thinking.

In economically emerging nations like India, most companies are oblivious about intangibles, or fail to recognize intangible value. When companies in sophisticated developed countries lose out on intangibles, they realize it, and work with the knowledge and mechanism they have towards regaining it. Apple Computers lost its intangibles several times; but through colorful monitors, the pearly transparent mouse, and now with the iPod, they've regained their intangible value.

The creative thought for iPod's product design emerged from associating it to a thin cigarette packet. When I read about this, I immediately understood that they wanted to create a relationship that went beyond being a packet in the pocket. It was the addictive value of cigarettes that they sought to instill in consumer mind. This addictive value of the iPod is the real intangible they have established. It goes beyond the device. People can copy the device, but it would be difficult to transplant the intangible addictive association from one product to another.

Every business model can easily be imitated today. The real challenge is to know how to add the intangible to your business model so your imitators cannot relocate it from your product or service. This intangible is Emotional Surplus value that will bring you surplus profit on a continuous basis.

I'm not sure how many software service providers in India are thinking about creating intangibles in the business that's outsourced to them. They mostly provide service that's negotiated down to a very low cost. Yet their overhead costs being low, they enjoy good margins. Is any of this an intangible? I doubt it. In the international market they still cannot command a price that sophisticated markets can. That's probably because they do not have a differentiating character in intangible format. Indian companies need to stretch their thoughts on how to add an intangible topping in business to achieve profit surplus.

I'm not questioning why any product or service sells at a low price. The denigrating issue I am raising is low price becoming the only selling factor of a business proposition.

Most rational factors in the planet stay hidden; you have to delve in deep to perceive them. Rational factors are very crucial in business (see Chapter 10 to understand the rational, non-visible attribute of any selling proposition that provides its intrinsic confidence of quality). In the glory of its growth, a company may tend to forget to qualitatively maintain this rational factor. But the consumer's subconscious back-of-mind confidence for a product or service is based on this hidden rational factor. Different businesses such as durables, FMCG, luxury or service have different intangible aspects.

Intangibles form and grow from a product's rational credibility. It may remain totally tacit with the user, but its unspoken layers are very crucial for business houses. Whatever size of business you may have, you just cannot afford to ignore those unarticulated layers. Starting at ground zero, you can grow to become gigantic tomorrow if you have the capacity to uniquely articulate what consumers and customers desire, but have not expressed.

durable products

Its very nomenclature spells reliability and quality for a durable product. But this durability is, in essence, a hidden rational factor that the consumer knows almost nothing about. A company manufacturing consumer durables products like TV sets for instance, cannot create its intangibles by just making the product look sophisticated or glamorous. The more the rational factor is improved, and through performance and aesthetics this change for the better becomes perceptible to the consumer, the more will its intangible score rise. Aesthetics and functional benefits can be a hook to create the difference. When the consumer's subconscious has implicit confidence on the product's rational factor, that product will be appreciated over others.

Buying a durable product can almost be a gamble because its intrinsic quality is hidden from the consumer's gaze. That's why it's indispensable for organizations to focus on uplifting the rational area. If consumers expect your product to be durable for 3 or 5 years, but it fails before that time, the damage to your brand's intangible value would be immense. A single consumer's bad mouthing reaches at least 50 people. Those 50 can communicate to another 2,500 people, and in multiples of 50 the figure can enlarge uncontrollably. It would be wise to remember that accurate quality cannot afford to have any tolerance level.

Poor quality is the root cause that kills intangibles. If you detect even a minor quality defect, or a product series has defects that can very likely occur post its year-long warranty period, you should be sensitive not to release such a durable product in the market. It can destroy your intangible value. The rational value should reach such heights that consumer confidence during usage is supreme.

Communication can play a pivotal role in making consumers understand, and implicitly believe in, a product's rational substance. It can translate rational excellence into credibility by creating an aspirational cue. When the only objective is the consumer's unconditional subconscious bonding with the rational attribute, communication can take the liberty of being provocative, perverted or even abusive. It should ensure that total belief in the product's rational substance is never displaced from the consumer's mind under any competitive situation.

FMCG

The hidden rational factor in fast moving consumer goods (FMCG) is extremely susceptible to damage. In a competitive scenario, no company in the world can depend on past record to win market share. No market leader is stable for long. It has to question its leadership on a daily basis, and check how consumers will appreciate and continue with its product.

Usage and habit are no indication that consumers will always buy your brand; newness is a very easy conversion reason. Among FMCG brands, whether old or new, consumers have understood that quality is more or less the same. There's very marginal space for introducing any differentiating character. The manufacturer's primary task here is to preserve newness at all times, to keep the intangible intact. Simultaneously, transparent focus on manufacturing excellence counts as the brand's rational factor when it is perceptible to consumers. Consistently and continuously upgrading intrinsic quality creates the brand's source credibility.

Regular usage FMCG brands have the opportunity of creating intimate relationships with consumers during the 5, 10 or 30 days it spends in a consumer's home. By fashioning excellent usage advantages, a brand can bond with the fickle mind consumers have about fast moving consumer products. Unlike durable brands, FMCG brands are susceptible in the consumer's hand, and this vulnerability needs to be broken. For FMCG brands to hold consumer mindshare, revitalization should become almost an everyday activity. The challenge for FMCG is to create extreme consumer proximity to its brand, organization and products.

Let's hypothetically see how much FMCG products have to stretch to display differentiation. In toothpaste, no new formula has emerged to make teeth brighter. So only a functional innovation can garner consumer mindshare. Hypothetically, immense proximity can perhaps be generated like this: when the toothpaste container touches the toothbrush, automatically, without pushing the tube, only that quantity of toothpaste that you like to use is released on the brush. The next innovation step would be to have this customizing facility adjusted separately for the whole family in the same toothpaste container. The consumer will feel very close to the brand and perhaps decode in it a value-for-money character. This economic solution can transcend to become an intangible that's surrounded by mystique. Such a mystique will place the brand far above its competitors. But if communicated vulgarly, the intangible character of this functional solution will slip very quickly. It will look like a gimmick, and competitors will follow just as fast in its wake.

Deploying hallucinating advertising with film star brand ambassadors does not compensate any hidden rational deficiency an FMCG product may have. Economically emerging countries should learn from the mistakes the developed countries made in the 1970s and 1980s. Consumption of FMCG products increased in the West when brands were converted to publicity stunts that used large advertising budgets. While doing that, they forgot to substantiate their brand's rational factor. Organized retail distribution took advantage of this shortcoming and created the private label.

Initially, branded companies disregarded private labels as mere me-too products. But consumers soon discovered that private label quality was not too dissimilar to national or international brands. The distinction that big brands sported was sexy television advertising, while private labels were confined to their retail outlets. In organized retails in the West, private labels engage in intense activation at the point of purchase. That's won them upto 50 percent share in consumer mindspace.

To flesh out its intangible, the FMCG brand's rational substance requires continuous endorsement with the organization's source credibility. When all competitive products look alike, the corporation's authenticity can play a decisive role in differentiating the brand from its competition. This legitimacy becomes the only intangible power in the FMCG brand. It also empowers premium value, which is the brand's real profitability.

luxury goods

Authenticity is the primary aspect in luxury brands. The intangibles in luxury brands have the ability to command astonishing prices, with the co-efficient of hundred going up 10, 20 or 50 times. Mercedes went back a hundred years to bring back the Maybach because starting a new brand with a new name will give them no advantage at ground zero. But transcending its legacy made credible the car's intangible aspect of genuineness. Consumers buying Maybach today may not have heard this history, but revealing authentic culture and meshing it with modernity has shaped an incredible intangible that has made Maybach more expensive than Rolls Royce. The rational factor of this proposition is legacy. This inheritance is the intangible.

It would be very difficult to have intangibles dominate over reality in a newly created luxury brand. You may sophisticate the new luxury brand by using outstanding technology, but it won't be able to compete with existing luxury brands. Even as they add incredible premium to their manufacturing and advertising costs, existing luxury brands are extremely cautious to uplift their product quality. Brands such as Mont Blanc, Louis Vuitton or Hermes have significantly improved the quality of their products compared to 20 or 30 years ago. This has permitted them to continue their perceptible superior value.

If you want to start a luxury brand, it is advisable to buy an existing small brand somewhere in the world on the condition that what it ever delivered was perceived to be good. It may not be well known, but at least it has legacy, which is its mystique. Retaining its legacy, you can improve its rational character to become contemporary. Do remember that advertising a luxury brand like a mass market product will make it lose its intangible, consequently all its value.

You will need immense patience to reap results after creating a new luxury brand. A beautiful presentation will not create the brand's intangible luxury platform. You have to exuberantly demonstrate its hidden rational factors to the consumer to prove that it is supreme. You need time, as seasoning is a critical factor. Lexus is an example of a new brand directly entering a sophisticated price category. It has taken a long time, and it may take even longer to overcome Mercedes, but having this patience is the key to success.

Comparing Mercedes and Lexus of a similar range, you may find the engineering performance and other functional benefits of Lexus to be higher than Mercedes. But with a life-size historical legacy of having performed through two World Wars, Mercedes carries its proven rational factor. This intangible has till today given Mercedes an edge over newcomers like Lexus.

service

The intangible in the service business spawns from stringent discipline. It is difficult to standardize a level of high quality service with an IT system, as service is dependent on the human touch and on relationships. The attitude and behavioral aspect of individuals counts enormously. The intangibles in service tend to become quite vulnerable. As a service provider you need to, at the initial stage, individually set the barometer of consumer and customer expectation as your back-end process.

Your customer is totally disinterested in the efforts you put in to maintain discipline at your back-end. He may never take any initiative to learn about it. But in the final analysis, this discipline, which is your customer's intangible association with your service from inception, will be your real advantage. You can set and instill service expectations in your customer's subconscious mind without ever disclosing your knowhow and back-end discipline. When your customer is able to articulate why he finds your service better than what the competition is offering, your business will gain.

This consumer endorsement is the rational and non-visible factor of your service business. This expectation barometer of the consumer is the intangible edge you have created. Let's look at a few services and how intangibles are formed there.

courier service

The crucial factor in courier services, irrespective of the size of the courier company, is the quality of the person who takes the package and how he delivers it. These comprise the most fundamental consumer or customer touch points. If your courier company has 10 different people collecting and delivering packages in 10 different ways, you will definitely not create any intangible aspect for your customers.

Let's say you provide a box for your client's merchandise. If this box has archaic systems not easy for the client to manipulate storage and closure, or even if the box looks ugly, you will lose out on intangibles in consumer and customer mindshare. The box is a rational factor, but if it is a hassle to open, your efficient and secure delivery will amount to very little in the aspect of retaining intangibles.

Courier companies tend to highlight on size, breadth of service, and facilities such as owning airplanes, ships or large fleets of surface vehicles. But what is their intangible association with the customer? The answer is being disciplined, predictable and rationally out-of-the-box at the two moments of recovery and delivery.

airline

All airline companies have the same vessel, the aircraft. So in-flight service is considered to be the key to creating intangibles. Actually, better consumer value can be constructed outside the aircraft. Consumers need taking care from the moment they reach the airport to the time they board the plane; and at the destination, from after they leave the aircraft upto baggage collection and exit to the taxi outside. Such rationally uplifting services are rarely to be found anywhere.

It's normal for a passenger to get into nail-biting consternation when his baggage is lost between destinations. For the airline this is not unusual; the misplaced baggage is generally found, when time is given to rectify human error. A passenger narrated an animalistic character he recently experienced in American air services and airports. The passenger, with only a numbered stub to go by, needed reassurance, but the airport staff behaved officiously and no one from the airline deigned to reply. The passenger was given a telephone number to call. Imagine his misgivings when he suddenly discovered the person at the end of the line is from a call center outside the US, and here he is, trying to locate his luggage lost somewhere between Dallas and New York!

You may marvel at modern technology that everything is handled through a boundaryless code number across geographies. But not at the precise time when you need to take a connecting flight to Rochester, NY, for a business meeting and can't locate your business suit. More importantly, you don't have access to the necessary files and material lying in that misplaced piece of baggage.

The airline staff may not know exactly when, where and how the luggage will be delivered to the passenger, but from past experience they have faith that the 'system' will retrieve the luggage. But there is no way the passenger can trust anyone when he does not encounter even a caring word to assuage his anxiety. All he gets subjected to is harried airline staff. If air travel in the

US had any intangible for this passenger, it has certainly flown out of the aircraft window into the clouds below.

banking

I find the doctor-patient relationship to be similar to the relationship between a consumer and his banker. Using technology as the interface, banks today are reducing face-to-face consumer relationships. Will this make all banks become generic on their product perspective, making them devoid of value in the near future? Outside of health, a person's most imperative concern is the security of the money he has worked so hard to earn. He goes to a bank to cosset this earning.

Core banking with digital proficiency provides high operational efficiency. But if by chance an ATM does not work when the consumer needs very quick service, there arises a total mismatch of the rational factor to consumer touch point. Digital codes alone cannot bring the intangible aspirational link with the bank. Relationships will always count in the banking business.

software services

Let's say you provide software coding services for your client's every technology need. Is there essentially any difference in the nature of the service you or your big and small competitors provide? Perhaps operational efficiency and size do matter. But does that give you the kind of premium that can be your intangible? Not really. Your current business is developed with either cost advantage or providing better manpower skills.

Can you develop a new dimension in coding, perhaps create a rational layer that your client may never have thought about? This extra will certainly improve your intangible value. You may need to invest in an innovation-led structure and team to work in parallel with the code writers. They can proactively ferret out some defect in the customer's brief which the customer has overlooked, and find ways to correct the defect. If you can make this a selling point, your deliverable will have a value that's much beyond your customer's expectation.

Through this initiative to uncover and set right a defect unknown to the customer, or by adding some other value, you are upgrading his business value. The customer did not expect it. This has become a precious intangible for you. Having invested in innovation, your profitability may be a little less for the short term. But you have strengthened your brand value. With such intangible brand value you can very soon charge a premium. Your organization need no longer depend on cost cutting to get operational efficiency.

Indian software development companies achieve operational efficiency through insensitive cost cutting and follow processes borrowed from foreign work cultures. That exposes them to attrition. The young generation trains in Indian companies, and then jumps to the international firms that fascinate them. Because GRCs have high brand value, the youngsters feel their careers here somehow have more worth. Indian software companies need to create the intangible in their brand. They will gain in reputation and premium value, impact global brand aspiration and reduce attrition levels.

I am not sure whether Indian IT companies think of intangibles in their delivery. They appear to me like enjoying the spring water of the huge worldwide demand for outsourced IT services. Whoever brings bigger and more containers can take more water. But when the spring dries up, what will they do? Wait with their containers.

The delicate nuances of the rational factor drive intangibles in business. When consumers and customers are more educated, their curiosity to understand the truth behind this hidden factor increases. When they perceive the built-up rational content, their comfort level rises, creating more intangibles for your organization.

Having had the opportunity to work for different companies across the world, I reiterate that my concerted effort has been to ensure that the companies and brands we help grow, persevere for the long term. In nearly 30 years since I've been in the profession, most of our work has sustained in the market. Many have created benchmarks in their categories. Companies in varied verticals we've consulted with have received remarkable growth, and their very crucial intangible aspects have been appropriated in different markets.

How and where in my creative business strategy have people connected so closely that our clients' businesses have sustained for the long term? Very curious to know, I sought answers among end consumers and B2B customers.

Our professional discipline involves delving into the psychological, sociological and historical aspects that surround different stakeholders. This association led me to closer interactions with philosophers, sociologists, anthropologists and historians in the European world. I wanted to figure out what that element could be which sustains in people's mind. With the help of these different professionals I discovered the subliminal aspect in every human being. This analysis of the subconscious took me back to 1925, the birth of Surrealism, the seminal exploration into new thought.

Surrealism actually illustrates nostalgia. Consciously you may not get involved quickly, but somehow it will work to connect to your subconscious. You may not be aware of an old subject, but surrealism provokes you to discover this nostalgia. The futuristic films of George Lucas and Steven Spielberg in the 1970s were replete with Surrealism established by visionary painters since 1925. An artist's observation is never mediocre unlike the general populace. The mass public does not generally get emotionally involved in futuristic advancement, which is the unknown. But the artist looks at the ordinary and gives it a gigantic thought and dimension. The West has very high regard for artists and their micro level involvement in society. Consequently, artistic expressions there have had awesome impact over several generations.

Such nuances have played an incomparable role in my attempt to understand different types of emotion people experience.

Surrealism intensified my in-depth search into emotion. I often remembered my mother's words from when I was a child. She insisted our economic poverty should not destroy our value of emotions. In fact, she said, poverty has its own strong emotion of how to drum up self-pressure to release yourself from poverty. Emotion is not for the affluent only. That truth is very visible in events like Lady Diana's death. Being royalty, affluent, and a celebrity, her fatal accident extracted from people across the world, intense emotion for a person defeated. But who cares for the thousands of people who die in similar conditions everywhere in the world? Obviously nobody but their own families.

Growing up in Western society from an impressionable age, I realized human beings have two types of emotion; one is futile and momentary, and the other, deep sustaining emotion.

Futile emotion is pure sentiment. In coping with any kind of difficult situation, a fragile mind can become very futile, and may respond with tears. This very basic emotion has no deeper value or sustainability. Exhibiting this emotion to another may evoke sympathy, or perhaps be seen as some deficiency or weakness, but it will not reach the other's deep sustaining emotion. This kind of volatile emotion is fragile. Such people are like the Yorkshire climate in England where it seems to rain throughout the year.

The other emotion of deeper meaning and profound substance is not fragile; it can sustain. This emotion is totally intangible and resides in the subconscious, not just in the conscious mind. Capturing this emotion to take proprietorship of it, I named the concept 'Emotional Surplus'.

The difference between emotion and Emotional Surplus can clearly be defined in every aspect of life. In the world of business that's only associated with the tangible rational, I found it important to mesh the Emotional Surplus thought with creative business strategy. When businessmen talk of adding emotion in HR projects, the thinking is clichéd and mathematical, more a formulated dictionary word. Only deep sustainable emotion can achieve the Emotional Surplus strategy that creates a value beyond the expectation of employees, consumers, customers and all other external stakeholders.

The private garden of Emotional Surplus is the outstanding blending of rational, functional and emotional attributes of business worth or human value (see Chapter 10 for details of measuring Emotional Surplus). This balanced blend makes business sustain, and shines the value of human character.

rational deflowering

How can rational attributes, so very critical in business, be made perceptible? Their hidden tangible dimension needs to get consumer appreciation as an intangible. This surely is a paradox. Only a Big Bang can absorb an ambiguity like this. The rational factor of business needs to be deflowered to bring it to maturity and fruition. This sensitive diaphragm touches the discerning nerve of consumers or customers. Let me take you through some of nature's habits of rational deflowering.

Deflowering of women has different rational parameters in diverse cultures. Being deflowered at an early age can be a matter of maturity in some cultures. In others, loss of virginity before social marriage is considered aggression that violates society's code of conduct. Sometimes both men and women are scared to enter the deflowering ceremony. Another unpalatable tackling of virginity is being given an ugly, unwanted souvenir like rape that mentally disturbs forever.

In certain societies, a woman deflowered gains in status of having achieved real womanhood. For women individually, this act is rational and tangible, with tremendous physical involvement. Deflowering, like most rational factors in this universe, is a hidden rational factor. Yet it's the intangible feelings post the breaking of the hymen that's of utmost consequence. After the event, the loss of the tissue is not a formidable outcome whatsoever.

In liberal societies, women are psychologically drawn to their first love in an unspoken attempt to be deflowered. It can even be a very clinical approach on 'how to make myself a woman.' Friends tease 16–17-year-old girls if they are still virgins. Among contemporary urban teenagers, virginity is old fashioned. So rational and tangible is the deflowering act in such societies that a virgin is almost considered abnormal. Seeing real proof of a broken hymen by curiously touching the blood with her three fingers spells satisfaction for these young women.

In conservative societies, deflowering is strongly consigned to the act of marriage alone. Here, the rational factor gets a score in a detective's report card. The only requirement is being able to provide physical proof of prior virginity. This practice prevails in British royalty too. Princess Diana had to undergo the virginity test as part of tradition before marrying the heir to the British Crown. In such a society, nobody gives credence to the woman's perspective, not even whether making love for the first time will scare or satisfy her.

In both these circumstances, the rational factor plays the life-size role. In a liberal society, a girl wants her personal glory of having already been deflowered. In a conservative society the man seeks the rational factor, that his wife has not been adulterated.

The genesis of human society is embedded in the rational factor. How and when procreation happens after deflowering is never really known. Making physical love is an action that's open to view, but the rational factor of procreation, the exact steps of sperm meeting egg, fertilization, and a baby growing in the womb, is physical yet hidden from sight. Generations start in a hidden way, as the exact moment cannot be recorded. Perhaps some high tech machine can record various activities, but it cannot really explain the mystery that is procreation.

A rose in a flower vase does not have rational characteristics. It is de-linked from the root, which would have provided it hidden strength to survive. The beauty of the rose in a vase is momentary. A rose growing in a garden has rational attributes.

Its beauty is longer lasting, and it will transform itself into seeds that dry and fall on the earth. From the seed the rose will pro-create its species.

In the same way, rational deflowering has to happen in business. The rational part of an organization, from every microtone angle, needs to deflower and impact every function. More par-ticularly, deflowering has to be perceptible in the functions of human resource, product development, manufacturing, market-ing and sales, and must happen continuously. The consumer must clearly understand and visibly see what hidden rational factors you have broken to bring consumer value. This is fundamental to establishing Emotional Surplus.

A child owes his strong bonding to his mother to rational fac-tors. Her ability to conceive, grow and sustain the baby in her body for nine months ingrains some intangibles in the child's subconscious mind, which sustains throughout his life. The father cannot replace this role of carrying the conception. His contrib-ution is providing the child with social recognition.

History says that Leonardo da Vinci was the illegitimate son born to a woman called Catarina. Being socially accepted and recognized with the da Vinci name was of such prime concern, that Leonardo took meticulous pain to hunt out the Florentine notary, Piaro da Vinci, whose unlawful son he was.

In today's world of business, all rational factors look very mas-culine. The future of business will seek subtlety and feminine traits in the rational factor, like deflowering and conceiving a child. These are not soft and easy qualities to imbibe. They re-quire immense tenacity, the ability to be steadfast against all odds, and to create with care and joy.

functional lick

The usage advantage of any system in our universe is its functional aspect (see Chapter 10 to understand the functional attribute which is usage advantage of any selling proposition). Usage needs smooth performance. In the business context a mechanical, digital or human physical process enables streamlined functioning. In the animal kingdom licking comprises performing various functional activities such as eating, drinking, repairing a wound, cleaning the newly born, testing the new and unknown. So a lick is a dexterous functional movement.

For human beings, licking starts as edible enjoyment. Mmmmm … that quick lick on the *jalebi* to savor a sugared trace on the tongue as it envelopes to become mouth-feel! From its birth, a child knows how to lick and suckle the mother's breast. This functional and vital activity of the child's first contact with the mother's breast ignites a deep sensitivity towards licking. From this nascent stage, the essence of the functional lick grows, grows and grows.

As the baby enters adulthood, its prediliction for licking takes on a new form. Intimate man-woman relationships can take licking to high ground hedonism. This sexual gratification of the lick distinguishes humans from animals. People attribute sensitive sexual prowess in enjoying a lick, whereas animals lick for pure functional purposes. Animals do not transfer any sexual connotations to licking the same female mammary organ that weaned them.

The female species experiences a unique functionality at childbirth that no male can even fathom. Giving birth, providing milk for the child's sustenance, nurturing the child's development in society are functional aspects. This complex relationship puts motherhood on a pedestal.

The functional lick in organizations is a dimension beyond the mechanical. While following a routine, the quality of an enjoyable lick can deteriorate, making it dull, flat, without action points, mundane or laborious. The *raison d'être* of society, and every improvement in it, has historically come from functional deployment. Whether it is in medicine, engineering, architecture, consuming products, music, cinema, entertainment, communication, technology or services, it is the functional lick that people have enjoyed, and that has given recognition to these functions.

As an organization if you want to give functional content a desirable rather than a routine character, you have to think about sensitive ergonomics. This is the psychological and physiological blend of a product or service. By closely refining the ergonomic blend, you will quickly reach your consumer's desire level.

utility product

In a utility product like a teacup, the handle is functional; its tangible benefit is to enable holding the cup. Buying a pair of shoes, you first check how smoothly you can walk in them. The shoes may be beautiful, adorning the signature of a famous designer, you may be very rich, but its unlikely you will ever pay even $10 unless you have tested both feet for walking comfort. Men and women not used to buying expensive dresses will not shop the same way for undergarments. For personal comfort they will definitely spend considerably more.

We easily recognize functional improvement in any product or service. With higher economic development and competition, functional benefit will provide the only differentiating factor.

Let's look at diverse functional areas. In an automobile, usage advantage can be tested through the steering, brake, clutch, accelerator, key, door handle, the door itself, foot board, wipers, internal and external lighting systems and seating comfort. In a refrigerator, the first consumer touch point is the handle that opens the door. Then comes inside packaging for storage, and the door itself. The bottle cap is the most important function in branded water bottles. The consumer's confidence in the water's purity entirely depends on whether the cap can be tampered with. A woman's purse or man's handbag must have many compartments to segregate different important need items.

How to comfortably grip a knife and fork to eat with, whether the knife cuts the food properly or the fork is sharp enough to pierce the food are important functional benefits. How easily can a mobile telephone send SMS, take pictures, send or receive mail? These are just a few examples of functional benefit as usage advantage. These touch points can mechanically respond to needs. Or they can be made so very desirable that they overcome their mechanical aspect.

Using a sense of ergonomics that covers psychological and physiological aspects, product functionality can be taken beyond the consumer's need level. People can have subtle and micro dimensions of a physical nature when touching a product. If a product's character is cold, check to see whether people want first contact with coldness. A metallic wrist-watch bracelet for men may be made to look heavy and masculine, but a man may not want a cold first feel. Being metal how can it be warm? A refrigerator ought to be cold inside, but nobody wants to touch coldness outside. Similarly most people don't like to touch a tap in the bathroom as a cold mechanical device. Women use cold cream for facial treatment, but they wouldn't like to touch a container that is stone cold. People's connection with the functional lick of products has such psychological characteristics.

Physiological aspects are more movement driven: a chair in a car, in front of a computer or a dressing table, in a plane for a long or short journey, in the garden, in a tractor or train, all have very different dimensions related to the human character. There is a very big physiological difference in designing a chair for moving transport or for static surface use. Fatigue grows slowly in a moving transport chair. The character of fatigue is very different at the beginning stage of travel, to the mid-stage and the last lap of the journey. Providing physiologic value to the consumer requires microtone sensitivity. Tomorrow's long journey chair needs to incorporate a continuous fatigue reduction system.

Static sitting conditions also have their own physiologic character. A static seating system must facilitate free user movement. The working table chair requires microtone physiology as continuous sitting in say, an assembly line with a repetitive process, causes fatigue in the mind.

Lets' say a convoy is moving at a certain speed and the perfection of a worker's ability to execute is recorded in a scoring barometer in front of him. Here both psychological and physiologic factors come into play. If the worker's appraisal is based on this online production quality, his stress level would be very high. So the chair he uses should specifically and continuously reduce his mental and physical stress. The assembly line is a robotic system. You may need to provide some human consideration of reducing the worker's effort through available ergonomic means. This is doubly important as his touch cannot be homogeneous throughout his work, and yet he must deliver a consumer sensitive product.

You spend a great deal of money to modernize your production line. Have you given thought to investing in another production requirement, that of human workmanship, how to reduce effort and increase comfort? In doing so, you add value to your product.

India has not started addressing these microtone functional sensitivities in the product. We address only what market pressure demands. Upgrading functional benefit through ergonomic attention can significantly change India's manufacturing strength, converting mundane functionality into a desirable functional lick.

The European art of product functionality envelopes a deeper sense of licking; the Japanese incredibly more so. In India a warm reception is with a cup of tea. If the tea is piping hot, your pleasurable sip is destroyed when you burn your lip. This does not connect to an intimate licking experience.

edible product

Deeply rooted social tradition changes from country to country. It conditions the sensorial and psychological approach with hyper functionality. Edible products are propelled by these sensorial, psychological and social acts. The aroma and taste of French cheese is deliciously charming for me. Accompanying my French-born son to delighting in French gastronomy, I acquired the taste for mature cheese, which my fellow Indians find detestable. Similarly our south Indian *sambar* is disliked in parts of the West where its unique flavor is not understood.

Today's new global culture absorbs influences of different traditional cultures. Indians or Chinese may find nothing exceptional in a hamburger. But the aura Americans have woven around fast food creating 'one world' that such social aspects outweigh the actual taste of the burger. Cultural manifestation can change the edible enjoyment of a dish, making it acquire a higher dimension, endowing it a more pleasurable functional lick. The hamburger's happy entry into France, the land of gastronomy connoisseurs with better control over the licking enjoyment, demonstrates how a global culture is building up.

Society has evolved in economic terms by co-opting functional usage. We are totally conditioned to search for better and better functional systems to rise above the obsolete. The more usage advantages we can find, the better we enjoy the functional lick. We certainly do that when biting into a *jalebi*.

You have experienced the *jalebi's* versatility in its different senses, nuances and connotations. In its variety the *jalebi* embodies a universe like no other, and makes a better bite through an exciting lick.

emotional shock

Our first emotional shock is getting yanked out of the womb to be born into the world. A mother's physical struggle with the labor pains of childbirth is not as excruciating as her mental anxiety. Will her baby be intact in all senses and form? Her experiencing childbirth, after conception, nine months of carrying, and readying herself for weaning, forms the rational factor. Her nurturing the baby in society is the functional factor. As the baby becomes a child, adolescent and adult, the Emotional Surplus relationship both mother and child enjoy transcends to a value beyond expectation. This emotional factor can rarely be changed.

Organizations normally associate the word emotion with advertising activities, which is very wrong. Emotion that sustains, not fragile emotion, should have power over an organization's culture, beginning from its grassroots. Just like a mother's emotion through procreation, organizational culture must ingrain emotion at every instance. High emotional content must be reflected in its deliverables every time to gain consumer proximity. This emotion can sustain only after proving rational and functional factors in a perceptible manner.

Having survived so many epochs without changing its core value in the many countries it is popular in, the *jalebi* has proved that it is endowed with Emotional Surplus value.

Emotional bonding must have a relevant factor in end delivery. An organization's unnecessary insistence on paternalistic family-like culture does not build sustainable emotion, nor does a fat salary check do that. An employee who spends the better part of his waking hours in his workplace needs high excitement and sustained emotion to keep his spirits and motivation up for productive delivery. Creating that sustaining emotion is tomorrow's organizational challenge. You cannot rely on sexy advertising, public relations, product or service imagery to sustain emotion. It comes from a delivery principle that has superior blending of its rational, functional and emotional attributes.

A brainless, emotionless robotic system can work unfailingly in a given system if all parameters are perfect. But people are never devoid of emotion. So in business, emotion has to be streamlined and managed.

I have defined a framework comprising the employee's attitude, behavior, action and delivery mechanism through which organizational emotional character can emerge. Attitude and behavior are decisive in bringing value to an action. This leads to high value delivery. When happenings in the external world arouse an organization's curiosity, when it observes society very keenly to action various opportunities, the organization can compete in a global perspective.

Wearisome routine amounts to a boring life in conjugal relationships, resulting in divorce. Lackluster work that becomes mind-numbing in organizations can also culminate in divorce-like attrition and souring of professional tie-ups. Unexciting activities kill emotion. They paralyze organizations into becoming monotonous stereotypes. More dangerously, the humdrum negatively impacts the channel and consumer's hand, resulting in low sales and lower share price.

Western society, post the two World Wars and anti Semite Nazi tortures, had struggled to rebuild its ravaged nation states. Several innovations have erupted from its survival tactics. This innovative character has somehow filtered into the blood of its young generation. But today, after more than half a century, young people in the West are inclined towards leisure. Their span of attention in any subject is low. Unlike the older generation for whom a job was life's central theme, youngsters don't consider legacy as an iconic character to follow.

India's youth scene

Unlike in the West, the Indian sub-continent did not face horrific, large scale, life-threatening violence. Our immediate past of following non-violence has given our young people a mild non-aggressive attitude.

ZAP 86

Indians born after 1986 comprise the future generation that can really understand and compete in a global economy. I call them the ZAP 86 generation. In 1991 when India's economic reforms were introduced, this age-group had reached the age of five. When you are five your consciousness is decisive, you have no past to remember, so you have no bias towards it. This age group does not value old Indian habits like sacrificing for savings, sacrificing for different aspects in the social, political or the working environment. They rebel against domination by elders. Not being submissive, they cannot understand why thoughts of sex should be suppressed. The security of a government job appears very boring to them.

Like zapping TV channels, ZAP 86 is the zapping crowd interested in everything, making all purchase decisions in every home and always looking for choice. With no inhibition from the pre-liberalized economy, no mental baggage whatsoever, they function in a new paradigm driven by the speed of technology, code language, egotism, global thought and knowledge, sexual liberation, flirtation with jobs. ZAP 86 is the strong visionary generation of tomorrow's India.

Being born before 1986 means harboring a compromised mentality. These people carry two kinds of baggage: pre- and post-liberalization outlook. In most Indian organizations, the majority of the middle and top managements have such a mentality of finding the middle ground. A 45–50-year-old senior manager clearly sees the difference between his and his own 20–25-year-old children's lives. But he does not realize he is living in the cusp of society's transition. He even talks about his life with his children like a story to others.

India's young people are not aggressive like their western counterparts. A subtle emotion gaining prominence with them is silent action. They seem to have tremendous admiration for the mystique. They love to get involved in proven true value; in minimalist under-statement but that must be perceptible to others. This generation is as well informed, and becoming as impatient as youngsters in the West. Organizations need to incline towards this restrained emotional attitude that's whirling in the melting pot of tomorrow's society.

To appropriately address this trend, your organization needs to create a very contrary emotional shock factor that will attract young talent and retain them. The principal aim of working professionals in the age group of 20–27 years is to acquire elaborate knowledge. They evaluate organizations on their ability to increase their market value with intricate and advanced skills. Working in developed countries or with GRCs possessing international brand value is still a big draw for Indian students. In time, when Indian thinking at university campuses becomes more global, this young generation with low attention span like their international brethren will avoid organizations that make them feel bored and unchallenged.

The more you bring your organizational attitude towards society's cauldron that's cooking sociocultural, economic and trend ingredients, the more subtly will your attitude be reflected in your delivery.

High drama is happening in the social cooking pot in areas unrelated to your business, in the media, the world of entertainment. You will get a strategic orientation towards the young consumer profile when you understand this hotch-potch brew. You won't become obsolete within a short period and your recruitment will stay contemporary.

Youth focus is not just to attract them as consumers. You need to be inspired by today's influencers of society to carve organizational culture and delivery accordingly.

I have been ripened in French and Western culture since 1973. So when, on May 12, 1990, I rediscovered the *jalebi* in Paris, you can imagine my delight. This time not overly sweetened in an Algerian street corner shop, but in sophisticated French zone.

To entertain a new client from Sweden in Paris, I chose a restaurant on the right bank, in Paris 8th district that I was still not very familiar with. Most of the haute couture fashion houses are just behind this restaurant, very close to the spot where Lady Diana had her fatal accident. In this Lasserre, I discovered one needed to reserve a table way in advance restaurant. But my fantastic assistant, Caroline, could do the impossible to help me take business forward. She managed the lunch table without advance reservation.

As we drove up Lasserre's independent house with two floors, we felt special even before reaching our table. People from the restaurant attended to us from the moment we stepped off the car, up to the ground floor, and then through the lift till we reached the first floor. The ground floor comprised the reception with a special room for private dinner. In a cage were a few doves. The ceiling was a fresco painted by an artist. After being seated, as the weather was good, the roof suddenly opened up to reveal the blue sky. This was a totally unexpected gesture. It's an example of a traditional French establishment indulging you with a difference in a cozy, sophisticated restaurant.

The *maitre* Monsieur Luis, greeted us cordially. Before taking the order he asked if I was a member of Lasserre. This enquiry in front of my new client offended me, but his hospitality and respectful salute prevented me from making a fuss. After some time, the garrulous wine taster arrived. Helping us select the right wine, he asked the same question. This time my voice was strong and unhappy as I said, 'No!' In anger I called the *maitre-d'hotel* to say I felt insulted. 'I may not be a member, but I have my reservation. So why ask this stupid question? I will never return to your restaurant!'

Suddenly, curiosity overtook me. 'Anyhow, tell me about your membership norms.' He replied that an existing Lasserre member has to acknowledge a new applicant. I waved away the possibility of my asking such a favor from anyone: 'I have connections to the *crème-de-la-creme* of French society and aristocracy, but not to approach for a restaurant membership!' I smirked.

My Swedish client was enjoying this engrossed interaction. It was her new learning on French establishment culture. The *maitre d'* was quite embarrassed now, and I too tried to let the situation move on. As in fine French dining, course after course of delicately stylized food was served accompanied by exquisite wine, each intercepted with ice sherbet. The restaurant was totally full.

Unexpectedly, on an adjacent table I noticed a waiter bring a beautiful dessert. It was a fine *jalebi* topping a mouth-watering dome of strawberry and cream filling in a cookie based tart. I was extraordinarily excited. I called the *maitre*, and ordered the same dessert. It was called '*Timbale d' Elysees*' he informed me. From the top it looked like a cage. When you lightly break into it, a luscious combined taste of strawberry, cream, biscuit and *jalebi* jostles for attention in each mouthful. I animatedly narrated my love for *jalebi*s to the *maitre*. 'This is a delicate version of the original,' I confided in him. The *jalebi* conversation took our dealings to the next higher level. He explained that the lace netting was caramel, and I confessed this was for me the quintessence of a French *jalebi*.

Our over-sensitive relationship became amiable and good humored by the end of lunch. He came nearer with a plateau tray and offered my client a miniature porcelain casserole. It seems Lasserre identifies its fine dining proficiency with the traditional casserole. Their special two-inch casserole gift to their women guests embodies this expertise. He also volunteered to make me a '*membre de casserole Lasserre,*' that is, Lasserre Casserole Member on my next visit. He declared he will arrange member acknowledgement without my making any request to anyone.

The next day I received a letter of apology from him in my office, and a formal offer of membership. The next time I wanted to visit the restaurant, we got the reservation within 48 hours. On arrival, the *maitre* presented me my membership token, a tiny, watch-sized stainless steel casserole with a handle. Its cover had threads so it could be tightly closed. My membership number was engraved at the back. The *maitre d'* discreetly gave me a glance of the membership list where at No. 1 spot was the name of the French President.

The *jalebi* gave me the opportunity to become a member of the French establishment. The emotional shock and then the connect between the *maitre d'hotel* and myself started from our *jalebi* conversation.

Different rational, functional and emotional parameters surround you, your family, your neighbor and society at large. Your organization can drive Emotional Surplus strategy when you sensitively comprehend people in society across the globe. Deploying the Emotional Surplus framework in your work culture and processes will help your business take a leap advantage.

her subconscious choice is multidimensional, not statistics

A statistical barometer can measure any given data to get a mathematical output. But a mathematical output cannot be used for visioning without understanding the subconscious mind of women. It's a well-researched fact that women in every country have an attraction, even an obsession, for buying. They are adept at shopping for men's personal products too. Unfortunately, the world of business being largely a masculine domain, the subtle subliminal dimensions of women remain unidentified in most industries.

Across the world, the psychological aspect is more pronounced in women who are the real consumers in any domain. It's very important to understand their psychological diaspora to run your business, even though it may be a very masculine, B2B business. Co-opting the characteristics of women can help you approach your consumer with subtlety and sensitivity, resulting in enhancing your business worth.

In parallel, I find the predominant attributes of women that need to be incorporated into business lattice very well with the *jalebi*'s traits that are invaluable in business. What are these attributes of women that can sway and control?

- Nurturing
- Lover of intangibles
- Patience
- Aesthetics

- Unlimited orgasm
- Subtlety
- Exuberance
- Networking
- Mystique

Don't you think you need such features for an organization's growth, profit and increase in share value? Check out their hidden value, and see how they become relevant for business success. Check out how closely these attributes mesh with the *jalebi* as well.

According to me, these attributes of women that I have identified are the unarticulated answers to business success. Your business may be missing these dimensions that address the subconscious of your consumer or customer.

nurturing

By nature, women are caring. Motherhood is associated with affection. A mother's nurturing practice links her to the experience of harmony. In business, you need to nurture your consumers in the same way to prevent them from going to others. Your people and partners need nurturing to deliver high quality in every aspect of their deliverables. Shareholders need continuous care as well. Nurturing must be a top management obsession to run a harmonious organization.

The *jalebi*'s value of nurturing is the healthy fermented nature of its dough which keeps you in the pink.

lover of intangibles

Creating the intangible in your business proposition will help get good talent, retain employees for the long-term, clinch better value from external partners, earn premiumness, better share value and market capitalization. The result is goodwill which totally connects to a woman's character as a lover of intangibles.

Women love intangibles. The way they appreciate a flower is at a high mental level. Men often use flowers to open the door of their relationships with women. In any function that welcomes guests with flowers, a woman will carefully keep the flower, whereas a man will carelessly leave it behind somewhere. The billion dollar perfume business is totally targeted at women. The price of a good perfume is beyond any justification of its manufacturing cost. Women can appreciate and absorb the intangible, evaporating value of perfumes, and are willing to pay for it.

Remembering a *jalebi*, or longing for one, is its intangible.

patience

Even as your organization is active and speedy, it needs to have extreme patience in all respects to better understand the latent trend and the market's microtone dimension. Otherwise you will not be able to capture tomorrow like a woman does. Patience does not mean slowing business down. Patience here is a consideration given to better understand the subject and internalize it. If women didn't have patience, they could not have carried a baby to fruition for nine months. They even accept and enjoy the physical pain of childbirth as control over the genesis of new life.

You can't hurry up a *jalebi* either. Until the fermentation process is complete, you cannot give birth to a real *jalebi*.

aesthetics

Women's consciousness about aesthetics starts from their physical structure. Harmonious anatomical construction gives a distinctive, soft character to her whole body, expressing sentimentality.

A man's body is very muscular, not sensitive. A woman can genu-inely admire another woman's nude body; but men in general don't like to see another nude man. Homosexuals, of course, are an exception.

Look at how women grew their profound sense of aesthet-ics along with civilization. They have always aesthetically orna-mented themselves to portray a pictorial image. They use color on the lips, draw a line on the eye, wear a chain around the neck, rings in the ear, bangles in the hand, high heeled shoes on their feet. These external elements add to a woman's beauty, making the female species the inheritor of the culture of aesthetics.

The *jalebi* has its own aesthetics, and differentiates itself from any other dessert. Its aesthetics is so profound that different bites give you diverse feelings of pleasure.

This aesthetic palette is very important for your organization. Your product or service must connect high class aesthetics in its very first contact or delivery to consumers or customers. Today sculpting aesthetics in any product or service deliverable has become a key differentiator. Aesthetics begins from the door that opens your office, and percolates to every aspect of action, tran-saction and space. The employee must be conditioned with un-conditional aesthetics. This will help avoid any dissonance in the organization's delivery to customers, and increase the employee's brand value among his colleagues.

An aesthetic working environment reduces monotony and rou-tine, and at the same time induces people to behave in a comple-mentary aesthetic manner. Employees coming from backgrounds not used to a sophisticated milieu can tend to get intimidated by high aesthetics alone. So a distinctive workplace rather than high aesthetics can help drive the employee to respect his surroundings and change his mentality towards aesthetics.

Aesthetics must address the entire value chain, beginning from back office activities to the front. Women pay ritualistic attention to their personal grooming. They are ready to spend great sums of money on lingerie, making sure their intimate wear is beautiful, perfect in fit and comfort, although it is not publicly seen. Maintaining an organization like sophisticated women's lingerie can improve its productivity and quality, and inculcate aesthetics in the work culture.

unlimited orgasm

Women's orgasm is known to be very subliminal and unlimited, whereas for men the climax of sexual pleasure is physical and momentary. The orgasmic character of your organization's delivery should relate to the continuous pleasure consumers can experience. Psychologically and in the social context, consumers go through their daily routine life (see Figure 9.1) which can fall towards daily economic crisis, health problem, work tension, family stress, social pressure, and general depression.

Figure 9.1   paradox of consumer mind

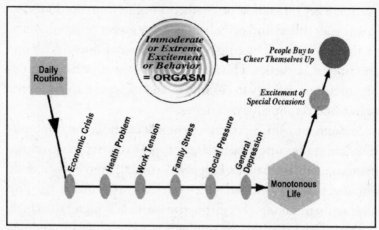

To overcome their daily woes, people spend to celebrate social occasions like festivals and anniversaries. There is another quite peculiar buying characteristic. People, particularly women, buy to cheer themselves up. It can happen at any moment, and it can transform itself into immoderate or extreme excitement, behavior just like an orgasm. Your organization should provoke this unlimited orgasmic character to get the best out of the employees or partners. You can excite your consumers and the channel by making your deliverables always orgasmic so they never stop buying from you.

In my childhood I remember *jalebi* was served in a big sal leaf made into a cone. You can get carried away in the pleasure of its bite, and eat *jalebi* after *jalebi* without stopping yourself. When biting into a *jalebi* you have to control yourself to stop the over-eating.

subtlety

Subtlety is a very female characteristic; men are on the face. It is the man who normally declares love or proposes marriage. The woman replies, 'I love you, too' or 'Yes, I will.' In critical situations men become violent either physically or with sarcasm. Women's softer handling of issues can result in tears or subtle understanding, which can ultimately win the game for her. Mothers cool down seemingly unsolvable father–child relationships with love, understanding and great subtlety.

Women can tantalize with subtle physical gestures. A European woman reveals her shapely legs by wearing frosted stockings or a garter. An Indian woman's sari covers her whole body, save that wee bit of a provocative belly that evokes subtle sensuality. Subtly revealing that little belly with a short top over trousers has become an international cult today. The cosmetics and color cosmetics industries are booming because women from all countries are giving shape to their faces.

A roadside *jalebi* in India or a *jalebi* in a North African sweet shop in Paris may not have subtlety, being bright in color and too sweet. But I was pleasantly surprised to enjoy tiny *jalebi*s of very light color, less sugary yet very crunchy in the home of a sophisticated friend in India. This proved to me that even in today's calorie conscious society, the *jalebi* can be subtle and delicious. The *jalebi* has this elasticity to meet a subtle requirement that's so essential in business relationships.

In the clutter of today's media, subtlety in business is very important. Screaming advertisements may get quick jerky sales, but the moment advertisements stop, you'll find those brands are not moving in the market. This means the brand has become a slave of advertising with no subtle value of the product. An organization has numerous subtle human aspects such as the difference between different people's intellectual capability, consistency in work, the leadership method or strength of teamwork. Creating passion and involvement for a common objective or operational goal needs subtle handling as also flowing a single consistent message across the organization. If you are managing these in a very statistical manner, you are negatively affecting the sensitivity of your people. You need to portray a woman's subtlety to implement the organization's culture to move forward harmoniously. This can give a valuable subtle character to all your deliverables.

Subtlety is also paradoxical. A loud devouring character can also carry a depth of profound values that's highly elevated. When you compare Bjorn Borg and John McEnroe, both are very good players, but Bjorn's subtlety may have made him the universal icon of tennis. Beckenbower and Maradona were both great players, but Beckenbower's subtlety puts him in a higher elevation in public esteem. If you compare German and Italian cars, the Italian car may be very flashy, but the German car's subtlety with high efficiency will win it consumer confidence.

exuberance

Somehow women by nature are exuberant, both in liberal and traditional societies. This exuberance always makes them good looking, giving them a better glow than the ordinary man. Women are careful about their appearance in every context, whether it is to open the door for a family guest or to appear in a social event. Nobody can challenge the implicit knowledge and stamina women have to create a difference for themselves. This energetic quality holds up in all cultures, religions, and social climates that women appear in.

By its very character and nature, if you put a *jalebi* on the dining table and compare its swirling, glistening visual enchantment to any dessert, its intrinsic character of exuberance will win hands down.

To increase the salience of your organization or brand you need exuberance as its focus. But exuberance has to have real cause. Richard Branson, Chairman of Virgin, displays exuberant coherence and tremendous interconnection between his personality and his business. Mont Blanc pen exuberantly exhibits the snowflake symbol so it's visible on a man's shirt pocket, but the pen has a very subtle character. Subtlety and exuberance are two perceptible platform faces of the same coin. To use them in your business, you need to find the right trade-off that will enable business to fly.

John Lennon and Yoko Ono's nude exhibition like Adam and Eve in their first album of *avant-garde* music called *Two Virgins* had the profound message of love and peace. John wanted to exuberantly share his obsessive love for Yoko by posing in the nude. His defense to the uproar of criticism this evoked was, 'The main hangup in the world today is hypocrisy and insecurity.... Being ourselves is what's important. If everyone practiced being themselves instead of pretending to be what they aren't, there would be peace.'

networking

Women of all economic strata are past masters at maintaining long-time relationships among family, friends, and even with friends of their children. They create and nurture networks in different subjects and keep them alive for no particular reason and with no ulterior motive. They come forward and enjoy participating in all kinds of social links, unlike men who network only if they need something out of that relationship.

The physical character of the *jalebi* is the spider's networked web. This is a dessert which has the capability, particularly in India, to connect a billion people. Everybody in India will know a *jalebi*. Inherently, a *jalebi* has for several centuries linked different regions and cultures, languages and religions in India.

Business needs tremendous networking too, as it is relevant in all circumstances. Whether it is the old boys' network of school and college friends, the industry associations, social organizations like the Rotary and Lions clubs, temple, church, or health club groups, if you can maintain your networking, you will find them useful for successfully carrying out different activities for your business.

If your organization is a conglomerate, you may find that employee rotation from one business to another is not so easy. Continuous networking inside the different business divisions of your organization is essential to facilitate job rotation as part of human resource management. When talent circulates inside the group companies you prevent attrition and satisfy the career aspirations of your employees. The corporate office of a diverse conglomerate needs to find time from operational pressures for networking among the human capital.

Why is networking a corporate concern? Because a vendor could be your consumer, a consumer or employee could be your shareholder. A women's dexterity in networking can be emulated to keep all stakeholders in the loop and keep you in their top of mind. To keep all systems active and running smoothly, the organization's networking skills has become a priority subject in today's business economy.

mystique

An air of mystery is the shell that envelops a woman. Just look at her accessories, each of which is selected carefully for an individual occasion, and connect with her desire to exhibit a certain aura for that instance. Her subtlety, her inscrutable subliminal need is her mystique. When women dress fashionably, their enigmatic attraction increases. Why do women create such allure? In any country a woman protects her inherent character of mystique as it gives her the power to control her destiny.

Your tongue touching a *jalebi* reveals one of its many aspects. This mystique is relevant when you bite your teeth into the sweet to get another taste. The taste has an aura that grabs you unexpectedly. The crunchiness of the *jalebi*, inspite of being in liquid syrup, is also its mystique. When you swallow it, the after-taste you experience is a pleasure of profound mystique that any organization will covet.

When organizational deliverables connect with the power of the mystique, intangible goodwill is created. Nurturing the mystique value reflects as premiumness which enhances shareholder value and profitability.

When your product or service loses its mystique value, your brand becomes generic. A brand's continuous usage in the consumer's hand can make it boring, or a habit could perhaps paralyze it. Arrival of new offerings in the market can make the brand even more mind-numbing and monotonous.

It is necessary to continuously protect a brand's mystique character, which essentially is its real goodwill. After plenty of usage, the brand mystique should intensify: the more its mystique, the more powerful will the brand become.

A certain school of marketing professionals work only in a statistical marketing process. Not understanding the psychological aspect of consumers, they kill the microtone mystique character of a brand. I call this 'justified marketing.' By nature when justification is the order of the day, consumer value loses out. Like answering a high school examination paper, if market pressure makes you justify the number of consumer benefits your brand offers over your competitors, there is a chance the brand's intrinsic value may be demystified.

Not every marketing professional may have the caliber to write product or service benefits incorporating an element of mystique. Such a marketer would do well to take help from a sociologist, doctor, psychologist, writer or singer, professionals who are more related to the human touch on an everyday basis. They will help find a path of mystique for your brand articulation.

A marketer should approach his work like a Western music conductor. A symphony orchestra conductor has to direct a variety of musical maestros playing different instruments in different scales to converge to a high tonal quality of musical harmony. Marketing and product development professionals cannot be unidirectional professionals like a soloist. They must become the conductor who creates, harbors and protects the brand's mystique dimension.

The nine characteristics of women: Nurturing, Lover of intangibles, Patience, Aesthetics, Unlimited orgasm, Subtlety, Exuberance, Networking, and Mystique are indispensable for today's organizational culture and action. These nine characteristics are connected to the consumer's psychological aspect, organizational culture or partner handling aspect. If you look at them independently and in a dispassionate way, they are more important than any initiative or process a company takes.

Delicate, subtle and unstated desires hide behind a woman's logical mind. In most purchases women are decision makers or influencers that sway decisions. Multiple dimensions including subconscious ones are factored into their choice, none of which are statistics driven.

Too many statistics and existing facts and data become the bane of an organization, an abscess that immobilizes action. Before women become your consumer it would be interesting to understand and deploy the inherent qualities of women into the organization culture. **It has now become very crucial to get a deeper understanding of women's characteristics in different societies of the world to take a strategic action for business growth.**

A woman's psychological paradigm is very fragile. Any kind of depression in society or in the family, a monotonous life, tension and stress, all can impact a purchase decision. Currently only health books and women's magazines talk about women's pre and post menstrual tension (PMT). Management circles can learn to talk about it and factor it in their operations scheme. This uniform monthly period has a big impact on women's desire level and spending. Menstruation is openly dealt with by sanitary pad manufacturing companies, and by pharmaceutical companies as their domain of business. In actual fact PMT's influence is very far reaching and mental. Sales of every other product are impacted on how the woman feels on those three to four days in the month. If you statistically analyze you may find women illogically spend more money at this time. This is by default. Has any organization taken into account this microtone aspect of consumers buying at PMT time?

The male species may be appropriate to maintain organizational processes for different kinds of work, in particular where physical strength is necessary. But if the total organizational system becomes masculine, it loses appreciation of the fragile subconscious choice of women at large and their spending habit.

women have influenced manufacturers to acquire multidimensional discipline

Traditionally, different products like the camera, television, computer and kitchen equipment were businesses of different competencies. Responding to a woman's subconscious choice, the compartmentalized outlook of manufacturing companies has been derailed as the user is the same person. Because of the home-maker's choice, a single manufacturing company has entered the total ecology of her home.

Of the identified psycho-socio factors that will drive tomorrow's business, behavior is quite assessable, but what about reckoning the mind? This varies (see Figure 9.2) from nation to nation, geography to geography, culture to culture, language to language, religion to religion, economic class to economic class, among political environments, different age groups, social and family environment, and is dependent on the self-confidence individuals have. If we have a population of say 6.5 billion people in the planet, upfront we can say there are 6.5 billion psychological strains to deal with. The accumulation of these strains comprises multidimensional consumer sensitivity.

Figure 9.2 pyramid of factors affecting human psychology

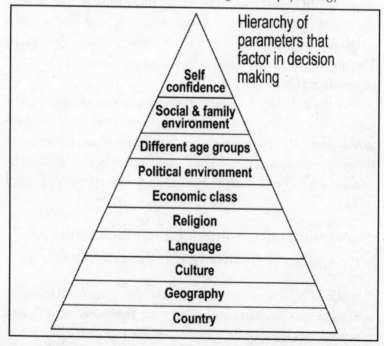

No management process has to date found a mechanism of how to understand and capture the multidimensional psychological content of the human race.

Want to discover this multidimensional psychological content? iPod is a perfect example of a multidimensional product. Put it on the table (see Table 9.1). Ask 20 people who may or may not possess an iPod, but who know the product, to surround the table and independently write down what the iPod is. You will find the 20 answers to be very different. People will note various perceptible features or qualities of the iPod depending on their experience, hearsay or assessment of the product. To further questions like what is their quality perception of iPod, the necessity of the product or its benefits, the answers will again vary widely. This simple exercise will reveal the multidimensional qualities of both the product and its perception by users and non-users.

Table 9.1   a matrix to analyze multidimensional customer sensitivity

Feedback from 5 people who know iPod, whether they own it or not				
iPod User	Understanding of the product	Quality perception	Need	Benefits & psychological involvement
Non-user	Small entertaining device in the pocket	Amazing music quality	Yes	Mental relaxation
Non-user	Smart & sleek technology	Defines quality	Yes	Instant solution for time pass
User	Compact innovative musical relief	Unbeatable sound	Yes	Multi-purpose entertainment
Non-user	Sleek music device	Good	Yes	Own music for own moments
User	Mobile companion	Good sound	Yes	Mobile entertainment whilealone

As the technology revolution escalates, people's sensitivity is intensifying. Our understanding of products and our psychological involvement in them have increased conspicuously from what it was 15–20 years ago. The diverse ways we approach a product or service to extract individual benefits is growing like elastic. Our collective perception of quality has severely augmented, but when it comes to choice, it's an individual who selects. Multidimensional psychological involvement encompasses the choice of tomorrow's consumers.

The primary requirement of any innovation center must be the invaluable knowledge of people's psychological dimension. Being tremendously sensitive to consumers will result in sustainable innovation. You may be serving your B2B customer, but your customer's end consumer will be very involved with the psychological paradigm.

In general, innovation centers employ technologists, engineers or scientists, but never consider recruiting psychologists or sociologists. The total absence of psychology or sociology from an innovation makes it take on a technical shape without human sensitivity. This results in technology-based products, which then become generic. If the innovation environment considers the cognitive and societal ramifications, the innovation can gain in differentiation and in capability to earn premium and sustain.

Sophisticated management theories to win against the competition are driven by numbers. Using modern technology, logic and mathematical matrix, they conjecture on given facts of the past. This is diametrically opposed to human development where intellectual facets grow at an individual level. Observing the market through standard statistics can generate enough data to paralyze an organization or create an abscess in a business segment. In a given activity sector, all competitors watch the market in this same angle. While losing the microtonal layers of the psyche, they end up dabbling in business mediocrity with most products and services looking alike.

Benchmarking with statistics is a global business process. At a local level, it bypasses the consumers' psychological facets. Business leaders featuring in *Fortune* 500 global companies who have good articulation skills and can number crunch often get accolades for their company's power, size, and business results. But if you ask these particular leaders what is the emotional level at which their product or service connects to the masses, will they be able to answer? They may score only with power and size.

In today's globalized temperature, industries are missing the microtonal dimension of curiosity. The curiosity level has to grow in a new breadth to engulf different societies and cultures that comprise of people from countries of a billion and million people. In this respect, since the end of the 1980s, sophisticated developed countries are becoming mediocre. Their curiosity level was high earlier, but that was adequate for countries populated by the millions. Curiosity now has to contour the billion population countries. In the business perspective, the curiosity of developing countries was always very low. That has to change and grow severely.

If I say COA (see Figure 9.3), what would your response be? You may perhaps try to check management books to see if the acronym exists. Should you have the patience, COA's power will unfold here. You'll discover it makes you penetrate people's multidimensional psychological traits.

Figure 9.3 curiosity, observation, and action

C is curiosity, O is observation, and A is action. Curiosity underpinned with self-discipline will lead to understanding the subconscious mind-frame of people. Curiosity has both negative and positive angles. You may be curious to understand human psychology with an unconstructive frame of mind, or in an upbeat stance. What you really need to discover is how to blend people's varied understanding, involve their emotions and confidence, and use this information to create strategy for quantum business growth opportunities.

If yours is a pessimistic outlook, your curiosity will swerve towards the negative. In my COA definition, when curiosity is innocent, it's possible to feel something totally new and fresh. An organization can take the initiative of running curiosity as an internal business process project. This experience can transform the business paradigm, making it quite vibrant.

You can measure your curiosity scale by checking how many businesses you have watched per year that were unrelated to yours and what incredible essence you have extracted from them. Such curiosity will impact the intensity of your watching, making it considerably different from any quantitative data, as well as different from how your competitors survey the market. Curiosity will drive you to infiltrate your consumer's psychological reckoning and improve your observation quality.

In today's business milieu, it's your unique observation quality that can give you a new dimension of profitable business. To make your business global, premium, and oriented towards quantum profit and growth, you have to imbibe the inventor's way of thinking. At the beginning of the last century inventors took into account people's unarticulated frustrations to create a new dimension of life that would benefit people either with more comfort or pleasure. Look at tomorrow's business in this way.

As market mediocrity is on the rise, in-depth curiosity and deeper observation will structure your mind to take up action powerfully. High quality curiosity and observation of the consumer's psychological area will create an unparalleled business platform for your strategy. Your action points would not be based on quantitative generic data, as you would have added your consumers' psycho-socio factors as a cushion. So your business model will be different, not obvious for others to imitate. This model will form your organizaton's intellectual property that runs your business in a unique direction.

Curiosity seems to have drastically reduced in developed countries. Replacing their earlier obsession to invent out-of the-box new things, they have started outsourcing from economically emerging countries to make better profitability. The time has come knocking on the door for India now to open a new chapter, that of innovative power. Business-to-business customers from sophisticated countries, presently only interested in rationalizing cost and outsourcing support services, can be taken by surprise with innovation.

Define the common factor among individual psychological layers of consumers: it's not easy to read the psychology of 6.5 billion people at any given time. But if understanding human psychology becomes a key result area in every deliverable of your corporate initiative and discipline, it could become an inbuilt process in your organization. You will find a common factor by filtering the different criteria of human psychology. On the other hand if you believe you can arrive at this common factor by internal brainstorming, it would not only be an introverted judgment, but also a gamble. You may win the market by chance, or you may cave in, which is a bigger probability.

On analyzing the findings after microtone understanding of the multidimensional human psychological condition, a common factor can emerge. You may find it to be a mechanism that works like a catalyst and can be used to deliver your product or service with plenty of multidimensional content. It will connect to a variety of people in the planet in different angles. In today's world, business delivery should not carry a unidirectional content. The focus has to be one, but it can be amplified to connect to a wider spectrum of people in a way unique to their individual, mystical private gardens.

The Indian education system formulates all learning into the question and answer mode (Q&A). Q&A is numerical and has a certain limit. Innovative power cannot emerge from an attitude of question and answer where reading is by rote, and has no personal accelerator from where you can drive the way you want to. Using COA can ultimately change our education system. COA invites people to increase their curiosity to improve their observation quality to put action on a fast forward mode.

COA for Britannia

The COA effect has stood by me throughout my global experience of working with 2,000 brands which includes corporate transformation, scientific and sensorial product design, branding and channel ownership and retail addiction. Let me give an Indian example to explain the COA discipline.

When Danone appointed us to work for Britannia in 1995, we observed that without a mass market product going from small towns into the rural it would be difficult for Britannia to gain future success. Britannia is a 90-year-old Indian biscuit company. When Danone acquired Nabisco in Asia, 24 percent of Britannia was a part of the portfolio they inherited.

One day in 1995 Jacques Vincent, the current Vice Chairman of Danone, asked me to accompany him to India. He said, 'You've worked for Danone in global projects spanning Europe, North and South America and many Asian markets. Now show me what you can do for your own country.' He gave me an appointment to meet his Singapore flight landing at 2300 hours at Kolkata airport.

On receiving him at the airport, I asked, 'If you want to enjoy Indian food, my mother has cooked something for you.' He was only too keen to experience the sociocultural ways of India, and willing to follow any itinerary I make. After dining at my mother's home, his curiosity enlarged. In subsequent days I arranged lunch with a joint family of middle class means, breakfast with an aristocratic family, a visit to a sweetmeat shop to watch their process from manufacturing to selling.

Before returning to the hotel that first night, I took Jacques to the cremation ground. In Europe, funerals are closed, family affairs. I wanted to show him how death acquires a spiritual dimension in India even as the dead are worshipped and given a social send-off. He found a certain serenity in the death ceremony where the dead person's face is open to view, unlike being inside a closed coffin. He saw something he could never fathom: several dead bodies waiting in line, either for burning on the wooden pyre or for the electric crematorium. He spent two hours at the burning *ghat*, and then we went to the hotel.

Jacques' curiosity was so powerful that two days later when he saw a marriage ceremony, he commented, 'This is cultural learning for me. The same white tuber rose flower can be used for death as well as for happiness.'

To establish the potential of Britannia in small towns, I organized a few consumer group interactions about 40 kilometers away from Kolkata. Always used to conversing in French with me, Jacques observantly commented that he was seeing another side of me that was so at home in animating the group in Bengali. He wanted to understand the consumer conversations, their lifestyle and trends influencing them. We arranged for a television camera to record the consumers as they spoke and for him to watch them from another room with a translator by his side. This is the way my Britannia journey started.

Biscuit has always been considered an on-the-move indulgence edible product. Month after month I went from metro to small towns and into interior rural settings to understand the psychological content of Indian consumers throughout the country. I understood then the possibility of introducing a new dimension relating health to the mind.

To position health as the platform, we had to highlight its most important tangible ingredient which was wheat. Each time consumers enjoy a biscuit, they are absorbing the health benefit of wheat. At that time, 1997, the awareness of, and consciousness about, health was not so high in India. But the COA discipline pushed us to get deeper into the psychological and social content. We extracted every microscopic element that empowers a consumer to finally lord it over a manufacturer with her purchasing power.

We found the consumer's unstated psychological desire was to get the same health benefit as a benefit for the mind as well. The power of COA enabled this insight. Continuity of the power of COA is Britannia *Eat Healthy, Think Better* which we have established as their strategic platform for the future.

How did we achieve the phenomenal growth for Britannia? Britannia was a well reputed, old economy brand in the country's metros. Sixty kilometers outside a city, the trace of Britannia would reduce. The challenge was to take Britannia to a wider geography.

Glucose has a wide platform. On the basis of quantitative data, glucose appeared a totally generic product. Nobody was ready to pay premium value for it apart from a particular competitor's product that was already riding the market. Several times earlier Britannia had done trials in the glucose category with brand names like Circus and Glucose D, but had failed to make a dent. It was very difficult to imagine then that another branded glucose biscuit would be viable in a market that had one giant and hundreds of generic Lilliputs.

Since 1995 I desperately believed that only with rural enlargement can Britannia fashion a new era of growth. I needed to establish a low cost, aspirational product that village India would wholeheartedly accept. I was confident that the growth and strength of the company will ensue from here. This accepted-in-rural-markets product will create a well trodden path into villages so that the other brands of Britannia can piggyback on it. This entry to the wide and exposed rural market will eventually make Britannia's foundation solid.

I engaged in research after research with consumers to convince the Britannia management that it was possible to succeed with a glucose brand. I started very unconventional interactions with rural people to understand their deeper psychological layer. Rural people told me that at 11 A.M., if they are very hungry, they take four to six of the particular category of biscuits and a glass of water. That gives them *takat*, meaning strength, to continue to work, and keeps hunger at bay.

This hidden consumer desire for acquiring on-the-move strength was the most relevant psychological factor. Our obsessive craving snowballed into finding ways to give shape to this psychological dimension of *takat*. How could we create another challenger national brand? I translated strength as the name 'Tiger', and the power of glucose as Health Force. A dominant red pack impacted rural consumers in the vital aspect of strength.

If we had chased statistical data, 'Tiger' would never have been born. This was the COA initiative. Curiosity pushed observation quality to unearth the psychological dimension. We then swung into action to drive for quantum growth and profit. With the symbiosis of body and mind we brought Britannia into a healthy new platform. Britannia's success, even after the entry of GRCs following India's economic liberalization, stays as one of the seminal examples of COA's efficacy in creating an Emotional Surplus brand.

Developed societies took a long time to understand the need of appreciating women's subconscious choice. This realization emerged from the competitive pressure of sophisticated markets.

Intense competition threw corporations off their thrones to check out ground reality with more consumer research to understand psychological gaps. An economically emerging country like India has several socio-economic layers of women with differing psychological subsets. Do Indian organizations factor this in as the real market space to drive future business in?

If there is no world war in future, the world of business will run only on the basis of the human psychological aspect. Indian companies that aspire to be GRCs have to venture into this area with substantial investment. Understanding the psychology of the world's women will win you an unending business platform. Just like understanding *Jalebi Management* is about applying intangibles that have Emotional Surplus to grow and sustain your business profitability.

consumer cold revolution singed by ReFinE value ladder

The mix of culture, laddering of technology, media influence, the concentration on individualism, radical growth of knowledge in general, the facility that brings the world's information into the consumer's grip; these have all combined to make organizations susceptible to the vagaries of rapid change. Irrespective of their size, organizations have become fragile puppets twirled in the fingers of the consumer.

Such revolutionary transformation is creating scope for organizations to prosper. How should they harvest this opportunity? Should we turn to the *jalebi* for help?

Branded at the high ground level of being a concept in culture, the *jalebi* is an evergreen delicacy. It has carried its patrons through joyful experiences in spite of competition from innumerable edible fares.

organizations are getting fragile

Availability, choice and alternatives in market offerings are creating, fulfilling and increasing the consumer's unexpected needs and desires, while equally clouding her mind. This makes her decisions vulnerable to unexpected change. You'll find eroding consumer fidelity in every product category. The proliferation of market offerings is making consumers experience a newfound discomfort in coping with plenty. But consumers are not only beginning to enjoy this continuous discomfort, they are getting used to it. It's becoming a habit. Brand registration is slipping out of focus in the consumer's subconscious mind. Desire is growing, simultaneously dreams are being fulfilled on demand. Can organizations cope with, or interface, with such stormy consumer behavior?

The Japanese have cleverly adopted processes that are in sync with their culture and way of being while keeping their traditional oriental lifestyle. They use these adapted formulae to challenge sophisticated Western markets and industries, and surprise global consumers with desirable products.

The quality processes the Japanese have followed includes the QFD (Quality Function Deployment) process which helps in consumer centricity. The total quality management (TQM) philosophy improves quality in all human processes and deliverables in an organization. These processes have helped Japanese companies perform successfully in the West and win world markets in different activity fields.

There is a saying in Japan, 'The nail that stands out is hit on the head.' This speaks of the homogeneity and team spirit of Japanese processes, where individualism is frowned upon. The Toyota Production System (TPS) is considered the best in Japanese management practices. In fact the largest number of doctoral studies in universities across the world have been done on TPS. Even companies in sophisticated countries have deployed Japan's brilliant quality systems for improving productivity activities.

These processes are clearly driven by Japanese culture that couples extreme tradition with extreme modernity and envelopes it with commitment. Japanese ethnicity has exceptionally disciplined ways of functioning, and all process innovations relate to their civilization. They have always had a killer instinct to rule the world. Post World War II treaties, this has now been shifted to win and own the global consumer's mindshare.

From the beginning of the 20th century, the Japanese took it upon themselves to master Western techniques to achieve their ambition of ruling the world. Translating the beauty of Zen and infusing it with European innovative style, they created and spread the minimalistic culture across the world. This is why Western society can easily relate and adapt to Japanese products as the root of that certain stringent decree which has its origin in Europe.

From feudalism to the Cultural Revolution to open, liberalized markets, China is also creating a reputation of being a high quality manufacturing hub. Their locally marketed products may still not be of high quality, but they are producing high-tech goods for global companies. The West has no hesitation today in buying an iPod that is made in China. So 'Made in China' branding is beginning to get established through such reputed global brands whose quality stringency is well established.

In the backdrop of such manufacturing excellence, where do countries like India stand?

discipline, creativity, process

Let me haphazardly give you three words, how will you hierarchically arrange them? The words are process, discipline, and creativity. Some people sequence them as process, discipline, and creativity. For others creativity comes first, followed by process and discipline, with the logic that if discipline or process rides over creativity, creativity will disappear. In reality this is not true. If an individual or a product, service or any theory, wants to get recognition and sustain day after day, decade after decade, or century after century, the cycle to follow would be discipline first, creativity second, and process third.

Creativity must be the central filling, sandwiched with discipline on the base and process on top. Why speak of only industry? If you take any famous creator, inventor, writer, philosopher, film star, painter or musician you will find serious and rigorous discipline has always been their first criterion. Discipline buttresses the streak of genius.

Let us visit a few geniuses at work to see how discipline was at their life's core in the domains they domineered in.

On April 27, 1937 when Guernica in Spain was burning with German bombs, the city became horrific. Witnessing the gruesome bloodshed, the Spaniard, Pablo Picasso, gave vent to his angry, torn emotions by the only way he could express his feeling, by thrusting paint to canvas. Oblivious to the horrendous scenes of war, he continued his brush strokes through screeching bombs, widespread burning and human cruelty, suffering and howling without getting disturbed, annoyed or disrupted.

Picasso was already an established painter then. The discipline in him chose painting as his medium of expression at that difficult moment. Today the bombing of Guernica is framed as history, the photographs of that time are part of the war archives, but Picasso's painting remains fresh and contemporary, a reminder of what people should never do.

His canvas emerged as the famed *Le Guernica*, outstanding in its philosophical and intriguing expression. The power of Picasso's discipline rendered this painting to become an anti-war tool, always used against anyone contemplating war or threatening humanity. In the 1960s it was a backdrop for anti-Vietnam activities. In 2003, a reproduction of *Le Guernica*, which hangs in the United Nations building in New York as a reminder against the ravages of war, had to be concealed by Colin Powell, the US Secretary of State, when he announced that the US would go to war against Saddam Hussein in Iraq.

In 1911, Pablo Picasso together with Georges Braque, had invented Cubism, and a new thought process. He painted *Le Guernica* in 1937 and died in 1973. In the 90 years he spent on earth, Picasso painted in different styles in different decades, representing the nostalgia of the 20th century. But through all those varying expressions there is a consistent, identifiable Picasso stroke that transcends his wide canvas spanning nearly a century. Without seeing his signature you can recognize his paintings. This shows how you can create your hallmark by incorporating discipline in extreme creativity.

Another example of discipline is the performance of rock 'n' roll king Elvis Presley. He stirred up controversy in his time with his unruly gyrating performing style and indisciplined personal life. But his discipline as a singer and entertainer, his ability to grab people's attention were unique. In a video film showing Elvis rehearsing with his musicians, the microphone falls from his hand, but that does not distract him or momentarily stop his rehearsal. Continuing without a break he performs in the full spirit of a live show even while rehearsing. There appears no difference in the discipline he maintains while rehearsing in the green room and performing live in front of a public audience.

Discipline sharpens the focus of your subject. It does not disturb your thinking differently or creating profusely. In different activity fields different masters may have led indisciplined lives, but on their core professional subjects, their priority on discipline was phenomenal. That's why masters produce creativity on a continuous basis, with the process becoming their slave.

Europe has a controversial dilemma with the word discipline. That's because Hitler with his murderous ways vulgarized it and made people anxious and fearful of the word. But the intrinsic meaning of discipline is not negative. My involvement of discipline is more with individual or organized creative expression.

Discipline is always a self-imposed state of mind. It streamlines creativity and processes. An organization will not benefit from hiring highly skilled people and acquiring state-of-the-art technology if all its other employees do not inculcate discipline in their work culture.

Let's say you have high quality, state-of-the-art tools in your factory. In the factory's three shifts a day, three different sets of workers operate the tools. They may be from totally different social and regional backgrounds. Unless their discipline is coherent with the discipline required for that work, the three shifts cannot all maintain the same harmonious production quality. If a few among the workers of diverse backgrounds fail to maintain discipline, the state-of-the-art machines will remain mere physical assets, rather than be tools for producing world-class products.

In a country like India it is quite possible to have factory hands from different states with differing cultures and mentality. Through a disciplined approach they must be specially trained on state-of-the-art machines to produce homogeneous results. The first aligning step would be to introduce a regimented, military-like uniform which would be aspirational, making them feel distinctive. It should not be like colonial British uniforms meant to make people look like servants.

Uniforms created by the British for their Indian servants were akin to the traditional dressing style of Indian royalty. This served the dual purpose of British officers openly dishonoring powerful Indian Maharajas and claiming colonial superiority. It gave the colonizers the cheap thrill of being served by make-believe princes! Such degrading thoughts should not get reflected at work today. Workers should look like skilled craftsmen, and they should feel proud to wear their uniforms.

State-of-the-art industrial machinery and work culture associated with it originated in the West, so it has links to the living style of workers there. Conversely, there is a big difference between the way Indian workers live at home vis-à-vis their sophisticated Western work environment and tools. As this difference will not mitigate in a hurry, harmonious discipline at work will connect everybody towards productivity and deriving job satisfaction. To achieve world class manufacturing excellence, it is essential to document and inculcate discipline with regular reviews as the organization's central focus.

I am not sure how the discipline of the Japanese process would be applicable in indisciplined and fast changing consuming societies. Being indisciplined is not a criticism. Actually it is just another human attitude that can be translated as flexibility. China could be very aligned to Japanese discipline. If you look back at the religions of yore such as Buddhism, Taoism, Islam, and Catholicism, they have thrived on dogma, which has a tremendous positive impact on discipline. A disciplinarian like Chairman Mao could lead the Chinese people through communism without allowing any disciplinary deviation.

A country like Russia composed of 72 percent Orthodox, 10 percent Muslims, and 2 percent Catholics will have strong discipline as these religions are dogmatic. Past political leaders have had great influence on the disciplined Russian masses, irrespective of whether it was good or bad.

India is composed of 80 percent Hindu, 14 percent Muslim, 2.4 percent Christians, 2 percent Sikhs, and less than a percent each of Buddhists, Jains, and other religions. As Hinduism is, in essence, a way of life without dogma, a billion plus population has enjoyed the liberty of choosing as many gods and goddesses they need for their mental peace. Any person can consider himself a Hindu without going through a religious ceremony. In spite of there being many dogmatic religions in India, Hinduism's way of life has highly influenced the living style of all societies in India.

Hinduism being a way of life provides liberty to people. So most Indians are averse to stringent control. Societies disciplined or undisciplined have their human values and intelligence, and of course consumers with consuming habits. It is indeed necessary to build organizational processes for products that will benefit emerging countries with their large consuming masses.

But the question is, when discipline is so feeble, can a process be created to streamline such a country for industrial development and global recognition?

India has an extremely large range in the levels of people, both in social life and the work environment. You may not find such gaps and differences in Japan. Mushrooming competition in every domain has companies from different parts of the world vying for a share of the same consuming pie. In contrast, industries in sophisticated countries are facing the problem of core and perceptible differentiation in their offerings. Consumers across the globe are now open to buying products from different countries. They have a different mindset now. They accept products that blend cultures reflecting perceptible difference and flawless quality, such as the iPod manufactured in China.

The innovative gene of people in advanced countries has always been so powerful that the products and services they invented have attracted everyone across the globe. But saturation has started creeping in now, and their needs and desires are diminishing. If they cannot offload their innovations somewhere, the fear is that their innovative superiority and economic growth will get curtailed.

Fifteen years ago, the presidents of these developed countries would come to India with the mission of showcasing how they help third world countries with wheat, milk and infrastructure building assistance. Today they come to India to sell sophisticated Airbus aircrafts or nuclear fuel worth billions of dollars. They come not to share their innovative power with India. They come to encash a consuming society and recruit low cost intellectuals to commercialize their innovative power.

Is this change phenomenal for India. Is India moving from being a political slave earlier to becoming a consuming society for Western products and providing cost-effective intellectual power to strengthen companies in the sophisticated countries of the West, Japan, and Korea? In this game, what is India's gain?

Chinese society is highly disciplined and hardworking, their work process is rigorous. They have assumed the role of being the world's low-cost manufacturing hub. But China is vulnerable with very perceptible issues. Just as Japan had to struggle to win the trust of people in different countries in 1952–75, the Chinese are in a credibility predicament. However, their assiduous regimentation and ability to correctly execute a process will see them succeed in becoming a world economic power within a short span of time. What they can do with now is some creativity to improve their innovative power.

In the work environment, Indians sometimes go through too much mental masturbation. Being deficient on discipline, the culture of efficiency and stringent following of processes is at a discount. But today with hundreds of thousands of knowledge workers filling up service seats in offshore outsourcing by multinational companies, the intelligence quotient of Indian manpower is acknowledged across the world. Unfortunately though, this has not contributed towards innovative manufacturing productivity of world class standards. Unless India pays attention to high discipline in creativity followed by a process, innovation will not emerge. The society will become a mere consuming one like all the Arab countries.

Discipline is essential in an organization, with every member performing his or her role without dilution and deviation. An organization should also have a blend of creativity and process (see Figure 10.1) with discipline at the core.

Creativity is the innovative stream in an organization. It determines a differentiating streak in products, services, customer relationships, partnerships, operating efficiency, and communication. It's like a twinkle from a star which characterizes and defines the star. An organization's global reputation can only come from this creative twinkle.

Creativity is mental extension. You cannot expect every individual in an organization to deliver creativity. But everyone is invited to participate on creativity on their function provided

Figure 10.1   an example of coherence, differentiation, and consistency

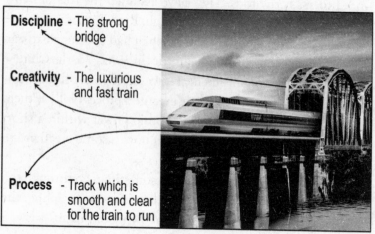

Discipline - The strong bridge

Creativity - The luxurious and fast train

Process - Track which is smooth and clear for the train to run

they follow the laid-down discipline and process. But for the organization's high profitability a group of insightful people combined with youngsters can give birth to a creative hub that will differentiate the business. The resultant innovation has to be exposed to one and all in the organization. It will inspire everyone to know how discipline and process were followed to arrive at this creative innovation which they will practice as a part of their daily work. Showing only the result will not institutionalize the path of discipline, creativity, and process.

For innovation to run as a process without being dependent on an individual creative genius, the framework of discipline, creativity and process is necessary (see Figure 10.2). This institutionalizes an innovative initiative. Innovation that's not converted to a process is a waste. It can disappear the moment the person or group responsible for it moves out. Process enables the common man to reap the benefits of innovation. Irrespective of their intellectual acumen, people in an organization should be able to use the innovation through a well-defined, standard documented process.

A process is both a slave and an asset, its good today, tomorrow it can be obsolete. It can never constitute an organization's

Figure 10.2 the framework of discipline, creativity, and process

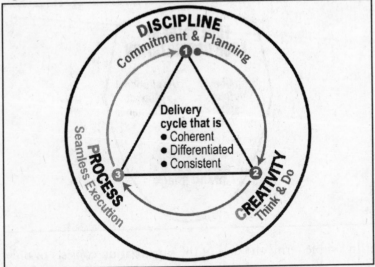

goodwill. A process is purchasable off the shelf. Discipline and creativity are the organization's genes, the real goodwill created by individuals. High discipline and creativity can result in the process becoming very superior. But a highly skilled process without discipline and creativity can make an organization very basic, not unique in any way.

consumer revolution

Is it possible to evolve a common benchmarking or quality parameter when there is so much diversity in consumer strata, and such varying types of products and services from different geographical regions? As I see it, today it is not enough to just have standard, required quality in a product or service. We need to simultaneously show and prove that it is the people in an organization who will, with their consumer perceptible quality sensitivity, uplift the product, service or system to surpass the level of consumer desire. They will then make the delivery unbeatable for the masses.

Figure 10.3   the three elements of the face of the organization

In simple terms the face of the organization consists of only three elements (see Figure 10.3): if the organization smiles, it means the corporation and brand has superior or unbeatable value. If the eyes are vibrant, one eye will carry high quality people, while the other eye will blink with products and services that will first have aspiration and quality, and then relevant cost.

Who's shaped the consuming society? Manufacturers of developed countries are credited with creating the lifecycle and purchase mentality so that people should want to consume, consume and consume. When this consuming system enslaves human beings they rebel in another way, somewhat like having a secret extra marital affair. Consumers, in the same way, opt for hidden choices. They bypass brands and head for 'choices' available in the market. This is a habit they can break at any moment.

More and more competitors are joining the market in almost all areas. Small players ride on the advertising done by bigger players. At the point of purchase they offer tremendous choice; and consumers are reveling in this choice.

If yours is a large organization, you can expect to dominate the market with huge advertising spends. This may create a spurt in sales, but the capital market can question, 'What if you stop this ad expense? Will the consumer still come to you?' If media focus is your only success factor, you are increasing your expenses, and drastically reducing your profitability. You are also making your brand value dependent on advertising gimmicks.

Even as you continue to increase your media spend, and consumers get entertained and recall your campaign, will they get involved with your product's core substance? Are consumers buying your brand regularly because you have captured their heart and mind with advertising? Or because your brand is carrying some core substance that the consumer will always look for?

Consumers never get connected with the brand's lifecycle from only seeing its image on TV, billboards or press ads. Their participation comes from experiencing a functional usage benefit that's supported by an unyielding rational base.

Thirty years ago consumers in the West revolted against Japanese and Chinese product quality, but these countries have since won over their adversaries. India is yet to admire 'Made in China' products. But China is fast improving quality and dropping prices, so will certainly overcome this hurdle quite soon.

The reality is that today's industries are training the masses to enjoy consuming choice, choice, choice. This obsession of unlimited orgasmic consumption has helped organizations grow. Then again, it has boomeranged on them by opening avenues for smaller and unorganized players to start ruling the roost. How can an organization protect its brands?

Through the revolutionary world events and changes in the last century, industry has always taken the lead to command people. The scenario is different today. With affordability having become rampant, people are pushing industry with a silent yet consistent revolutionary power. This is not obvious, nor manifested on the street through big rallies. It is the psychological, rebellious character of human beings that is silently creating a 'cold consuming revolution.' Every person has his or her reason to choose a product or service.

Just like the political Cold War since the 1960s when everybody knew the US–USSR acrimony existed though not always out in the open, industries today are grappling with ways to service the 'cold revolution' of consumption. How should they avoid getting slapped by unseen competition at every step?

Five intertwining factors comprise today's consuming movement of the masses (see Figure 10.4):

Figure 10.4 organizations overlook the five factors that influence consumers

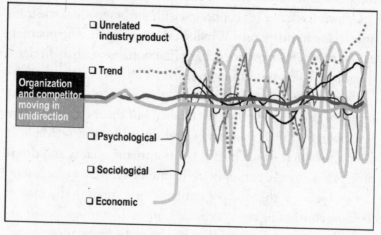

(*i*) **The psychological mindframe** of consumers has constantly changing sensitive curves of lows and peaks. It is conditioned by several factors ranging from an individual's country of origin to his self-confidence (see also Figure 9.2).

(*ii*) **The sociological moves** are undulating (see Figure 10.4). That's because society is a collective consciousness that's without the sharp shenanigans the mind plays with.

(*iii*) **The curvature of the trend** rides on the psychological and sociological aspects, so it has both arcs and deep bends. Consumers have a curious eye for trends. A trend always grows from some forbidden character, what people want to do but social norms prevent them from giving vent to that desire. When a trend is really thought provoking, it takes an anti-establishment direction and slowly becomes outsize. Trends break the monotony of consumer life.

(*iv*) **The economic graph** is more cyclical and structured, but has its share of spurts and slurs.

(*v*) **Unrelated industry's business:** Then there is business that is unrelated to the specific industry which is examining the market. Today when consumers have affordability and multiple choices, what is it that comprises their consideration set for purchase? Unfortunately for industries not sensitive to consumers, this is unknown. But the answer lies in the 'cold revolution' the consumer is a part of. Her decision will be impacted by her mental make-up, her position or aspiration to be in a certain social domain, and the trends that are driving people and the cultures they live in.

It's very important to look at business that's indirectly related to yours. You may think it is not related to you, but in the frame of your consumer's ecosystem, some unrelated product might have totally changed her mental conception. It may cause her to look at your product as a boring habit. For example, being an automobile manufacturer, if you look at say the iPod as an independent gadget, you may be making a mistake. You have to factor into your car the fact that consumers will now lose patience to load or unload the cassettes or CDs while driving, or dealing with too many buttons in the instrument panel. Perhaps auto Bluetooth content transfer can be a future option.

Let's assume you are in the apparel business in a developing country. If an international company is selling hair color in the rural market, you have to take into account and understand the logic of why consumers have shifted from hair dye to hair color. If consumers are willing to experiment on their god-given bodies, turning their simple black and white hair to color, won't they want to experiment with clothing that is external, a social factor?

Unless you care to understand the consumer's inner mind, you will not be addressing your apparel sales in consumer language. Similarly, unrelated products are impacting the consumer's mind in multiple domains.

take-out for you and your competitor

Look at how your organization and your direct competitor are moving so straight over these graphic psychological, sociological, trend, economic and unrelated industries curves. You may find that both your organizations are more or less following the straight and narrow path, like twin lines of a parallel railroad track.

In this world's multi-perfumed society, how do you bring excellence to your product or service? To win in the consumer's 'cold consuming revolution' paradigm, you need a new way of thinking. You need in-depth penetration into how society's five movements in the graph (see Figure 10.4) are forming and plotting their courses.

These five consumer-influencing factors create a cloud in the consumer mind at all times. Your real challenge is to enter these five factors to better understand consumers, and see how your products and services need to be delivered. Once you have entered here, you will no longer be in the parallel railroad track, but will flow with the five influencing factors.

The understanding of consumer and customer sensitivity in companies from sophisticated countries like Western Europe, North America, and Japan is very high. These countries had full-bodied innovative power yesterday. Today their GDP growth has become incremental. That's because their societies are plagued (see Figure 10.5) with the panic of terrorism, anxiety over AIDS, fear of their de-growing population, being overpowered by colored immigrants, and the dread of being economically swallowed up by China, India, and other emerging nations.

Figure 10.5 reasons for decrease in desire level in the West

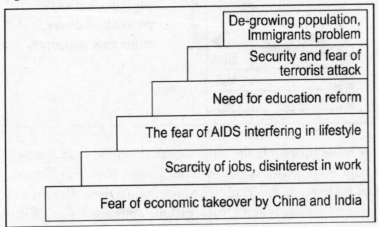

This huge mental instability created in the Western mind has led to reducing their level of desire (see Figure 10.6). Consequently, society has reached saturation point, consumers expect and receive no excitement or surprise. The paucity of demand has made their organizations use normal processes where growth is incremental, sustained by mere continuous quality improvement. What they need is quantum innovation, which is missing. This causes low GDP (gross domestic product) growth.

To leapfrog growth in their sophisticated markets they require a different type of quality process; a process that ladders their value proposition and breaks incremental improvement towards quantum innovative power. They desperately need to bring back this real innovative character for the future.

Conversely in emerging countries the quality platform has several layers. As local employees are not adequately sensitized to

Figure 10.6 economic reforms reversed desire level in India

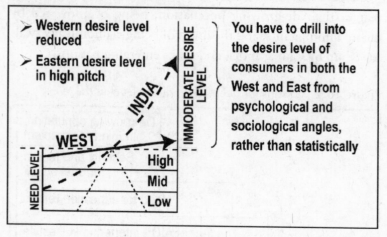

- Western desire level reduced
- Eastern desire level in high pitch

You have to drill into the desire level of consumers in both the West and East from psychological and sociological angles, rather than statistically

the nuances of using the sophisticated imported tools and processes, work gets executed without human sensitivity. The result is a lower quality platform which thwarts these Western and Japanese quality systems from reaching optimum levels. Global manufacturing companies that want to expand their businesses to economically emerging countries face quality problems.

think, feel, and lick consumer

The goodwill of any market offer is intangible; it is beyond the physical level of any product. Intangibles in some businesses can be associated with perceptible functional superiority. For example, it is obvious why people prefer a plasma television to a traditional CRT (cathode ray tube) inspite of the huge pricing difference between them, which in future will drastically reduce. The plasma TV is slim, can be put on the wall, the screen is flat, the picture quality is better. The consumer decodes only visible and tangible appearance here. But because of the new product's functional superiority, people will covet it for some time with an intangible greed and temptation to own it.

However, intangibles can also go beyond reliability, into the realm of sophistication in the same product segment. That's when brand value comes into the picture. Among competing plasma TV sets the cost could range several times higher in a given format. If the manufacturer has proven quality superiority in other products in the market, the consumer perceives this brand's quality as a tangible aspect which is actually not visible. It's a rational attribute in the ReFinE Value Ladder process (see Figure 10.8).

A brand acquires salience and premium value when its non-visible rational factors are perceived to be of superior quality in the consumer's subconscious mind.

Consumer experience with a product or service goes through four different stages:

(*i*)   **Trial** after becoming aware of the product/service
(*ii*) **Involvement** with usage
(*iii*) **Admiration** when the product/service feels secure
(*iv*) **Blind follower** so go for repeat purchase

trial

When consumers initially try out a product or service, the fundamental rational factors of quality and sustainability, and functional factor of usage advantage, make their mark felt. The brand must have these proven attributes.

If by showcasing the product's look, touch and feel an organization plays on fragile emotion alone, the consumer is actually being cheated. A brand with a beautiful advertisement that uses a charming star as brand ambassador can fail to connect to consumers post the trial run, at decision-making time.

Brands can create and sustain consumer aspiration at the trial stage by proving their rational and functional factors. Usage advantage is the functional factor; while the rational factor is the quality support that makes the function durable and faithful at any moment. Of course the product or service must have an aspirational look, touch and feel, but consumer mindshare can be won over only by first proving its rational and functional factors.

involvement

The purchase of a product or service for the second time, either in the same category or the same brand in another category, shows involvement with the brand. If the product has proved its worth in the first purchase, the consumer will return because of having experienced its positive rational and functional factors which has implicitly increased confidence in the brand. The consumer may not be able to articulate the rational and functional factors that are implicit in her mind. You as a marketer or product development person can dig out the cause of return by accurately focusing your questions to her.

admiration

When do consumers start admiring your product? When you have significantly meshed the product's lifecycle with continuous usage in the consumer's lifecycle. When the consumer grows to trust the rational and functional parts of your product, the next emotional level of the product's look, touch and feel will count enormously.

As technology advancement is spiraling, you need to anticipate the consumer's future frustration. When competitors come with low cost products with added features, admiration for your product gets eroded. Calculate the time cycle so the consumer does not regret having bought a lower version product from you at a higher cost in the near past. Consumers should never ever feel cheated when they compare your product with others. This way your brand continues to be admired.

blind follower

When your consumer becomes your blind follower it means that your organization thinks more about your consumer's sense of desire. Your delivery of the product's rational, functional and emotional balance is so powerful that it goes beyond consumer requirement. Your consumer looks forward to the surprise you have in store for her.

At this stage your brand perception has become unbeatable based on proven results on the rational and functional aspects. To sustain this aspiration, you need to continuously create and upgrade differentiation from the market. This means upgrading the product's rational and functional factors so they reflect on its look, touch, and feel.

If you happen to be a newcomer or local player in a market where global giants stomp, can you become big? The answer is yes. The rider is that the product you introduce must have extreme functional benefit with uncompromised rational support that exhibits sustaining quality. It must have breakaway differentiating character to make consumers aspire differently and become yours. Of course you have to be different in look, touch and feel; but it's critical to remember that this is not the initial focus area.

When the product traverses the four stages of trial, involvement, admiration, and blind follower, the company's internal team will be motivated to continuously surpass the consumer's sense of desire.

'Aqcurate gain'

In companies that act as though cost is the fulcrum of a deliverable, employees naturally focus only on adhering to cost parameters. This may satisfy the promoter or shareholder, and earn the employee a good appraisal, but it directly affects the brand, reducing it to a generic position.

There's no question about profitability being the priority, but an organization's sustainability clearly needs consumers and their

Figure 10.7   aqcurate gain

continuous bonding. When satisfied with the cost structure as operational efficiency, an organization fails to address the consumer or customer's key aspirations and quality requirement. This lack of sensitivity will certainly distance consumers and customers in the long run.

When cost is the fulcrum, employee knowledge, skill and its deployment in different functions get paralyzed. No attention is paid to consumer aspiration and quality beyond the base industrial norm. Quality becomes a mundane jargon manifested in quality policies hung in factory and office walls. Is this the quality consumers are looking for? Have you considered responding to deliver real consumer proximity in a product or service?

An organization acquires '*Aqcurate Gain*' when it spotlights aspiration as the fulcrum of its deliverable. Here A = Aspiration,

Q = Quality, and C = Cost. When consumers seek aspiration, they take quality for granted. The consumer micro sensitive quality is driven by his dense external demands, not by following an introverted quality system.

Aspiration and quality can be equated to human rights, while cost is like a religious sect that has to follow some obligatory rules and regulations (see Figure 10.7). Your organization will achieve '*Aqcurate Gain*' if aspiration is the fulcrum followed by quality and cost. The result would be market sustainability and leadership, profitability and high shareholder value.

'What's the price?' Upto 2000, this was the Indian consumer's top-of-mind query in a decision to buy any product.

India's economy was liberalized in 1991. Although international brands started entering the country, people did not immediately change their prevalent cultural mindset of savings. By 2002, the new generation teenagers and previously deprived-of-choice Indian consumers became exposed to high quality international products in Indian markets. By 2005, India's Parliament formally agreed to the Trade Related Intellectual Property Rights of World Trade Organization (WTO), and markets became flooded with foreign goods. Aspiration and quality started gaining ground, while intense competition brought the cost of products down.

'*Aqcurate Gain*' *can make price into a hygiene factor*. Faced with vast choice, the consuming Indian's attention diverted to quality of international standard. Quality is now equated with the achievement of global reputation, and receiving that same quality locally. With quality goods being available at more or less the right price point everywhere, the accent has shifted to aspiration, which has started to rise.

Post 15 years of economic reforms, by 2005 Indian consumers reversed their purchase cycle of first seeking price, then quality. Aspiration is the priority today, followed by quality; while price has become a hygiene factor. Organizations competing in the Indian market cannot afford to think that the consumer's first consideration is price. That mentality is over. Consumers no longer zoom in on price sensitive products and services where aspiration and quality are missing.

Should an organization nevertheless look at cost as a market segment, a type of category in an industry, the focus should be more on aspiration and quality to fit inside a price band, not as price alone that ignores aspirational quality.

The consumer's perception of quality from her every touch or relationship point should become the industry's quality benchmark, not traditional quality management programs which are too introverted. When high quality becomes the market standard by virtue of technology advancement, the differentiating character that defines customer involvement in quality becomes microtone.

The microtone of a consumer or customer can be tapped to be incorporated in the quality program and make it more aspirational.

'Aqcurate Gain' can optimize volumes to bring cost down. The advantage in a country like India is volume. In any business, volumes determine the cost. Looking at a market domain through aspiration and quality, you will find volume decreases the cost factor. Developed countries in Europe did not factor in volume when they concentrated on aspiration and quality. Consequently products of aspiration and quality got aligned with high cost.

European luxury products are in the premium range today where American, Japanese or Korean products cannot fit. Europeans have a problem entering the global mass market as the aspiration and quality of their products have become so high that they become sophisticated premium products.

Americans introduced the concept of mass scale consumption of products. The Japanese and Koreans adopted their scale to be for mass consumption too, but injected it with aspiration as the priority, and with inbuilt quality. Price was used for segmentation of the product category into different consumer and customer targets.

The global market is waiting for India, a representative of the billions, to show how the billion population scale can bring down cost while delivering high aspiration and quality in everyday consuming products.

'Aqcurate Gain' in Toyota's Oobeya

I hugely admire Toyota. Toyota is not the inventor of the automobile but this company has redefined the automobile to connect to a million people of the world while being extremely sensitive to the cost, but never at the cost of aspiration and quality. Let me share this example I read about the real application of quality and cost.

Corolla, which carries the Toyota DNA in terms of quality, reliability and affordability, is an excellent example of evoking consumer aspiration with a top quality product delivered at an extremely reasonable price. In 1998, Toyota's Chief Engineer Takeshi Yoshida took on the big task of redesigning the Corolla at a price under $15,000 while reinvigorating the design and adding high-tech options that would win over young drivers. Yoshida adopted *Oobeya*, a new approach to planning and engineering that promotes more innovation, lower costs, higher quality, and fewer last-minute changes.

Oobeya is Japanese for big, open office and is about the power of open minds. It allowed Toyota to think differently, **cut costs and boost quality.** Cross functional teams from design, engineering, manufacturing, logistics and sales came together, tore down silos in engineering and manufacturing, and created more communication among people.

'We had never looked at a car that way,' said Yoshida. 'In the past, each of us had a budget, and we were fine if we stayed under that.' Subsequently, savings in all areas, big and small, came into being.

In North America, Toyota was making Corollas with sunroofs mostly in Canada while a California plant was not outfitted to make them. When logistics told manufacturing that transporting sunroof-equipped vehicles south from Canada cost $300 per car, executives revised the assembly process at a cost $600,000. This unexpected expenditure will end up saving millions for Toyota in the long run.

An *Oobeya* set up in Torrance, California, on expensive four-color brochures that dealers could not afford was resolved by including them in the Toyota Website for dealers or customers to download. This saved them $2 million. But *Oobeya*-based insights also added costs by adding features like sleek wheel covers, and a 60–40 split backseat to help sell Corollas to younger people. If Toyota didn't include them then, dealers would have to discount those optionless cars in future.

In March 2002, the under $15,000 Corolla was ready with first time quality so good that Toyota did not have to make a single change to the car from the final design. This is unheard of in the automobile industry. Explains Yoshida: 'There are no taboos in *Oobeya*. Everyone in that room is an expert. They all have a part to play in building the car. With everyone being equally important to the process, we don't confine ourselves to just one way of thinking our way out of a problem.'

To get the best advantage on cost it is essential to try every method such as outsourcing, various types of negotiations and wisely managing vendors. But in the 21st century, those who design their cost factoring in consumer aspiration and quality consciousness will become the sustaining winner in the future. When you design the cost, you are obliged to design the total deliverable where aspiration and quality become integral. But when an organization only engages in cost cutting, it becomes like a butcher of consumer sensitivity.

one world quality system

Business houses catering to sophisticated markets have raised their quality parameters much beyond expected levels. That's because different economic classes have upgraded their living standards to become sensitive about every aspect of their quality of life. So industries here focus business on continuous improvement, and the outcome has become incremental growth.

The requirement of sophisticated markets has become so uniform, albeit of high quality, that differentiation is minimal and competition extremely high. To improve operational efficiency and reduce cost, all industries have learnt to break-up work into independent bit-size packets. These are outsourced from economically emerging countries.

But sooner or later sophisticated developed countries will need an innovative leapfrog in their own markets. The only way they can differentiate is through a creative quantum leap in the quality character of their products. Currently they are busy catering to the consuming craze of economically emerging countries.

Displaying quality performance, newcomers like Samsung, LG, and Hyundai have made a dent in global markets as well as in people's minds. Many existing players that failed to meet the consumers' sense of desire with superior innovative quality in their propositions have had to exit. With increasing competition, newcomers with new offers have used quality that's tangible to prove their difference. Providing extreme consumer sensitivity in products is another immediate consumer win.

The masses in Western society were attuned with a certain layer of quality before World War II. The integrity of manufacturers and their skill of craftsmanship brought in this quality consciousness. After World War II, the skill of individual crafts-manship was transcended into quality in mass production. The obvious next step was to invent a processed industrial quality man-agement program.

Upto 1980, a few world famous industries could still claim their unique product recipes to be superior, and have mystic value. Technological advancement has more or less democrat-ized all recipes today. Secret recipes have been bared open to the world in the new, uniform way that technology is making every-one function.

Mass production had become very important for large con-sumption. Simultaneously the cost of living in sophisticated economic systems skyrocketed. To avoid the social responsi-bility of providing employee health and social benefits, reputed multinational corporations started outsourcing from econom-ically emerging countries.

Outsourcing has become a vigorous and dynamic feature of business today, consuming every management issue, much like how the industrial revolution created a new way of working. When 90 percent of the materials and processes are outsourced, how can quality standards be enhanced? Can consumer sen-sitivity find its due respect from outsourced systems and leader-ship? The quality parameter of sophisticated countries will be higher because of the exigency of their sophisticated consumers. Work outsourced to economically emerging countries has to meet those standards.

On the other hand, knowledge about quality is very low in economically emerging countries as the quality movement has not been part of their heritage. They have imported the concept of quality and its processes from developed countries. So they are yet to understand and address the subtlety and nuances of the kind of quality Western consumers demand.

As economically emerging countries lack quality appreciation, sophisticated markets do not consider their product offerings to be of high value. They find merit only when they dictate the service processes they outsource from economically emerging countries, and that too, when cost arbitrage is met.

Simultaneously, consumers in economically emerging countries are getting demanding too. Their influence is aspiration from sophisticated countries with superior quality products and brands. Consciousness of quality is growing faster in India than industry can keep pace with. Indian consumers can now distinguish between high and low-quality products coming from sophisticated markets from the wares Indian industry can offer.

Global companies addressing Indian markets are trying to match their cost to what they believe Indian consumers can pay. But in doing so, they sometimes compromise by not maintaining quality at par with sophisticated markets. This tenet will not work for the long-term. When some American companies enter emerging economies like India their attention to quality diminishes from the exigencies their own country obliges them to follow. For example, two globally reputed American water manufacturers are profiting from the lack of quality consciousness in India. The quality of the plastic bottle and the cap is very poor, the ring of authenticity that keeps the bottle sealed comes off very easily, as does the sticker, even before the first usage of the water. The other water company fills its bottles to the brim, and water splashes on the consumer every time the tight cap is unsealed.

Quality difference becomes visible when a global brand manufactures locally in economically emerging countries. An automobile brand from a sophisticated developed country can lose its credibility when the sheen of the car and other functional elements do not look to be of their reputed quality. Consumers will slowly discover these differences and feel cheated. Sooner than later, the quality consciousness of both Indian and Western consumers will become the same.

Isn't it important to sell a product of single homogeneous quality across the world? For different reasons, if it's not possible to launch the same brand with the same quality, then why use the same brand name? There could be some difference in the functional approach of the product due to geographical differences, but the total substance should be the same. There are many globally reputed companies not maintaining the same quality across the world. I hear this buzz very often in different consumer fora as people travel a lot today.

In this context Indian companies need to strappingly leapfrog on quality sensitivity, and very rapidly. Global players may need to define a 'one world quality system.' Otherwise they will be hit by the 'cold revolution' of consumers and melt.

dream latent, think latent, and act latent to refine the active agent

I entered the management arena in 1980 after seven years of grazing on, piercing and permeating into Western mores. It was in management committee meetings that I understood differentiation to be the one thing that counts in Western society. But if differentiation was the hot coveted subject, how come all management people dress in the same way?

In the corporate showground where I carried no heavyweight degree from Harvard, Columbia, INSEAD or the London School of Economics, how should I, a creative person in their midst, differentiate myself? I decided to grab the opportunity of making a personal and perceptible distinction through breakaway dressing style. My brashly printed shirts, unusually colorful jackets, vibrant matching ties, sarcastic socks have since been highly accepted in boardrooms across the globe. Premier international management institutions that invite me to share with their students the management techniques I have developed, and my experience of transforming organizations across the world enjoy my unconventional attire too.

I quip to my corporate colleagues:

When you were writing dissertations at an educational institute or creating organizational strategy at corporate board rooms, I was busy sitting on public benches. I observed the vagaries of people's moods, interacted with what interests and occupies them. I extracted invitations into their homes, I drew insights from how they behave there, on the street, in the market. From the psychological mindframe of people I discovered how fragile and crucial sensitivity is. Being consumers, it's these people of all hues and sensitivities who determine the survival of an organization.

From consumers I understood quality, its complexity and nuances, and how it counts in the world of business. These experiences helped me to formulate and formally give birth in 2002 to a process I called ReFinE Value Ladder process.

The practical, comprehensive and insightful innovative process that is the ReFinE Value Ladder can mirror the future economic development of any organization. Whether yours is a sophisticated business house or an emerging one, you can take the initiative to leapfrog the quality of your delivery. To do so, you need to know whether the consumer or customer has comprehended the perceptible tangible quality of your product or service which results in intangible goodwill.

elaborating ReFinE value ladder

ReFinE Value Ladder is a process I have created to benchmark an organization in its competitive environment, the quality of its people to meet the market need, and how it can develop a product or service that can surpass the consumer's needs and desire. It is a tool which can, stage by stage, help you **leapfrog innovative power** in your organization. The objective is to achieve or reinforce global premiumness with high growth resulting in a high bottomline that sustains.

The semantic expression of ReFinE is refining perceptible superiority in quality. It can motivate your organization's employee as an ever-active agent. By definition the concept of this process asks everybody to refine. Simultaneously, with the Value Ladder you are addressing a quantifiable system to measure growth that happens on a quantum basis.

the refining attributes

The ReFinE Value Ladder process was created based on how human beings operate in society. Its validity is as obvious as living life (see Figure 10.8).

Figure 10.8   the refining attributes

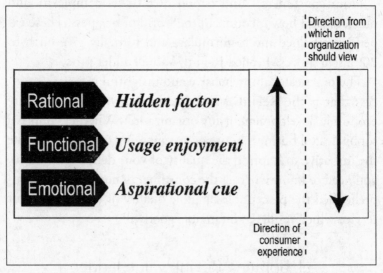

In ReFinE, R stands for Rational, F for Functional, and E for Emotional. Instead of using the acronym of RFE, I prefer a message rich name that also describes the benefit of the process. This prevents the process from becoming mechanical or inhuman. In normal course, people in industry work in a robotic manner with processes whose acronyms are not meaningful. This loses its finesse in human contact.

ReFinE Value Ladder has four fundamental approaches to differentiate the product or service in any market condition. It helps avoid presumption. It's a process that's not personality driven. It's led by a team, not an individual.

(*i*) **All-sides comparative scale:** It compares products and services in the same category in all price segments.

(*ii*) **Innovation catalyst:** It provokes consumers to think and respond in an imaginative way. That's because it is always assisted with a visual cue of an exploratory product image that associates with a future possibility.

(*iii*) **Deep dive into the subject:** The substance of the existing delivery, as seen through the consumer's eye, is distinguished in the parameters of the consumer's approach, usage and feeling.

(*iv*) **Ingeniously applying elements from unrelated industries:** You can bring the influence of unrelated industries in your product delivery.

Let me invite you to walk through the **ReFinE Value Ladder**. Evolving from my 30 years of practical experience in strategic consulting with senior management across Europe, North and South America, India, South East Asia, and Japan, I have already applied the ReFinE process in different organizations where it's giving the intended quantum results. I have used ReFinE in four activity domains: corporate transformation, scientific and sensorial product design, branding and channel ownership and retail addiction in both sophisticated developed countries and emerging nations.

Hailing from a striving background, I have always looked at the practical side of life and struggled against the tide. If I hadn't resisted the wave, my life would have run smoothly on it, or perhaps I would have drowned under it. Instinctively confronting the wave in every aspect of life since childhood, I have understood differentiation to be the key success factor.

ReFinE differentiates all the way

The ReFinE Value Ladder helps us in coming to grips with assessing, measuring and performing in this multi-perfumed society. My self-inflicted boundary in creating this tool was that it had to be understood by people of all nations, and be so simple to apply that people from the bottom to the topmost layer in an organization can embrace it. The nature of this process is to make any business anywhere in the world take a quantum leap in both growth and profitability which can sustain.

Rational, functional, and emotional attributes are universal to human sensitivity. Life starts from these three attributes, and finishes with the closure of its rational and functional factors. The balancing of the three attributes stays on as the soul or the mark a person leaves behind. This is Emotional Surplus, and it does not evaporate.

Organizational culture starts from the living human spirit, balanced with mechanical systems to bring in productivity. If the living human system is not perfect, the result will not come. ReFinE Value Ladder transcends the human living spirit and organizational complexity, and connects the organization's output to the subconscious mind of the masses. In essence, every human act in every step of your life has a balance of these three attributes.

functional platform is usage advantage
Functionality is visible and experiential. It comprises any significant improvement that has the benefit of usage advantage and surpasses human need and desire. Society's intelligent growth and development always emerges from functional benefit.

rational support is the substance

All reliable factors such as human trust or engineering quality are always non-visible for an outsider. The robustness of this non-visible factor can make the functional benefit powerful and make it sustain. The rational factor is initially non-comprehendible. It is understood after getting a number of usage experiences.

emotional take-out establishes the character

Once a functional advantage is strengthened by the rational support, the ensuing benefit becomes very powerful. Continuous positive experience arising out of the functional advantage and rational support results in emotional bonding. Giving it an identifiable character can further strengthen the emotional bonding to create emotional attachment. An emotional character is look, touch or feel.

Every individual looks different, our digital fingerprints are all different, and so from birth we associate a differentiating character with every person. Similarly, the looks of the product, or the tangible aspects surrounding a service, are the characters that identify them differently. Touch is physical appreciation, and leverages the feel. There is another feel that you don't touch. This is the intangible experience emanating from the perfect or high laddering of the rational and functional attributes. Hence the emotional content of look, touch or feel can be sustained with the supporting balance of the rational and functional attributes.

What is the difference between emotion and Emotional Surplus (see Figure 10.9)? Emotion by itself is ephemeral, can be fragile and is not sustainable. An individual can cry at the slightest instance to display emotion. This actually shows no depth, just the vulnerability of this individual. Such emotion does not sustain, nor does it relate to others. If someone expresses the same issue without tears but with considered thought and feeling, a depth of emotion is experienced. This emotion will have a strong balance of rational and functional factors. Emotion, which has

Figure 10.9   equilibrium of selling attributes

| TOPPING | USAGE | FOUNDATION | | EMOTIONAL | FUNCTIONAL | RATIONAL |

Universal human sensitivity always lies in the rational, functional, and emotional attributes

Differentiated look, touch & feel emanating from strong Rational & Functional support. This takes the stakeholders' mindshare

Any significant improvement that gives the benefit of usage advantage, that surpasses stakeholders' needs and desires

Reliable technical and intrinsic quality support that makes the Functional benefit robust, credible and sustainable

the supporting balance of rational and functional content, can sustain as Emotional Surplus.

Just as crying at the slightest instance is considered frivolous, when a service or product brand tries to evoke consumer or customer emotion with multiple advertising gimmicks, it represents flimsy emotion. Unless the rational and functional attributes are focused to explain the product's benefit, the target customer may enjoy an entertaining communication when in a relaxed mood, but will his purchase inclination be ignited?

mother and child relationship has emotional surplus

The rational and functional factors in a mother and child relationship are very powerful. A mother nurtures her child through conception, through its link with her umbilical cord, up to breast-feeding. A stronger mother–child emotional bonding results from these functional attachments than the father–child relationship that is devoid of such biological elements. This leads to a child feeling more intimate with its mother than father.

If a couple separates when the child is at an early age the mother's priority will always include the child in her decision of a new life with a new man. She'd never like to sacrifice her child.

But generally the case of the father is the opposite. The father may not ignore his children, but his priority would be to build up his new life.

Barring a few exceptions, the mother–child bonding has a cocooning effect by nature. It flows from inception up to adulthood, without ever becoming an adult relationship. This sustaining emotion is Emotional Surplus. A product or service has to similarly find a balance of the rational, functional and emotional attributes, connect to consumers and customers and so sustain premium business results.

Emotional Surplus attributes in products and services or in organizational culture can be prioritized to counter the 'cold consuming revolution' characteristics of consumers across the world.

the ReFinE structure

ReFinE is about the identification, macro and micro segregation, benchmarking and laddering-balancing of the rational, functional and emotional content of any subject in an organization in the context of its competitive barriers to result in a refined output. Climbing the ReFinE Value Ladder will land you at the summit of differentiating quality in consumer or customer perception at any given time.

laddering hierarchy

In general, organizations in the world can experience four types of competitive environments at any given time (see Table 10.1):

Table 10.1 laddering hierarchy

4 LAYERS OF COMPETITORS	Unbeatable advantage
	Superior preference
	Good mediocrity
	Basic proliferation

1. competitors in the basic proliferation layer

This layer is price sensitive. The only competitive advantage here is low price; the organization's product, service or human capital has no significant value program that is sustainable. Innovation is non-existent, the only tactic is to drive volume with low price. Even the profitability percentage is low. The company's cash flow is its billing. Earning can go as low as 2–3 percent, sometimes even touching zero. Sustainability is an issue here.

Several organizations here promising the benefits of low price have had to exit the area because of business not being sustainable. When low price means being insensitive to quality and to the quality of the organization's people, only a fog gets created in the market, not a benchmark.

Several low priced, insensitive service driven airline companies have been trampled over in business. When investors are presented with low cost business models, they often get charged up seeing exaggerated future volumes. But unless they consider the quality of the product or service, human capital strategy and an outstanding corporate value program, there can be no future sustainability.

Non-specific basic products will always find consumers and customers. But to sustain in business, there should be a difference between low cost, low quality on one side, and aspirational quality and relevant cost on the other. Just as Swatch watch is low in cost but its aspiration and quality are very high.

Competition from low cost, low quality will always create a market storm to destroy high value brands, but they cannot sustain. If you are a basic proliferation competitor, you can migrate towards the high value chain. ReFinE Value Ladder can very explicitly and perceptibly take basic proliferation products up the value chain. If you are a high value product getting disturbed by basic proliferation products you can climb another step in the ReFinE Value Ladder.

Even as a basic player, never look at your business in a low profile way. Perhaps your only possibility was starting from the basic layer. You will face real challenge and get true satisfaction if you can transfer yourself to the good mediocre layer and graduate higher from there onwards.

2. competitors in the good mediocre layer

With average quality of products or services, the good mediocre layer has a brand value that can be recognized a little more than the basic layer, which allows it to command a decent price. Human capital is average, better than in the basic zone. Brand value starts from here. Organizations in this layer can be sandwiched between the superior and basic layers.

You can be good mediocre, but must have the willingness to migrate to a higher level. You will find your organization has created sedimentation of a reactive nature. People love to sit in the comfort zone. Here your organization needs a pinprick in the backside, which I call being in the discomfort zone (see Table 2.1). Use the ReFinE Value Ladder to see where you can ladder in year 1, year 2, and year 3 to escape this situation. It can show you the cost of laddering and returns.

A basic proliferation competitor can shift to the good mediocre layer, but making this shift can be very tedious. It does not happen overnight as the company needs time to gain credibility with consumers and customers and change its working culture. A mindframe for strategic business vision in both short and long-term perspectives is required. It may take a minimum of 18 months for basic players to shift to this layer. A radical shift in the minds of its employees, and selection of a few products that can be uplifted in quality are essential.

It's true that the operational costs of a basic zone organization can shoot up once it enters the good level. It's not possible to get quick, short-term results while moving to the good mediocre layer. If you are a company graduating to the good mediocre layer, after telescoping the market, look to see what advantage you can create for your consumer and customer. Based on that, check the value added delivery you can make, what your return would be three years down the line, gauge whether your sustaining character can become powerful, and how you can make your human capital more knowledge driven.

Should your organization want to go for an IPO (initial public offer), you have to first create brand value in this layer. Your human capital and product quality relating to consumer and customer sensitivity can create an impact.

3. competitors in the superior preference layer

This layer is better than, and uplifted from, the good mediocre layer. Its better brand value can command better pricing. Its human resource will be superior, but its attrition level will also be high because of the company's superior preference position in the market. Such an organization's major challenge would be to keep talent motivated at all times. Both the unbeatable and good mediocre layers will exercise enormous pull to attract these employees exposed to a superior way of working.

The quality of products and services of the superior layer has a certain reputation in the market. However, if tangible differentiation is not exhibited upfront, the good or basic zone competitors will suck up the brand and its product superiority. The quality delivery character of your product or service has to be proven and significant in this layer. Shortcomings can suffocate you with unbeatable advantage above, and good and basic layers at the bottom. So you have little choice but to push your value chain towards the unbeatable layer.

It is not only organizational size that matters in climbing from superior to unbeatable advantage. A small company can always reach the unbeatable layer with high knowledgeable people who have innovative power which can create superior brand value. But it needs an ambitious desire to move up the value chain. It is difficult to double promote from basic to superior advantage without going through the good mediocre layer. But once in the superior layer, you only need to think of how to become unbeatable.

The ReFinE Value Ladder can help you to migrate to the unbeatable area. But to reach there you should not look at your direct unbeatable competitor face to face. If you do that you will be merely playing squash with the ball returning to you. ReFinEing will help you to benchmark with unrelated industry products, bring some new element in your product that will enable you to change the market rules. Suddenly you will find your unbeatable competitor getting stuck in a situation because you are getting tremendous consumer support by aligning your product to their unexpected desire level.

4. competitors in the unbeatable advantage layer

Companies here have premium brand value. This highest hierarchical layer has outstanding human capital and outstanding quality of product or service. You can undoubtedly get premium price from your consumer and customer as your brand aspirational cue is very high. But this is an extremely vulnerable layer. It needs meticulous 360-degree observation to avoid the Titantic syndrome. Being big and unbeatable may create different kinds of small holes that nobody is watching out for. If these accumulate, they may drown your ship within a short time.

Internal complacency is the malaise this layer often faces. They generally always mirror their past experience and successes on future projects. But they forget to look back to see how society has since changed, and whether they have kept pace with it. In such organizations that carry a lot of fat, people may not even look themselves in the eye on how they should be connecting to the latent trend. So here too a pinprick in the backside to create discomfort is essential.

The real need of organizations in this layer is to be in the discomfort zone. Are they connecting to society's behavior and economic factors? What is the impact of businesses not related to theirs having in their business? Do they know how different layers of competitors are relating to the consumer or customer's hidden psychological mindspace? Only when in search of such answers will they find a zone of discomfort, which is not exposed in the market. If these organizations can ride the discomfort zone, they can stabilize their unbeatable advantage with premium command. Activities to seek discomfort and unearth solutions have to be a continuous movement, not a one-time affair.

Should you be ReFinEing your organization's value ladder, whatever may your level be, try to benchmark your organization's value chain against these four layers of competition in the laddering hierarchy. From stakeholder research that's not biased, and from comparing competitors, you will find your fit in the market. What is the strength of your brand or corporate value, the real status of your people, products and services? Once you discover that, you can refine your value pro-position for consumers and customers.

laddering system of rational, functional, emotional attributes

The inverse triangle (Figure 10.10) has three converging facets: rational is on the left, on the right is functional, and on top emotional. At the bottom of the triangle is a horizontal column of the basic zone with a score of zero. This has no significant rational, functional, and emotional attribute to claim a value proposition, so it is non-specific.

The ReFinE Value Ladder is always a combination of three attributes: rational, functional, and emotional. That's why in any situation, three figures are required to ReFinE. It means that ReFinE will not happen if three figures reflecting the three attri-butes are not used.

Figure 10.10 laddering system of rational, functional, and emotional attributes

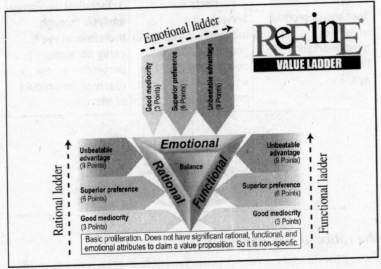

How can an organization find the trade-off to score high on the ReFinE Value Ladder? The value of a product, service or any selling proposition can be determined through three aspects (see Figure 10.11) comprising the consumer's eye and the professional eye. Your organization's total competitive scenario can be evaluated and benchmarked through the consumer's eye. In a consumer's life, no product or service is ever considered in isolation of the ecosystem the consumer resides in. So it's important to get the consumer eye perspective of products or services that are unrelated to your business and brand but very much a part of the consumer's daily life.

To check and verify whether the assessment of the consumer has any bearing on reality in terms of product or service competence, a technical analysis can be done in the laboratory through 'professional eye.' If the product or service is just as good as its competitors but consumers have rated it low, it means the value of the brand has faded or is not recognized. This will be an indicator of the kind of work that's required for the brand to score high on the ReFinE Value Ladder.

Figure 10.11 refining the value in three aspects

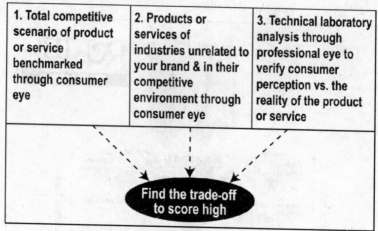

1. Total competitive scenario of product or service benchmarked through consumer eye	2. Products or services of industries unrelated to your brand & in their competitive environment through consumer eye	3. Technical laboratory analysis through professional eye to verify consumer perception vs. the reality of the product or service

Find the trade-off to score high

the rational ladder system

Good mediocrity scores 3 points, superior preference 6 points, and unbeatable advantage would score 9 points.

rational good mediocrity

In moving up from basic to good mediocrity, the rational attribute, which means the hidden component, has to be significantly different and value added. This significant, value added differentiation from the basic zone has to be perceptible to establish its difference. If a deliverable's rational attribute is not understood at this good mediocre layer, progress to the next layer could fail. It's important to take the initiative to uplift the non-visible rational factor as it contributes to creating high aspiration for consumers and customers at the good advantage layer.

rational superior preference

In this layer, a competitor can at any moment challenge what's perceptible of your product's rational non-visible factor. Consumers or customers can also ignore the value of your rational factor. That's why it's necessary to restore in consumer and customer mind the rational attribute of superior preference to ensure it becomes top-of-mind at any given time. Unlike many global conglomerates, Japanese and German companies very proactively make the rational factor perceptible to consumers and customers. Organizations should seek to present it in a very aspirational way.

In benchmarking Mercedes, Lexus, Skoda, and Jaguar cars (see Figure 10.12), Mercedes evokes trust. Mercedes has been reliably used through two World Wars, so its rational score is above everyone else. With unbeatable ergonomics as well, Mercedes acquires Emotional Surplus value in the customers' mind and scores 26 on a 27-point scale. The newcomer Lexus scores high in look, touch and feel but has no legacy up to now to evoke faith in the rational area. Skoda has improved its quality in all rational, functional, and emotional areas since its poor pre-World War II reputation. Jaguar is a beautiful, aspirational automobile, but its over-engineering reduces its rational value.

Figure 10.12   ReFinE benchmarking with automobiles

ReFinE VALUE LADDER		**R** Engineering	**F** Ergonomics	**E** Look and touch
Score	Value ladder	Non-visible perceived reliable factor	Usage advantage with physical involvement	Aspirational cue, from initial contact—look & touch
RFE 19 - 27	Unbeatable 9.0 8.5 8.0 7.5 7.0 6.5	9	9	Lexus / Mercedes / Jaguar / Skoda
RFE 10 - 18	Superior 6.0 5.5 5.0 4.5 4.0 3.5	6	6	6
RFE 1 - 9	Good 3.0 2.5 2.0 1.5 1.0 0.5	3	3	3
0	Basic			

Mercedes = 26 / Lexus = 22.5 / Skoda = 18 / Jaguar = 17

the rational unbeatable advantage

In most cases, Western sophisticated countries still score on the rational attribute in the unbeatable advantage layer. There is no doubt that most innovations have emerged from Western society, with Europe being the hub of inventive genius since ancient Greek time. These innovations have contributed enormously towards bringing in better living, thinking, and knowledge power.

America was discovered and dominated by a bunch of Europeans, so the innovative gene has traveled there through their blood. Western society has, decade after decade, instilled the rational factor into people's mind through their unbeatable advantage layer. Nobody will question the rational factor and unbeatable advantage of companies like Proctor & Gamble or Johnson & Johnson in USA. Similarly, Mercedes has established rational excellence globally.

Economically emerging countries neglect addressing the rational factor. Organizations think beautiful advertising can compensate the rational factor in consumer and customer mind. This is not true. When you refine Japanese or Korean companies you find they very exuberantly display the rational excellence of their deliverable at every step. This brings their brand's aspirational level at par with sophisticated Western society. Such an initiative improves an organization's quality program.

The rational part of the ReFinE Value Ladder is critical for an organization to ladder or sustain its value. Sophisticated companies with unbeatable advantage in the rational factor should continuously strengthen their rational position and take it to newer levels, thereby setting a benchmark for the industry.

the functional ladder system

Good mediocrity has 3 points, superior preference has 6 points, and the unbeatable advantage has 9 points.

functional good mediocrity

The functional factor is visible so everybody can see, appreciate and understand the subject very easily. Laddering from the basic zone to the good mediocre area needs stability in functional benefit. A low cost Chinese product can look fancy in the basic area, but without rational support, it can be very fragile.

The functional benefit in the basic advantage layer needs strengthening with rational support to make the product or service sustainable, such as a motorbike having an easy grip or a courier service making on-time delivery of goods.

functional superior preference

As technology is very easily available today, a company in this layer can really score high. If you have the curiosity to extract a breakaway usage advantage from the consumer's usage habit, you can deliver superior preference in functional benefit. Curiosity leads to fine observation quality that's molded with passion. First-rate observation has a hawk's eye for detail, and here, work and personal life do not have any dichotomy. Action that follows intense curiosity and observation will obviously display a marked functional benefit and differentiation.

Nokia's biggest success is that, across its range, it is user friendly. I found this to be its functional superior preference in every consumer interaction I've had all over the world.

the functional unbeatable advantage

Nobody has a monopoly of unbeatable advantage in the functional benefit area today. Even a reputed brand with substantial rational acknowledgment from consumers in sophisticated countries can fail in a developing country. Consumer sensitivity at every microtone angle has to be plugged in very meticulously.

Excellent functional benefit can emerge from cultural influence too. In the iPod example, after Thomas Alva Edison's invention of the phonograph, it was no surprise that American Steve Jobs brought in the next innovation in the sound business. Steve Jobs and his Western team were raised in a society where the level of musical understanding is very different from Eastern society.

The last hundred years have seen hundreds of types of music being created in the West. In a casual roadside interaction, young or old alike would be able to name at least 10 different types of music such as blues, jazz, rock 'n' roll, classic symphony, R&B, funk, hard rock, country music, world music or raggae. For them to have a device in hand that can escort them through the multiplicity of music is an immediate connect. The thought of this enjoyment can inspire the creation of a functional benefit like the iPod, complete with necessary and desirable features.

Corporations in South East Asia, Japan, or Korea may regret not having created the iPod first. But actually the need for it was purely cultural. An innovation of this kind could only have come from the West because of their need to shuffle different musical genres. The runaway success that the iPod is proves that functional benefit driven by unbeatable advantage can originate from any country's culture, but other cultures can see enough advantage in it, so it can become a big hit in the world.

India, for example, can represent a billion people's car. The car's functional benefit could be customized as per the diversity of people. Culture, religion and different sociocultural trends could all impact the product.

The country has huge diversity in its geographical conditions with deserts, tropical, humid and temperate zones, and diverse infrastructure issues such as road conditions in metros, urban, semi-urban and rural not being the same. The way people use a vehicle is also very different in India. People combine livelihood and pleasure in the same vehicle.

A car that's used as a workhorse for diverse purposes, on both roads and dirt tracks could represent a billion people's car that combines livelihood and lifestyle.

A snapshot of the functional benefit areas of the world's automobile industry reveals how sociocultural aspects have been ingrained in the way different European countries have represented the automobile. In France the automobile represents a piece of art; in Italy it is like a come-hither girlfriend. It represents excellence of quality in Germany, and in England it spells the comfort of Royal Highnesses. The Swedish automobile evokes security, while in the US it's a toy game. Japan has perfected miniaturization into extreme customer sensitive features; and the Koreans are now gambling with Europeanizing the car.

the emotional ladder system
Good mediocrity has 3 point, superior preference has 6 points, and the unbeatable advantage has 9 points.

emotional good mediocrity
If you have reached the good mediocre level in the rational and functional content, don't make the emotional attribute layer too flighty. If your product or service output is very fancy and tries to fight with superior and unbeatable layers, it will not work, it may instead backfire on you. There is a temptation in this layer to advertise for gaining market share, although this may not sustain in the long run. But your emotional content cannot be ugly; its standard must be maintained.

To strengthen the good mediocrity layer you need to focus on your consumer or customer target. When rational and functional attributes are in the good mediocre layer, don't try infusing superior or unbeatable advantage in the emotional content. The ideal is a balance of the attributes, so your credibility will not unnecessarily get tarnished.

When emerging economy countries entered the World Trade Organization, smaller brands of developed countries started to enter these countries. Such opportunistic manufacturing and servicing companies tried raising their brand value with emotional content without correcting any consumer connect or rational/functional deficiencies they may have. Consumers who may have never seen such brands in a global perspective will not believe in them if there is no proof of their credibility.

emotional superior preference

This layer is vulnerable too. When quality levels of all products in a country are at par, you can play to move up a nick. But when there are huge hills and valleys in the quality graph, making outstanding emotional output can boomerang on you.

the emotional unbeatable advantage

You can create unbeatable advantage in emotional content only if your rational layer is at superior preference and functional layer at unbeatable advantage. Don't try notching up the emotional layer without this balance.

Emotional Surplus can be gauged in any area, but only if its three attributes are segregated, benchmarked, laddered, and balanced.

The ReFinE process is simple, effective, and universal. It can be used to measure and uplift any performance across people, process, organization, and products. Let's benchmark four soccer champions (see Figure 10.13): Pele, Beckenbauer, Maradona,

Figure 10.13 ReFinE benchmarking with soccer champions

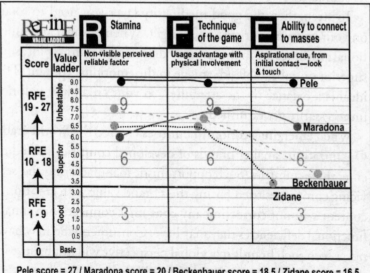

Pele score = 27 / Maradona score = 20 / Beckenbauer score = 18.5 / Zidane score = 16.5

and Zidane on the ReFinE Value Ladder. The three most critical attributes we will segregate are stamina (rational), technique of the game (functional), and ability to connect to the masses (emotional).

ReFinE process for different functions in an organization

The substance of ReFinE Value Ladder is such that it allows you to diagnose a business subject at any moment by segregating its rational non-visible attribute, functional usage advantage factor and emotional attribute of being an aspirational cue. As you work with the ReFinE process, you will get the scope to think about and segregate each attribute in a subject so that it can be addressed separately. Contemplate and activate improvements in the rational attribute; similarly repeat the action for the functional, and emotional attributes as well.

Macro and micro segregation of content in each attribute box of the score sheet is the most decisive step in ReFinEing. You need the consensus approach of strong cross-functional teams to ReFinE. In an automobile for example, you can take every component and separately refine its rational, functional, and emotional attributes based on human need and desire.

To illustrate, Table 10.2 shows the segregation of rational, functional, and emotional attributes in different verticals of business.

functions for refining
On one hand you have society's behavior and economic factors, on the other the impact of businesses not related to yours. All the different departments of your organization surround the ReFinE Value Ladder which occupies the center of gravity of this cauldron because its perspective is consumer and customer benefit (see Figure 10.14).

Table 10.2 segregation of rational, functional, and emotional attributes of different industries

Industries	Rational	Functional	Emotional
FOOD	Quality of ingredient	Edible enjoyment and/or benefit of health. Filling the stomach	Positive image association of intangibles. Tasty enjoyment
COSMETICS	Not being harmful	Application comfort	Subliminal look, touch, feel of the presentation & bold image of confidence
TECHNOLOGY	Proven R&D power — — — — — — — — Uninterrupted usage	Processing speed & consumer friendliness — — — — — — — — Easy to use	Thought leadership, indicator of latent trend, Breakaway look, touch and feel of the vehicle — — — — — — — — Humanized image
AUTOMOBILE	Engineering excellence as proven quality	Unstated need	Look, touch, feel and pleasure of driving the vehicle
FASHION	Quality of material, design and stitching	Magnification of the product is relevant factors at point of purchase	Look, touch, feel and hallucinating (breakaway trendy image) image association
BANKING	Backend coherency speed with technology and integrity	Productized, predictable knowledge-oriented service driven by overwhelming hospitality	Surpassing customer need
DETERGENTS	Efficacy of harmless ingredients	Visible cleaning	Confidence

Figure 10.14 for consumer benefit, an organization's functions can be refined in two aspects

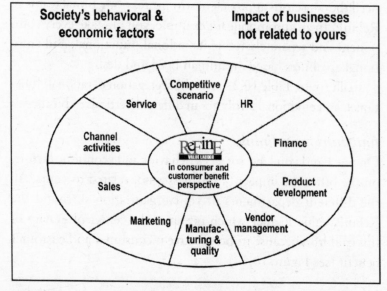

Now stitch your organization's complete value chain together for refining it in the perspective of the consumer and customer's sense of desire. This will encompass the competitive scenario, together with your organization's internal functions: HR, finance, product development, vendor management, manufacturing/quality, marketing, sales and channel activities, and service after sales.

activities for refining

A ReFinE segregation reference chart (see Table 10.3) shows how every function can be refined in an organization. This can vary from company to company depending on the industry vertical the company belongs to.

When benchmarking your organization with competitors, human capital would be the rational attribute, product quality the functional attribute, and brand value the emotional attribute.

In your own organization, if you were to ReFinE your human resource, an employee's intellectual capital would comprise the rational factor, his delivery capability would be the functional factor and his ability to lead and work as a team would be the emotional factor.

Under each function, all its sub-activities can be refined separately. If marketing is the function being refined, the sub-activities would be branding quality, mass communication, direct marketing, marketing vision for three to five years down the line, and the organization's quality of consumer understanding.

use ReFinE to uplift various functions and deliverables in an organization

There are three stages in ReFinEing:

Stage 1. Identification and segregation of parameters
Here you identify the attributes that affect consumers and customers, and which are critical to associating value to the product or

Table 10.3 ReFinE segregation

The parameters to evaluate the competitor with		
R Human capital	F Product quality	E Brand value

Your organization		
HR		
R Intellectual acumen	F Delivery capability	E Teamwork/Leadership
Finance		
R Corporate governance	F Maintaining financial health	E Aspiring commitment
Business planning		
R Understanding of latent market dynamics	F Precise operational plan	E Strong capability to foresee the market
Product development		
R Engineering	F Ergonomic	E Look, touch and feel
Vendor management		
R Intrinsic knowledge of technology and engineering requirement	F Cost design through volume and efficiency	E Upgrading partner relationship
Manufacturing		
R Reduction of defects	F Surpass all existing quality standards	E Customer sensitive in delivery
Quality		
R Comprehensive understanding of quality tools	F Deployment capability	E Sustaining discipline
Marketing		
R Microtone understanding of customer and consumer	F Translating business strategy to execution	E Guardian of brand health
Sales		
R Planning master	F Sustainable target achievement	E Relationship
Channel activities		
R Relationship	F Trade proximity	E Sensitive trade
Service		
R Assurance	F Friendly / Proactive	E Sensitive steering

service. For example in a car, the headlamp, steering wheel and suspension, are three important factors which can differentiate it from competitors (*a ReFinE exercise on these vehicle parts follows* with Figure 10.16). They are also critical to customer experience and in making the purchase decision.

In the car, you first get consumers to identify the various parts that will impact the car's value in the market, and then segregate these parts for their rational, functional, and emotional attributes. Any attribute which can be experienced only on usage is rational (such as mileage, suspension, engine efficiency); attributes which can be tested prior to purchase are functional (such as ergonomic design of steering wheel, braking); the points of look, touch and feel are emotional attributes (such as lamp design, contours of the vehicle, color, finish).

Segregating parameters should emerge from indepth exploratory interaction with consumers, customers or stakeholders on their connect, needs and desire for the product and service. You can discover the parameters that are sensitive by getting them to physically see and experience the product or service and react on-the-spot on their reality experience. Be attentive to listen to what they say about their perception. Segregation of attributes cannot happen based on your presumption. What consumers perceive should be divided into three baskets, rational, functional, and emotional. Your probing questions have to derive answers for these three baskets.

The right identification with macro and micro segregation of the attributes will result in effective output after ReFinE. ReFinE is also done for areas like organization value, human capital, quality systems, marketing, and sales. Every ReFinE exercise should be preceded by capturing customer needs and hidden desires which are often unarticulated.

Stage 2. benchmarking

The factors identified for ReFinE have to be benchmarked with products across different ladders. For benchmarking, it is preferable to use an unbiased external research partner. This will ensure the exercise is scientific and clearly filters out perception. Deep and subtle analysis is essential. An internal benchmark scoring team can be set up in collaboration with the external partner so no presumption or bias gets admitted.

The rational, functional, and emotional scores have nine points each of which the consumer or stakeholder has to rate. Ask for his qualitative rating on the 0–9 scale individually for the rational, functional and emotional attributes. Overall, the scoring is basic (0), good (1–9), superior (10–18), and unbeatable (19–27). You can also do a technical laboratory analysis to verify consumer perception versus reality, where the match is, and where the gap (see Figure 10.11). To climb the ladder and bring exceptional ideas you can benchmark with industries unrelated to yours.

Stage 3: the two steps of laddering-balancing

Based on the results of benchmarking the identified and segregated attributes, the ReFinE team can decide to ladder (leapfrog) selected attributes to varying levels on the Value Ladder. Preparation for this stakeholder research has to be very creative. Consumers must be provoked to think and respond in an imaginative way. The visual cue must be the 'innovation catalyst' that associates with a future possibility.

For example, if the group finds a laddering possibility on several attributes of the organization's existing capabilities, these can initially be chosen for ReFinEing. Some attributes may require higher investment such as infusion of human talent, or investment in machinery or partnerships. These attributes may need a longer time to ReFinE. They become a point for management decision. This can be the next stage for ReFinE. If the situation is critical then these need to be done on an emergency basis.

After laddering different attributes, balancing is the next critical action. Balancing ensures that the laddering is not lopsided in any way. This means we cannot be at the unbeatable level in the rational and functional attributes, and be at the basic level for the emotional attribute. There needs to be a balance which can also be cost driven. You have to see benefit in the laddering output to take an investment decision. A trade-off will be required now: what benefit does the consumer or customer want, how much can I stretch, and what is the return?

refining score sheet

Each quality layer of good, superior and unbeatable has a score of 3, which can be further divided into 0.5 to measure quality in micro detail. The basic layer will always be zero (see Figure 10.15).

Figure 10.15 ReFinE score sheet

ReFinE VALUE LADDER		**R** Segregated attribute	**F** Segregated attribute	**E** Segregated attribute
Score	Value ladder	Non-visible perceived reliable factor	Usage advantage with physical involvement	Aspirational cue, from initial contact—look & touch
RFE 19 - 27	Unbeatable 9.0 8.5 8.0 7.5 7.0 6.5	9	9	9
RFE 10 - 18	Superior 6.0 5.5 5.0 4.5 4.0 3.5	6	6	6
RFE 1 - 9	Good 3.0 2.5 2.0 1.5 1.0 0.5	3	3	3
0	Basic			

- Total score: 27
- Each block of Rational, Functional & Emotional has 9 points
- Any interactive benchmarking session with consumers or R&D team should be on the scale of 9 each for R, F & E

To illustrate the process, let's refine three functions: product development of a manufacturing company, human resource, and overall corporate value.

product development

I. segregating a subject to identify its attributes for diagnosis

If your general physician wants to diagnose your health, he will segregate the treatment you need. He will send you to a pathologist to check your blood, a cardiologist to examine your heart, and to a psychoanalyst to clean up any cobwebs in your mind. If a lacuna is seen he will take action to cure that area specifically to make you perfect. The segregating system in the ReFinE Value Ladder works exactly in this way. As every offer has the combination of rational, functional, and emotional attributes, its three factors have to be segregated.

macro segregation

In macro segregation through the consumer eye, the consumer will identify multiple features, but let's illustrate by taking three vehicle parts, the headlamp, steering wheel and suspension (see Figure 10.16). At the first moment of the consumer's contact with the vehicle she registers the headlamp. Her second moment of contact is when she checks the functional usage aspects, namely, the steering wheel. The third moment of contact is the suspension, which she does not see, but through which she gets the confidence of the car's quality. This is called macro segregation.

The headlamp is an emotional factor as it provides the aspirational cue from its initial contact and through its lifecycle relationship with the consumer. The steering wheel has usage advantage through regular physical involvement with the consumer. The suspension is a rational, totally non-visible factor perceived as reliable in the consumer's subconscious mind.

Analysis from the consumer's perspective will make the headlamp, steering wheel, and suspension, as emotional, functional, and rational attributes respectively.

Figure 10.16 ReFinE macro segregation method with three vehicle parts

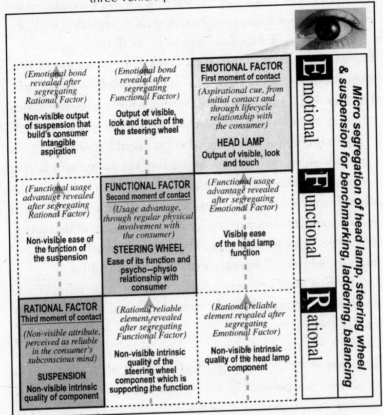

headlamp (emotional factor, first moment of contact): The visible look, touch, and feel of the headlamp, the consumer's emotional aspiration, can be further segregated to reveal its functional usage advantage. This is the way the light moves directionally, according to the driving movement. The headlamp can be segregated to reveal its reliable rational element as well, which is its components' intrinsic quality that consumers don't see.

Aspirational styling has rational and functional factors too. Designing a beautiful headlamp may not capture the consumer's subconscious aspiration if its functional and rational attributes do not function satisfactorily.

steering wheel (functional factor, second moment of contact): The quality of the steering wheel's function establishes its psychological and physiological relationship with the consumer. How it functions would be its ReFinE segregation. The intrinsic quality of the components that support its function is the rational reliable element that's not visible to consumers. The functional attribute of the steering wheel can be segregated to reveal its emotional bond, which is its look, touch, and feel.

If you think of the steering wheel as just the controller of the car's movement, you are not addressing the consumer's deeper pleasure of driving. What's the kind of enjoyment he experiences when firmly holding the steering wheel in his hand? The first visible manifestation is its look, touch and the feel of that touch. The impeccable functioning of the steering wheel is its rational support, which will finally clinch a pleasurable drive.

The functional part is sandwiched between rational and emotional attributes. Here the emotion is visible, but the rational part is not.

suspension (rational factor, third moment of contact): The quality of components in the suspension that's non-visible to consumers, intrinsically determines the vehicle's reliability. This rational factor can be segregated to reveal its functional usage advantage, which is the quality of the suspension's functioning. The suspension can be further segregated to determine its emotional bond. This converts the non-visible output of the suspension's function into the consumer's intangible aspiration.

A better suspension provides better comfort during the consumer's travel. So consumers don't experience jerks from traversing bad roads and feel fresh at the end of a journey. Through the vehicle's lifecycle in the consumer's life, a bonding and pride of ownership develops, an unarticulated feeling of comfort that reinforces the consumer's sensitivity towards the product. This is an example of non-visible rational factor resulting in consumer emotion that's not articulated.

The ReFinE process macro segregates the emotional (head-lamp), functional (steering wheel), and rational (suspension) attributes to diagnose every action and aspect. The purpose is to **ladder and balance value to make the product or service either reach the benchmark or create the Next-mark.**

micro segregation

Micro segregation is detailing for benchmarking, laddering, and balancing. Let us now take only the suspension to micro segregate.

The macro segregated individual suspension component chosen by consumers has to be further micro segregated to inter-act with consumers in detail once again (see Figure 10.17). This detailed diagnosis in conjunction with consumers is the key of ReFinE Value Ladder. This focuses on perfecting each factor of the consumer's first, second, and third moments of contact for benchmarking, laddering, and balancing of micro elements.

Figure 10.17   ReFinE macro segregation of supension

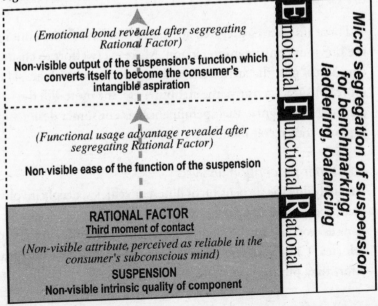

Perfecting the micro segregated individual components from the consumers' first, second, and third moments of contact for benchmarking with other competitors is totally the manufacturer's discretion. Doing so will allow the manufacturer to deliver consumer value on the intrinsic component quality of the suspension, ease of the suspension's functioning so that the consumer experiences a comfortable drive from the suspension.

II. benchmarking a vehicle's suspension with competition to gauge all performance parameters

Let's now take the micro segregated suspension to benchmark. ReFinE Value Ladder recommends that four layers of competition be taken: basic, good, superior, and unbeatable competitors (see Figure 10.18). Suppose your vehicle costs $7,000. To start laddering your vehicle's suspension, segregate its attributes as follows:

- Rational is intrinsic component quality.
- Functional is ease of the suspension's functioning.
- Emotional is the experience of a comfortable drive.

These are micro segregated attributes that have fleshed out in the previous consumer interaction. Make every effort to ensure consumers give the attributes, and you don't create them. The more consumer sensitive the attributes are, the more will the organization recognize their genuineness as consumer desire and support your recommendation for investment.

consumer perception analysis

For analyzing the suspension of different vehicles, deeply involve consumers to extract their perception. Give them as much freedom as possible to thoroughly experience these four layers of vehicles. Closely observe the psychological and physiological effort they put in.

Figure 10.18 ReFinE benchmarking matrix for your $7,000 vehicle' suspension

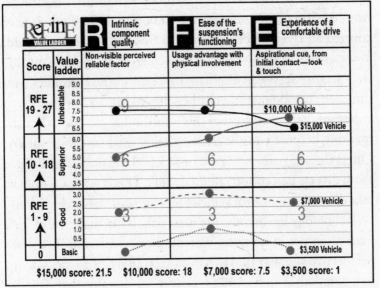

Try to find hidden meanings that they never thought to articulate, nor had you ever considered as areas to check to gather research data. The more curious you are to discover, the more will you press consumers to experience and articulate in depth. What will then emerge are hidden, microtone consumer subconscious points.

Be attentive so your camera captures every angle of a consumer's approach, usage and feeling to the vehicle's suspension (see Chapter 11 for explanation of approach, usage, feeling). Consider yourself a stupid observer with no preconceived ideas and expectations. Experiencing emotionally with the consumer will give you sensitive results. You can deploy the data you intelligently collect to improve your product.

How should you select vehicles for benchmarking? Take vehicles that are 50 percent more or less in cost than the subject to be benchmarked. Also take a vehicle that is 100 percent more expensive. This will ensure your benchmarking aspires to the best quality. If your vehicle is $7,000, select others beginning from $3,500, then going from $10,000 to $15,000. You have covered all layers of competitors to find out where you stand. You can take as many vehicles in each layer. If a vehicle outside the category serves an alternate function to the consumer, you can even include that in your benchmarking.

ReFinE Value Ladder uses this unorthodox method of benchmarking because consumers are getting used to a wide variety. Offers that range from $3,500 to $15,000 will undoubtedly give them diverse perceptions about quality. This is why you need to take diverse categories of vehicles for competitive benchmarking.

Technology has become the maverick. It can make a high cost item plummet in no time. Watching competition from a wide perspective you may find two things: (*i*) In trying to measure up to a competitor that's 100 percent more superior than you, its an easy climb to achieve up to 70 percent. (*ii*) On the other side, the competitor with a price 50 percent lower than yours also has a high-quality suspension, but because of low brand value it cannot command a high price. What's the moral of the story? Don't ignore either inferior or superior competitors. Extract the value that's better than yours, and deploy it in your offer.

In the hypothetical scenario shown in Figure 10.18, the consumer perception scores are: 21.5 points for the $15,000 vehicle, 18 points for the $10,000 category, 7.5 points for the $7,000 vehicle, and 1 point for the $3,500 vehicle. The suspension in your $7,000 vehicle scores 7.5. Now what? Go for technical analysis to find out what the reality is.

reality technical analysis

Do a technical laboratory analysis through 'professional eye' to verify consumer perception versus the reality of the product or service. This will give you the trade-off to score high. In the

R&D laboratory you can verify the suspension's rational and functional factors. All competing vehicles used for benchmarking can be opened up and the technical aspects checked. This will reveal how real the score is vis-à-vis consumer perception. Don't be biased about the suspension's emotional attribute; only the consumer can take that judgment, definitely not the manufacturer.

Your job as the manufacturer is unbiased sensitive analysis. Use your R&D knowledge to verify the correctness of the consumer's rational and functional scores. You may find that your suspension is as good or better than $10,000 competitor who's superior in consumer perception. This will translate to mean that consumers perceive your brand with lower value.

What is the element that's disturbing your brand and giving it this low perceptive value? You need to study that. The suspension itself may be fine, but it is not connecting to the consumer's aspirational level. There obviously is a flaw.

To resolve this low score, you'll need to take a call on perception vs. reality. If perception is the only problem, you may need to address it through communication. If consumer perception and reality are the same as per the R&D laboratory analysis, you have to improve that component which is disturbing consumer aspiration of the suspension.

III. first laddering then balancing your vehicle's suspension to establish consumer credibility

To start laddering your $7,000 vehicle's suspension, segregate its attributes in the same way you did for benchmarking, that is: Rational is intrinsic component quality, Functional is the ease of the suspension's functioning, and Emotional is the consumer's experience of a comfortable drive.

From an initial score of 7.5 (see Figure 10.19) your initiative should be on how to significantly improve the quality of your

Figure 10.19   ReFinE laddering-balancing method for your $7,000 vehicle suspension

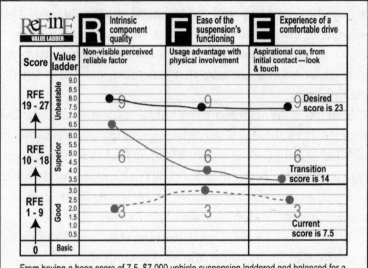

From having a base score of 7.5, $7,000 vehicle suspension laddered and balanced for a superior transitional score of 14 and finally reaching the desired unbeatable score of 23

suspension's rational component. While doing that, don't try to thrust up your functional and emotional scores. That would unnecessarily take you to a high layer in consumer perception, and if your rational component is still not up to the mark you will not be credible in the market.

To establish credibility in consumer mindspace, you will need to stabilize your functional benefit in the market for a certain time. At this time don't over-promise by provocative advertising or other promotional means. Remember that your deliverable quality needs a certain time to get seasoned and settled sustainably in the consumer's mind. You may have a desire to go to 23 but you need a transition stage. That's why from an overall current score of 7.5 your transition score may be 14 to stabilize and give you a trade-off for investment. Also, it will make consumers understand that you are going step by step.

But the business viability situation may compel you to go to 23 directly. This is balancing, the call you take as to where you can afford to go, both from the perspective of your investment capability and market demands. Having in-house skill and knowledge are prime factors for achieving this score.

transition score

On the rational score the jump is 4.5 points, from 2 to 6.5. This means you have really worked hard on reliability that's totally non-visible for consumers. Ladder and balance the functional score from 3 to 4 points and the emotional score from 2.5 to 3.5 points. If you can stabilize here for a year or two and accordingly communicate your rational factor, your brand's consumer credibility will rise. Following that, work out on how to improve the functional and emotional attributes.

desired score

The desired score to be achieved is 23, with rational being 8, functional 7.5, and emotional 7.5 points. This will give you a proper balance to rule in the premium price segment. As you can see in the matrix, the rational factor should always dominate with a few points more in this case of the suspension.

Even as you go through the exercise of laddering-balancing, your very important job is to ensure continuous consumer interaction throughout this period. Should the consumer not perceive your laddering-balancing activities, you would just be wasting your money and time. If your innovative R&D people are isolated from consumer experience in thought and working process, they can never perfect design to what the consumer is looking for.

Don't think and action your personal viewpoint on the consumer's behalf during laddering-balancing. Instead it's critical to be able to say, 'We have displaced the consumer's requirement with what the consumer desires.' To get deeper insight into suspension development, the consumer interaction activities need to be filmed on camera so you can get up close to their unstated psycho-physiological involvement.

Laddering-balancing are two key steps in the third stage of the ReFinE Value Ladder process. After laddering, the attributes are balanced for market credibility and to create quantum change. That means you are not over-designing as British automobiles have a reputation of doing. The British are one of the pioneering and most innovative of automobile designers, yet no viable British automobile industry exists any more because of this urge for over-design. If you superimpose the British Isles over the Japanese islands, the size may be the same, but in customer sensitivity the Japanese win hands down because they always come to the optimum instead of over designing (see Figure 7.1).

You can use the ReFinE Value Ladder process in whatever domain or subject you work with, and connect with it to consumer or customer perception, the most important element of purchase and repurchase behavior.

human resource

The articulated content segregated in each attribute box is as follows: Rational is intellectual acumen, Functional is delivery capability, and Emotional is teamwork and leadership quality. This is an example of segregation. According to your organization's need, you can segregate other attributes. But whatever attributes you create, don't make it introverted. You must be able to benchmark and ladder-balance with competition (see Table 10.4).

overall corporate value

In laddering-balancing (see Table 10.5), it is most important to balance the quality of human capital, products, services, and

Table 10.4 ReFinE human capital

	R Intellectual acumen	**F** Delivery capability	**E** Team work & leadership
UNBEATABLE	*Anticipate customer needs and surprise customers*	*Continuously institutionalize the work so as to deskill the job*	*Become a role model in the sphere of work*
Likely inputs required for moving from Superior to Unbeatable	1. Spends sufficient time in a job and specializes the same 2. Organization's priority to proactive functioning	1. Well structured knowledge management system 2. Continuous challenges on the job	1. Recognition and reward program 2. Professional management without personality dominance
SUPERIOR	*Prioritize customer needs and capability to analyze the root cause of every customer need*	*Capability to continuously improve productivity of his/her work so as to deliver more*	*Champion and create a cohesive team environment. Takes lead in setting team objectives*
Likely inputs required for moving from Good to Superior	1. Training 2. Infusion of new talent	1. Measurement linked compensation 2. Technology enhancement	1. Career path well defined 2. Has an active role in team selection
GOOD	*Ability to listen and understand customer needs*	*Capability to do his/her job without errors*	*Works for the team by keeping aside any ego*
Likely inputs required for moving from Basic to Good	Customer orientation programs to create awareness and transform people thinking	1. Quality initiatives like ISO, 6 Sigma, TQM 2. Process changes 3. Skill development programs	1. Suggestion schemes 2. Team Building 3. IT usage for removing person dependence
BASIC	*Inward looking, lacks customer understanding*	*Inconsistent quality in job*	*Person dependent organization, no sharing of knowledge*

organizational value and promise. Force fitting to ladder will only create dissonance; there will not be compatibility either inside or outside the organization.

This is the ReFinE Value Ladder recipe. If your company is already in an unbeatable position, but you see no growth in your market, it means you too have become insensitive to the consumer or customer. Check how you can ladder inside the

Table 10.5 ReFinEing Value Ladder for overall corporate value

	R Quality of human capital	F Quality of product & service	E Organizational value & promise
UNBEATABLE	*Pioneering efforts in the market by the leadership.* *Customer satisfaction and societal results given prime importance.* *Highly process driven.* *Performance driven by healthy enablers.*	*Leadership in the business.* *Takes responsibility for shaping up the industry for the future.* *Customers and consumers look up to the company as a benchmark in the Industry.*	*Balances customer and consumer promise and delivery.* *Societal results given equal importance.* *Trusted and paternal image in the industry.*
Likely inputs required for moving from Superior to Unbeatable	Intense Leadership skill development PR and networking skills enhancement of leaders to take active role in industry forums	Clear and well structured programs to work on future generation projects Continous effort on products and serices to improve systems efficiency	Brand building and PR to enhance organization image Focus on world market
SUPERIOR	*Has leadership which is ambitious.* *Good mix of young talent and experience.* *Leaders creates a sense of urgency.* *Highly performance driven.*	*Products and services differentiated well from competition.* *Gains leadership in some markets and some products.* *Overall considered as an aggressive marketer.*	*Has a well articulated promise and organization values.* *Performance driven by management policy and company vision.* *Aggressive in customer promise and delivery.*
Likely inputs required for moving from Good to Superior	Create discomfort through building a performance driven environment and infusion of new talent	Bring in product and service innovations to gain competitive edge Investments in R&D and cutting edge technologies	Matrix organization to build synergy and cross learning Well articulated career path for people
GOOD	*Has people with necessary talent, good understanding of market and competition.* *Happy with the company position.*	*Products and services competitively priced.* *Focus on timely delivery and acceptable quality levels.*	*Has good work ethics.* *Drives performance through individual and team objectives.* *Sales driven culture.*
Likely inputs required for moving from Basic to Good	Customer orientation programs to create awareness and transform people thinking Skill development	Company wide quality program Technology improvements in core business domain Infusion of talented people with capability in core business domain	Corporate Transformation and Branding program to remove the generic character
BASIC	*Inward looking, lacks customer understanding.* *Inconsistent quality in job.*	*Products sell mainly on price advantage.* *Inconsistent quality with high rejections.* *Inspection based quality.*	*Person dependent organization, no sharing of knowledge.* *Not an Aspirational company to work for and hence cannot attract and retain good talent.*

unbeatable zone. Compared to companies in advanced countries you may find you are not really unbeatable in the quality of your product and service. Perhaps you are the same as your superior or basic competitor in a blind test. Accordingly draw up your benchmarking graph in rational, functional, and emotional attributes to significantly improve in product and service quality.

As you already have high value human capital, and your organizational value and promise are established, the only game you need to play is with the upliftment of your product and service quality. Create the Next-mark with your own initiative. This can become another reference in the market.

If the good and superior level competitors want to improve earnings and profits, they need to think of laddering-balancing on the ReFinE Value Ladder. When growth is good, but profitability not there in spite of undertaking operational efficiency measures, it means your delivery is not aspirational enough. Instead of force-fitting hardcore sales to increase volume, first ladder your human capital. Hire a few new professionals who have the knowledge and skill to sell intangible value. Simultaneously train core employees in the organization on how to create intangibles that generate profitability. ReFinE Value Ladder can help here.

Drive the organization's values and promise with intangibles that external stakeholders can understand. In doing so, you will find your laddering-balancing will generate better profit. Better profitability cannot come from one source. It has to be system driven with the collective effort of everyone in the organization admiring and worshipping the intangible.

Here's a bird's eye view of four layers of organizations on the ReFinE Value Ladder (Table 10.6). Their brand value becomes perceptible as premium, better, good or led only by price, and connects directly to the quality of the organization's employees and product. The more your organization ladders the quality of human capital in intellect (rational), delivery on time (functional), teamwork and leadership (emotional), the better you can sustain your brand value at a higher order level.

Your organization can achieve the concept of Emotional Surplus (see Figure 10.20) when every aspect of business first

Table 10.6 bird's eye view on four layers of organizations ReFinEd

		R HUMAN CAPITAL	*F* PRODUCT PERFORMANCE	*E* BRAND VALUE
Score	BENCHMARKING	HUMAN CAPITAL	PRODUCT PERFORMANCE	BRAND VALUE
RFE 19 - 27 ↑	*Competitors in Unbeatable advantage layer*	PREMIUM Outstanding human resource	PREMIUM Outstanding quality of product and service	PREMIUM Can acquire outstanding market position as a leader and command high price
RFE 10 - 18 ↑	*Competitors in Superior preference layer*	BETTER Superior human resource	BETTER Superior quality product and service	BETTER Can have superior market position and command a better price
RFE 1 - 9 ↑	*Competitors in Good mediocrity layer*	GOOD Average human resource	GOOD Average quality product and service	GOOD Little higher than commodity and can command a decent price
0	*Competitors in in Basic layer*	Low profile	Below standard	ONLY PRICE Price sensitive market

Figure 10.20 ReFinE to achieve emotional surplus for organizational premium value

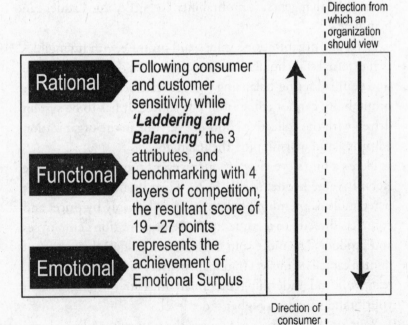

Direction from which an organization should view

Rational
Functional
Emotional

Following consumer and customer sensitivity while *'Laddering and Balancing'* the 3 attributes, and benchmarking with 4 layers of competition, the resultant score of 19–27 points represents the achievement of Emotional Surplus

Direction of consumer experience

segregates its rational, functional and emotional attributes, then benchmarks with four layers of competition. You can include unrelated business competitors to bring newness and ingenious laddering-balancing.

Next, use external stakeholder perception to realize your actual strength and analyze your real position in the market. Then make your business plan while laddering each aspect of your rational, functional, and emotional attribute. This can help give you clarity on how much investment you require for strong innovative support. The final step is balancing these three attributes. Doing so will tell you the areas you have to work on to differentiate and sustain business. This process can help your business take a quantum leap and sustain either in sophisticated developed countries or in emerging economy countries.

ReFinE summary

ReFinE Value Ladder is a three-stage process that pivots around consumer or customer involvement and your observation quality. The non-negotiable *leitmotif* of ReFinE Value Ladder is (1) segregation, (2) benchmarking, (3) laddering-balancing comprising two steps (see Figure 10.21).

Figure 10.21   the three-stage process of ReFinE Value Ladder

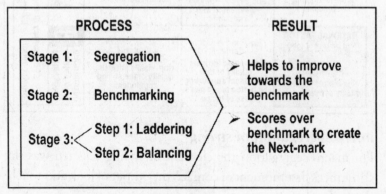

Stage 1: macro segregation through consumer eye

Let's ReFinE the styling of a mobile phone in this exercise. The consumer's first moment of contact with the mobile phone starts from its styling, the look, touch and feel that's an emotional attribute. The second moment of contact is the object's functional usage benefit. The rational factor, the third moment of contact, is unseen but provides the confidence. In the three-layered diagram, the consumer eye penetrates diagonally (see Figure 10.22). The look-touch-feel box, aside from being the emotional layer, has its rational and functional layers too. Similarly, the functional and rational layers have the other two attributes as layers as well.

Figure 10.22   ReFinE macro segregation method for mobile phone

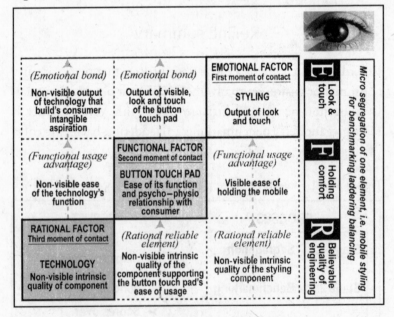

micro segregation of styling

For macro segregation the element of styling selected was the consumer's first moment of contact, the output of look and touch.

The micro segregation has functional usage advantage, which is visible ease of holding the mobile. Its rational reliable element is the non-visible intrinsic quality of the styling component.

Stage 2: benchmarking

Take every type of competitive mobile phone available, premium, high, mid and low priced. The consumer is already exposed to this variety; her competitive judgment is the insight you seek. You can even put in something new she has not seen to cue her. Having taken the phone's styling (look), its emotional content, we will now benchmark the three attributes (emotional, functional, and rational) of the phone's look among competitors through consumer judgment. The benchmark will clearly show, as per consumer perception, which phones are basic, good, superior and unbeatable in their styling. Simultaneously, the functional benefit the consumer sees in the shape, and the rational confidence she has in it will be revealed in this benchmarking stage. In the illustration Figure 10.23, suppose Mobile D is your phone, you have scored 13.

If you want to make a new product, the scores flesh out what's valued by consumers. If yours is an existing product, benchmarking it in the competitive scenario through the consumer eye tells you where to go to win the market.

Stage 3: laddering-balancing, a two-step process

Step 1: laddering

With the benchmarked emotional, functional, and rational scores of the phone's styling you can now start laddering each area. To change the phone's look may not cost you much unless you want to blend a new material. If you want to give a specific change

Figure 10.23 benchmarking mobile styling

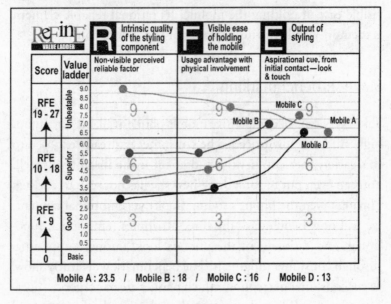

Mobile A : 23.5 / Mobile B : 18 / Mobile C : 16 / Mobile D : 13

in the functional area, cost will be incurred. Ensuring durability of the new shape, which is rational, may also incur cost, perhaps because of a different process that has to be used. Suppose you have laddered Mobile D from 13 to 18 (see Figure 10.24). You have to take a call on how much laddering you can afford because at the end of the day your mobile phone has to generate profit. Next return to the consumer to check if she connects to your laddered position in the same competitive environment. Your laddering may or may not involve cost, but without significant laddering your deficiency will be visible as it will not impact sales.

Step 2: balancing

After laddering the rational, functional, and emotional scores of the phone's styling, your final judgment will be of balancing these three attributes. Let's say the functional and emotional attributes have been laddered very high, but the rational attribute

Figure 10.24 laddering mobile styling D = 18

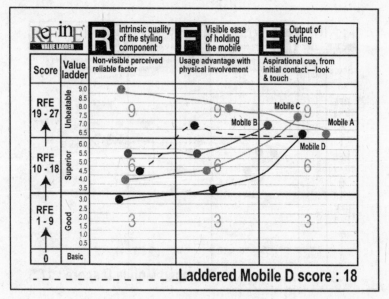

Laddered Mobile D score : 18

is low, the phone's durability will be hampered. This then is not the right balance. Alternatively, if you raise high the rational area, reduce functional advantage and increase emotional look, the model will be static, will not impact consumers to buy, so negatively affect your sales. Or if you emphasize the look, and don't take care of the functional and rational areas, the phone will become a museum piece without use. That's why a judgment on how much and where to balance is critical. In the balanced Mobile D scoring 17.5 (see Figure 10.25), the 3 attributes are prudently balanced.

After balancing, recheck with the consumer in the same competitive environment. Have you really created the difference of the Next-mark or are you matching the benchmark? Now it is your call if you want to take the route of benchmark or Next-mark. The marketing strategy flows from here. Either way you have a blue print ready of reaching the benchmark or the Next-mark.

Figure 10.25 balancing mobile styling D = 17.5

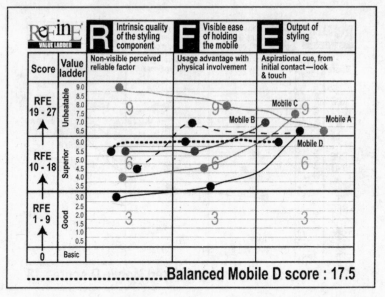

can a billion people's *jalebi* be ReFinEd to become global?

If Americans can transform home made potato chips into a branded product, sell it globally with a price more premium than any local potato chip maker can, why can't *jalebi* make that grade?

Can India brand *jalebi* like potato chips is branded? A long time ago potato chips were considered very fragile for manufacturing, transportation, or to even put on retail shelves. All this has become possible today. There was only one type to start with, salted chips. Look at the tremendous variety now. Can the fragile *jalebi* not be processed like this without losing its authenticity, and by creating variety?

Most American brands have been created from traditional, local, and home-made backgrounds. If you take the initiative to ReFinE the *jalebi* for a quantum leap in its rational, functional, and emotional attributes, it's quite possible to make it a repre-sentative of a billion people's crunchy, snacky dessert either at home or on-the-move. Modern food store shelves across the world can possibly stock it.

To find the rational ingredient for the *jalebi* will require advanced innovation. This has to be a highly researched project to find added health benefits that can be packaged for a certain duration as packaged food. The functional area would be a big science too. While keeping the *jalebi*'s format, there could be sweet and spicy *jalebi*s, and flavored *jalebi*s. The emotional aspect of the *jalebi* could be its representing a billion people's snacking enjoyment.

Look at how Indian food habits are shifting today, from trad-itional food to burgers, crumb fried chicken, pizza, noodles to cookies. India does not have any contribution in the innovative area of creating or marketing these different food items. Can we make a *jalebi* which can anchor India's innovative power, and make a favorite Indian sweetmeat a business success worldwide? If Americans can sell a basic product of American culture to dif-ferent people of the world, why can't India do the same with a product representing a billion people? Does India have this pas-sion to struggle and find answers for innovation and commercial success?

high voltage consumer sensitivity

Unstated in society's flair is consumer and customer sensitivity. When organizations sincerely and without bias seek to continuously unearth consumer and customer behavior, they can land in the elevated plane of 'High Voltage Consumer Sensitivity.'

What is the difference between consumer sensitivity and consumer satisfaction? Any roadside *jalebi* may satisfy you, but perhaps you have reason to return to a specific *jalebi* shop that indulges you with warm ambience and taste that tickles your taste buds. Consumer satisfaction is the momentary roadside pleasure, whereas the *jalebi* shop you sought out has understood your sensitivity. Satisfaction is reactive; sensitivity is proactive.

A brothel, devoid of emotional connect, is the symbol of satisfaction. It serves a basic physical purpose. A man–woman relationship filled with love and affection creates sensitivity. Likewise, consumer sensitivity absorbs consumer mindspace resulting in proactive delivery. In today's competitive scenario, business culture needs this sensitivity of emotional love and affection towards consumers. Your organization needs to understand the consumer's sensitivity, how to help her attain personal, family or working pleasure.

Whatever your business may be, connecting in-depth to the Sensitivity Steering, which is the psychological, sociological and trend paradigm (Figure 2.2) of your customers and consumers, will assure you of business growth and profitability. When consumer and customer sensitivity drive organizational culture, it reflects in a brand that sustains, in scientific product design that is sensorial, and in the retail business.

Composed of lifecycle in the centre, lifestyle surrounding it and trend as the periphery, the *Sensitivity Steering* helps in deeper understanding of society (see Figure 11.1). You can use it to unearth hidden factors that can be healthy for your business. Just focus devoutly on society's sensitivity steering. It can take your organization forward with customer and consumer sensitive insight, renovate your existing proposition or innovate for the future.

Figure 11.1   consumer sensitivity steering drives organizations into the latent

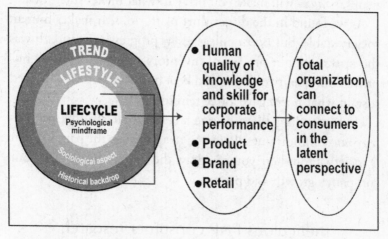

Spanish art, their incredible 20th century paintings, architecture, music and films fascinate me. A Spanish friend of mine explained the content of *seny* (sane) and *rauxa* (crazy energy); two opposites. Picasso, Salvadore Dali or Miro's works are all very *rauxa*. They created discomfort in the minds of people across the world through their painting style. But in the thought behind the painting was the balance of *seny* and *rauxa*, a vision so powerful that the art form has continued to create waves across cultures since inception.

Antoine Gaudi's architecture was totally *rauxa* in that he translated brick and mortar into human flesh. But his architectural plan was seeped in *seny*. The fanatical guitarist Pacadilucia brought *rauxa* in his guitar stroke and sound, but was totally *seny* in accurately following the scientific grammar of Western musical notes. Luis Buneul drew the *rauxa* character in his films based on *seny* societal paradox.

In the same way, if you drive the Sensitive Steering to understand people's *seny* and *rauxa* streaks, you'll get some real live insight. Industry normally tries to understand *seny* practices that do not upset society's sensitive graph. *Seny* provides the mathematical answer, which everybody else also knows in the market. Being on the surface, it is not an insight. But understanding people's *rauxa* will make you privy to what makes them tick.

As we found in the **discomfort** platform, *seny* makes human society stable, but *rauxa* unleashes its progressive nature. It was the *rauxa* thought process of inventors and creators that's improved our quality of living and kept our spirits up. *Seny* helped sustain what *rauxa* gave a free rein to.

Understanding the sensitive steering that absorbs people's *seny rauxa* mindframe allows you to appreciate the paradox that is society. From here you can draw the strategic vision for your company's growth and profit.

meticulous P&P consumer research

The Perception and Potential Value (P&P) Research is a two-step qualitative research process I have mastered to drill deep into the consumer's subconscious mind. The first P stands for extracting perception, and the other P for digging up potential value. The research is driven by the ripples emanating from consumer lifecycle, lifestyle, and trend (Figure 11.2). The super-blending of this human potpourri in the subliminal layer gives birth to the intangible substance that's driven by tangible rationality.

Microtone understanding and analysis after actioning the human potpourri helps envision business. It indicates where to go, how to go, and how to win.

Figure 11.2   understanding lifecycle, lifestyle, and trend

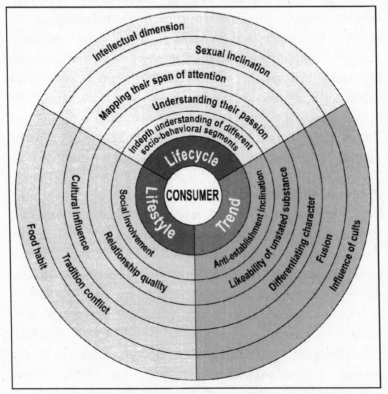

The fundamental and unique process of P&P Research is that it is totally driven by visual interaction. These could be pictorial, audio visual or audio. I find that without probing stimuli, consumers cannot open up to talk. Multiple images as stimuli help different types of consumers talk on the same subject.

perception research
In any subject that's sensitive to consumers and customers, you first need to prioritize the perception of the current situation

using the ReFinE score sheet. This will remove all presumption and sedimentation aspects in the value building exercise. Perception analysis means you find out your exact situation in the market. This is the time to listen and absorb, not bring a solution.

Perception research has to be totally unbiased. During perception interaction, people in the organization could complacently ignore or be sensitive to it. So reality portrayal must be authentic and pure, without interpretation. Perception analysis must be articulated in a way that allows decision makers to understand it and deal with the current scenario. You'll find virgin, unadulterated areas that nobody has perhaps thought of when delving deep into perception analysis. Take an opportune direction in one such area. The direction of strategy can start from here.

potential value research

The stimuli for potential value research should not be restricted in direction to elicit a question-answer scenario. While being in the subject, it has to be imaginative. This research gives consumers a structure to talk differently, and takes them far into the subconscious layer to extract the latent perspective. Deriving as it does from perception research, you unearth potential new ideas to bring a strong differentiable value in your deliverable.

Psychologists, sociologists, anthropologists, philosophers, and artists are welcome to be observers in this research. With their insight, implement a strategic step in your value proposition.

fil conducteur

I have appropriated the French words *fil conducteur* to the world of business. I use it as a strong concept for bringing coherency into different aspects of an organization. Equating *fil conducteur* to a sensitive nerve that can activate different cells, I have branded *fil conducteur* as a tool for making organizations coherent.

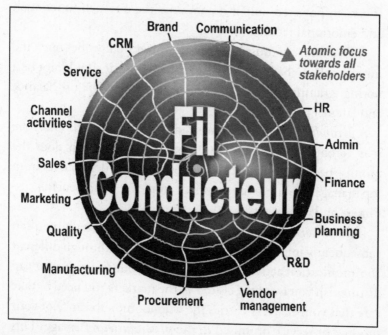

Every organization has its own character, its own kind of employee management style and skill. What customers and consumers expect from an organization and its deliverables can be detected only after deeper understanding of the latent needs and desire in their subconscious mind which is formed by the psycho-socio-trend paradigm.

Consumers need to understand the promise an organization is delivering. This promise has to be the reflection of the organization's core substance. It must define a communicating concept, which has the balance of rational, functional, and emotional attributes of the organization's deliverables. This concept is the *fil conducteur*, which must have the power of atomic function and communication so it forms a part of colloquial conversation (see Figure 11.3).

Figure 11.3   the nerve that connects and drives all activities with seamless coherency

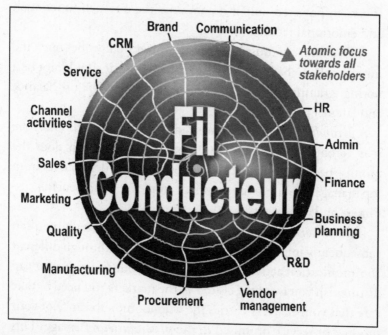

To give an example, '*Eat Healthy, Think Better*' is the *fil conducteur* and promise I established for Britannia in India in 1997. This was the first time in the world that a biscuit company was being associated with health leading to a fertile mind. 'Eat' is the functional factor, 'Healthy' is the rational factor while 'Think Better' the emotional factor. We spent 18 months working hard to understand the consumers' lifecycle, lifestyle, and trend in India at the end of the 20th century. Then in conjunction with the company's deliverable capability, we formulated and implemented this positioning statement that's become the company's promise delivery. The impact of '*Eat Healthy, Think Better*' was extraordinary. Ninety-year-old Britannia has become a breakaway success since the beginning of the economic reforms in India.

The *fil conducteur* must be understood, internalized and actioned by everyone at every level in an organization, in every aspect of their jobs. A highly researched *fil conducteur* that's arrived at after deep consumer insight can traverse several decades. It gets empowered only if it combines the rational, functional, and emotional factors.

A *fil conducteur* must have mystic power that probes open the inner mind. To be intriguing and memorable, it should not be a boring, grammatically correct phrase, but be crisp, off-balance and latent.

A *fil conducteur* is a discipline inside the organization. The more it is verbalized internally, the more word-of-mouth does the promise become. This helps bring coherency on deliverables from top management upto the shopfloor employees, and benefits customers and consumers.

If the *fil conducteur* substance is cultivated internally, you can subsequently implement it in the outside world through different communication activities. The power of your *fil conducteur* can distinguish you from the clutter of the market. You need to take care that your delivery carries the wholesome substance of your product or service promised in the *fil conducteur* message. This will ensure there is no dissonance between your delivery promise which is the *fil conducteur*. Otherwise the *fil conducteur* becomes just a grammatical phrase or jargon without action.

An organization's unique *fil conducteur* can drive its business to seamlessly interconnect key aspects across all deliverables, generation after generation. Internal and external clarity can always be driven by the *fil conducteur*. This coherency driver needs to be continuously marketed internally, like a project, to ingrain employees with its strength.

Fil conducteur brings customer focused value alignment in a manufacturing or service organization. It can become the harmonizer among the organization, partners, consumers and future talent. The MD, CEO, and Chief Operating Officer (COO) can amplify their top-line and bottom-line objectives if they can establish the *fil conducteur* with employees. Imbibing the *fil conducteur*, employees deliver value beyond expectation to customers through products, services and solutions.

This business driving *fil conducteur* is applied to business in different ways for organizational coherency, product design, branding or retail design.

fil conducteur for organization coherency

A *fil conducteur* positioning should not be mistaken for a tagline, which is an advertising claim accompanied with fashionable advertising charm. Slick and appealing taglines may not last or transcend the organization through different social epochs. Most often, the tagline is not understood or supported by the organization's back-end processes. It is somehow isolated from employees as it's mainly concerned with how the outer shell of the organization could be focused in the market.

In contrast, the *fil conducteur* creates the organization's driving principle. Inherent in the *fil conducteur* process is a thrust on activating the organization's internal substance, upto its outer shell image. To articulate the *fil conducteur* positioning, you need to have a deeper understanding of the market, consumers and competitors. The articulation need not be gimmicky or clever semantics. The deeper meaning of its substance is the key that describes its discipline and action of delivery. This *fil conducteur* has to drive the organization for the long-term, ensuring that the strategy does not change frequently.

An organization's articulated vision can be its *fil conducteur* and positioning statement. '*The future of the car*' is what Mercedes says. This can be considered its *fil conducteur* if at any given time, every aspect of the car has a futuristic outlook. Or in its renovation or innovation cycle, the consumer feels and experiences that Mercedes' substance is futuristic. This means the car's driving experience and features should not be the same as any other competitor.

To deliver '*The future of the car*,' the whole organization has to work keeping this principle active. If a shopfloor Mercedes employee in any country cannot connect to or articulate the work culture of '*The future of the car*,' it means the *fil conducteur* has not penetrated everywhere.

Driving a *fil conducteur* both within and outside the organization makes the *fil conducteur* a genuine corporate promise.

Corporate positioning must have robust substance. While radiating to all internal functions and the external world, it must create a difference in the competitive world. For example, Toyota's *fil conducteur* positioning, '*Touch the Perfection*' is very impactful, and without over-promise. The company can prove the strength of this positioning in every activity, as it happens to be aligned both internally and externally.

It's a mammoth task for Toyota's back-end activities to customize '*Touch the Perfection*' with their different employees, vendors, and dealers. This *fil conducteur* invites everyone to work under a single delivery umbrella, the touch of perfection, a continuous improvement towards perfection. Here is the rational, functional, and emotional break-up of this *fil conducteur*: *Touch* is functional and *Perfection* is rational; the combination of the two can render emotional content.

fil conducteur in product design

The *fil conducteur* can work like a design element when used in product design. In my experience, I have found seven different possibilities to apply *fil conducteur* in product design:

(*i*)   process discipline
(*ii*)   productization of a service
(*iii*) product sound, if the product generates it
(*iv*)   user friendliness
(*v*)   a hallmark sign
(*vi*)   reappearance of an element
(*vii*) consistency of a style.

process discipline

To develop a product, be it food, machinery, luxury product or service, you need a certain time and involvement of different types of people, both from inside or outside the company. Sometimes if product development takes too long and people work in silos, they can lose focus on the real value they want to create.

In such an instance, if the ultimate delivery concept is used as a *fil conducteur* or process discipline, everybody's predisposition will be spotlit on this parameter. Say '*Active healthy indulgence*' is established as the *fil conducteur* concept in a food product after sufficient research has been done. This could be used month after month as a blue print, and people of all the different departments can work with '*Active healthy indulgence*' as their direction. The lengthy work of product development will then be coherent using this process discipline. That's because everyone's focus will be on this one subject.

productization of a service

The *fil conducteur* in the service business can be the employees' physical approach. The stewardesses of Singapore Airlines are consistent in the way they approach a customer on board. From one aircraft to another you will get the same service, smell, and dialog, which is extreme politeness and a caring attitude.

The attitude and behavior of employees can be driven by stringent discipline as the *fil conducteur* in any service business. This will protect deviation from one person to another. In the service business, a product has to be like a train track that is not straight, but with curves to keep alive different microtone nuances of customer sensitivity. Its inherent discipline is that the distance between the two parallel lines cannot be compromized. But the parallel lines should join after the curvy journey to form a single consolidated service. This can be repeated seamlessly in a cyclical manner, and be driven by the *fil conducteur* process.

product sound, if the product generates it

There are physical products that have sound by default. If you cannot avoid sound, turn it into your differentiating advantage by creating a unique sound. Musicians can help to create some incredible sounds that can touch the emotional chord of consumers or customers. Sound can be so powerful that you can create a recognition factor from one product design cycle to another.

The Harley Davidson motorbike has a specific sound, which has been maintained for more than a century. If you manufacture printers that emit a continuous tiresome sound, you can totally avoid cacophony by creating a soothing sound. This sound can become part of your corporate identity for the printer product. You can even introduce the same sound in other products you may be manufacturing from your company. This sound can then become the reference of your company's recognition.

user friendliness

A *fil conducteur* in product design could be its user friendly systems from one product to another. Among existing Nokia mobile phone models and its many innovations, you will always find some similarity in its usage parameter from one product to another.

a hallmark sign

Another way the *fil conducteur* can be used is by having a single principle for a component that remains visibly similar in look, decade after decade, even as the component is restyled in accordance with the trend. The front grill of the BMW is an example of carrying an element consistently over time. Initially they called it the kidney grill. Now the BMW has restyled it to be smaller and more ornamental while maintaining the spirit of the kidney style.

This is the single *fil conducteur* component that the organization has kept consistent in its evolution. This visibly keeps the vehicle's authenticity so it cannot get diluted in contemporary competition (see Figure 11.4). BMW styling has changed so much since its inception that only by its radiator can you distinguish BMW's authenticity and recognition in a vehicle.

Figure 11.4   *fil conducteur* in BMW grill

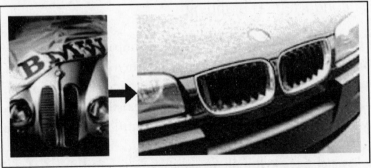

reappearance of an element

It can be an element that repeats itself, decade after decade. Japanese cosmetics major Shiseido maintains the *fil conducteur* in a different layer. Art form in cosmetics was their guiding principle from the initial stage. From traditional Japanese style they successfully transformed to have oriental and occidental balance in the last 125 years. They have modernized the container design but it visually carries the idea of the art form in cosmetology through the Zen expression.

In food products, Danone and Nestlé have significantly taken consumer mindshare in Europe with the taste and health concepts as their respective *fil conducteurs*. As Nestlé stands for good quality taste, consumers find a consistency in taste in Nestlé chocolates even as the products are different. Danone chose the platform of health. Consumers find a health association through different dairy products of Danone, even upto indulgence products which they believe will not harm their bodies.

consistency of a style

The Porche, for example, has since its inception, maintained an ovalness that is replicated across different components. The automobile's overall styling still maintains this effect.

fil conducteur in branding

The *fil conducteur* has a tremendous impact on branding. A brand's intrinsic content in its product often gets diluted in retail activities, advertising, promotions, and trade relationship management. If the core benefit of the brand is laddered and balanced with rational, functional, and emotional attributes, the brand can very strongly be empowered with all marketing activities.

Swatch has a well-built *fil conducteur* which is also an art form. For the first time in the watch market Swatch has shifted watches from being sophisticated, useful and snobby jewelry to being trendy art. Its communicating platform has a strong *fil conducteur* effect which straddles its brand, product and retail activities and societal involvement.

The non-conformist effect overcomes the humdrum of the watch category. In over two decades, Swatch has been established as the way to be. There are many varieties in Swatch products, but the art form translated as addiction is its *fil conducteur* that anchors all its products. This also proves that you can create variety while keeping a very strong platform as a pulley. The pulley can be very small, but in this context it has content so it can carry very large loads.

fil conducteur in retail business

The positioning concept of the organized retail offer, either for different brands or own private label and unpacked speciality products, is its *fil conducteur*. It is important to establish how this *fil conducteur* aligns with the total back-end and front-end, and how it is different from any other retail business.

The major retail crisis worldwide is how to make a given brand consistent across multi-brand or single brand retails through-out the world. Different aspects of the retailing business can be focused on the *fil conducteur* effect, such as in-shop service quality of employees. McDonald's is an apt example of having established a recognizable service *fil conducteur* across the world.

Retail signage, while being very strong, also allows locality cus-tomization from one place to another. Starbucks Café has per-fected this as a *fil conducteur*. When you go to Starbucks outlets you will find them similar and subtle, unlike other flashy fast food restaurants. Aside from subtlety, refreshing coffee aroma is another distinctive *fil conducteur* characteristic in the café.

You need a *fil conducteur* system in retail merchandizing as well. It defines the character of the retail and how it should approach the consumer. The behavior of shop employees can be defined as a *fil conducteur* too, an approach which Wal-Mart has mastered.

Let me take you on a high voltage customer sensitivity journey into four areas where I have worked intensely in:

- Corporate Transformation
- Scientific and Sensorial Product Design
- Branding and Channel Ownership
- Retail Addiction

corporate transformation

Deliverables from an organization invariably reflect its culture. If an organization's culture scores at the unbeatable level, its products or services will be unbeatable. Similarly, when deliverables score at the superior, good and basic levels, organizational culture will correspondingly reflect these levels. The capacity for, and inclination towards, improving products or services depend on organizational culture.

Distinct societal trends tremendously impact human society. Your organization cannot afford to isolate itself from societal trends. Riding the trend and reading it in latent perspective, your organization will automatically see a transformation towards growth. Ignoring the trend will get you left behind with tangible assets only. The advent of technology and its rapid upgradation is pushing the world towards thinking and acting for quick progress.

Those who want to transform take their own initiative. Transformation cannot be generalized. It can happen in three motifs. These motifs reflect in human character and can be equated to organizations as well. They are

(*a*) Proactive transformation: Self initiative and urge to transform

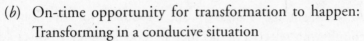

(*b*) On-time opportunity for transformation to happen: Transforming in a conducive situation

(*c*) Do or die transformation: Craving to overcome deprivation propels transformation

proactive transformation: self initiative and urge to transform

at a personal level

It was Mohammed Ali's own initiative to realize the dream of 'I'm the greatest!' From his early age gestures, much before he became a leading boxer, it was clear he was pushing hard to become the greatest. Whatever number of laps his trainer instructed him to run for body tone up, he would double it in his impatience to get to the top. His was an urge to transform into the greatest boxer on earth, and he took every initiative to fulfill that urge.

at the corporate level

Look at Toyota, a loom manufacturer in 1927 transformed to occupy a place among the world's automobile leaders. Toyota's disposition towards transformation in the reign of sophisticated Western markets is phenomenal. In fact GM and Ford who figure among pioneers of the automobile are getting left behind by the galloping Toyota.

on-time opportunity for transformation to happen: transforming in a conducive situation

at the human level

This reminds me of how classical Western opera singer Kiri Te Kanawa hurtled to fame.

Kiri Te Kanawa, an orphaned Mauri, an aborigine tribe in New Zealand, was on an adoption list with social workers there.

At the fragile age of a month, she was offered for adoption to a couple who rejected her as they were looking for a boy child. After five months of looking for, and not finding a male child, the social workers offered up Kiri for adopted again. No one else had taken her till then. 'Out of pity, my parents adopted me,' is how Kiri describes her homecoming. Her adopted mother was Irish, and the father was a Mauri.

Kiri's adopted mother found the young Kiri to have immense talent in her voice. She encouraged her and tried to open all avenues so Kiri could excel as a soprano singer. In spite of her adopted mother being part of the white society, Kiri faced racial problems. At the age of 13, her school mates would exclude her from social parties as her origin was not white. But this did not deter her adopted mother. She achieved the ambition of transforming Kiri from an orphaned Mauri to becoming a celebrated Western classical opera singer.

Kiri explained in her film autobiography that she had to observe strict discipline so her voice does not get corrupted with easy modern songs. Later she revealed that she wanted to be a singer like Tina Turner, but her adopted parents would hear of nothing less than her being a Western classical singer. Kiri went on to become one of the biggest opera singers of the world, with a strong foundation of musical grammar and an outstanding voice that is superior than any pop, jazz, funk or country music singer.

Growing in the environment of strict musical discipline quickly shot her into fame in New Zealand. She then applied to study in the London Opera Center in 1965 where she was accepted without an audition. Hers is an unimaginable journey of how the environment can transform human personality and create a genius.

Imagine if she were not adopted, had remained in the neglected aborigine society, who could have known her? The love and courage her adopted parents gave her resulted in her being an outstanding, graceful, beautiful, out-of-the-box soprano opera singer today. At over the age of 60 she represented excellence in precision for Rolex whose advertisement of their most prestigious and expensive watch they related to Kiri's meticulous accuracy in song and tempo.

This is the most inspiring example of transforming in a conducive situation: from an abandoned orphan to dominating the sophisticated world with her highly disciplined, emotional soprano voice.

at the corporate level

A corporate example of transforming in a conducive situation would be the Indian company, Wipro, which grew from the vision of its Chairman, Azim Hasham Premji. Inheriting an edible oil (*vanaspati*) business from his father, he diversified to get growth under a protected economy. In 1980–81 Wipro's turnover was $60 million (Rs 523 million at $ = Rs 8.6). He meticulously pumped his profits from the edible oil business into information technology and other businesses.

Premji's confidence in being able to fulfill his dream, made him buy his own company's shares whenever he could find them. In the early years when the company was small and unknown, everybody knew that if they wanted to sell Wipro shares, Premji would be more than happy to buy them. This ended up making Premji own about 85 percent of the company. It shows that his faith on trans-formation was so high that he knew he can grow without depending on shareholders.

In 1998 we helped Wipro transform to enter the global competitive league with the *fil conducteur* of '*Applying Thought.*' Post this transformation exercise focused on IT services, the company saw exponential financial growth and high market capitalization, catapulting Premji to occupy the *Forbes* billionaires listing by topping India's Working Rich list. In 2006–07, Wipro is transformed into a $3.4 billion (Rs 150,000 million at $1 = Rs 44) global company specializing in IT software services.

do or die transformation: craving to overcome
deprivation propels transformation

at the personal level

My obsessive urge to bracket with transformation started as
I rocked in my mother's knees. Allow me to give you a glimpse
of my transformation from a poverty struck life in a refugee
colony to my personally attaining a corporate guise. Recalling
my mother's conviction and attempts to expose me to different
cultures, I salute the spirit in all mothers that seeks the best for
their children, from inception upto their adult lives.

My mother's training was: never say you have nothing, because
you have high spirit and a constructive outlook that inspires you
to transform. When I look back my 50 years, I marvel: what a
mother! She supported the joint family in a simple schoolteacher's
salary. My father, a communist party leader, was always engaged in
neighborhood survival activities as many refugees like us squatted
in Sahidnagar, about 30 kilometers from Kolkata. Political
upheaval made us leave everything we owned in erstwhile East
Pakistan, now Bangladesh, to find living space in India.

We didn't have electricity at home, no water connection or
sewage system. Our 20 × 10 feet mud house had bamboo walls
and paddy hay roof and two verandahs of 20 × 5 feet accessible by
a sliding door and a fixed movable door, both made of bamboo.
I remember when I was growing up, our single bed needed to
be enlarged. It was a great day when my mother added more
bamboos to make it 3 feet more. My mother also created a mud
table for my studies. I could sit on the floor and put the reading
material atop the mud table.

A kind neighbour, on leaving the village sold us two pieces of
used furniture at a price low enough to be affordable for us. My
father kept his Lenin and Chairman Mao books in the almirah
we bought, while a set of drawers with a dressing table held our
clothes. In front of the small mirror atop the drawers were kept

two combs and a tiny round box containing my mother's *sindur*, the red powder Indian women use on their foreheads as a symbol of marriage.

A harmonium adorned one side of the room. My mother's uncle had received it as a gift on release from a British prison in Andaman Islands where he was held for political activities. It seems my mother was a good singer before I was born so he gave her the harmonium.

The harmonium is a legacy of the British Raj. Inspired by the organ with pedals, the harmonium was created in India as a simple instrument for song accompaniment. Much later in Paris, I saw a painting of August Renoir which also had a harmonium with a woman. So obviously this musical instrument never gained popularity in Europe, but it's become irreplaceable for Indian music.

Music is a passion in India, and particularly in Bengali culture, both rich and poor people have a great desire to sing. So the harmonium always occupied a pride of place in our home. Being malnourished at the time she gave birth to me, my mother impaired her health. Unfortunately she never really recovered enough, or even got the free time and energy from school work and housework, to pursue her musical inclination.

Even though we had no choice, there were two things my heart couldn't accept at childhood. The first was night time, which was a regular nightmare with me. I remember at 5 o'clock every afternoon my grandmother, and sometimes my mother, would take ash off their self-made mud cooking stove to clean the glass of the kerosene lantern we used after sundown. We had to switch off the lantern at night before going to bed to save on kerosene.

My father used to put his bicycle between the bed and the set of drawers, and chain it with a lock on one leg of the bed. Even in those striving times we had the problem of thieves. They would dig a tunnel from outside, enter the room when we were asleep, grab whatever they found, and leave by opening the door. This lack of security haunts me till today.

My other fear was with the roof. In the rainy season, a large storm would blow out part of the roof leaving big leaks in its wake. We would scuttle inside trying to find buckets and plastics and save whatever we could. But nature often overpowered our efforts, alarming us with more show of strength like making the walls of the house move dramatically in the howling wind.

The roof being made of hay used to regularly attract birds to make their nests here. These nests in turn were magnets for snakes. While stretched out on the bed in deep sleep, I several times awoke to discover snakes precariously above on the ceiling enjoying the taste of birds.

This remote Sahidnagar refugee colony in Kachrapara sub-district housed refugees who entered different professions. We had barbers who would go home to home to give haircuts and shave beards. Vegetable sellers, maidservants, carpenters, schoolteachers, shop floor workers in a railway workshop, rickshaw pullers and small shop owners. The water carriers who brought potable water from afar had two containers supported by ropes on both edges of a wooden rod that they carried on one shoulder. When the containers were full the rod bent over to become a bow at the end of the man's neck, as he swung hippity-hop in a structured momentum carrying the water to sell and make his livelihood.

My mother's contribution in my transformation was unimaginable. Divided by a train line, the other side of Kanchrapara was quite chic and more affluent, with the British heritage of a railway wagon making workshop being located here. This workshop owned a town hall called Bell Institution. A cine club here regularly projected films. Just think of my mother's quiet determination to transport me to a worldview away from Sahidnagar refugee colony. She used to take me to Bell Institution to see Shakespeare films when I was just seven or eight years old.

I remember those black and white films where I understood Hamlet to be a big sword player, and his stepmother as evil for putting poison in his father's ear to kill him. I obviously could not express these learnings to my friends at my village as the films had no relevance to Sahidnagar's poverty and environs.

My mother attempted to make me feel there are lots and lots of big things happening out there in the world. I should not resort to traditional nativity, but think very differently. Her dreamy stories were about events and achievements of different kinds in diverse places across the world, mostly in Europe. I cannot believe now that without any exposure to affluent societies or European culture, how she had learnt so much.

Immediately after her high school graduation, my parents were married. Within her meager salary of Rs 110 to run the household, she struggled to get both Bachelor of Arts and then Bachelor of Education degrees. It was her courage and belief in transformation that always spurred me on. Even as I lived in this refugee colony, she tried to continuously engage my mind in transformation, which has since become a way of life for me.

Whenever I return to my village to meet my childhood friends, I can see how my life has since transformed. I was exactly like them. I marvel at how a person like my mother could have such influence over me to escape this place. I don't think I have gained more spiritually; I find my village friends have a certain innocence that I have lost. But my expression to the world is at a different level today.

You, my reader, may not understand the disparity without having experienced life in my village in the 1950s and 1960s of the last century. Saying thanks to my mother for influencing my transformation feels totally inadequate.

Organizations in general are averse to a radical shift strategy. If after our research process and analysis I found transformation was needed, it is always quite a task to convince my clients. But I pursue with honest conviction, pointing out the benefits of the prescribed change. Perhaps it is this fervor in my body and mind that makes them believe in my proposition to take the transformation route with me for their betterment.

My inbuilt character to transform for betterment was surely a result of my personal transformation inherited from my mother. Her training was: 'Never accept mediocrity. Break the rules if you must, as rules are all man made.'

at the corporate level

A corporate example of transformation propelled by a craving to overcome deprivation was Sony's vision articulated in 1950. This was just after Japan was defeated in World War II:

> We will create products that become pervasive around the world. We will be the first Japanese company to go into the American market and distribute directly. We will succeed with innovations like transistor radio that American companies have failed at. Fifty years from now our brand name will be as well known as any on earth. And will signify innovation and quality that rivals the most innovative companies anywhere. 'Made in Japan' will mean some-thing fine, not shoddy.

These are three types of transformation triggers I can see. It is possible for organizations to trigger one of these motifs to start their own transformation chapter.

An organization that's keen to grow exponentially can try finding itself amongst any one of the three motifs of transformation. Organizational culture that's in tune with the trend and consumer sensitivity can influence an employee at work, allowing him to deliver accordingly. In one way or another this culture will always reflect in the product or service that reaches the end consumer's hand. If an organizational culture is neutral, the deliverable also becomes neutral. If it is introverted the deliverable will reflect this, and if it is outstanding, the consumer's acceptance of the product will be outstanding.

Let me reiterate my market observation: 'Philips invents, Sony markets.' Philips invented the hardware for portable music, but Sony with a more open culture very successfully marketed this concept as the Walkman. This is a living example of the balance between organization culture and the deliverable. This balance is the indicator of an organization's profit, growth, and share value. Today punctuality, discipline, quality and on-time delivery have become hygiene factors. What's important is how you convince the consumer by entering his/her subliminal context.

When an entrepreneur with tremendous conviction creates an outstanding success in his time, why do his inheritors fail to reach the same type of success? Perhaps the company enlarged in size but didn't change its culture according to the world's trend movement. This is a very valid reason for financial results heating up.

Henry Ford's automobile passion and vision in 1910 was that anybody who worked in his car manufacturing plant should be able to afford the car. So he increased wages from $2.34 for a 9 hour shift to $5 per day. This enabled employees to work ingeniously for a surprising delivery. Check out the beauty of the vision implemented a hundred years ago. The employee who promises a perfect car to his end consumer, himself becomes a consumer. Employee satisfaction and end consumer promise guarantor become the same person. This is an iconic example of organizational culture. Simultaneously, Henry's whole idea was to increase the sales volume of the car.

But today's competitive scenario is undoubtedly more intense than that time. You need to bring in an incredible culture into your organization to emotionally inspire your people, failing which the organization will likely face a dissonance from the market. A work culture that's hypnotic can create a dynamic bond with your employee so he/she continuously energizes the organization with care.

A high salary alone, without a unique culture, will not make your organization visionary. Instead, growing complacency will creep in putting all employees into a comfort zone, and making them risk averse. In such a situation, personal wealth protection gains priority, and employees deliver only what is required, without proactive quantum leap in delivery.

To return to Henry Ford, the automobile industry culture that he pioneered with inventive organic growth has, until recently, been in the maintenance mode. But now Ford has shifted towards acquisitions. When companies have enough money, they indulge in acquisition after acquisition. Little do they think about the fact that the culture required for organic growth is very different from what inorganic growth needs. The automobile companies that Ford acquired such as Range Rover and Jaguar have totally different cultures. Such acquisitions took Ford's existing culture to the realm of total dissonance. Ford may have miscalculated on the transformation its traditional business needed to handle inorganic growth. Ford has certainly displaced its funds into a loss, but transformation has not happened.

Of the three corporate transformation motifs—(*a*) Proactive transformation, (*b*) On-time opportunity for transformation to happen, and (*c*) Do or die transformation—you need to figure out which transformation motif is more suitable and aligned to your organization. The discomfort framework (see Chapter 2) can be used as a stimulator. Choose the platform of displacement, rupture or maintaining aspiration and use the means of renovation, innovation or both (see Chapter 5), as per your business requirement. Then using the ReFinE Value Ladder (see Chapter 10), you can upgrade your organization to take your business to a position of good, superior or unbeatable in the market.

According to our ReFinE Value Ladder, if yours is a basic company, you can upgrade to the next level of good. A good company can upgrade to superior, and a superior company can upgrade to the unbeatable position. If you are already in the unbeatable level, your organization has to strongly use the discomfort framework to unearth unexpected value which can give you outstanding growth and profit that sustain.

If you are currently in the basic situation, don't try to quickly jump to the unbeatable, not even superior area. First top the good level with a total displacement platform. Your stakeholders need some lead time to accept that you have really upgraded from basic to good. Strategically work out with further proactive transformation how to move up from good to superior deploying the rupture platform. Don't rush for the unbeatable area; continue to work hard in laddering and balancing your deliverable. The unbeatable area will come when the time is mature.

Here is a matrix of three possible corporate transformation motifs (see Figure 11.5) stimulated by discomfort framework to go through the platform of displacement, rupture or maintaining aspiration. The means could be breakaway renovation or innovation while using ReFinE Value Ladder. This framework can help you to escalate from basic to good, good to superior or superior to unbeatable. If you are already in unbeatable you can further escalate for the long-term.

Figure 11.5   three possible corporate transformation motifs stimulated by discomfort

Stimulator	Transformation Motifs	Platforms	Means	Process	End result in the market
Discomfort	1. Proactive transformation	DISPLACEMENT or / and RUPTURE or / and MAINTAINING ASPIRATION	Breakaway RENOVATION or / and INNOVATION	ReFinE Value Ladder	Basic to good
	2. On-time opportunity for transformation to happen				Good to superior
	3. Do or die transformation				Superior to unbeatable

Here are some examples showing how different companies have used the three transformation motifs (see Figure 11.6). I cannot use discomfort as stimulator in these examples. That would be judgmental on my part as I do not have internal details of these companies. But from my experience in corporate transformation for different companies across the world, I have clearly understood that transformation that's looking for quantum results will require the discomfort platform as stimulator. Otherwise the organization will become like stagnant water that tends to get polluted.

Figure 11.6 transformation examples

Company	Transformation Motifs	Platforms	Means	End result in the market
GE, L'Oréal, Nestlé & Mercedes	Proactive transformation	Continuous rupture & maintaining aspiration	Breakaway renovation & innovation	Superior to unbeatable
Sony & Toyota	On-time opportunity for transformation to happen	Displacement & continuous rupture	Breakaway renovation	Basic to superior & unbeatable
LG, Samsung & Skoda	Do or die transformation	Displacement	Breakaway renovation	Basic to superior

If you are sensitive to the external world's diverse activities, and realize that your company's fortunes are linked to them, you will also be sensitive to corporate transformation. Only an extrovert outlook can understand the requirement for transformation of both an organization and its business strategy. Corporate transformation has to manifest to the external world. It must simultaneously be impactful and visible internally. One of its visible elements is the corporate identity and its message, which is the primary contact with all stakeholders.

If your company is transforming to go up the value chain from a basic or good level using the displacement platform, it may need to change its name to grab the stakeholders' attention on the displacement.

Why should a name be changed? If a company has kept the semantic connotation of its name neutral and harmless, and the name carries no old or negative baggage, it is possible to create displacement without changing the name. But if the name is associated with some negative relating to its past, a name change would be beneficial.

However, this depends largely on your past delivery perception and association with the image. If the image has a neutral association, you can change its perception without changing the name. But if the image has a negative association you need to take a call on whether to change the name. This is always a tough decision for an organization. But if the negative association of the name creates some contamination in the growth path, you may consider it as a zonal disease. Try to knock it out to avoid contamination.

If your organization is in a superior position and growth has been stagnant, you may need to create a rupture to change the market perception of oldness in your product or service which impacts your corporate message and identity. Here the name of the company can be translated in a totally different form to change the perception without changing the name. You cannot be in the superior position if your activities were not superior. That's why there's no need to change the name.

In the unbeatable position, your product, service and image are at peak position. Your challenge is to maintain this aspiration on a continuous basis. Corporate image becomes very iconic here so difficult to change. But why should you want to change? The dilemma here is how to achieve grand innovation in your product or service to authenticate your corporate value and take a certain leap forward.

Creating a beautiful logo without a core message or an elaborate internal rejuvenation program will not obtain financial result (see Figure 11.7). Such an exercise triggers just a beautiful logo, yet isolates this identity from the organization's back-end and front-end alignment.

Figure 11.7 beauty vs strategy

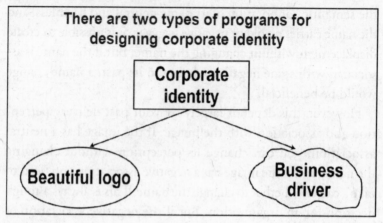

Whereas when the corporate identity drives business in the corporate transformation program, it can become a visible manifestation that radiates different activities. It needs at least two years to establish and manage internal change so it is internalized perfectly.

In my experience of transforming several corporations in different countries, there are nine satellites that must get positively impacted when corporate transformation drives them (see Figure 11.8).

Figure 11.8 corporate business driver

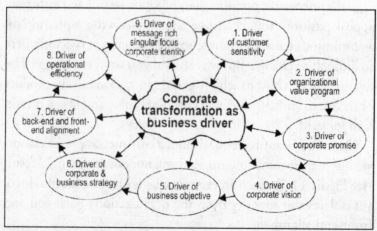

Corporate transformation as business driver for coherence can have a central theme of how to understand consumers and customers in the competitive environment. It can set the direction on how to win their hearts with a *fil conducteur* positioning as per the company's deliverable excellence.

The single value system deriving from consumer and customer sensitive offers can independently drive the organization. These values can be drilled into employees of different functions inside the organization by accurately addressing their actionable points.

I have designed an actionable value matrix that can be used to seamlessly interconnect the back-end and front-end of any organization to its market dynamics. This value matrix comprises four human demeanors: attitude, behavior, action, and delivery. The matrix will not change, but the articulation of employees' attitude behavior, action and delivery will be different for different organizations depending on the gaps they need to plug to run the organization coherently and with fluidity in their competitive environment. A unique employee brand can be created primarily for internal purpose, but which external stakeholders can understand and connect to as well.

attitude

An individual's attitude to work is important. The attitude of different people and organizational attitude have to meet at a point to create coherence. This resonating point should be able to match the needs and desires of consumers and customers.

Attitude can be built as organizational philosophy that encompasses:

(*a*) distinct global and local sociocultural observation in a deeper manner to collect and extract information relevant to business, and

(*b*) curiosity to discover society's fast moving and distinct trends that can contribute to business enhancement.

You can create an organization policy on how different functions should look at distinct and relevant-to-business societal trends with consumer sensitivity. Information should be filtered for the requirements of different functions, and then distributed for cross-functional purposes.

behavior

Behavior is conduct that coherently incorporates customer sensitivity across the organization. A structured, defined attitude should guide the behavior of employees to bring coherence across the organization. Without this structured attitude impacting behavior at work, decision-making for any functional or corporate action will be made vulnerable.

action

Action points become coherent once attitude and behavior are inculcated in this way. The definite upshot of this coherence is that the organization will never face a crisis situation at any point. That's because the attitude and behavior of employees have been streamlined so they can anticipate the trend and the competitive scale, and take requisite action.

With such structured attitude and behavior, action inputs of employees can result in an Emotional Surplus experience for the consumers and customers. And this can sustain by making products and services vibrant and efficacious. Of course, the core attributes have to be laddered and balanced as per the ReFinE Value Ladder flow.

delivery promise

Experience tells me that a delivery mechanism has to be promise driven because a promise is measurable. Consumers or customers always choose a brand based on its promise of delivering excellence. So deliverables must be proactively woven with a *fil conducteur* that is the result of the attitude, behavior, and action of employees (see Figure 11.9).

Figure 11.9 ABoArD value framework

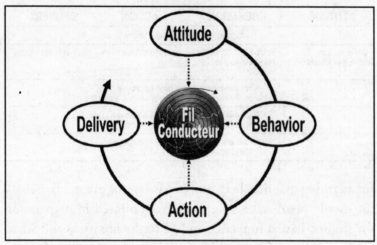

The four progressive steps of attitude, behavior, action and delivery (ABoArD) promise of an organization's employees can be articulated and linked to one another as a value program. These values must be specific to the organization in the competitive scenario. Like a jet aircraft where all parameters are regulated for speed and rationality, you come aboard this value framework for a continuous journey. Every individual in the organization can practically use the ABoArD value framework for his everyday work.

The values have to be translated distinctly to three types of employees, the desk employee, mobile employee, and shop floor employee (see Table 11.1) as per different department functions such as HR, Sales, Manufacturing, and others. This framework can be harmoniously internalized across all employees so they understand the meaning and action points of the articulated values. The result will be cohesive performance.

A specific team needs to drive this corporate value program, which is sensitive to consumers and customers.

Let us apply this framework to an out-of-industry experience, that of a student who needs to pass an examination. His attitude should be to learn without any ego, have no shame in asking questions to clear any doubt he has, keep his eyes and ears open

Table 11.1 framework for corporate transformation

ATTITUDE	BEHAVIOR	ACTION	DELIVERY
(Hypothetical articulation below)			
Strive to be part of consumer fantasy	Behave with consumer like she is your family member	Translate chore into fantasy	Make alive the fantasy
What this means to the desk employee HR, Admin, Finance, Planning, Vendor management, IT, Marketing, R&D			
What this means to the mobile employee Sales, Customer service, Procurement			
What this means to the shop floor employee Manufacturing, Quality, Maintenance			

for anything that may help him in passing the exam. His behavior should be to wake up early, refresh himself in preparation for studies, have a timetable and go to the library as and when required. His action should be to take and make notes for preparation of serious studies. The delivery would be to concentrate on the paper during the exam and ensure he writes clearly and well.

You could be a very good student but fail miserably in your professional life. Because you may have studied by rote for your exams, your attitude was not very open to the external world. This makes you behave in an introverted manner. You may have scored high marks, but in practical business life you need action and delivery, in which you are weak. In the competitive professional world, the strategy of studying by heart, memorizing, and spitting it out on an examination paper does not work.

The quality of organizational delivery and success depend on the organizational attitude to learning and behaving accordingly, then putting in action to make a deliverable which can positively surprise consumers and customers.

process of corporate transformation

I have developed a process to get unbiased information through an audit of an organization's business strategy and practices with a large sample size of all kinds of internal and external stakeholders. The core objective of the audit is to align an organization with consumer and customer sensitivity, from strategy to the delivery (see Figure 11.10).

Every organization needs multiple visual expressions to connect with different people. The transformation process I have developed has visual communication for interaction with various stakeholders. This makes every interactive session very dynamic and fruitful.

Step 1. audit of organization strategy to understand its culture, unearth its strengths and identify the shortcomings

This is an elaborate audit with senior, middle, and junior management and upto the shop floor on consumer and customer sensitivity in all functions of the organization. How coherently is everybody working in the direction of consumer and customer sensitivity? The auditor at this stage should be very neutral, not give any subjective input, just be a good objective listener.

Quantitative questions are a waste of time here as such data can always be had without an interactive session. The interaction has to be emotionally driven to find the inner sense of the organization's culture, practice and the participant's involvement. If this audit appears like spying, or an appraisal system to the respondent, the direction of corporate transformation will never emerge as the loopholes will not be exposed.

In this strategy audit session, if managers of one function cannot give any idea about another function, it means the organization is working in silos. Managers may be responsible about their own work, but not being able to articulate a strategic outline of the company's vision is the first verification of incoherency within an organization. At this stage no information needs to be given to top management on the rational, functional, and emotional data collected.

Figure 11.10 eight-step stakeholder sensitive corporate transformation process

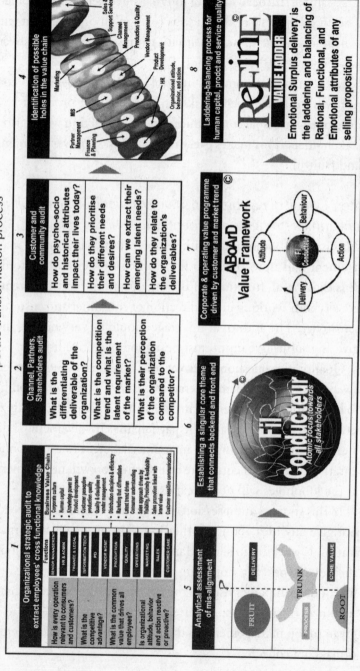

1
Organizational strategic audit to extract employees' cross functional knowledge

How is every operation relevant to consumers and customers?

What is the competitive advantage?

What is the common value that drives all employees?

Is organizational attitude, behavior and action reactive or proactive?

Business Value Chain

Functions	
SENIOR MANAGEMENT	• Corporate culture • Human capital
HR & ADMIN	• Knowledge power in
FINANCE & LEGAL	• Product development
INFORMATION TECH	• Customer perceptive production quality
PD	• Quality & discipline in vendor management
VENDOR MGMT	• Distribution discipline & efficiency
PRODUCTION	• Marketing that differentiates
QUALITY	• Consumer understanding
OPERATIONS	• Latest trend driven • Sales approach driven by Visibility, Proximity & Availability
SALES	• Sales promotion linked with brand value
CUSTOMER CARE	• Customer sensible communication

2
Channel, Partners, Shareholders audit

What is the differentiating deliverable of the organization?

What is the competition trend and what is the latent requirement of the market?

What is their perception of the organization compared to the competitor?

3
Customer and community audit

How do psycho-socio and historical attributes impact their lives today?

How do they prioritise their different needs and desires?

How can we extract their emerging latent needs?

How do they relate to the organization's deliverables?

4
Identification of possible holes in the value chain

Partner Management — Finance & Planning — MIS — Marketing — Sales & Support Service — Channel Management — Production & Quality — Vendor Management — Product Development — HR — Organizational attitude, behavior, and action

5
Analytical assessment of mis-alignment

FRUIT — DELIVERY
TRUNK — PROCESS
ROOT — CORE VALUE

6
Establishing a singular core theme that connects backend and front end

Fil Conducteur — atomic focus towards all stakeholders ©

7
Corporate & operating value programme driven by customer and market trend

ABoArD Value Framework ©

Attitude — Behaviour — Action — Delivery — Fil Conducteur

8
Laddering-balancing process for human capital, prodct and service quality

ReFiNE © VALUE LADDER

Emotional Surplus delivery is the laddering and balancing of Rational, Functional, and Emotional attributes of any selling proposition

Step 2. partner feedback

From the cues that emerge from Step 1, the audit of business strategy, a questionnaire is drawn up. The central theme of the questions is always consumer and customer sensitivity as they relate to different external functions. These are vendors, partners, talent pool, financial institutes and shareholders from whom we collect feedback of their understanding of the organization and its market area. What comes to light is their experience, trust and faith in the given organization.

An analytical workout of the cohesive factor between the organization audit and the external stakeholder audit is benchmarked through the ReFinE Value Ladder. At this stage, the strengths and weaknesses of the company flesh out. It is now necessary to make a senior management presentation in the presence of all line heads of each function, but also advisable not to divulge specific names against specific information.

Step 3. consumer and community audit through perception research

Its time now to blend questions from the two audits for interactions with consumers, customers, the community and talent pool. This elaborate research has to be very insightful and potent to verify the perception of the organization in a competitive scenario. The ReFinE Value Ladder benchmarks the organization on consumer perception of its Rational, Functional, and Emotional attributes.

Step 4: identification of possible holes in the value chain

The holistic perception of the organization that emerges from amalgamating the internal and external audits with consumers, customers, talent pool and community research has to be informed to the client's management team in a very structured manner. Major resonance and dissonance will transpire at this stage, as the organization's true character with all its pockmarks is revealed from senior management discussions. Any consequential tension needs to be cooled down in a positive way so that you get to see the future in a very outsized way. The reactions from the management can vary like this:

Category 1: The organization accepts the dissonance as a positive need gap. People become highly charged to go further.

Category 2: The organization gets demoralized. If the dissonance is too disheartening, complacency starts to set in.

Category 3: The organization gets totally scared even among themselves.

Category 4: The organization agrees to its resonance, and wants to further take a bold step forward.

Category 5: The organization has good resonance but complacency is very high, making it difficult to manage.

I have experienced these five kinds of reactions on presenting the corporate audit results. With the objective of delivering beyond the clients' expectation we have somehow managed to grow the clients' businesses in a quantum way with our promise of:

We experience emotionally,
We deliver rationally,
We help grow our client's bottomline significantly.

Step 5. potential research on how to align the organization
In this transformation step the direction of the future is established. The organization's deliverables need a character with which we can bounce with consumer, customer, talent pool and community. This indepth qualitative research tries to discover the business potential, and define a strategy on where and how to land in success.

In preparation of potential research, I always invite aboard different types of professionals like advocates, judges, sociologists, psychologists, scientists, writers, and artists to get multidimensional angles and a larger diaphragm. Such an unbiased council of different types of people who do not know the organization helps it to generate big, new ideas.

This projective research combines the lifecycle, lifestyle, and trend of stakeholders. Using the ReFinE Value Ladder, a strategic platform to transform the organization becomes very clear.

Upto this stage the research generates a great deal of content. To simplify dissonance and resonance factors for an organization's management, I have created the tree tool that divides an organization into three parts, the root, trunk and fruit (see Figure 11.11).

Figure 11.11   the root, the trunk, and the fruit of an organization

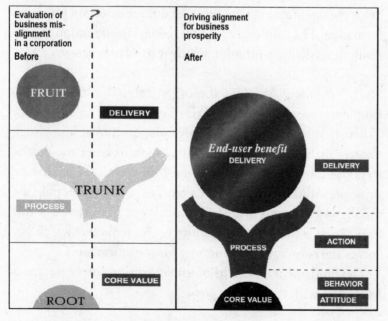

The root stands for the organization's core value driven by attitude and behavior. The trunk can be equated to the processes

with which the organization functions, and is the action in the ABoArD value framework. The fruit is the delivery that goes to consumers, customers, the talent pool and the community. If the root, trunk and fruit are not aligned, stakeholders get a raw deal.

The dissonance identified during research can be segregated to fit into the root, trunk or fruit. This uncomplicated pictorial image is an easy way to present the organization's visible manifestation of dissonance. This image hammers home misalignment points in the organization's core values, process or delivery. These can be registered in the mind quite simply for subsequent correction of the structure.

Step 6. defining fil conductuer

The correction of the misalignment combined with the organization's potential for growth gives birth to a strategic *fil conducteur*. The *fil conducteur* drives coherency across every function, and helps the organization take-off in an unique direction for transformation. The employees' attitude, behavior, and action should result in its delivery promise, which is its *fil conductuer*.

Step 7. instilling ABoArD, the organizational mould

Employees need to get ABoArD the operating value system. Whether they are thinkers, innovators, executors, knowledge masters or business generators, they have to enter the organizational mould for corporate transformation. The operating principles of ABoArD must be creatively crafted so they plug the misalignment points in an aspirational way. The essence of this framework is the delivery promise or *fil conducteur* which becomes the corporate repositioning for transformation.

The fundamental benefits of implementing corporate transformation with this process are:

- The CEO, vice presidents, and other managers can drive the organization with seamless coherency.

- Employees get obliged to think and act in the direction of the organization vision and goal.
- The organization becomes relevant to the external society.
- Back-end becomes dynamic and proactive.
- Vendor management gets driven by and high volume.
- People in the organization get passionate at work.
- It becomes easy to retain and recruit talent.
- Quantum growth with premium earning is achieved.
- The share value in the share market goes up significantly.

Corporate transformation impacts product design, which includes service that is productized for tangible delivery like a physical product. The ABoArD framework creates transformation in product design which specifically impacts the business result. Defined ABoArD values can contemporarize product design to surpass market expectations. As an example, let's get ABoArD for a hypothetical product design:

attitude: *Strive to be part of the consumer's fantasy.* The product design has to be driven by consumer fantasy.

behavior: *Behave with the consumer like she is your family member.* Product design character to have a family approach.

action: *Translate chore into fantasy.* If your existing product has become a chore for consumers, following this attitude and behavior process will push you into action to transform your product design into creating a fantasy for consumers. That's because the input of attitude is fantasy.

delivery: *Make alive the fantasy.* With this principle, the delivery promise of your product design will become fantasy driven.

Getting ABoArD, your tired product concept will become contemporary and efficacious. In this example, the delivery promise of fantasy is the *fil conducteur*. So the guiding principle and output of product design has to represent fantasy. This is the way your product design will ABoArD a disciplined framework year after year. ABoArd value framework has one objective: align all functions with external partners to deliver high value to consumers and customers, and thereby increase corporate growth and profitability. When you have aligned your total organization with ABoArD you have done an aspirational corporate *jalebi* which everyone can bite into.

Step 8: ReFinE Value Ladder

To achieve and transact the Emotional Surplus strategy to deliver value beyond the expectation of customers and consumers, you have to go through the ReFinE process. For a snapshot of how to segregate, benchmark and ladder-balance the rational, functional and emotional attributes of your corporate value proposition, turn back to the end of Chapter 10.

scientific and sensorial product design

The Loire Valley has, for centuries, described the French art of living. The fascinating castles of Loire attract tourists, even the French, who want to know more about France. They take long drives on either side of the beautiful Loire river, which meanders to become very narrow or wide. They stop to visit a chateau or to wade in the river.

River Loire passes through Amboise, a small and lovely village town with a bridge connecting both river banks. From the bridge, as they step down to the riverside road, people get hypnotically drawn to the main attraction, Chateau d'Amboise where King Francois Ist had lived. But if this desire to go into the chateau can be controlled, a surprise awaits the visitor just a short walk away. The road slowly narrows as you enter the workplace of a genius of all time who reinvented human need and lifestyle.

This 600-year-old shrine inspired the enigmatic genius to write his theories like the flow of a river's calligraphy. His unbelievable thinking process was so totally ahead of his time, so displaced and crazy that the genius was afraid to declare it openly for fear of being ostracized as a madman. He wrote everything in reverse. As you walk on this road with heavy concentration, with nostalgia for the theories that transformed your life, you get sensitized to the overwhelming power of the human mind.

My visits to Amboise are frequent because they draw out in me a burning passion to walk down and sense the very same street this incredible genius had used. What was his style of walking from the King's chateau to his own house? How did he dress? What did passers by think of him then, did he talk to anyone as he traversed that one kilometer? If he suddenly had a new thought, did he sit by a corner of the street to make a drawing or write in a notebook? When he was very hungry, did he run fast? Did he read while he was walking? Perhaps he had a luxurious time, enjoying the privileges of being an artist patronized by the king.

His home in Clos Luce connected to the Chateau by an underground passage is small, not flashy. You may even miss it as you walk by, but for the few cars and visitors outside indicating something of interest. At the age of 39, he himself declared 'Je'suis un genie' or 'I am a genius.' Did such an audacious man really exist? Today after 600 years, nobody can deny that he was the genius of all time in an extreme variety of fields.

This was the house of artist, engineer, scientist, medical expert Leonardo da Vinci, the genius who wrote: 'A day with a full load of work gives better sleep; only a life totally covered with work gives a tranquil death.' King Francois Ist brought him from

Italy to France as his personal guest artist when Leonardo was 63 years old. He stayed at Clos Luce for five years, and breathed his last here.

Ardent fervor pulsates through my being as I walk through Leonardo's beautiful home where he struggled to overcome monotony and invented what we cannot do without today—the aircraft, infrastructure, anatomical studies. Was it unlimited passion, craziness, expression of masculine power, a show-off attitude or absolute madness that made such an irreplaceable genius? In this incomparable pilgrimage paradise, such questions crop up. I need to discover the wholesome struggle he went through to bring human society out of its monotony. But that my questions don't get answered gives me that inevitable, thrill-seeking reason to visit Amboise again and again.

Why did a painter like Leonardo da Vinci need to go beyond his painting canvas where he has shown sensorialism unbeatable till today? Through scientific invention he provided people the benefit of science in everyday life. The 20th century marketing jargon of being consumer friendly can actually be attributed to Leonardo da Vinci.

Reputed as the world's best painter with *Mona Lisa*, Leonardo went on to apply his mind for the upgradation of human life. He found engineers were mere introverted theoreticians who did not think about people. The genius of his vision took him several hundred years ahead of his time. He broke the mould of being known as just a painter and sculptor. His inventions were varied and unimaginable, which future generations are still enjoying.

A painting or a sculpture is hung or erected in a museum, but design that is applied through functional improvement for bettering human quality of life represents an artist's strong discipline. When Leonardo went beyond painting to becoming a designer, he became the future builder of the world. Design that can be used has tremendous balance of rational, functional, and emotional

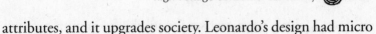

attributes, and it upgrades society. Leonardo's design had micro detailing. Never before him did people think like that.

My curiosity and knowledge of product design developed from delving into the roots of European culture. I observed how they address every aspect of human comfort in product design. Compared to developed countries like USA and Japan, it cannot be denied that the discipline, creativity and process of European design are the authentic source of the world's best knowledge and knowhow of product design. As a designer you should go beyond the surface or output of any innovative work to the root of the mechanism Europeans use to enter the subject. It will help you to reorganize your discipline and creativity.

The nut and the bolt depict scientific product design for me. In the advance of technology people may have forgotten that product design fundamentally starts with the simple nut/bolt mechanism. Without this, where would scientific design and invention for better living be today? The nut/bolt mechanism's every aspect with holistic male-female plugs represents super precision in design.

I equate sensorialism in product design to the touch of a rose, which universally has the power to take a physical metaphor into the mental level. If you superimpose the nut/bolt invention and mechanism to the touch and feeling a rose evokes, you will realize my obsession for scientific and sensorial product design. The heady combination of scientific and sensorial substance cannot fail to surprise the consumer.

consumer's approach, usage, and feeling towards a product

While designing a product I have observed that three primary factors can gain us entry to the scientific and sensorial paradigm. They are the consumer's approach, usage and feeling towards a product. Making consumer sensitivity the fulcrum of product design, we need to follow the consumer's inclination to a product.

first, the consumer's approach to a product

Without assistance, the consumer should get convinced that she can easily approach the product, especially a new product she is unfamiliar with. The product's immediate appearance must be easy, inviting, glamorous, and psychologically in sync with the consumer's mind (see Figure 11.12).

Figure 11.12 approach parameters

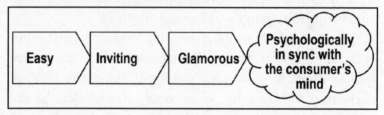

These four parameters should get linked in the product due to regular usage after purchase, but they should not become boring. That's why before designing the product, consumer approach must be put through the ReFinE Value Ladder to raise these four parameters you are addressing. The designer's deep understanding of the consumer's microtone approach will determine the product's approachability in the consumer's first glance and usage pattern.

second, the consumer's usage of the product

The initial involvement of product usage should be magnetic, provide independence, be devoid of intimidation, easy to use, and ergonomically in sync with consumer usage habit (see Figure 11.13). This is valid for after purchase too. The product's user friendliness depends on how the designer has ReFinEd the usage area linking it to consumer usage habit prior to design.

Figure 11.13 usage parameters

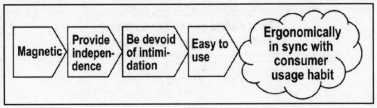

third, the consumer's feeling of the product

The aspect that's hidden and impacts the consumer's acceptance of the product is her feeling, and that's intangible. As a designer, if you can gauge the consumer's feeling after she has approached and used the product, you can mastermind a strong concept for the design. If the consumer's feeling is not distinctive, you can be sure there will be no word-of-mouth nor excessive commercial success. Your product will remain mundane.

While initiating product design you need to carefully carry out the ReFinE exercise to understand the consumer's feeling parameters at that stage. These are eye expression, facial expression, body language, and making the consumer articulate her unstated feelings (see Figure 11.14).

Figure 11.14 feeling parameters

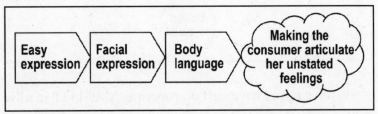

Approach, usage and feeling of a product should trigger a thorough design principle. This will help you create a design blueprint with a process that is consumer centric (Figure 11.15).

Figure 11.15 process to define design blueprint

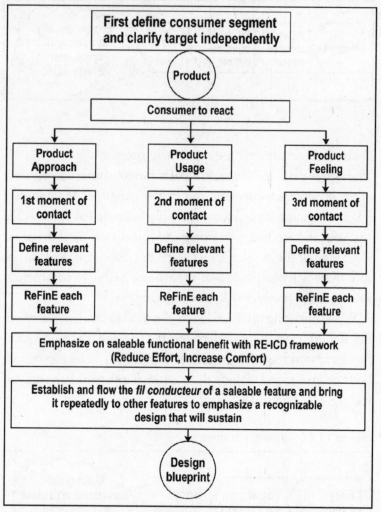

As an example, I have used the American MAGLITE in a live consumer research project with Indian farmers who desperately need the torchlight (see Table 11.2). I was not working for any torch company but introduced this as a product from an unrelated industry to see how farmers take to a sophisticated torch.

This was achieved following the COA (curiosity, observation, action) framework.

Table 11.2 Indian farmer's approach, usage, and feeling towards product MAGLITE torch

RESEARCH PARAMETER	OBJECT MAGLITE	CURIOSITY	OBSERVATION	ACTION FOR PRODUCT DESIGN	DESIGN PARAMETER FOR NEW PRODUCT
APPROACH—Relationship between product and human beings	How he touches and holds a Maglite	Unfamiliar, hesitating approch	Product needs to be more simple to invite the consumer	All product design should invite consumers the first time he glances at it	What it is the first impression you want to create with your product
USAGE—Benefit of product to human beings	How he uses it	Difficult to use	Complicated, not user friendly	Make the usage benefit of the product extremely friendly to any type of consumer	How do you design all touch points to be user friendly and aspirational
FEELING—Psychological and physiological aspect of design	What does he feel about the product	Surprised	Touching to verify both the smooth surface and graphic surface	Use material of different types of textures to increase the sensorial feel of the product	What are the elements that will lead to consumer bonding

product design's core sensitivity and its relation to eight universal categories

Europeans invented product design that has extreme functional benefit for human beings. Americans mass customized it to get economic scale for selling it. The Japanese miniturized design to bring it close to consumers in a cozy, friendly output.

In this paradigm, I have developed a theory of design culture that surpasses functional benefit. The principle of functional benefit excellence touches the fully outstretched human being with

unlimited sensorial advantage to always increase comfort and reduce effort across the eight areas of universal product design.

eight universal product categories through RE-ICD principle

RE-ICD means reduce effort and increase comfort design
(see Figure 11.16). It is the ideal metaphor of human living and
reflects people's psychological and physical craving. RE-ICD
plays a major role in making product design sensorial and driven
by commerce as it directly connects to consumers' psychological
and physiological behavior. It is the platform of fundamental
physical benefit that can differentiate your product as pay-off.
RE-ICD discipline can be deployed in any type of product design
in any category.

Figure 11.16   the RE-ICD discipline

My style has always been to approach work through the consumer's eye, heart, and soul. This has given me the advantage of
easily entering and accomplishing a required design. Having
lived in consumer context, I arrived at the logic of eight universal

product design categories (see Table 11.3) as the value upliftment and excellence of any product category is led through its functional benefit.

Table 11.3 eight universal product design categories

Engineering design	Technology design	Habitat design	Luxury product design
FMCG design	Fashion design	Service design	Infrastructure design

If you are a designer in one of these eight design categories, don't get disinterested in the other seven as they too influence your target consumer. Consider them instead as industries unrelated to yours, and use them to help you think differently of your design output. To avoid monotony and stereotyping in your specific product design work, bring their design input or output into your subject. Today's product design thinking and application cannot be merely a mechanical process and technology centric because you may get a high class design but if it does not connect with consumers, you may not get good financial results.

Let's get a little deep into each of these eight different product design categories (see Table 11.3):

engineering products are precision driven

When engineering components dominate a product, their alignment, cohesiveness, and a particular shape either with metal or wood, plastic or any new material, need tremendous discipline of blend before creativity comes into the picture. The design world is moving towards using a mix of different materials. That's why creativity now needs to assume the detailing skills of classic master Leonardo da Vinci. The physical object of engineering design, which reflects the use of these different new materials, should have great detailing and refinement in its physical parts so as to create genuine aspiration for consumers.

RE-ICD

A water tap can be given an air of mystery by reducing the effort required in using it. In fact all bathroom accessories can be dramatized for consumer functional benefit through RE-ICD discipline as people enjoy relaxation in the bathroom.

technology design is multidimensional

Technology intrinsically has no physical expression like mechanical engineering, but improves the product's feel or unstated advantage in usage. Digital language being totally non-human, design that's driven by digital technology has to be obsessed with humanization. Technology is used in three different angles: to improve mechanical engineering as in automobiles, technology as design as in computers, and technology as non-visible output as in sound. Consumer and customer sensitivity takes priority in these three technology involvement areas.

A designer driven by technology alone cannot bring out-of-the-box, consumer sensitive, commercially successful products. But a designer who is more sensitive to consumers, and who can adapt technology, can certainly sell his products. The credo is: think first, design will follow, either mechanically or technologically. Today when technology is commoditized, goes through continuous advancement, and is freely available, it's a consumer sensitive driven latent concept that's required for commercial success.

When a design has extraordinary usage advantage, it is the thought or concept behind it that has led to its success. Technology designers across the world can think and observe consumers with curiosity, and then take the advan-tage of technology to act with speed.

RE-ICD

The wider masses always find a technology product to be quite complicated to use. When such a product is user friendly for the tech savvy consumer only, the product will not bring in high sales. RE-ICD discipline can reduce the mental torture most consumers go through with technology products, and so get them to buy such products. Computer usage, for example, is still not RE-ICD for the wider masses.

habitat is comfort and personification

The art of living incorporates habitat product design with its mix of physical engineering and digital back-end support. It will always be very difficult to bring a single style of lifestyle products for different types of people. Consumer choice has its own illogical and continuous demands for change. IKEA in Europe started mass consumption in habitat products. This is poised to be a vast economic sector as future generations dream to live in their own unique dimensions.

RE-ICD

An easy approach fitted kitchen could be marketed by the RE-ICD discipline. There would be more functional than show off advantage here, with everything fitted within arms length for continuous usage. If you are a readymade kitchen manufacturer, using RE-ICD could benefit the consumer in her every operation in the kitchen. This could then become your marketing selling proposition.

FMCG design is convenience centric

FMCG product design tends to maintain a habit. As the designer, you may think a consumer's habit needs nurturing, but in actual fact you may be inducing a sense of boredom in the consumer's mind with your product. Commoditization can set in. The world is witnessing mushrooming competition in the lower price FMCG segments. If the consumer and retailer are acquainted with a particular low price category product's quality, the retailer pushes the product and the consumer gets accustomed to it and creates the pull.

In such regular purchase acts, it would be dangerous to imagine the consumer pays only for the brand's name and its sophisticated television campaign. This category is like a husband–wife relationship. It needs to be continuously renovated so the consumer and product do not lead a boring life together. If product rectifications are incremental, consumers can easily shift. That's why FMCG products need a strong differentiating character to kick-off the 21st century.

RE-ICD
Breaking a fresh egg by tapping the shell with a metal instrument can be quite slapdash, and tossing the shell can make the kitchen untidy. A container can be designed with RE-ICD discipline so a simple hole is created in the egg which also separates the white and the yolk. Consumers can confidently use it without spilling the egg.

fashion design is feel good and personality centric

This is the part of human life where they want to get an orgasmic feel. It doesn't have any rational justification. It is desire level. It makes the society sophisticated and gives allure. It also gives the distinction of different individual characters.

Today four layers of fashion exist in the world:

(*i*)   *Popular:* Value for money fashion which is generated from mass appeal with a marketing treatment, like GAP, Adidas, Nike, NAF NAF, Swatch, L'Oréal.

(*ii*)   *Trendy:* Fashion for the trendy with a marketing approach like Zara, Esprit, Tommy Hilfiger.

(*iii*)   *Selective:* Fashion that's personality driven for selective consumers like Kenzo, Hugo Boss.

(*iv*)   *Exclusive:* Fashion that's driven by a designer's unique, limited collection like Christian Dior, YSL, Armani, Chanel.

In general all these four layers have a certain quality undoubtedly superior than basic price sensitive products. The discipline of this category is irrational. As all these products help consumers in an ephemeral area, they try to indulge. Intangible association is very strong here, as also image magnification. Retail expression and the kind of product experience you create at the retail are a part of this kind of product. Creating the illogical base is a must here.

RE-ICD
Instead of a thread cap or flip top cap, a lipstick could be a single integrated system with RE-ICD. As you push a button on the bottom, the top of the lipstick opens like a tulip releasing the color stick for application. With a sliding movement on one side, the petals can envelope the lipstick to close: a one piece lipstick.

luxury product design is refinement
Most luxury products emanated from Europe's monarchical affiliation. They reflect the traditional artistic craftsmanship and the designer's passion patronized by European royalty during their rule. Today brands like Cartier, Mont Blanc, Lalique, Remy Martin, Don Perignon, Rolex cater to the rich and mighty. Design refinement and the fame of old Houses get highlighted, and intangible association is very, very high. You may be able to buy the same type of product at a price hundred times lower, but you will miss out on brand value. Luxury product brands will never compromise on their quality which is out-of-the-box.

RE-ICD
Bring RE-ICD in the latent perspective to luxury products to keep trend alive in them. Using RE-ICD through technology in the hidden aspect of luxury products without destroying their

look of authenticity can help it to advance in the latent trend. With infra-ray treatment, the nib of the pen will come out at the time of writing, otherwise the nib will pull back inside. There'll be no tension that the nib can break.

service design is productization

This can be a tedious domain as service quality varies from person to person. The route to designing an outstanding service is a written process, discipline and its application as in the military barracks. For example, if you say 'smiling' is your service output in the hospitality business, you should design the contour of a smile and train people across your organization on the accurate smiling expression they should have. To productize the service, technology has to be used as backbone support. Technology is a mere process. Delivery will always come through the human aspect. That's why human service activity productization is the key for service designing productization.

As relationship is the key factor in service individuals cannot be left to function according to their moods. Everybody must converge to a directional mood as defined by the service value.

RE-ICD

Today customers find it a hassle to open a secure courier packet. As a courier service provider, you may consider a box with RE-ICD, with a defined cutting point that will not be damaged in travel, and will ease the customer to open it elegantly.

infrastructure design is philosophical

Infrastructure could be considered an art form. Regular replenishment is not required here as in other design forms. Infrastructure design needs vision at inception to look at how it will never go out of fashion. The thought behind is how to endure permanency. Infrastructure construction can represent the flair of its time, but it must have a universal yet trendy appeal to withstand decades and centuries. That's why past data like the track record of human evolution becomes very important while designing infrastructure.

At the moment of conceiving, the designer-architect has to visualize the infinite expression of his design. He has to worry about how after 10, 25, 50, and 100 years, people will live in this design environment even as they cross different trends over epochs. If infrastructure design becomes obsolete within 10 to 20 years then it was not a design, it was just a requirement. If on the other hand, a piece of infrastructure design was abandoned from human living, it means that the design was too cold and so got obsolete.

Georges Haussmann, appointed to the post of Councilor of Paris on June 23, 1853 from a rural district in France, used great political and administrative ingenuity to fulfill his passion of changing the face of Paris. From being a medieval city, he transformed Paris to become a modern capital with grand masterpieces of unique infrastructure within 16 years, upto 1870.

Haussmann imposed a pattern on Paris based on great suburban routes, radial roads to the suburbs, strategic nodal points and circular boulevards. It was a town planned for public security. From the air Paris represented another beauty of geometrical figures, which no other city in the world can boast of. From the ground the buildings and roads were imposed with a uniform structure of gardens and trees.

Paris remains unchallenged as the most beautiful city in the world. Amidst the marvelous 19th century infrastructure of Paris, any mediocre modern architecture has failed to gain public approval. To match with Haussmann ingenious city design, only a breakaway, out-of-the-box architecture like the Cultural Center of Georges Pompideau can stand scrutiny.

But this magnificent city came too close to destruction during the German occupation of France in World War II. Hitler had instructed his army that should German defeat in France be imminent, the Nazis must bomb the city of Paris before surrendering it. Fortunately the Allies entered on time for the liberation of Paris on August 25, 1944.

Archives recall that Haussmann's theory was based on how to benefit the public. This out-of-the-box vision of a Prefect has created inimitable city infrastructure, which is timeless.

RE-ICD

Those parts of infrastructure design that have functional usage can deploy the RE-ICD discipline. If the maintenance system is designed in RE-ICD from inception, the infrastructure product's maintenance will be better and long lasting.

In the eight universal product categories when RE-ICD is at the core of product design, it connects very well to consumer usage of the product. So RE-ICD becomes a strong marketing proposition for better commercial value realization. In product design the RE-ICD metaphor can radically shift the functional benefit of product design to create the Next-mark. The rider is that its rational attributes be strongly supported, and the emotional content of look, touch and feel are in the latent perspective.

design discipline

There are four facets to scientific and sensorial design that result in thought, concept, design, prototype, tooling and the final product (see Figure 11.17). From design logic to design expression, to design execution to design output are four scientific and sensorial elements which create the four dimensions of product design. The human being in the rhombus is linked with

Figure 11.17   scientific and sensorial 4D to profitably sell design with quality that is unbeatable

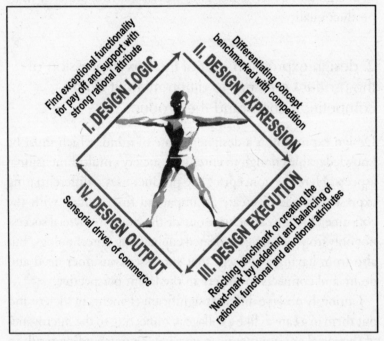

every aspect signifying that product design should never carry a method or process against the human touch.

This visual framework establishes that design starts with the human living aspect surrounded by design logic, expression, execution, and output. If you are designing a product with these four aspects without having a human being in the middle, your product will not become scientific and sensorial to respect human need and desire.

1. design logic: strengthening the rational and functional attributes

This means the functional attributes of the design need to be strengthened with reduce effort-increase comfort then supported by rational substance. So consumers will receive a surprise benefit of ergonomic excellence. They will also have confidence in its product quality.

2. design expression: out-of-the-box expression of the product concept to differentiate it from competition and brand the product

Design expression is a designer's state of mind, which must be knowledgeable enough to enter into society's multidimensional aspects. Here the concept of the product uses a differentiating expressive mode to create an impactful first contact with the consumer. Design can achieve out-of-the-box commercial success not only from using sophisticated engineering or technology, but also from having a concept that surpasses consumer need and desire and connects to society in the latent perspective.

Curiously observe different significant elements in society and put them in a canvas like a collage. Connecting to the microtones of the social environment can give you an outstanding result in design concept.

In spite of you and your competitor working separately in different environments, your design logic may perhaps be quite mathematical and more or less the same as the market is the same too. But if you use the ReFinE Value Ladder process to help you create design logic and expression, you can make that clinching difference.

Every economically successful design has an out-of-the-box concept. For a suitably complex design logic of a sophisticated product, you may find that a simple form of an orange or pumpkin will create the difference. It can make your wife, mother, friend or children connect to it spontaneously as the first consumer.

A concept in a totally different paradigm, can generate commercial success for your product design.

3. design execution: laddering and balancing the ReFinE attributes

This is the ReFinE stage of laddering and balancing the total design through a combination of its rational, functional, and emotional attributes (see Figure 11.18).

Figure 11.18　scientific and sensorial design path

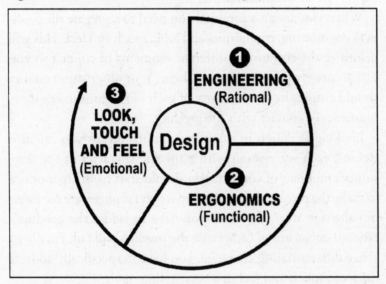

The rational element could be its mechanical engineering or technology. Design needs to deliver defect free products. This will happen if Step 1, Design logic, is respected. This early stage prevents defects in manufacturing delivery. It must link and upgrade technology to reach the consumer's aspiration for reliability. The functional elements equate to ergonomic benefits. The consumer's psycho-physio movement must be harmoniously translated into functional benefit that uplifts the senses. The emotional element is the product's aesthetics. You can curiously observe worldwide trends and apply a sense of aesthetics in the consumer touch, feel and visible points.

The key driver of a manufacturing business is product design. When linked with consumer or customer lifecycle, lifestyle and trend, the design connects to them. It's important to get consumer perspective for the product at the time of design execution too. The first moment of contact is the consumer's inclination towards the product. The second moment of contact is consumer usage of the product. The third moment of contact is consumer experience of the product.

When you design a product, you need to segregate the product's engineering, ergonomics and look, touch and feel. This will prioritize the consumer's different moments of contact so you can accurately pay attention to them. Your observation quality should emphasize the intensity of each of the consumer's three moments of contact with the product.

Looking at design in three segregations means you can also ReFinE each segregation with a specific character of the consumer's moment of contact. You should start from ergonomics to make the product robust. The more you sophisticate the functional usage areas, the more you have to ladder the product's rational engineering. Otherwise the product will fail. Finally to give a differentiating character, you have to specifically address the look, touch and feel in a very styling mode.

styling

A product, from the time it's conceived through its development, market launch and reach to the consumer, takes a few years. That's why the latent trend has a big impact on styling. As the first visible contact of a product's design is its look, touch and feel, too many people in the organization feel free to give their comments. But not everyone will have the caliber to judge the product's styling.

Styling has to be judged not only by its ephemeral look, but driven by touch, feel and your deeper thoughts on consumer association in the latent perspective. A professionally competent styling council must be appointed with people of exceptional quality sensitized to the latent trend.

Sophisticated developed countries use professionals like sociologists, psychologists and trend forecasters to enrich management decision making with some structure on styling. Indian manufacturers very often outsource styling to Western professionals. However, irrespective of the competence of Western stylists, the main point is that styling has to flow from four market areas as explained later here in the ReFinE product development process (see Figure 11.20).

As a designer you can effectively educate the design styling council in four market areas:

(*i*) Consumer lifecycle, lifestyle and trend.

(*ii*) Impact of sophisticated developed countries in the product or service in the society.

(*iii*) Impact of technology in society.

(*iv*) The five factors impacting consumers namely, the psychological, sociological, economical factors, the trend and industries unrelated to yours.

The exceptional people in the design styling council would be more driven by emotional content. Motivate them through strong visuals and short audio-visuals to take a decision in the latent perspective.

Efficient project management for product features: Product features can be managed by checking them against the consumer's first, second, and third moments of contact (see Figure 11.19).

To strategize the overall design perspective from the design table, use cost design along with vendor management, manufacturing and the consumer's three moments of contact. This will show the selling character of the design and help alert your marketing person in advance.

Figure 11.19   product features driven by the consumer's three moments of contact

Determine the number of features required for selling	The first moment of contact is the consumer's inclination towards the product	**AT THE TIME OF PURCHASE** • Societal influence • Media influence • Personal and collective ego	
	Define the number of useful features	The second moment of contact is the consumer usage of the product	**AT THE TIME OF USAGE** • Starting point of hate or love • Service becomes a given factor
		Assure guarantee of feature durability	The third moment of contact is consumer experience of the product	**HABITUATED TO BE IN CONSUMER LIFECYCLE** • Spread of word-of-mouth to create brand value • Service is the vital factor

Of the total number of features in the design, let us hypothetically say that 10 percent could impact the consumer in the first moment of contact, 20 percent in the second moment, and 30 percent in the third moment of contact. The balance 40 percent will be the inner structure where it's difficult to get consumer insight. The insight from the 10 percent of features impacting consumers in the first moment of contact has to be so powerful that they help sell the product like hot cakes. You can then invest accordingly as you will know exactly what will sell your product.

The second moment of contact is critical as the consumer's love and hate factor emanates from usage. The consumer's third moment of contact, which is product experience, is not visible. This moment will bring your credibility to the consumer and help make your product and brand successful for the future.

This framework will provide clarity on product investment vis-à-vis its success on the condition that each moment of contact has consumer connect in the ReFinE Value Ladder.

4. design output: sensorial driver of commerce

Design output should not become technical substance, but substance that helps human evolution. When design output is a manufactured product, its performance must be tested in the market for a few months, and defects, if any, corrected. A defect free product launch is crucial to get good word-of-mouth in the market, especially in an emerging country where such a track record is rare.

conclusion

Scientific and sensorial product design in engineering, technology and habitat areas are driven by engineering excellence. So engineering has to flesh out and lead marketing. If marketing gimmicks take center stage with these three product design areas, market success will escape the product.

business case for projects

Whether you are renovating an old product or creating a new one, projecting a business case with mere statistical analysis cannot make business success today. Statistical analysis is cold and driven by financial calculations. It has no strong customer interface.

From experiencing project management in different verticals, I have developed a consumer and society-driven funnel of perception (see Figure 11.20) that strongly fleshes out the real opportunity of business. If you extract indepth insight from the four parameters in the funnel, and add it to your statistical analysis,

Figure 11.20 ReFinE product development process through COA framework by applying perceived and potential value research

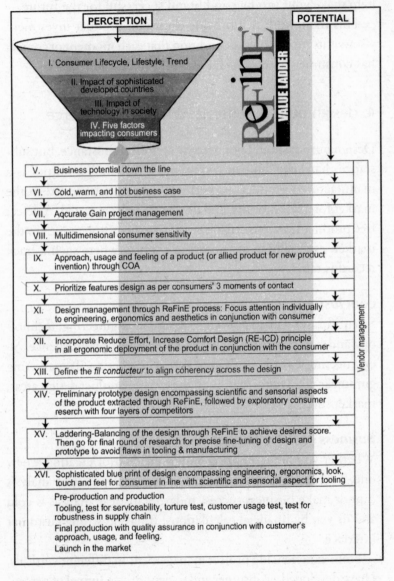

you will get a genuine feel of whether your product needs renovation or innovation. You will clearly see if your business case is for low volume (cold), mid volume (warm), or large volume (hot business case). A cold business case arrived at from statistical analysis can be warmed up to become hot after going through this funnel of consumer interactions. As we all know, volume always drives cost down, thereby expanding the market with high quality products.

application of ReFinE process for engineering, technology, habitat, and luxury products

In Figure 11.20 is a summary of how the different frameworks, tools and processes I have designed can help managements grow their business. This configuration can be applied in the areas of engineering, technology, habitat, and luxury products. To apply these processes in other areas, the configurations from No. 9 to No. 16 have to be accordingly customized and changed.

Look at the *jalebi* in the perspective of product design. It is round, but not totally. Ergonomically, a *jalebi* bite in any area feels like a single crunchy object in your mouth, and its engineering holds it together. Product design must also give you the same yummy pleasure as the *jalebi* does. Look, touch and feel are integral to the *jalebi*, its ergonomics of a crunchy bite is equivalent to scientific and sensorial design.

branding and channel ownership

Branding is a specialist activity with specific actions in different categories of products and services. Just as medical science has precise and different categories of diagnosis and treatment for every part of the human body, with diverse professionals corresponding to these categories, the science of branding has categories too, each of which is very different from the others.

A hospital has to equip itself with specific departments to treat different illnesses in the same person. Every specialist doctor has specific processes of looking at and analyzing the health symptom of a patient. In the same way, branding cannot have a generalist approach. It's very specific to the category and has to be specialized on the health symptom subject of different brands.

Branding means consistently selling and earning premium value that has a recall pull for consumers and customers. This brand strategy relates to a wide category of products and services. The buyer could be the same for diverse categories, but the approach of each of these categories obviously needs its individual focus.

Drawing from my long years of personal global experience working in multi-vertical categories for repositioning or new branding, I have made a branding platform chart for a variety of categories (see Tables 11.4 and 11.5). Consider these holistic platforms of high ground significance to be the basis of ideal brand characteristics for different specialities. Taking any of them will not per se give your branding a differentiating character. But based on them, you find a specific language or positioning for your brand.

sensorial approach to the brand

The branding approach needs to have different sensorial connects to its consumers and customers. Whatever the approach in branding may be, you will never know how your consumers are getting attracted to your brand: is it by seeing, smelling, tasting, hearing, or touching? Of course unprivileged persons like the blind can connect with senses other that the visual, or the deaf and dumb can be disconnected from sound, but connect with the rest of their senses.

Table 11.4 branding platform of different categories

CATEGORY	BRANDING PLATFORM
Branding for vehicle	
Vehicle for pleasure	Engineering to pleasurable drive
Vehicle for livelihood	Robustness and need customization
Vehicle for livelihood-lifestyle	Mixture of robustness and pleasure
Vehicle for Transportation	Comfort and durability
Branding for home application	
White goods	Companionship
Brown goods	Fidelity
Electronic	Immoderate pleasure
Branding for entertainment	Infinite pleasure
Branding for FMCG	
Food & beverage	Hedonism, active health
Carbonated drink	Taste and excitement
Personal care	Harmless pleasurable efficacy
Home care	Eco-friendly efficacy
Laundry	Confident efficacy
Branding for fashion	
Garments	Individual personality
Shoes	Glamor that gets noticed
Branding for lifestyle product	Instant sensation
Branding for luxury product	
Cosmetics	Preservation of beauty
Accessories	Immoderate desire
Jewelery	Show-off possession
Branding for habitat	
Furniture	Living differentiation
Home decor	Vibrancy in daily life
Linen	Mix and match
Kitchen	Art of practicality
Bath	Aqua dream
Branding for IT	
Hardware equipment office	Trendy workhorse
Hardware equipment home	Fantasy
Hardware equipment personal	Companion
Software	Profound knowledge
Branding for NGO	Serve and act with integrity
Branding for political party	Selfless social responsibility
Corporate branding	
Domain specific	Magnifying the core
Multi-conglomerate	Principle of cohesive union
Specialist	Insightful
B2B software	Adaptability with speed
B2B component	Consistency and speed
B2B consulting	Knowledge of the future

To connect all types of people in society to a brand, a branding jewel box (see Figure 11.21) can unfold the real treasure of the brand. Why a jewel box? That's because like a jewel, a product is always kept in the center of its packaging box. It is covered with different types of protective layers to give it glamor and sensorialism.

Table 11.5 branding platform of different categories

CATEGORY	BRANDING PLATFORM
Celebrity branding	Character magnification
Branding for learning centers	Assurance of knowledge gain
Branding for services	
Hospitality	Maternal care
Travel	Stressless tour
Airlines	Cocooning service
Banking	Proactive partnering
Insurance	Assurance for tomorrow
Railways	Cost saving convenience
Courier service	Delivery done
Supply chain management	Networking precision
Branding for government departments	
Tourism	Assurance of infrastructure facilities
Public service	Better quality of life
Investment	Proximity, availability, and security
Health care	Living comfort
Education	Responsible for the future
Security	Assured of safety
Branding for state councils	Value of progress
Branding for Media	
Newspapers	Analytical authenticity of the day
Electronic (TV)	Crisp, unadulterated enjoyment
Radio	Day long companion
Magazines	Enlarging information on the present
Books	Past, present, and future knowledge
Internet	Friendly and intimate relation
Outdoor	Provocative capsule
Branding for sports	
Garments	Fresh and active and vitality
Accessories	Body language
Sports persons	Emotional bulldozer
Branding for health & fitness	
Hospitals	High-tech peace of life
Clinic	Hygiene and sincerity
Pharmacist	Sober and disciplined
Drugs OTC	Self-explanatory
Drugs prescriptions	Trust and relief
Fitness equipment	Vibration of life
Branding for recreation & holidays	
Hotels	Hygiene, leisure, and pleasure
Time share	Immoderate anticipation
Travel agents	The peacock spirit

Let me take you through my branding jewel box where every protection has glamor and communicating power. A consumer's approach to a brand is conditioned by the five elements of form, color, symbol, semantics and the personality of a living character. In the branding jewel box they are protected in the inner circle, inside the pentagon. Use the branding jewel box metaphor as a

Figure 11.21   branding jewel box

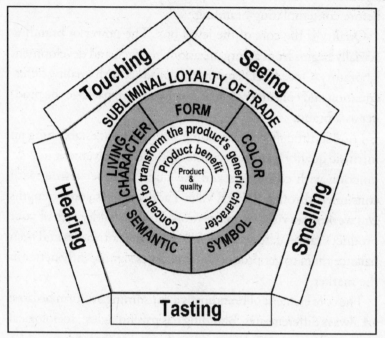

framework. Your brand activities can be sensitized to the consumer and customers' varied ways of using your brand.

In my practice, branding doesn't exist without product or service quality performance. If product quality is inferior to its competition or consumer expectation, branding becomes superficial plastic surgery. Only if product quality is at par with, or better than, its superior level of competition, can branding start. Branding as a makeover exercise to hide a product's quality deficiency is being totally unfaithful to the consumer and customer.

product quality

In every product or service-branding exercise I have undertaken anywhere in the world, I have always sensitized my client about significantly improving the quality of the product or service before contemplating branding.

Quality is the core of the jewel box. The power of branding actually begins from an organization's research and development laboratory. Once R&D empowers a product with quality, differentiation and consumer benefit, marketers can package the product as a brand.

I find it difficult to do branding work without establishing an intrinsic quality standard with total R&D involvement in conjunction with consumers and the trade. Product testing with consumers through ReFinE Value Ladder reveals your strengths and weaknesses vis-à-vis competitors. You can ladder each of your product's rational, functional and emotional attributes and then balance them to get product quality that's significantly better in the market.

The core element of branding is a consuming art form because art always differentiates. Branding has psychological, sociological and trend parameters bolstered with an economic sense.

benefit

The first radius of the jewel box surrounding the product has a tremendous sensitivity to give glamor and protection to the product and its quality. The consumer or customer's only interest in the product is its benefit, and this is what they pay for. So branding activities have to start from product benefit.

R&D's real job is to find a unique product benefit, which may not be easy to propagate in all categories. There are two types of benefit manifestation, the intrinsic and the imagery-driven brand difference. Between Coca-Cola and Pepsi the differentiation is more imagery driven; while Toblerone chocolate manifests intrinsic product benefit through its shape.

In general, a blind test reveals intrinsic product quality difference where people can recall the brand. Imagery-driven branded products may not be differentiated from competitors in a blind test; the support of an established image will be required to recall the brand.

Even when it's conceptual, use the ReFinE Value Ladder to get a spark from consumers on whether differentiation will come from the rational, functional, or emotional element. Only from consumers and customers, not from the industry back-end, will you get the real understanding of product benefit.

It is crucial for a brand to register a unique product benefit in consumer mind. A brand that performs better in its category usually has a clear product benefit, even in the basic level where product differentiation is very difficult to create. The dairy category Danone, for example, has a clear distinguished benefit in its *Actimel*. You need a strong corporate vision to achieve that, and behavior that sustains it. In time this benefit can become a tangible asset that creates strong goodwill. Similarly, Nokia's goodwill is its user-friendliness, Sony television is respected for its color and image, and Dolby for its sound quality. This cannot happen by itself, the organization has to take the right initiative and build on it.

Both differentiating and non-differentiating characters need a strong conceptual transformation. This is the concept which transforms a product's generic character.

concept

The idea that determines the selling ability of a product or service is its concept. A brand's concept must always be in an altitude higher than its technical substance. It cannot be substituted by any mechanical or technology-driven industrial process, no matter how sophisticated that is. If a brand's core concept is powerful from inception, it can withstand change. Evolving through different decades, it can modernize the intrinsic quality of its products, and sustain its brand value.

You need a large canvas to build the concept of a product or service. The work involves the total diaspora of living, a collage of consumer lifecycle, the social aspects, existing and latent trends. Just as consumers never occupy themselves with just a factor or two, the branding concept should reflect their multidimensional life. The specific product or service idea should be instilled here to find the brand's concept.

The branding concept needs a potent balance of reality and mystique. The more canvas-like the concept is, the more will brand sustainability increase. Being grounded on reality for selling products like toothpaste or body lotion is important but this reality will not grow the brand's power. It is the element of mystique you inject into the brand that will spiral, making it grow and grow and grow.

The conceptual area of branding is critical for brand success. At the initial stage, the concept is an intellectual substance of your marketing strength. But if the concept is driven by monocentric thinking with good language articulation, it will not connect to the consumer. The concept's formation should be consumer or customer psychology driven.

Organizations very often end up doing conceptual work at two levels. For corporate consumption, the brand's concept is written in boring text, explaining it at length so employees can understand it. Then a professional branding company or advertising agency is given the task of communicating to consumers in grammatically correct wording as though it's a mathematical equation. The brand concept's mystique dimension gets lost here.

Actually there should be just one concept that's relevant to the product. Its mystique power should connect to consumers, and the corporation should follow it. In creating such a single communication you will be putting back pressure on your R&D and marketing teams to work together with external research and branding partners to come out with a concept that becomes a real differentiator.

After establishing it, the concept can get the practical form, color, symbol, semantics and living character, the five elements in the third radius of the branding jewel box. This can radiate the core focus of the product's benefit and concept to bring glamor.

what is form in branding?

Form is the metaphysics of a product. When a product or service needs to be branded, a form must first establish its visible character, which people can keep in mind. A brand without a physical form cannot last. A simple example is bottled water. It can have a label and sealed cap, but without a differentiating silhouette of the bottle with specific usage advantage, the brand of water can become very generic.

Form is the decisive factor that establishes FMCG, technology, engineering, luxury, habitat, fashion, service or infrastructure products. To garner cost advantage, a generic form has often been used by different FMCG brands in the same category, sometimes even the same form in other categories. Consumers find themselves at a loss to appreciate the category's premium brand. Advertisement investment becomes its only sales tool. Plastic sachets or standard carton boxes make the brand vulnerable, more in FMCG than in other product areas.

Product containers of brands like Perrier, Nescafé instant coffee and Saffola oil have the silhouette character in themselves. Kinder is a surprise egg-shaped product container made of chocolate and milk you can bite into directly. Toblerone is a triangular chocolate product which is visible in its packaging on the shelf. These brands have tremendous premium and uniqueness in consumer connect.

In service companies the staff uniform, greeting courtesies, attitude and behavior create the productization form. The successful courier company, UPS, has proven to the world that service productization makes sound business sense.

Software development companies in general do not worry about the metaphysics of their deliverables. These are in digital format with no branding or established delivery form, making their business vulnerable and price sensitive. Companies are running software and voice process businesses with size, manpower, and facilities. The same service can be obtained from any company irrespective of size.

Apart from their size, facilities, manpower and relationship, they don't have any element that elevates them from the generic category and distinguishes them as a brand to their customers. If they can create a physical form surrounding their deliverables, they can distinguish their fundamental business character and sustain their margins in any competitive scenario in the future. I think there is a need to give form to this virtual business delivery. Companies can establish their differentiating delivery mechanism through a form. It can create continuous proximity to the customer through physical presence.

If four competitive biscuit brands with more or less the same recipe can create different forms, why not software development and voice companies? Similarly, they can give their deliverables a form.

Form means the shape. Being identified as having an unique form has tremendous commercial impact. A brand's consumer and customer contact through its form can humanize the man and product relationship. Even a blind consumer can be mesmerized with an original shape like the Coca-Cola bottle or Toblerone chocolate.

what is color in branding?

The marketing world has many preconceived notions that categorize color into specific domains, an approach I find to be totally illogical, even wrong. Color is a matter of combination and mix. The union of the product's function with the psychology of consumers and customers determines color usage. So any color that maintains and communicates the essence of the brand in absolute terms is acceptable.

A brand can become outstanding when a breakaway color is blended to make a product relevant. I have very often used unconventional colors in branding, and that has given sustainable leadership to the brands.

At the initial stage, people in Europe found my use of color to be an extension of my painting canvas. But when my color alchemy enlarged their businesses and sustained them, it was proven that colors do connect businesses to consumers. I appreciate French and European society for encouraging my experiments in color usage as that gave me the opportunity to create the Next-mark in this field, and help clients to reach the Next-mark in their businesses.

When I used green for Bio, the new yoghurt brand I created for Danone in Europe in 1987, it shocked Western society markets. Using this unconventional, bold color for the first time in the all white yoghurt category made the brand distinctive and successful. The Bio name has since been shifted to Activia to become a global brand. The color green created no difficulty, instead helped in brand recognition when this big brand changed its name recently.

What was the thought behind using color to bring this success? It all started with *bifidus actif*, a new bacteria created by Pasteur Institute. This formulation was extremely effective for digestion. I realized Danone could be the first to exploit such an active agent and create a displacement in traditional yoghurt. Christian Koffman, Managing Director of Danone France who considered me a 'crazy creative' egged me on by saying, 'Sen, show me your creativity.' Fondly naming me 'Sen of the Indian holy cow heritage' the French always appreciated the aspect of spiritualism I tried to bring into Western consumption habits.

Bifidus actif was a great formulation, but it was available to all manufacturers. Even as we were the second company to utilize *bifidus actif*, sooner or later it would no longer be a differentiator. I had to think out-of-the-box. The scientific effect of *bifidus actif* would make everyone arrive at scientific solutions, so I started to dream big and different.

Social stress in France at that time, and easy access to medication and tranquillizers led to a common complaint of constipation, especially with women. Coping with office and home issues, getting old, losing glamor were mental blocks that multiplied along with poor digestion. I understood *bifidus actif* could be the solution for faster and systematic cleansing of body and mind.

Before Bio, the yoghurt market had military regimentation, strictly highlighting the product's functionality. It was almost like discussing detergent as a cleansing agent. Marketing professionals and technocrats saw yoghurt as a good-for-basic-digestion product belonging to the cold distribution chain. So yoghurt identities were all white or with a blue effect, to represent refrigeration and freshness.

In time the bacteria's efficacy would become commoditized. People would remember yoghurt as just a dairy product. Are cows found on mountain-tops in snowy cold altitude? Not at all! Cows graze on green fields.

The psycho-drama of the consumer's stressful life, its efficacious scientific solution with *bifidus actif*, the green habitat of cows: they all swirled in my mind. And bing! came the idea: a breakaway yoghurt brand in the color of Nature where cows are found. The cure for the socially created ailments is also natural, so what should the name be? An extract of nature: Bio.

On dark green packaging, Bio was written in yoghurt-white. At the center of the packaging was a vertical corridor that communicated its intestinal cleaning properties. A graphical yellow scientific sun over the letter 'i' illustrated the yoghurt's progressive curing and flushing of the body. At that time, green was rarely used for frequent consumption food products. What Bio's color alchemy established in consumer mind is that this was the only brand with a natural active agent that cleansed the body to elevate the mind.

Green Bio made the difference on the shelf, in the consumer mind, in distribution, and Danone brand became a talking point in society. A new culture was created. Other yoghurt manufacturers soon followed with the *bifidus actif* formula. But till today Bio de Danone resides as a state of mind that's understood beyond the physical product.

But to achieve that, the type of unconventional research I undertook then made people consider me a crazy man. I went into the provinces of France for consumer research and market visits to understand the consumer's social aspect. I appeared at odd times like 2 o'clock in the afternoon in consumer homes to ask if there was any place to eat somewhere nearby. My main curiosity and wish was to get invited to their homes to see how they use their refrigerator. Quite a few times people accepted my friendly manner, and I got the chance to visit their homes, have some snacks with them and see how they consume yoghurt. My objective was to gauge the importance of yoghurt in the consumer's core of life.

I broke the color code in different fields of work. But if you consider breakaway color to be just a clutter-breaker proposition, you are making a mistake. Only when color plays a role as subconscious phenomenon for the consumer, can the impact last.

what is symbol in branding?

A symbol is a distinction in the crowd. It has the power of recognition, plus the power of silent communication. Symbols have been used by monarchies, prophets and in politics as the origin of a distinctive character. The silent message of a symbol can take a brand higher from it physical product or service substance.

A symbol can play a social role too, as Shell Petroleum has done by raising awareness of the ecology. By default petrol and gas connote pollution in people's mind. But Shell's shell symbol isolates its commercial aspect. Instead, it highlights the origin of petroleum from delicate sea-shells, a million years old, and preserved in the bowels of the earth.

The symbol of Bibendum from Michelin, the world-famous tyre company, establishes a human character. This Bibendum symbol has humanized the tyre, considered by many as the dirtiest part of the car as it plies on unhygienic roads.

A thought provoking, visionary symbol can empower brand recognition, bridge language problems and last century after century. Unfortunately marketers in industry are generally more semantic driven. They trust written communication as that competency is under their control. That's probably why you will find, across the world, a large number of branding without symbols, just driven by semantics. Companies that have focused on symbols to build the brand, undoubtedly have non-traditional marketing thinking processes.

Another way of expressing the symbol is through the brand name typography. In the last century, Coca-Cola came up with a symbolic expression in their typography. Another example is IBM. A recent example is Sony's laptop where Vaio brand is a symbolic typography representing today's technology world.

I always incline towards making unique typography to represent the brand symbol. Calligraphy is an established art form in the West, exhibitions are held on calligraphy alone. I spent enormous time in Paris understanding calligraphy grammar with famed European calligrapher, Paul Gabor of Poland. He trained me on the nuances of typographical grammar, how the force of your handwriting creates typography style, how typography can be drawn with concentration similar to drawing the human figure. You can invent symbolic expression by writing typography. I gave the same importance to calligraphy with Paul Gabor as I did in sketching human or animal bodies when in the Calcutta Government College of Art and Craft.

Calligraphy has fascinated me since childhood when I made secret political posters and wall paintings for my father. Digital calligraphy fonts irritate me today as they rarely follow the grammar of typography. It's unfortunate the young generation is losing the grammatical foundation of typography. I should mention that in the 2,000 branding exercises I have been involved in, I have never allowed any member of my team to use typography available in readymade fonts for branding work.

There are different expressions of symbols. In the liquor, alcohol, and beer markets, symbols can express traditionalism. In olden times a trademark symbol was used for legal protection of the brand. But the best symbolic expression of a brand is when it communicates the brand's value and shows its futuristic approach.

Making a symbolic brand expression involves tedious research in anthropology, sociology and the consumers' psychological aspect. The combination of these three elements can result in a brand's enduring symbolic expression. This static expression of the brand can become a powerful communicating and recognizable tool.

what is semantic in branding?

A brand's semantic expression is strategically advantageous to create awareness. There was a time when company names were very elaborate, but with expansion a crisp substance was required. So acronyms became popular like The Hongkong and Shanghai Bank became HSBC, and Imperial Chemical Industry became ICI. Of course ICI's objective was also to avoid 'imperialism' in its brand as it may have been difficult to enter sophisticated markets with an imperial connotation.

Another type of semantic branding expression is a word like Sony with beautiful pronunciation, but meaningless for global people. A very sensitive area is using the name of the creator in brand expression like Ford, Bell, Nestlé, Bose where the inventor's heritage of authenticity and his personality made the brand relevant and created the reference of a segment. The marketer can make such a brand into a cult. In semantic brand expression you need a terrific innovative substance to substitute the brand's future stability.

Many companies in emerging economy countries use the founder's name as branding. Most times, the founder is more a businessman than an inventor so the brand may encounter dissonance or a credibility dilemma, especially if the personality is not charismatic or innovative.

A composed name of different words that make a meaning, like Volkswagen 'the people's car' can be very powerful because the meaning is translating the ultimate benefit of the product. The semantic name becomes the communicator.

Semantics can be effective in branding when the name itself is meaningful, like Windows from Microsoft. There is complex alchemy in coming up with a nostalgic effect name like Oracle, a Greek goddess, and connecting that to ultra-modern technology the company deploys in its operations.

Semantics can be creatively crafted for writing positioning statements associated with a brand, and for concept verbalization, the third radius of the jewel box. Thought provoking and unique semantics will give distinctive substance to the brand character. Nike means nothing, but '*Just do it*' reflects its substance. Similarly Wipro does not communicate anything. The semantics of '*Applying Thought*' make sense and indicate Wipro's deliverables anywhere in the world.

what is living character in branding?

A brand's living character is its connectivity to contemporary social flavor and latent trends. The advertising medium can create this living character by connecting it to the product, concept, form, color, symbol, and semantics of its given character. When isolated from these elements, advertising becomes a gimmick that consumers may enjoy, but it may not influence them to buy.

The comic character Popeye is an example. When Popeye needs remarkable strength to perform a daring feat he opens a can of spinach and achieves his mission. This character endeared spinach to children and reduced the mother's labor of convincing them to eat their greens. Communication from such a living character can sustain a brand decade after decade in people's minds.

Today's advertising needs a distinctive character to meticulously describe the brand concept, form, color, symbol, and semantics. At the same time the message must be entertaining, impactful and suggest the product's benefit to increase the consumer's purchase inclination. People's attention span is reducing, yet opportunities of different activities engaging their time is increasing.

Take television. There is juicy news from every corner of the world, a large variety of entertaining programs, share market information, and multiple channels from several satellites. Cyber time also occupies a great deal of time as the Internet's bandwidth is overflowing with content and reach. In this media bazaar, advertising has to break clutter. By following the living character and driving it meticulously from product, concept, form, color, symbol and semantics, advertising can consistently create a mystique effect of the brand.

Somehow, advertising needs an art form totally different from other shows and activities on television. For example, a clear directional art form distinguishes the specific entertaining characters of feature films, the theater, television serials, and reality shows. Advertising will also benefit from its own art form to communicate among programs competing for the consumer's mindspace. As advertising has almost become mandatory for most companies, and with heavy expenditure too, the domain has become a consuming industry.

In earlier times, established thinkers like David Ogilvy were used for advertising to bring alive a brand's living character. Today marketers, technocrats and businessmen are amalgamating to set up advertising agencies to focus on media planning and create the power of the big. Thought and creativity have fallen by the wayside. The result? A large number of advertisements look like one another.

There is a huge difference between Ogilvy, Bernbach and Saatchi brothers versus Martin Sorrel. The first three are all creative geniuses but Sir Martin Sorrell is a business tycoon. The expansion of the companies of Ogilvy, Bernbach, Saatchi & Saatchi was driven by their strong thinking power processed to successfully replicate and develop in different countries to better sell brands. A process like this was totally like blood infusion. Sir Martin may influence business but how could he manage the creative gene?

As a global corporation, you may believe that an advertising agency with global reach can simplify your handling system in different countries, reduce your cost and bring coherency. You may get reduction of cost and coherency, but will you get the creativity that connects to your consumers and customers across different parts of the world with an excellent blend of local and global atmosphere?

Creative geniuses of advertising should be nurtured to govern advertising with a creative source. They should be propelled to powerfully bring alive the living character of the brand and make it accessible to consumers. Advertising should not be relegated to become a mere media buying business source.

what is subliminal loyalty of the trade in branding?

The first customer of the brand is the trade. If the trade does not understand the brand's character, focus and product quality, it will never reach to the consumer the way you desire it to. Trade marketing is a major factor in the branding exercise.

A manufacturing company does not directly interact with consumers; so their sensitivity to consumers is, in effect, behind the wall. But the retailer and distributor have direct frontal contact, which is why their shopper sensitivity is higher. They have a great advantage of being able to observe the psychological, sociological and the trend aspects of shoppers in their own premise, the retail outlet. Using these observations as research samples, the retailer can improve his retail's value proposition in a continuous manner.

The priority for manufacturing companies that are totally dependent on their channel of dealers, distributors and resellers to make their fortune, is definitely channel ownership.

Manufacturing companies deploy different processes to understand the consumer and shopper, and try connecting through the media. Having worked for both manufacturers and retailers, I can vouch for retail business houses having an upper hand here. The 'last mile' point-of-purchase shopper connect of the manufacturer's product goes through the retailer's hand. As the via media to shoppers, the retailer is privileged in being the last point influence of every purchase decision.

The manufacturing company can overcome this lack of direct shopper proximity by putting in place a process to own his channel partner's mindshare. Even before your product sees the consumer's face, your channel's decision can endorse or reject your product. You need to win over your channel with very sensitive actions. Aside from hard number deals, use about 60 percent soft skill methods to own his loyalty. The money you spend for brand building will then fetch desirable results.

Achieving channel ownership is an intense, specific act. The retail activities of manufacturing companies who sell brands can be taken through the ReFinE Value Ladder process (see Figure 11.22), with the rational, functional, and emotional attributes addressed specifically.

Figure 11.22 rational, functional, and emotional attributes for retail activities of manufacturing companies who sell brands

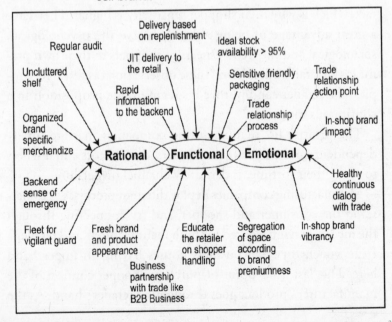

Brand pull is a major factor to successfully own channel mindshare. Brand pull does not come from advertising and promotional offers only. Interconnecting, laddering and balancing of the rational, functional and emotional attributes can make your brand grow and be profitable. When you are deficient in brand pull, retailers can ruin you with excessive pressure to pay exorbitant commissions. Your sales may grow, but at the cost of low profit because of heavy spends in advertising, consumer promotion offers and distributor margin.

Brand pull also comes from trade relationship management. Your mutually cordial and profitable relations with your channel can ensure that shoppers always see your brand at the retail. You brand must never face stock-out at the outlet, and shoppers need to experience a positive approach to your brand at the point-of-purchase. After media and marketing spend, brand pull will be created when your brand achieves high visibility, availability and proximity at the retail.

We created outstanding brand pull for a small manufacturer in Europe by sensitive retail marketing with the channel (see Figure 11.23). We did not spend on advertising, but concentrated on making the brand visible and available on the shelf so it can reach consumer proximity. This hundred-year-old, $15 million fabric protection company has, within 10 years, grown to achieve $300 million in sales.

Thirty to forty years ago, the organized retail chain was at a embryonic stage in the West too. It has now matured; the learning curve has risen high. These learnings are readily available in India. As a manufacturer, realize that retailing will not stay the trading business it currently is. The sophistication of organized retail houses is growing. The channel is small today, but its knowledge and skill are on the rise.

Sensitive trade relationship is the project for manufacturers to win consumer heart and mind.

Figure 11.23 direction for trade relationship branding project

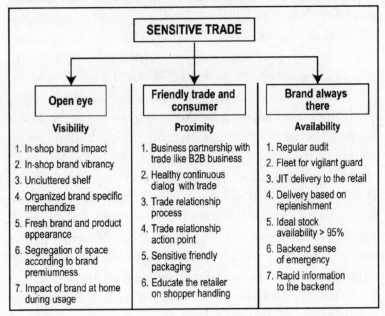

what are the five external facets of the branding jewel box?

The branding jewel box is framed with five sensorial facets through which the brand reaches the consumer's custody. Once wrapped with glamor and quality, the branding jewel box can radiate sensorialism with the five senses of seeing, smelling, tasting, hearing, and touching.

This is the way you can create a brand that becomes universal and global, traversing large geographies and making your business big and profitable. Yes, I call it a jewel box. As a manufacturer or service provider, you should protect your brand very cautiously like a jewel. Your brand's jewel box will always be in the hands of the public. Your brand must enter their spirit and mind like a precious jewel to be treasured.

brand substance evaluation parameter

The marketing chapter first opened up in business when industrial mass-consuming products were manufactured in the West after World War II. Educating consumers was a challenge then. So was transferring trade from small-scale home production to mass scale industrial production.

The 21st century consumer is excessively knowledgeable, so the branding exercise needs a different treatment today. You need philosophers, anthropologists, sociologists, psychologists, and artists to feed and nurture brand content. Psychologists, sociologists, and anthropologists will translate society in a structured form, philosophers will bring in futuristic imagination, and artists will portray the visual expression in a latent perspective.

Why involve professionals not evidently related to business growth? Because the five senses of the branding jewel box are not statistically rational. Just image, you as an industrialist are totally dependant on these five sensorial attachments of the end user to make your growth and profit.

How can these professionals be put through the organizational process? Artists may be outsourced, but most organizations would benefit from having a psychologist, sociologist, anthropologist and/or philosopher on board. These specialists may lack economic sense, but they are proficient to nurture and feed the brand.

The marketing department can drive branding content through psychological, sociological, anthropological and philosophical knowledge and approach. Unfortunately, marketing professionals are becoming like technocrats, more inclined to statistics. However, to generate business, keep consistency and sustain the brand and its activities you definitely also need the technocrat.

Branding activities are akin to theatre acting. You have to remember to connect with the spectator. No matter what grave turn of events a theater actor may have faced during the day, when he's on stage his stage character rules supreme. An organization must drive the brand as the actor, and consumers and customers as spectators. Strong branding will happen when attention is given to every activity that interfaces the consumer. These would include working culture, product quality, retail magnification and the message rich communication of a living character. It's a total *fil conducteur* act. Every element has to be embedded to make the brand successful.

When it comes to aspiration, boasting quality, being value for money or a trendsetter, where does your brand score with consumers? What is your brand's relevance to consumer lifecycle and lifestyle? What is its domestic and global image? Does it have a techy character, youthfulness, femininity and any benefit output (see Figure 11.24)? These are the 11 brand substances you can put through the ReFinE Value Ladder. You can see that even unbeatable brand scores are not uniform in these 11 criteria. Whether you are a superior or good brand, your score cannot be uniform. Any recognized consumer brand would at least start at the level of good and go up to the superior and unbeatable levels.

This scoring system can help identify where to micro focus your brand to improve its consumer perception. You may find that being a superior brand, your quality scores very high, but you may be short in the trendsetter score. That definitely has a negative impact on aspiration. If you are a high quality product but not scoring in different criteria, perhaps your proposition has over design or you have not connected to the other 10 areas that consumers link with.

During research, it's necessary to also benchmark with basic category products that integrate the rational, functional, and emotional attributes but score 0 as per the ReFinE Value Ladder. This will show your brand's position among the lowest and highest market competitors.

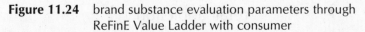

Figure 11.24   brand substance evaluation parameters through ReFinE Value Ladder with consumer

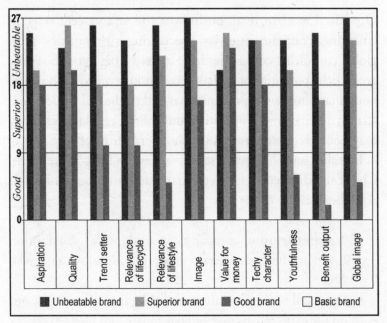

Evaluating an existing brand's substance can help arrive at its core strengths and weaknesses. In Figure 11.24, an unbeatable brand is at the summit of the category, a superior brand is a little lower while a good brand reaches the unbeatable score in certain areas.

Check whether your brand is in the unbeatable, superior, good, or basic position. Accordingly ReFinE your value in conjunction with the consumer and trade. If you are creating a new brand first master the current market composition. You may find a gap you can appropriate to achieve quick success.

Jalebi when served in its original dried *sal* leaves, instead of sophisticated crockery, feels like the real thing. The soothing, dry smell of this leaf adds value to the *jalebi*. You can take the consumer's heart by making the product's branding jewel box as natural to its origin as possible. Don't adulterate it.

retail addiction

Organized modern retail business is still at a nascent stage in emerging economic countries. Speculating with statistics, a few global consulting companies have created a big hype about the green field potential of India's retail industry. Indian business houses tapping this opportunity have taken the real estate route, setting up large and plush brick-and-mortar retail spaces. They may not have gone through the shoppers' sensitive core.

In reality, retail business is sensitive, fresh and fragile like a rose. Check the differences between manufacturing companies and retail business:

- A manufacturing company can multiply its distribution to sell products in different geographical areas at any given time.
- But retail business is not mobile like that. If you miss out on the expected average bill per square foot on an everyday basis, it means the retail is losing money. That's why the shopper's permanent addiction to the organized retail is the only solution for success.

Within the next 10–15 years India will undoubtedly be the hub of the world's organized retail business. But to achieve and sustain with reasonable profit will not be easy. Patience and passion will be required in plenty to understand the shopper's sensitive areas.

I have made an exhaustive classification of the complexity of retailing that an emerging market like India should focus on. The shopper purchase act is linked to the type of outlet and its merchandize. When a shopper goes to different types of outlets, her purchase act is not the same. It is the store plan and its merchandizing that creates the impact. The type of outlet defines the type of merchandize, and the purchase act responds to that through the psychological parameter (see Table 11.6).

Table 11.6 exhaustive classification of retail formats

TYPE OF OUTLET	(1) Grocery	(2) Multi-segment	(3) Single brand outlets – require a brand pull					(4) Specialized multi-product outlets			
TYPE OF MERCHANDIZE	Convenience outlets Super market Hyper market	Departmental store	Apparel	Automobile	Banking	Personal grooming	Petrol pump	IT Hardware	Consumer durables	Snacks / restaurant	Chemists / medicines
PURCHASE ACT	Regular & periodic	Instant & periodic	Instant & planned	Planned			Regular	Periodic & regular			
PSYCHOLOGICAL PARAMETER	I will fulfill my need without spending more	I will be surprised	I am orgasmic	I am happy with my choice			In a mood to stretch out	Fulfilment of need & desire	Happiness		Secured hygiene / clean and brightness

As a retailer you need to anticipate shopper psychography in her purchase behavior and involvement with the product in your retail premise. You have to address shoppers who arrive carrying different moods (see Table 11.7). The retail store management team needs to recognize these moods to increase their wallet share. The retail experience must be powerfully customized to be very shopper-centric. This means she gets what she wants as well as gets surprised to refresh her desires.

To capture the shopper's eyeball, particularly in emerging countries, organized retail needs to overpower the three other distractions pulling at it at any given time (see Figure 11.25). These are:

(a) Unorganized hawkers on the road or visiting homes
(b) Unorganized local traditional retail with no price consistency
(c) Small modern independent store

Table 11.7 shopper psychography in the purchase act

Purchase behavior	Involvement with product
• Serious buyer	• Curious
• Bored buyer	• Techy
• Snobby buyer	• Playful
• Show-off buyer	• Sporty
• Window shopper	• Show-off
• Trend driven buyer	• Cranky
• Romancing buyer	• Funky
• Love smitten buyer	• Low key
• Arrogant buyer	• Freaky
• Speculative buyer	• Conservative techy
• Impulsive buyer	• Need based
• Value seeker	• Classic
	• Classic contemporary
	• Techno classy
	• Conservative

Figure 11.25 different directions pulling at the shopper's eye

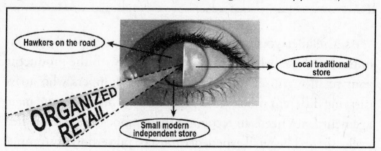

The shopper's mind and eye are always in a Yes/No mental wrestle. Have I made the right choice? Is the price right? Have I seen enough variety? Was my bargaining satisfactory, or is there something here that legitimately substitutes my bargaining temperament? Finally, did I make a clever purchase?

For organized retail business to be viable, you need to see how you can enlarge the shopper's eyeball space. Your three types of competitors are trying to distract the shopper, and increase the proportion of the shopper's eye towards them. Grass roots retail strategy is no more than a focus into how to occupy and maximize the shopper's eye space. What addiction will you offer the shopper so they converge and occupy your organized modern retail space?

Check out the distractions organized retail has to fight in the Indian subcontinent compared to the West. Walking along an American or European city sidewalk, what will you see? Different vehicles on the street, a cop or two, stylish men and women in a hurry, perhaps a rebellious or nasty character you'll be careful about, a couple, either of the same gender or girl and boy, kissing and lost in themselves, pets on leashes. On both sides are large retail stores and corporate houses that seem an extension of the neat sidewalk especially as certain retails are designed in open format. The absence of a boundary between the footpath and shop, even in –5 degree temperature, encourages shopper footfall. You are out cold in winter, but just a few meters inside the shop you feel a warm, welcoming wave. This is extreme shopper sensitivity that creates overwhelming footfall.

In a city footpath in India, organized retail has grave competition to catch the shopper's eye and mind. On one side are several kinds of honking vehicles, from taxis to auto rickshaws, trucks to cycles, buses spilling over with people, stopping anywhere without notice, traffic police trying to control those who duck traffic signals. Jostling with you for footpath space are hawkers of various kinds, parked two-wheelers, a broken tap with people washing dishes or bathing, open drains or unsteady, broken pavement, both stylish and dirtily dressed men and women rushing past, and children playing games. You have to be careful about pick pockets here too, or beggars who whine, or a sudden motorcycle crossing the footpath.

As a retailer, you have to clearly be very imaginative to attract shoppers from such an environment. Unless you have a hypnotic retail façade, internal merchandize that cues shoppers to enter, you may not be able to attract footfall from both planned and impulse shoppers.

In-shop experience can change the metaphor of a product or brand. The more hallucinating an in-shop experience is, the more the shopper returns to spend more here. It's easier to create vibrant shopping for one-time luxurious product purchase. Enticing the shopper for regular daily need purchase is easy if price is the only factor. While doing that, are you making profit? To retain the shopper and make profits, the retailer must provide an unparalleled shopping experience. This will increase footfall, conversion, retention, repurchase and increased wallet share. Merchandize that's unparalleled, coupled with the right price, can give you the power to sustain an ethical retail practice.

Let's examine four types of outlets given in Table 11.6:

1. Grocery
2. Multi-segment
3. Single brand outlet
4. Specialized multi-product outlet.

grocery retail

Traditional retail still dominates in Asian countries. In China, 68 percent is traditional trade, just 32 percent is modern retail. In India 97 percent is still traditional, and 3 percent modern.

Traditional trade has high shopper proximity. This prevents different retail styles imported from developed sophisticated countries from getting a foothold here. Sophisticated retails have suddenly mushroomed in Indian metros. Shoppers are in the process of getting familiarized with organized malls. They appear like a museum of consuming products, basically because people seem to have a good time in air-conditioned comfort but are not loaded with shopping bags when they exit. In a museum you don't touch the product, you just see.

GRC brands and outlets of global standard attract people to these malls. Most successful retail businesses in the world are associated with stringent discipline. They minutely calculate latent lifestyle, almost as in millimeters, taking a million people's sensitivity into account. I remember 15 years ago a famed hypermarket retailer in Europe put plastic jackets in the metal trolleys. This would avoid sound when they are rearranged in the counter alleys.

Million population consumers of sophisticated developed countries are disciplined because they have regimented societies. In India's billion population, people's lifestyle is not homogeneous nor is discipline high, and consciousness on hygiene is very low. With huge disparity in living style from urban to micro/macro rural levels, from province to province, in different or the same economic strata of different religions or castes, retail business in India will need a different approach. Western style retails intimidate these shoppers. Bring the so-called chaos as seen in roadside markets, inside organized retail to invite everyone and create differentiation.

Retails that cater to every day needs are always driven by the masses. The 'masses' in India are very different from the West. If retailers in India only cater to higher society to maintain aspiration, the masses will never get close to them. Chaos organized inside could be the ideal implementation for retail business in India.

How does an ideal business conversion happens in a hyper or supermarket?

Purchase can have five motivation purposes: essential, secondary planned, occasional, festive, and gifting (see Figure 11.26). The shopper's wallet share is approximately divided like this: essential purchase 60 percent, secondary planned purchase 15 percent, occasional purchase 10 percent, festive purchase 5 percent, and gifting purchase 10 percent. This purchase motivation percentage can change depending on the retailer's understanding of the shopper. As the retailer, you can rearrange your merchandize to correspond with shoppers' needs.

Figure 11.26 retail strategy for footfall, conversion, retention, repurchase, and increase in wallet share

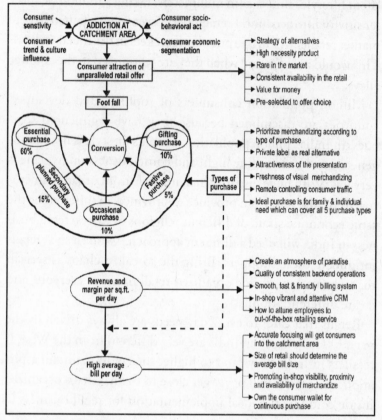

Create addiction for your retail at the catchment area. This will achieve repeat footfall, conversion, retention and your increase of their wallet share. What could be considered addiction at the retail's catchment area?

specific merchandize as unparalleled purchase offer

If a shopper gets a particular product in a retail in her catchment area, which is normally not easily available in most outlets, it will be a reason to return. This shopping experience itself could be unparalleled. The item could be as simple as a rare branded jam or a particular vegetable like lettuce. If this is a regular purchase for her, it will motivate her to visit this retail for her every other need as well. She will never go far away for any purchase. This attraction of finding her specific requirement that she doesn't easily get anywhere else is an unparalleled purchase act.

Understanding the shoppers' different needs, the retail should be sensitive to expose the merchandize in a way that entices shoppers to return. The retail then becomes an addiction.

Retail catchment areas are very specific in India, quite unlike anywhere else in the world. The critical points to analyze to better understand the catchment area are environmental aspects, varying age groups, socio-behavioral clusters in different economic strata, the complex of religion and caste, food habits of being vegetarian or non-vegetarian, and whether or not selling alcohol along with groceries will matter.

Economic reforms have made Indian consumers, whether poor, middle class, rich or affluent, become behavioral driven. From our unique, insightful market watch we have identified eight different behavioral clusters emerging in India's metros, urban and macro rural areas. These are people who have individual traits, such as

(*i*)   **Low key**: he/she seeks simple living with quality of life

(*ii*) **Value seeker**: gets involved only when a worthwhile pay-off is seen

(*iii*) **Sober**: goes for quiet efficiency

(*iv*) **Flamboyant**: exhibitionist, out to grab attention

(*v*)   **Critical**: perfectionist, not easy to satisfy

(*vi*) **Novelty seeker**: curious for the new

(*vii*) **Techy**: goes for the digital mode of life

(*viii*) **Gizmo lover**: likes gadgets and goes for differentiation

We have continuously tracked these behavioral clusters since 2001 and found that people across monthly earnings of Rs 5,000 to Rs 100,000 and above have these behavioral dispositions.

On a sample size of 1,000 ranging from children to 45-year-olds throughout India we have found people with Low key temperament comprise 30 percent, Value seekers comprise 22 percent, traits of Sober are 18 percent, Flamboyant 12 percent, Critical 8 percent, Novelty seeker 7 percent, Techy 2 percent, and Gizmo lover 1 percent. Over the years we can see that the percentage of Sober and Low key are diminishing while the percentage of people with Novelty seeker and Critical traits are growing.

With these eight behavioral clusters reflecting in every income segment, the efficacy of economic segmentation is diminishing in India. Economic classification tells you people's buying capacity in macro level while behavioral clusters indicate people's inclinations in the micro level. If you can superimpose the buying capacity with the behavioral leanings we have identified, conversion, retention and wallet share increase will become very powerful.

Behavioral consumer clusters can help to analyze the catchment areas so retail merchandize can be customized.

Another indispensable catchment analysis to be done is availability of different unorganized market products that can disturb organized retails by severely breaking price down. Your top-of-mind must beware of such unpredictable happenstance. If you are selling oranges, for example, a hawker can put up a temporary stall in front of your outlet selling similar oranges at 30–50 percent lower price. Its critical to analyze the catchment area's predictable and unpredictable clutter and take preventive measures before setting up your retail.

You can garner microtone understanding by observing the shopper's in-shop eye and body movement, psychological attachment, sensitivity to trends, and the spending capacity of different segments. The collected data can be used to improve footfall and conversion, and increase the shoppers' spend.

In sum, two parameters will define your retail business success. First, continuously microscope your catchment area in a 3–7 km radius, refine its analysis, and internalize the findings before entering the business. Second is continuously observing the shoppers' every movement, filter the data and take the essence to remote control the shopper movement to optimize conversion possibilities.

Use international benchmarks and standard operating procedures for logistics and back-end supply chain systems. You may face human resource and infrastructure volatility and some chaos at start-up. Manage human-related issues the Indian way while reinforcing the passion of shopper sensitivity with strong discipline. Never try benchmarking the shoppers' catchment area with Western influences, as the Indian pulse is unique. Even replicating a merchandizing system for daily need supermarkets or hypermarkets may not be homogeneous for the country. Merchandizing can differ about 30–40 percent from one region to another, and even within a region.

private label

Private label and fresh products are a big source of income for supermarkets, hypermarkets or convenient stores. Here is how private label has undergone a six-stage evolution in the last 40 years in Europe:

1. Using a different brand only for private label.
2. Total copy of the national big brand with different brand names for each category to create low cost, me-too brands.
3. A European global retail giant tried to bring the concept of '*produit libre* (freedom product).' White was used across all packaging in every category. They liberally played with the value of low cost and simplicity but the consumer ended up getting a clinical interface. It dominated the shelves, created monotony and looked like a communist regime market of Eastern Europe. The consumers thought they

were sacrificing choice and totally rejected the expression of low cost and monotony. Low cost does not mean sacrificing aspiration. Fortunately this giant retailer radically changed its face within a short time.

4. The retail shop name itself carries forward the private label.

5. Intelligent co-branding of the private label with a reputed manufacturer especially for products that need special competence. Co-branding was the innovation of a large Anglophone retailer. His retailing business made excellent partnerships with gigantic manufacturers to co-brand special products with private label. This retailer's credibility spiraled being seen as the value creator of consumer benefit.

6. Private label can suffer from imitating a manufacturer's branding strategy which has several line extensions in a category.

I personally worked with retail chains in Europe where we captured detailed consumer understanding on such product segmentation. We created a few core products and offered restricted variety within them. This reduced the range, occupied less shelf space and was more efficacious for consumer recognition and category growth.

To associate with the consumer's Aqcurate Gain, its better for the private label to be an alternative to other brands in the retail. It should have a differentiating character, extreme consumer benefit, and be a responsible guardian for the growth of consumer lifecycle, lifestyle, and trend. Private label should not vampire the shelf with monotonous, overpowering exposure. You have to subtly keep shopper choice alive with variety so they feel they have done well to buy private label. Being able to touch the product is indulging for shoppers. It has democratized the capitalistic world. Private label needs to respect this democracy.

Its difficult to advertise all private-label categories in the media as the shopper cost advantage will be destroyed. That's why private label needs extreme 'self-selling provocation' as its branding alchemy. The sustaining success of a retail's private label is sophistication, easy understanding, high quality, benefit driven, easy usage, friendly pricing and differentiating character.

seamless back-end alignment is the core of retail success

If retail has a key executional point, it is coherency. Commercial success in retail business will come from proactive back-end alignment. Excellence in negotiating for purchase, brilliant selection, consistency of quality, speed and time management all need to be interlinked like a honeycomb. This is the coherence of retail business.

Unlike a manufacturing company where automatic systems can be exploited, the retail business has profuse human interventions. No manufacturing company will have such wide versatility of products that a retail has to manage. That's why seamless coherence in every function is the keystone of retail business. A coherent back-end and sensitive, microtone shopper catchment area comprise the real source of retail success.

Effective and honeycombed back-end coherence is the driver of shopper footfall conversion, retention, repurchase and increase in wallet share.

If a single honeycomb cell gets disconnected, the business will suffer. How should this honeycomb back-end employee culture be instituted and ingrained by the staff? A simple, fun way for them to understand the different back-end support functions is to compare these functions with some symbolic expression as aspirational element. Handling the human factory with coherency everyday is a Herculean job. That's why it's important to bring some amusement into everyday life by recharging the coherency factor to escape boredom. Here is one of my thoughts to make a coherent honeycomb:

- A merchandizer/category management procurer should be like a **cow**, a holistic provider of the company.

- A procurer for private label should be smart like a **chimpanzee**, and be able to surprise shoppers with real alternatives.
- Consignment purchase/payment-after-sales person should be like a **monkey**. He should be tricky and play around for a while.
- Concessionaire/shop-in-shop negotiator. Like a **swan**, get classy products but also be able to make a noise when things don't go right.
- Warehousing personnel must do correct bar coding. Like an **elephant**, he should be reliable with a sharp memory and provide ample space.
- Store manager. He should be alert like a **wolf** before issues escalate.
- Department manager. He should handle all personnel and functions to create unique differentiation, just like every **zebra** is unique in their black-and-white lines.
- Sales associate. He should be opportunistic like a **fox** to close deals.
- Support service. Hardworking and diligent like **ants**, they should work in teams and provide all necessary service.
- Security. Like a trained **German shepherd** he should guard the premise and equipment with full loyalty.
- Housekeeping should be like the **weaverbird**, neat, meticulous, respecting time, and pay attention to details.
- The most crucial function is Customer Care. Like a **sheep dog**, he should provide overwhelming service and assure shopper comfort.
- Marketing is the strategic function. Like a **rabbit**, the marketer should multiply business by leapfrogging growth and profitability.
- MIS should be proactive, sensitive and provide silent yet effective networking like a **spider**.

- Human resource. Like a **goose** he should have extreme human sensitivity and the ability to choose the right people. He should enable streamlining of all operations.
- Billing system/cashier should be smooth, fast and friendly, not succumb to pressure and be interactive like a **cat**.
- The entire back-end attitude, behavior, and action should be like a **honeycomb**, all interlinked with extraordinary teamwork.

multi-segment retail

Departmental stores have merchandize in multiple segments. The shopper's purchase act can be both instant buys as well as planned periodic purchase in the same shop, so high caliber knowledge of merchandize decor is essential. An ongoing, full-fledged in-shop merchandizing design team needs to be put in place. It can be outsourced or be integrated in the organization. The caliber of this design team to create an exhibitionist, artistic selling approach will pivot the shopper in the retail.

Instant purchase will be provoked when the shopper is surprised and tempted to buy at every turn. The more surprised they are, the more they will spend as people do in an Arabian Medina bazaar. A Medina shopping experience is so enjoyable and fast moving because everything is available openly. From selling slaves to women (allegedly done surreptitiously even now) to animals or products, every sales person has only one motive, how to magnify his product to empty the shopper's wallet.

Periodic purchase shoppers also want to brighten their everyday lives. Shoppers will open their wallets based on how an an artistically done up departmental store differentiates its presentation to match the consumer's lifecycle, lifestyle, and trend. The art of merchandizing is the identity of the multi-segment retail of the departmental store. It goes on to become its landmark like Bloomingdale and Macy's in USA.

As this segment caters to both instant and periodic purchase shoppers, the merchandize design team has to find a trade-off that's attractive to both sets of shoppers. Instant buyers are provoked by newness, whereas changing merchandize can depress periodic shoppers who don't find the product in the place they had earlier bought it from. The design work for display needs absolute understanding of the shoppers' ergonomic movement, which covers both psychological as well physiological factors, and of course the influence of the trend.

single brand outlets require a brand pull

Specific product brand pull is the prime attraction for such outlets. Shoppers will come here if it totally corresponds to their needs and desires. So creating addictive purchase motivation is the key.

Apparel comprises both instant and periodic planned purchase. The apparel retailer should become the shopper's confidant, mirroring her psychological expressions. A heightened purchase experience is more important here than the product bought.

People cannot gauge the cost of the apparel you wear. The experience in the shop perhaps made you pay a hundred times more than some basic apparel. This cost will not be seen on wearing the apparel, but it was your personal hedonism in buying it. Apparel shops are very personality driven. Its overwhelming experience gives it character. The personal touch stands out. Artistic sense of décor must ooze from every centimeter of the shop. Meticulous art direction makes the merchandize bigger than its reality.

Being very rational in your merchandize will sell only low price products. When you have proven quality, the more irrational or *rauxa* your shop is, the more you invite the shopper to put money into your retail bank. This kind of retail does not sport variety. It understands the types of shoppers and surpasses their desire. They first fashion the shop with retail merchandizing and then a purchase experience so exquisite that the business becomes robust.

Automobile, banking, and personal grooming are all part of periodic planned purchase. Shoppers want to be pampered to the extreme from these retails. These are all high sensitive, knowledge, skill and service driven product or service retails. Deficiency of knowledge and skill leads to total destruction of this business.

Petrol is regular planned purchase. The differentiating character of the product from one brand to another is not evident. That's why creating a sense of perk up in the petrol station is the direction to make this retail outlet inviting. In general, when consumers stop for petrol they would love to stretch and do some childish shopping. Extreme hygienic conditions and availability of impulse purchase attractions while stretching would make this regular purchase for petrol more sensitive. A small range of 'in case' products to pull in consumers are welcome in these outlets.

specialist multi-product outlet

Outlets with merchandize such as IT hardware, consumer durables, medicines, and restaurants are considered specialists. Shoppers frequent them for periodic and regular planned purchase.

Snacking is an instant unplanned consumption.

The psychological parameter is very crucial in the specialist multi-product outlets that are driven by skill and knowledge of the product. IT hardware and consumer durables psychologically fulfill needs and desire of getting an evolved product with added features. At one time such an item was an asset purchase. Today shoppers check not their requirement for work, leisure or the home, but about whether they are acquiring the latest innovation. Retail merchandizing has to be inventive and of substance for this type of very futuristic business.

A snacking place breaks monotony on the road and at work. It has to recharge you for your next destination. It combines whimsical hunger with real hunger. Many consumers think of snacking as an alternative to a meal for four reasons: 'It costs less, I eat less, I indulge, I eat in hygienic conditions.' A snacking place can become regular for a consumer if it can consistently satisfy these four reasons, particularly the hygienic ambience, which is not negotiable. Indian snacking outlets often miss out on the hygienic sense. McDonald's has created a benchmark by selling a burger at Rs 20, and visibly providing consumers these four reasons to enjoy themselves.

Organized restaurant chains need to be places of happiness, an extra dimension from eating at home. The medicine retail can create difference by having a bright organized look of secure hygiene and cleanliness.

While working with different retailers of the organized retail business in Europe I have experienced that they have tremendous proactive shopper sensitivity and practical sense. As their business is entirely related to watching the steps shoppers take, they are extraordinarily accustomed to shopper language. In their outlets, one can easily identify different kinds of shoppers, their varied sensitivity parameters, and closely validate every element with observable facts.

Indian shopper's paradigm of convenience retails

What is a convenience store for Indian shoppers? Large retail outlets that they visit once a month, that has groceries, personal care, apparel, consumer durables all under one roof, somewhat like a hypermarket, is considered their ideal convenience store. Understanding shopper language, I have identified four shopping frequencies for groceries and provisions in India:

The first is **emergency shopping** for SOS requirements done closest to home. The spend would be from Rs 2 to Rs 50. **Daily shopping** is the second frequency. It includes fresh and dairy products with a spend of Rs 50–100 within a distance of 1 km. It's very difficult to strategize and get shopper fidelity for both emergency and daily needs as they are very vulnerable. If a stack of bananas in your retail looks fresh on one day and wilted in any other day, you've lost your shopper. So consistency of merchandize, its freshness and the distance from the shopper's home, including no queues at the outlet are important to get this shopper who's in a hurry. The bill size here is small, so trying to drag in volume for this volatile shopper is necessary, but is a tough task.

Weekly shopping is the third frequency where Rs 400–800 is spent. Shoppers would normally go upto 3 kms from home but depending on unparalleled purchase offers in a store she may even travel 5 kms every week. This is a very interesting space and format for retails to target. As the retailer, if you create excitement every Tuesday, Thursday, and Saturday, you can get your shopper to come in on her convenient day, and by default buy her emergency and daily needs for a couple of days too. But never put emergency and daily needs at the front of your store or you will miss the weekly, leisurely shopper who goes inside the store. If your differentiation is really big, you can try converting the shopper into making this her monthly purchase destination, but for that you will need more merchandize and special offers.

The fourth frequency is **monthly shopping** that comprises both need plus desire items. Here, store distance of upto 7–10 kms translates as sweet anticipation. Shoppers indulge to change the monotony of their lives. Emergency and daily buys are boring. Weekly gets in the serious shoppers whereas monthly is a bigger bill as it enters the shopper's yearning level. She would love to visit a large and entertaining outlet with many promotions and a food court for the family's enjoyable outing.

The hidden aspects for shopper addiction are shopper hyper-sensitivity, strategic merchandize, back-end coherency and service for shoppers. And shopper addiction is the key for retail business.

Retail business is coherent and consistent precision of seam-less supply chain management. It's like the way the coherency and consistency that's followed from *jalebi* ingredient to its dough to the professional's spontaneous hand skill. The seamlessly right mixture, right crafting in the pan, the right fry and right syrup bath contribute to the real pleasure of the *jalebi*.

The *jalebi*'s relevance in the retail is the innovative way it cap-tures shopper sensitivity. Being spongy and sticky, the *jalebi* dough flows easily to form its rippled shape as it is expertly poured from a distance of at least six inches on to the pan of hot fat it fries in. It requires skill and a disciplined hand to make a *jalebi*.

A retailer can draw an analogy of how to skillfully create a retail ambience that makes individual shoppers 'spongy' so they soak into the offerings and ripple their wallet contents inside the retail. Like frying a well-fermented *jalebi*, today's retail needs to observe shoppers innovatively and guide them towards the hot fat of the billing counter.

think victory

At the dawn of this 21st century, innovation is looking very tired and saturated. Innovation took a leap from the 19th to the 20th century. Western society had high thoughts in other centuries too, but in the 20th century we have enjoyed the application of unparalleled innovation. The last century went through exceptional turbulence as well. Did society intentionally generate discomfort to create a hunger for innovation where the innovator gains as well as imposes power? Innovations prove the strength of human intelligence to enhance living comfort.

My adventures into different human dimensions culminate in an aspirational direction, which makes you think of victory (see Figure 12.1). 'Think Victory' is the winning character of a business vision. In the battle of negatives and positives that a thought process goes through, victory can come faster and smoother if you avoid arithmetical number crunching. Aim to nurture the subliminal intangible that always wins.

Using statistical information alone can give you a narrow vision, either in professional or personal life. The word arithmetic, by default, starts with an A which is symbolically constrained with a closed horizon and blocked vision; you can do what you see but nothing beyond. On the other hand, the letter V is open at the top, so more powerful. It not only opens up, it also becomes wider. V means being visionary for victory. If corporate or product strategy is put in the V platform, you bring continuity into different generations of deliverables.

Figure 12.1 think and drive victory

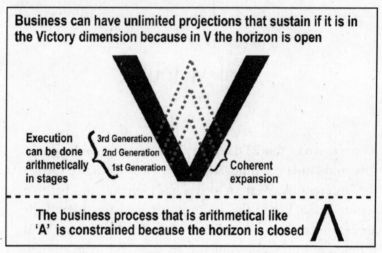

My corporate positioning experience of *Eat Healthy, Think Better* for Britannia or *Active Health* for Danone are driven by the V platform which is so universal that it can grow and grow and grow. Toyota's Corolla grew robust in the V platform since 1966, connecting to consumer trends by upgrading value. Being in the V platform, iPod continues to addict different generations. Placing corporate transformation or product design in the V platform from inception can take you far and make you unique. Even in personal life if you continuously nurture your thought process in the V platform, your intellectual capacity will build up to take you into leadership mode.

What crime, tumult and turmoil have mankind gone through, how many lives have we sacrificed to reach today's global advancement through innovation! As a responsible world citizen, I regret the destruction and human loss before I set out to enjoy the innovative facilities the 20th century threw up.

I marvel at today's outstanding musical device of the Bose sound system, that brings me close to the dazzling music of György Cziffra. This most celebrated Hungarian piano virtuoso had barely survived Communist torture. When I listen to him play Liszt's *Hungarian Rhapsody* and Chopin's *Polonaise*, I'm really at a loss. Should I appreciate the emotion of this incredible man's music, or the emotion of his miserable life transformed?

Born to a poor gypsy family in 1921, he saw his father and younger sister die of starvation, even as he was improvising requests from a circus audience at age five. Cziffra learned the piano by watching his sister take lessons. When Communists gained power in Hungary they imprisoned him for political reasons. Realizing he was a pianist, they tortured him further by beating up his hands and making him carry heavy stones. When released, the ligaments on Cziffra's hands were so loose that he could barely transmit the power of his arms to his fingers.

When Cziffra finally recovered his form, his records were circulated in Western Europe, and he was propelled to legendary status as a music composer par excellence. Nobody can destroy the musical emotion his innovative interpretations give us through modern technology today. He proves to us that a self-struggle agenda through stamina, passion and perseverance, an inventive character and thrust on the mission can unleash innovation.

This bears out that human innovative power can beat the finite advances of man-made technology and mechanics. In any field, the maverick's knowledge and skill will always be ahead of its time. Society should always encourage deviant thinkers without conditions, so they can contribute by becoming more and more ground-breaking in their own specialized fields.

Cziffra did not immerse himself into the piano in the A (arithmetic) way; he took the initiative to enter through the V (victory) route. His pathetic life and fractured body did not destroy his inherent virtuoso's passion to be victorious. He exercised his musical notes arithmetically on the V platform and grew to become a world famous pianist.

Innovative power is the weapon to become superior. A new type of struggle must emerge in this century. Out-of-the-box innovation should now bypass the destructive ways of human beings and Nature and cater to a higher level of human need and desire.

There is appalling inequilibrium on the innovative platform among people from the West, East, and South. Caucasian Western society has usurped superiority status upto now through innovations. In my view, all emerging economy nations should dive into innovation to change global power equations. Basic Caucasian racism will roll to a stop if the 21st century's innovative power emerges and grows from Asia, Africa, and Latin America; a balanced power equation will result between the West and the rest of the world. How can this be done? Be curious, develop an innovative mindset, take up the challenge to achieve a determined, time-bound action.

mixing art with commerce

With a foundation in fine arts I have been a global consultant to top managements for two-and-a-half decades on corporate transformation, branding and channel ownership, product design and retail addiction. I have experienced that an artistic temperament and my family's refugee status and economic crisis during my childhood have combined to give me a balance of art and commerce.

Having studied a few years in Government College of Art and Craft in Kolkata, I left India in 1973 without any educational degree. My destination of Paris was very clear to me. For better careers, people from India were then leaving for the UK, US, or Middle East. But I chose the land where art flourished. I braved discomfort, an unknown language and economic insecurity to create the self-struggle of growth. So I have since seen the world through the window of art and economics.

My economic predicament prevented my studying whole time. While working as a sweeper in Paris, I got the rare opportunity of entering the world's most prestigious, proficient, and famous fine arts college, Ecole de Beauxart in Paris. I also attended a graphic design school called Esag. But nowhere could I finish or obtain any degree because managing time for work and studies was very difficult, and money was scarce. The French education system was not as in Anglophone countries where you can work and study at the same time. I had no choice but to prioritize my livelihood to feed my family.

These two art colleges taught me how to see things differently. I learnt what the synthesis of art is, how to avoid overdoing the canvas, how to give strength and a sensitive nerve to a line with charcoal, a pencil, or a brush. What is the infinite line in an architectural perspective drawing? How can a brush stroke be simplified? I have understood that painting has three stages: First, it is a white canvas. Second, when you put color, it becomes a colorful canvas. But this canvas is just like a wall, it does not have anything behind it.

When you throw color from a brush, while it becomes a colorful surface, what is its difference from a famous painter's canvas? For example, Rembrandt's painting called *Nightwatch* makes you travel a great distance inside the canvas. You can go back a few centuries. You can really feel that time, that momentum, that phantasm of light, telling expressions on different people, all these multifarious layers in the same canvas. This hallucination is the third stage of art, which can change a surface towards a philosophical road.

While sweeping the lithographic studio, I got acquainted with Maitre Arte, a famous painter. Russian in origin, he met great success in USA with his art deco style drawings and sculptures. I once asked his advice about my career. I confessed I didn't have the luxury to become a whole-time painter, but that I'd like to be in the design and graphic art domain where I can earn but with a little less adventure that a painter undergoes. He was very empathetic.

But more than that, to Maitre Arte I owe the big idea that changed my perspective on life. He told me to read a few books, but keeping an economic perspective. These books, he said, would at the same time develop my wider perspective of the world in different areas. His prescription was to simultaneously read Karl Marx, Vladimir Lenin, Sigmund Freud, Mao Zedong, Adolf Hitler's *Mein Kampf*, Victor Hugo, Bhagavad Gita, Koran, and Bible. I did non-stop reading of all these books all at the same time. My biggest learning of life and business came from these readings.

Karl Marx's *Das Kapital*: communism leads to capitalism

I understood from him that communism or socialism is the path to reach capitalism while destroying monarchy. Also that a symbol has great power: the hammer and sickle is the combination of industry and agriculture, while the color red is the manifestation of human blood, a will to succeed from struggle.

Lenin: maturity of time

Visiting France before his successful Russian Revolution was very fruitful. He learned the word comrade from the French word *camarade*, which means union of friendship. He canceled the 1905 revolutionary call, which later happened in 1917. That learning achieves successful action came to him with the maturity of time.

Sigmund Freud: subconscious acts

He taught me that apart from chemistry, physics, biology, and medical science, there exists another science, and that is psychology. Psychological parameters are important for human beings as human relationships and acts are imbibed with subconscious acts. Psychodrama is human evolution with the subtlety of psychology. This is Freud.

Mao Zedong: cultural equilibrium

To create equilibrium in society, discipline and the balance of human culture are most important.

Hitler's Mein Kampf: leadership at any cost

What he did is what we as human beings should never do ever again.

Victor Hugo: symbiosis of thought and scribble

His vivid description of France inspired me to enter French culture. His writing and simultaneous drawings portray the anatomy of his thinking process in a mystic environment.

Bhagavad Gita: no dogma

Hinduism has no dogmatic system. Love, greed, passion, and hate are combined in human society. Religion sans dogma can transport people into boundaryless humanism.

Koran: single focus communication has big power and consistency

The core statement of the Prophet is homogeneous in every corner of the world. Consistency and focus of the core is the Koran.

Bible: taboos to create discomfort

In Catholic religion, sex outside of procreation is taboo. Western society rebels against this with incredible sexual perversion. This prohibition has made sex a priority of life. Taboo creates sensation; taboo breaks monotony. Sex provocations are always fresh and new, and attract human society. Contradictions with the Bible have created several new trends and social cultures.

This was my recipe for attaining knowledge, to fill up my gaps of formal education. I am indebted to Maitre Arte for his advice. My personal willingness to learn the principal acts of famous people helped me to transform the business of different organizations in the world.

Learning is not a one-time activity, it is ongoing. After a certain experience of life, if one feels that all achievement is done, the learning curve becomes stagnant. Such overconfidence is never productive. The more I age, I yearn to indulge the child in me, to leapfrog my learning curve so I can absorb and address new subjects easily and forcefully.

India's young generation will continue to be the world's biggest youth population. An innovative entrepreneur is yet to emerge who will change the rule in fundamental human need and desire. India has role models of many successful businessmen, but there has been no innovator like Thomas Edison, Henry Ford, or Carl Zeiss who have enmeshed business and fundamental innovation together.

The Indian flag symbolically represents a country of spirituality and the world's biggest democracy. Can this flag one day acquire the positive values of innovation, and be pointed out as the center of Asian innovative power? By breaking a few rules as is the essence of innovation, Indians can work to translate the flag's future identity to be a combination of nature (green), peace (white), and hedonism (orange) whirlpooled by the central (navy blue) wheel of innovation to surprise the world and surpass human need. The Indian flag should not become a folklore gimmick of Bollywood which does not reflect any unconventional intellectual thought to develop the mind of the masses. It must connect to the power of human intelligence and vision.

The Japanese flag, with its stark red circle in a white surface connotes the bull's eye of 'think different' power. It also translates the tremendous power of getting the first glimpse of the sun, and represents Japan with high-tech professionalism absorbing the all time rising sun.

Working on business process outsourcing and providing support services to developed countries is good for one section of India's economy. For society to withdraw from the poverty line and acquire superior global leadership, it is important to deploy highly sophisticated manufacturing. This way, everyone can enjoy a sophisticated *jalebi*.

Being a popular sweet in India, *jalebi* is in high demand from all classes of society. The more healthy and innovative you can make the *jalebi*, the more unconditional will its acceptance be. It will become a coveted benchmark among all other sweets, biscuits and even savory snacks. Our manufacturing should pick up this cue of achieving excellence.

In the IT software business, Indian companies perfect the coding requirements of their clients in developed countries. Do the IT employees understand the deeper sociocultural and economic requirements of their foreign clients and their end consumers? Knowing the end use of their coding work, they further develop their intellectual capacity beyond the client's coding requirements. Can India ever dream of one day being able to innovate such an out-of-the-box a chip, for say an advanced refrigerator, that nobody in the world can run the advanced refrigerator without this chip?

It's important to recognize that innovative power will always be generated by your own initiative. Make a pedagogic effort to understand the root of Western innovation in every industry vertical. If your organization is working for GRC body shopping requirements, you may not have the access to find out the practical utilization of their work for end-users. Once you learn of end-user requirement, by imbibing the COA inspiration, you can find an innovative platform to independently enter the finished product market to address the latent trend. Just look at the dichotomy in your own life, how your parents and grandparents lived in their time, your own advanced education, and how well your career is progressing. The excellence you have achieved is the credit of your own intelligence and how you chose to deploy it.

To pursue business, the innovation formula to understand end user sensitivity has four wings:

1. Discover unstated frustrations and tacit needs and desires of human beings.
2. Accordingly design the product or service on the V platform.
3. Think victory; challenge the world's sophisticated society so you get the requisite recognition.
4. Simplify the output even if it is highly complicated. Make it approachable for the common man on the road anywhere in the world.

Here is the dilemma though. Sophisticated developed countries will never think of taking the initiative to disclose the physical and mental labor their innovative mechanism went through. The learning curiosity must be ours. We need to mastermind the mechanism of how Western and Japanese societies created discomfort that unearthed their innovative streak. Meticulously absorbing their methods as the base, our future innovations can surpass the past, and the nation's collective learning will improve. When our execution is superior the world will stand up and recognize our innovative power.

Mediocrity kills vision and innovative power. If you accept mediocrity when you are poor, you won't be able to overcome your economic status, because society at large pushes people to stay mediocre. A successful businessman who is intellectually mediocre makes all his subordinates run-of-the-mill in spirit. The corollary in business is that no matter how much investment is made, mediocrity will prevent innovation, cuddling you into a thick comfort layer. The more you wallow in that comfort, mediocrity will contaminate you into social oblivion.

Do billion-mindset business houses raise money from foreign investors or capital market for innovation or merely to further volume expansion? Volumes will increase business for the short term, but with no innovation, your profit will be low, as is the character of volume business.

It will be fantastic if the new generation of professionals places innovation at the center of their careers. A hundred years ago Western business leaders, through passion and curiosity, had to prove themselves with fundamental innovation. Not any longer. An alternative to your existing business model could be marketing innovation that steers you into a totally new path.

Just look around at a domain unrelated to your business. You may find a terrific, readymade source of innovation already available in some knowledge bank. Just invite yourself to get fully involved. Your innovative thinking process to challenge innovations existing in a canvas can change the market rules.

Create such an alternative innovation and change the shareholders' mind. Raise funds for innovation, give a timeframe for the output and achieve it with your operational team. Quarterly performance results must focus on the inclination and action on innovation. Within a decade India must bring forth innovative organizations like Cisco, Intel, Sony, Toyota, GE, LVMH, Apple, and Samsung. Innovative power is not a monopoly for any country, process or individual. So don't think small, create self-revolt. Chairman Mao created the cultural revolution, we need the innovation revolution.

A curious mindframe needs to ignite the innovative root. Every domain has an innovative possibility, a phenomenal data bank exists in the world today. Connecting different data unrelated to one another can perhaps surprise tomorrow's need of human society. Young business leaders, convince your shareholders that innovation is always high-rise, so quarterly results should not become a barrier for investment. Ask for the space to innovate, with discipline to fuel business. It will bring sustainability and premium value, a value beyond expectation.

expansion of INDIA is innovative nation driving inventive action

Innovative Nation Driving Inventive Action is my expansion of India, were it an acronym. Becoming also the country's *fil conducteur*, it can sensitize our people to see the future differently, creating back-pressure for innovation to happen. By 2015, it's possible to make India the hub of innovative power in the world. How?

1. initiate curiosity
Curiosity generates from intellectual development at the individual level. It can then be imposed to a team, and then the society. Being consistently curious in a subject can help grow intellect to discover innovation. An individual's business capacity is not inherent or derived from knowledge read in a book, but more related with practical experience that comes from diagonal reading.

2. diagonal reading
Reading from top left to bottom right befits the perfect leader. Diagonal reading can result in unique and brief action points

that can translate into a successful business strategy. Its different from readings such as horizontal and vertical. Horizontal is analytical and elaborate reading of a subject required in business, but not by the leader. Crucial action points must emerge from elaborate analytical work. Vertical reading is necessary observation that gives the perspective of depth of the business, but this alone can result in no action at all.

But diagonal reading takes into account other sensorial factors in decision-making. The strategy has a concise smell and enough power to generate an environment for innovation to take place in the organization. Communication can be atomic and of meaningful content.

3. observation quality

Try looking for information on any subject. You will drown in the ocean of knowledge that's available. In the innovative movement, it is the quality of observation and span of attention that will elevate you over competition.

Birds have been flying in the sky since civilization began. But it was only in the 16th century that a man curiously observed the bird's movement and thought with consistency. That led him to innovation. He envisioned a flying machine. Centuries later, this became the airplane we fly in today. A billion people had seen birds before him, but the spark of 'Can people fly?' did not occur to others. Leonardo da Vinci's thought process of a flying machine is out-of-the-box observation quality.

Some people see a subject very differently from others. Observation quality in Indian business is driven by need and readily-available-reading-material. To increase your observation quality you need intellectual acumen and self-imposed curiosity, not even business school training. Check it out like this: let's say you want to make a specific knife to pare apples into many portions. Take a sample of 25 people, individually give them an apple and knife, and film their different approaches to cutting and eating the apple. Your curious observation power will find a solution using ergonomics to design a unique knife that matches everybody's way of paring an apple. Think next of how to design a knife and make it a worldwide economic success.

4. passion to invent

Don't feel victimized about not having big funds for invention like Americans have. Without a vision that is innovative and powerful to translate into big business, nobody in the US, Germany, Japan, or India will get funds. A large number of Indian companies have raised funds based on quick business opportunity aligned to GDP growth. But we need to have the passion of innovation, to achieve a high platform in the global arena. At least 40 percent of a business leader's perspective should target alternative opportunities to create incredible innovation. That should be the investment perspective.

India should not remain synonymous to good labor for sophisticated developed countries. We have every possibility to become inventive and create breakaway alternatives in all domains in the world.

bonding emotionally

In today's multidimensional world, job satisfaction is very important for employees at every level. How do you inspire every layer of your employees on a continuous basis? Before focusing on your consumer or customer in the marketplace, you have an internal consumer you need to inspire, and that is the employee.

You cannot be innovative alone; you have to take your organization totally in the platform of innovation. When you have inspired each and everyone to collectively become innovative, only then can you get a high mach reactor.

Have you tried to find out how different employees introduce their professional activities to their families, or in a social gathering? You may very well find that apart from your managers, the other support or factory staff may not be clear how to identify themselves or how to introduce the organization they work for.

In today's multidimensional world, job satisfaction is very important for employees at every level, and work designations work like an incentive. Just as you undertake value creation projects for consumers and customers where your deliverables reach an aspirational level, you can similarly take on projects with the objective of creative inspiration that drives the employees. When high attrition is a stark reality and competition is stiff for the right talent, retaining employees should become a fine-tuned innovative challenge. And bonding with the company should be elevated to an emotional, aspirational level while balancing the rational and functional attributes.

If you consider your employee as your corporation's internal consumer you should know what inspires him and his family. It is important to focus on understanding your employees' multidimensional background because such factors influence their productivity at work. You may not be able to create individual inspirational level for everybody, but if you do a subconscious analysis of your employees and their families, you will be able to establish an ideal platform to inspire them more easily from.

As an entrepreneur it is worth paying attention to the micro details of your employee's work atmosphere to ensure it is better than mediocre. For example, your 45-year-old shop floor workers returning home may find a totally changed milieu as their children are part of today's high tech trend with access to the techno-world. In such a situation has his working environment become very mundane? Phenomenon like this is more prevalent in emerging economic countries. In absolute terms, contemporary work culture that's influenced by society will bring you better productivity and deliverable quality in the innovative platform.

the pride of belongingness

Why shouldn't pride of ownership and belongingness be relevant for all employees in your corporation? By the very nature of work in an organization, employees know whether they belong to the operational or support services team.

The operational team is always seen as the key result unit, they manufacture, they sell, they bring in the money. What about the support service teams? They are made to appear as pure expenditure. Every cost-cutting measure is always applied to the services they handle like stringently regulating stationery, consumables for the pantry, for cleaning, security measures and for fresh plants at office.

Such a divided world in an organization is not healthy. The CEO is responsible for weaving strong employee emotional bonding in every activity sector to achieve the organization's goals with different competencies.

Establishing and articulating a set of corporate values that communicates in an interactive way to every individual can become a very dynamic emotional bonding tool. These values must drive attitude, behavior, action and deliverables through a promise that connects to the final consumer or customer. When employees converge on an organizational promise to consumers, they can achieve the desired corporate vision by delivering the most effective result.

Corporate values exist only to coherently and consistently deliver consumer or customer value beyond their expectation. Very often corporate values are used as mere jargon to be with the times. They may even be lifted from management books without worrying about their perfect fit with the organization. In such an instance, employees cannot internalize these pedagogic values at work resulting in mismatch of consumer value and corporate value.

When subordinates ostensibly pay respect to superiors by mouthing 'Sir' or 'Boss', they are actually disrespecting professionalism. They pay attention to fragile etiquette as per India's cultural conditioning of slavery; but looking up to a superior's competence is more inspiring for tomorrow's business orientation to become GRC.

The organization will flourish when you inspire employees to use the intrinsic knowledge they possess, and make them more competent professionals than you are. We are no longer in the feudal mode. Professionalism should become the ethos of India's corporate culture. Good professionals will stay for the long haul if their career challenges are valued and met. If not, they'll switch to another company.

A top-down vision and mission will hang on the office walls like a template without any efficacy. Bottom up has more relevance. The more you listen to the lower-level workers in your corporation the more you'll find the real picture of your organization and your market.

structure your need

Structuring the need of your working hours will help in constructively absorbing objectives to channelize the efficiency of your innovative thinking process.

Individuals need to prioritize on their strategic or tactical moves and focus on a selected subject to achieve an objective. During corporate strategy planning, a plethora of information and ideas emerge. Competitors have access to the same data collected from public sources, so its uniqueness is limited. How can top managers focus when they are bombarded with layer after cloudy layer of generic information?

The magnitude of data can overshadow or subvert the objective of catering to market needs. We may believe that exhaustive data will take us forward, but it deters our ability to effectively filter inputs. And we lose sight of the specific target.

The mind can work efficiently if our needs are structured. When a need is mentally structured in different steps, pertinent information can be stored in each step for deployment of an effective solution at the right time.

Structuring the need in scouting for business: If you've been sent on a business opportunity search to a foreign country, you may take the fast, easy route of getting data on the country and your area of business. Such information collection will make you a business tourist.

Alternatively, you may choose to see the market differently. You can ask questions like what people in different socio cultural contexts eat for breakfast here; what is the social relationship between men and women in general; what comprises the zones of stress, or of being carefree.

Analyzing the socio-psycho and historical context of any specific subject may give you insights into the meaning and uniqueness of this country. You may, perhaps, take just the men–women relationship to check out your business opportunity.

outsourcing a service

Structuring the need of outsourcing a service depends on the quality of human intelligence. A company may need to outsource certain services to reduce responsibility of directly managing extra manpower in their organization. But focusing only on cost reduction and disengaging responsibility will not help upgrade your outsourcing partners. Consequently your requirement from them will not meet quality standards.

If you structure your need to get quality from your outsourcing partners, you must first educate them on the culture of your organization, the value of your need, and make them feel a part of your organization. You can then extract diligent and knowledge-based service. If you consider your outsourcing partner as a mere supplier, you can never upgrade your own value chain.

purchase of raw material

Raw material purchase is among the biggest recurring costs that affect operational efficiency. In structuring your need here, the main issue would be quality assessment and ideal boundary, but companies tend to compromise on quality to get price efficiency.

For instance, in sourcing for soap you may give priority to fragrance presuming that to be the selling hook. If a consumer buys the soap for fragrance, but pimples occur because another ingredient had sub-optimal quality, that consumer will never return to the brand.

Similarly in branded water, which people buy for purity, if the label and advertising are beautiful, but the sealing ring of the cap uproots on opening, the bottled water violates its guarantee. If this happens even in a single bottle, the consumer feels cheated, and considers the water spurious.

ancillary parts

In outsourcing an ancillary part, companies normally find multiple vendors with competitive pricing, and then look for the lowest price with acceptable quality to achieve operation efficiency. In doing so, your need structure has shifted to cost rather than delivery ingenuity, where the accuracy of the engineering drawing must first be established.

Structuring your need does not limit you, nor do you lose any insight. Instead you constructively absorb the objective to provide better end user value. You get better time management, your agenda will be fulfilled by action of value creation in every step.

breed of exceptional people

Invention doesn't only come from the laboratory. To innovate an alternative in business, create an intellectual community who can nurture one another in an innovative jacuzzi where intellectual power takes a collective bath to reach a new diaspora. India needs a new breed of business people who can aspire.

This aspiration will generate from a fusion of the talents of philosophers, painters, film-makers, singers, sociologists, historians, psychologists, sports professionals, physicians, and engineers:

- **Philosophers** will draw the vision of the future.
- **Painters** will eccentrically break the canvas to draw the thought of the unknown. Artist painters have exceptional liberty of expression. These boundaryless creators should always be inspired to draw their imagination to shape human evolution. They need not bother explaining their visual thoughts; people will put in the effort to understand them. The world is multidimensional. Various people will understand a piece of art differently.
- **Film-makers** will draw surrealism in society and evoke emotion with visual arts.
- **Singers** will drive entertainment with intellect, words rich in message.
- **Sociologists** will define the complexity of human lifestyle.
- **Historians** will continuously revive the past to look for that big idea that was not used before.
- **Psychologists** will unearth society's psychodrama that impacts economic growth. Without independent analysis of people at the psychological level, it is not possible to read the latent.
- **Sports professionals** will use self-stamina that influences people to develop the winning mentality.
- **Actors** will enact society's unstated messages that become immortal. Cerebral actors like Charlie Chaplin and Dustin Hoffman are unforgettable symbols of social messages.
- **Writers** create fiction that throws up contradiction, and dynamizes society to think differently.

- **Physicians** with knowledge of human health will show the step forward for tomorrow's well-being, the basis of the innovative step.

A fertile mixture of these professionals can result in an innovative social platform. Involving different layers of intellectuals, will not only address innovative business; the intellectual level of other social activities will simultaneously increase. With such productive actionables, you can shock the future.

'Don't allow economic poverty to contaminate intellectual growth to make you mediocre,' was the most inspirational vision, and the biggest goodwill, my mother gave me when I was 14 and living sans electricity under a leaky thatched roof in our refugee colony. These words ringing in my mind, I had to strategise to evict myself from mediocrity and grow.

People like me, underprivileged at childhood, exist everywhere in the world. In my management consulting life I have executed the vision, strategy and implementation of hundreds of organizations in the world, but my mother's vision is so universal, every individual can apply it. You too may have profited from valuable advice given and received on life or business. My mother's message for me may perhaps inspire another person to overcome mediocrity.

Emotion is the most important capital for the human race; it's what remains after people pass away. Implementing my mother's vision at every step I have established a simple message in the last 20 years: love and courage. Love is above any institution, it's for everybody. This is the biggest gift the human race can distribute across the globe. Courage is the route to overcome mediocrity. Courage can overcome any obstacle in life. I find love and courage to be the super balance of emotion and self-confidence. Whoever has received a letter from me in the last 20 years would have found this message as a sign off: 'Love and courage.'

My business associates very often censor my 'Love and courage' sign off when writing to persons I don't yet know. They think new clients may not take me seriously. Making me write 'Sincerely yours' kills me. I feel stupid that I have to be so mediocre for business etiquette.

My Emotional Surplus strategy emanated with the 'Love and courage' notion in my mind and soul. Emotional Surplus is becoming more and more indispensable for tomorrow. Using the Emotional Surplus strategy results in an organization's consistent and sustainable high value business. Of course it must be laddered and balanced with rational, functional, and emotional attributes in every activity to overcome the benchmark to reach the Next-mark.

This is the end of my *Jalebi Management* journey. The way I love *jalebis*, I love the human race. The longing for it never finishes. Once you finish a *jalebi*, you want to bite into another crunchy syrupy one, and try to get another *jalebi*. None of the rippling *jalebis* look alike. Human psychology is exactly like the *jalebi* structure. We are all made differently but we have a certain commune of love and affection, which is totally universal notwithstanding geography, tradition, culture, and politics.

People across the world have endowed me with a vast array of subjects that I have happily meshed into thoughts to transform corporations. With immense passion and curiosity have I interacted with people of different cultures and nations in the world to mastermind customer and consumer sensitivity. Let me stay with you in gratitude with all my love and courage.

index